D.K. Printworld

The Toraṇa

Parul Pandya Dhar

in Indian
and Southeast
Asian
Architecture

IMAGE CAPTIONS

pp.ii-iii : *Āndola-citra-toraṇas*, Kiradu, Viṣṇu temple, *raṅgmaṇḍapa*, c. 975-985 CE.

pp.iv-v : *Nāsī toraṇas,* Ittagi, Mahādeva temple, c. early 12th century.

pp.vi-vii : *Illikā toraṇa* (reassembled fragments), Kiradu, now in VAM, London, c. early 11th century.

p.viii : Architectural drawing of a *toraṇa* for *ḍolā-yātrā*, c. 1816-1822 CE, VAM, London.

pp.xii : *Toraṇa,* Barabudur, c. 800-835 CE.

pp.xvi : *Toraṇa,* Barabudur, c. 800-835 CE.

p.xviii : *Āndola toraṇas*, Ranakpur, Dharaṇavihāra, c. 15th century.

Cataloging in Publication Data - DK
[Courtesy: D.K. Agencies (P) Ltd. <docinfo@dkagencies.com>]

Dhar, Parul Pandya, 1966-
The toraṇa in Indian and Southeast Asian architecture / Parul Pandya Dhar.
p. cm.
Includes bibliographical references (p.).
Includes index.
ISBN 13: 9788124605349 (Hb)
ISBN 10: 8124605343 (Hb)

1. Gateways — India. 2. Hindu architecture — India. 3. Buddhist architecture — India. 4. Temples, Hindu India. 5. Buddhist temples — India. 6. Symbolism in art — India. 7. India — Antiquities. 8. Gateways — Southeast Asia. 9. Religious architecture — Southeast Asia.
I. Title.

DDC 725.960954 22

First published in India, 2010
ISBN 13: 978-81-246-0534-9 (Hb)
ISBN 10: 81-246-0534-3

Book design: Designations, New Delhi.

Published and printed by:

D.K. Printworld (P) Ltd.
Regd. office: 'Srikunj,' F-52, Bali Nagar
Ramesh Nagar Metro Station
New Delhi - 110 015
Phones : (011) 2545 3975, 2546 6019
Fax : (011) 2546 5926
E-mail: indology@dkprintworld.com
Web: www.dkprintworld.com

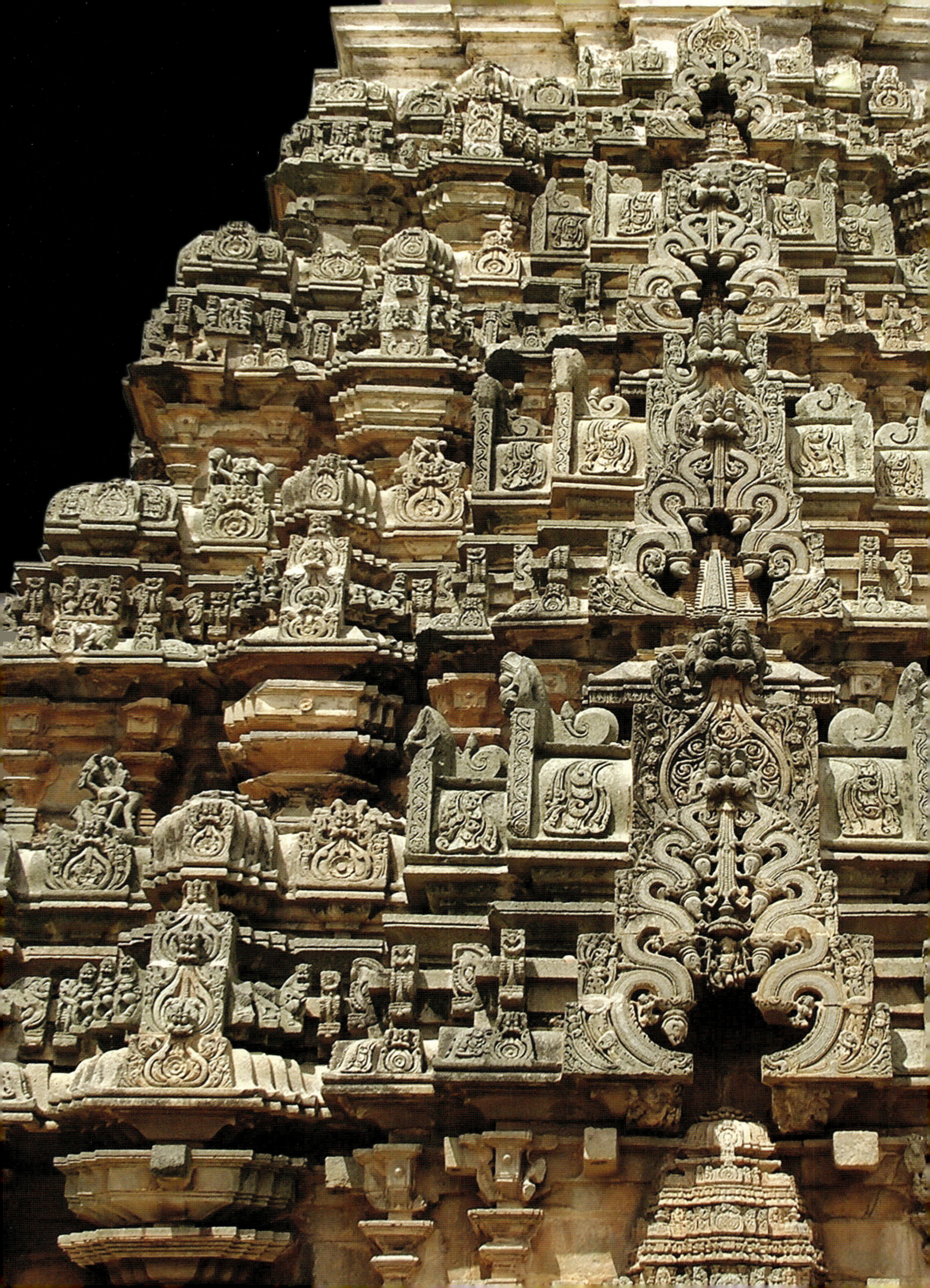

To
Prof. M.A. Dhaky

Architectural Elevation
Stone Arch near the
ple of Juggernaut in Orissa
ring the Celebration of the
Festival Dole Jattra

Contents

Foreword

Indian art-historical studies have covered considerable ground, changing course several times during the last hundred and fifty years. When Alexander Cunningham argued for a separate body for this study, the focus of his argument was on the survey of India's antiquities, and when it was established in 1871, this term received centre space in its name, Archaeological Survey of India. However, the results of the first comprehensive survey of Indian monuments under the title *History of Indian and Eastern Architecture* were presented by an enterprising architectural historian, James Fergusson, in the year 1876. He wrote this as a complement to his grand series, *History of Architecture in All Countries*, begun earlier. Though Fergusson made a pioneering attempt at synthesizing a vast monumental material collected across the country, the traditional context of the monuments was felt missing in his *History*. Rajendralal Mitra and others had already engaged themselves with this issue, though not to the full liking of Fergusson, but to be fair, we must note that Fergusson himself had been bitten by Indian mythologies almost a decade before he began to study the history of architecture. His *Tree and Serpent Worship, or Illustration of Mythology and Art in India* (1868) had preceded his *History*.

The textual studies on Indian traditional arts received momentum in the early part of the 20th century. This is made evident by the publications of Ganapati Sastri (1913, 1919), T.A. Gopinatha Rao (1916), Jouveau Dubreuil (1917), E.B. Havell (1915, 1920), P.K. Acharya (1921, 1927, 1933, 1946), P.N. Bose (1926), Bhattashali (1929), Gravely and Ramachandran (1936), H. Zimmer (1946), M.V. Mallayya (1949) and others. A Dictionary (1927) as well as an Encyclopaedia (1946) of Hindu Architecture also came out during this period. More studies followed, covering not only the *vāstu, śilpa,* and *citra,* but also symbols, motifs, myths, and legends. While all these may have pointed out the missing links in the study of Indian architecture by the early western scholars, Fergusson's masterly synthesis of Indian architecture could not be surpassed by his successors. This is true despite the expansive and extensive coverage of V.A. Smith on Fine Art, E.B. Havell and Ananda Coomaraswamy on Art, F.H. Gravely, O.C. Ganguly, and Percy Brown on Architecture, and S. Kramrisch on Temples.

During this period the archaeological reporting, that had occupied the centre stage in art-historical studies, was continued both at the national and provincial levels alongside studies in iconography, iconology, mythology, philosophy, aesthetics, chronology, composition, ritual, technique, artisanship, and such other aspects. Some of these studies were made in isolation, while some others were made across boundaries. Some maintained a balance between the archaeological material and textual terminology; some others ignored one for the other. Excessive application of Indian textual terminology caused as much discomfort as excessive employment of western jargons and clichés. Whatever virtuosity one may find in such excesses, there is no doubt that it made the reading difficult and the meaning distant. On occasions, exposition in unintelligible vocabulary became the hallmark of scholarship and this was true of both Indian textual scholars and western-oriented Indian art-historians. While this state continues even now - especially among those engaged in modern arts or modern interpretation of traditional arts - the situation is made bearable by some at least who try to balance tradition with modernity and write to convince rather than to confound.

It is in this background that I read Parul's *Toraṇa* and found it very refreshing. She writes to convince without abandoning Indian textual terminologies but without parading them.

Parul has made a massive attempt to study a single but very striking architectural member of Indian monumental art. It is massive because she covers nearly the entire history of the *toraṇa*-motif, beginning from the earliest Buddhist and Jain instances (Bharhut, Sanchi, Mathura) and ending with those of Indo-Islamic times (notably of the Sultanate and Mughal periods). The spread is also vast. It includes examples from the major part of South Asia (Afghanistan, Pakistan, Nepal, and Sri Lanka) and Southeast Asia (Myanmar, Cambodia, Thailand, Indonesia, and Champa or Vietnam). We find among the examples, religious (cave and structural) establishments, civil, civic, ceremonial, and defence architecture, free-standing ones, and many more of this kind. In the temple complex, this architectural member is situated at the entrance to the temple as well as the sanctum-cella, in the halls, as decorative adjunct to the vestibule, as arched frame of niches, as the *prabhā* or aureole of the deities in the sanctum and on the outer wall, and as decorative frame on the parapet and tower.

Outside of the temple-complex, examples associated with forts, streets, mountain paths, and tank bunds are also covered. The memorial *(kīrti-toraṇa)* and ceremonial *(tulābhāra, hiṇḍola)* pavilions are also not left out.

Parul frames her arguments effectively, making use of more than two dozen ancient and medieval texts. But the weight of the scholarship is so carefully concealed that the labour gone into it is hardly felt. The reading is made easy though the subject matter is complex. This is achieved by employing textual terminology only where it is inevitable, but always ascertaining its meaning first. The clarity is enhanced by an amazing variety of illustrations – photographic and hand-drawn – chosen with considerable care and placed in appropriate contexts. This makes consultation easy and the context and the content clear.

P.K. Acharya was perhaps among the first to draw attention to the term *Toraṇa* in his *Dictionary,* though Cunningham, Alexander Rea, Fergusson, and Smith had noticed its architectural contexts. He instanced descriptions occurring in three major texts on architecture, two epics, two *purāṇas*, and the *Arthaśāstra*, besides a dozen and a half inscriptions. Parul has added more texts and inscriptions. For the first time, we learn about two dozen types of *toraṇas* found in South Asian and Southeast Asian monuments. Some attempts have been already made to study the temple towers, ceilings, traceries, and gateways *(gopuras)*, but the depth of inquiry is far more formidable here than in any I have read so far.

Parul briefly discusses the etymon of *toraṇa (tur-tvaraṇe)*, but quickly passes on to concentrate on its variety, form, and context. This creates scope to explore the other dimensions of this architectural member. The provincial styles presented here provide firm clues to the existence of several regional language texts and traditions, especially in Gujarat, Rajasthan, and Karnataka. To sample how a study of these could be rewarding, I may instance one or two of what I am aware of in Karnataka.

Though this term occurs first in the Pali-Prakrit records, its entry in Sanskrit and then in the regional languages was not delayed far too long. I have not been able to locate this term either in the Vedic texts or the Sangam compendium, but its occurrence in the epics, *purāṇas,* and *śāstras* (especially *Arthaśāstra*) and the *Cilappatikāram* (5,104) and *Maṇimekalai* (1, 45), cannot be disputed. Parul has drawn attention to several references occurring in the *Rāmāyaṇa* and *Mahābhārata*, but the *Toraṇasphaṭika* built by Dhritarashtra for the dice play, mentioned in the *Sabhā Parva*, seems to have eluded her. This was obviously a pavilion of palatial scale built of crystals or a creeper, as the term *sphaṭika* carries both these meanings.

I have not been able to trace the term *toraṇa* in the Kannada inscriptions of the first millennium CE, but its occurrence, though somewhat sparingly, in Kannada literary works and Sanskrit inscriptions of this period cannot be doubted. However, from about the beginning of the second millennium, its occurrence becomes as common in Kannada texts and Karnataka inscriptions as in monumental representation. I may present a couple of unusual instances which may or may not be found elsewhere. Some records in Karnataka assign auspicious *(maṅgala)* and honorific *(vaibhava)* significance to *toraṇas* and also make them moving objects on the model of the moving idols *(utsava vigrahas)* of divinities. A Vijayanagara copper plate (1450) associated with the Rāghottama Maṭha describes how its pontiff was honoured with auspicious symbols that could accompany him wherever he travelled in the four directions of the empire. These symbols comprised the throne, crown, palanquin, white-parasol, double-whisk, fan, day-torch, cymbals, yellow and red flags, auspicious musical instruments including cymbals and conch, and the *toraṇa*. Interestingly, the record which makes this declaration is called *vaibhava* (pomp, glory)-*tāmra-śāsana* (copper plate record).

Just as the receipt of the *makara-toraṇa* was a matter of great pride and privilege, the loss of it was a matter of great insult and humiliation. That capturing the *makara-toraṇa* of the vanquished adversary (like capturing of the enemy's tutelary deity) was an act of great bravery is proven by an 11th century Tamil record found in Karnataka. It describes how, after defeating the Chalukyan king in a celebrated battle, the Chola king captured not only his wives, family treasure, conches, umbrella, trumpets, white-whisks, the royal banner, the camel force but also his *makara-toraṇa*. While this *makara-toraṇa* was one of the regal paraphernalia of the king, there was also an immovable one called *vicchādira- (vidyādhara-) toraṇa* at the war gate of the enemy's extensive capital-city, which he had already captured along with the splendid wicket door set with large jewels.

Another point of interest is the deification of *toraṇa*. This seems to have a hoary history, for one of the thousand names of Śiva is stated to be Toraṇa and Tārāmbikā's alternative name is mentioned as Toraṇeśvarī in the *purāṇas*. The worship of *toraṇas,* especially those attached to tanks, was not uncommon. Like the goddess Lakṣmī, this deity seems to have been associated with water and lotuses. A medieval Kannada Jain *purāṇa* describes a lofty stone *Toraṇa* located amidst lotuses. This kind of deification seems to have continued through the ages, making the images of Śiva, Viṣṇu, Gaṇeśa, Lakṣmī, Saraswatī or Śakti, Indra, and such other gods located in the centre of the architrave. These are pointed out only to show what kind of provocation could be provided by this study and what more could be added to it by exploring the regional sources, both textual and monumental. Parul's observation on the ritualistic significance accorded to the *toraṇa* in the worship of goddess Pattini in Sri Lanka is to be understood in this background.

Parul has tread in the path of Professor M.A. Dhaky, who besides his encyclopaedic pursuits, has also pioneered such in-depth studies as an author of a couple of monographs on temple ceilings and traceries. Professor Dhaky should be pleased to accept the dedication of this book, not only because it is a continuation of his work but also because it is satisfying in scholarship. I am sure other art-historians will not be far behind in welcoming this very gratifying study.

S. Settar
National Institute of Advanced Studies,
Bangalore.

Acknowledgements

This work owes its present structure to the goodwill and efforts of a number of people and institutions. Foremost is the contribution of Professor M.A. Dhaky, veteran scholar, under whose guidance I first researched the subject as my doctoral thesis at the National Museum Institute, New Delhi (NMI). His generous nature led me to integrate my understanding of the subject with his profound erudition, even as he inspired me to chart my course. His wife, Geetanjali Dhaky, welcomed me as a part of the family, an association I continue to cherish.

At the NMI, the successive Vice-Chancellors, Dr. R.D. Choudhury, Dr. K.K. Chakravarty, and Dr. A.K.V.S. Reddy, facilitated the work in many ways. In the Department of History of Art, at first Professor Lolita Nehru and then Professor Arputha Rani Sengupta, were always helpful. The libraries of the NMI and the National Museum, New Delhi (NM) have been a very valuable resource. I would like to especially mention Pratibha Parashar and Dr. B.N. Singh for all the help rendered. My gratitude extends equally to J.E. Dawson, Curator, Archaeology, for his help in sourcing the NM collections. Suman Lata at the NMI as well as S. Pandian and N. Ravi at the American Institute of Indian Studies, Gurgaon (AIIS), have painstakingly prepared the line drawings that illustrate the various chapters. To them I am indebted.

The library and archives of the AIIS have been a most significant resource. Thanks are due to the Vice-President of the AIIS, Dr. Pradeep Mehendiretta and its Director-General, Purnima Mehta, as also to Jagdish Yadav, Dr. Vandana Sinha, Dr. P. Bilimale, Dr. U.S. Moorti, Amrit Kaur, D.P. Nanda, S.E. Rizvi, V.K. Venkatavardhan, Raju Prasad, and Jagannath Kushwaha. I am also grateful to the Archaeological Survey of India (ASI) for photographs from their archives and for permissions during the various site visits. The collections and resources of the NM, the Indian Museum, Kolkata, the State Museums in Lucknow, Mathura, Sarnath, and Chennai, the Institut Français de Pondichèry, the British Museum, the British Library, and the Victoria and Albert Museum in London (VAM), the Musée national des arts Asiatiques (Guimet) in Paris, the Istituto Italiano per l'Africa e l'Oriente in Rome, and the Staatsbibliothek in Berlin, have proved very useful. Affectionate acknowledgements are due especially to Dr. Chedha Tingsanchali and also to Dr. Joachim Bautze, Gerd Mevissen, Dr. A. K. Singh, and A. K. Sharma for sharing photographs from their personal collections.

A Research Fellowship awarded by the University Grants Commission for pursuing doctoral research in Indian Art History brought welcome relief on the financial front. The Nehru Trust for the Indian Collections at the VAM awarded a research grant that facilitated visits to libraries in the U.K. Later, a 14-month long research stay as an Alexander von Humboldt post-doctoral fellow affiliated to the Kunsthistorisches Institut, Kunstgeschichte Südasiens, at the Freie Universität (FU) in Berlin, enabled me to broaden my horizons through academic presentations and interactions with the German academic fraternity. Special mention should be made of Professor Dr. Adalbert J. Gail, the host-supervisor for my post-doctoral research at the FU in Berlin. Professor Dr. Klaus Bruhn, Dr. Gouriswar Bhattacharya, Dr. Christian Luczanits, Dr. Claudine Picron-Bautze, Dr. Joachim Bautze, Gerd Mevissen, Martina Stoye, and Dr. Corinna Wessels-Mevissen offered many valuable suggestions. These reflect in the final shape that the work has taken.

My parents, Jyoti and Arun Pandya, have been pillars of faith and strength and have stood by me throughout this endeavour, as always. To them I owe more than words could say.
Urvi Dhar, my daughter, lovingly cultivated a heightened '*toraṇa*-consciousness' and has demonstrated remarkable solidarity with her preoccupied mother! Sincere gratitude extends to Sanjay Dhar, who took keen interest in this work since its inception and has waited long to see it in print. To Dr. Parag and Priya Pandya, and to all my friends, colleagues, and students who did so much to see this through, I am very grateful.

Vinay Jain, self-effacing yet well-known for his subtle design sensibilities, has transformed the visual appeal of this book. Surender Sejwal at Designations, New Delhi, has also been most helpful. It has been a pleasure to collaborate with the publishers, D.K. Printworld (P) Limited, New Delhi, and their chief, Susheel Mittal. Distinguished historian and art-historian, Professor S. Settar, spared precious time to read this manuscript and offered valuable suggestions to refine the text. The Foreword written by him is a privilege that I shall always cherish. The last leaf in this *toraṇa* of acknowledgements is to him.

Parul Pandya Dhar
2009

Introduction

As the architectural expressions of ancient and medieval India grew in dimensions and complexity, detailed attention was lavished on specific members such as pillars, traceries, ceilings, doorframes, and archways. Consequently, each of these gained a rich repertoire replete with intricate relationships between form and function, symbol and significance, structure and ornament. A study of the rationale, grammar, and visual formulations of the units of traditional Indian architecture expectedly provides significant ground for art historical research, one that has so far received limited attention.[1] The present work focuses on a specific architectural entity, the *toraṇa* (arched portal or festoon), and examines the ways in which intent, function, artistic criteria, and cultural contexts determined its manifestations in different architectural settings during the ancient and medieval periods.

Semantic Concerns

Though difficult to translate into English, the *toraṇa* may best be described as an arched portal or festoon associated with traditional Indian architecture. The etymon of the word *toraṇa (tur-tvaraṇe)*[2] implies 'to forge forwards' or 'to rush forth', plausibly relating to a portal or passage which enabled efficient entry and exit. An associated root word, *tṝ*, means 'to pass or cross over,' or 'to attain an end or aim.'[3] The latter, though grammatically not the correct root word for *toraṇa*, none-the-less suggests its role as an architectural symbol of a rite of passage or liminality. The gloss of *toraṇa* in the *Amarakośa* (c. sixth century) mentions its function in early Indian architecture as an outer gateway *(bahirdvāram)*, as compared to the *gopura*, which is defined there as a city gateway *(puradvāram)*.[4] The *Halāyudhakośa (Abhidhānaratnamālā)*, a medieval lexicon (c. 11th century), identifies the festooned garland *(vandanamālā)* itself as the *toraṇa*.[5] The commentator of the *Abhidhānaratnamālā* refers to its context, configuration, and constituent units: It is bow-shaped, ornamented with a variety of jewels and clothes, placed in the upper regions between two pillars, and situated in front of an outer entrance.[6] The *toraṇa* made up of such festoons is seen in several parts of the country to this day. The dual implication of the term as a free-standing archway and an arched festoon encountered in the lexicons can also be observed in practice. The first interpretation alludes to the free-standing *toraṇa* comprising the base, pillars, lintel, and pediment, with or without the arched festoon *(vandanamālā* or *toraṇamālā)* between the pillars, whereas the second refers to the festoon itself as the *toraṇa*. As per the *Abhidhānacintāmaṇi* of

Hemacandra, a *toraṇa* is the free-standing structure at the outer entrance and includes an auspicious garland (*vandanamālikā)* in its upper portion.[7] The twin connotations are merged in one architectural unit in this text, as seen also in practice in the free-standing examples and the miniature versions carved in relief on temples.

Early texts such as Kauṭilya's *Arthaśāstra* (c. third century BCE to first century), the *Bṛhat Saṁhitā* (c. 560 CE) and the *Viṣṇudharmottara Purāṇa* (c. seventh century), as also Nirgrantha texts such as the *Rājapraśnīya Sūtra* and the *Jīvājīvābhigama Sūtra* (c. second to third century), Buddhist *jātakas*, and the epics [the *Rāmāyaṇa* (c. first century) and the *Mahābhārata* (c. second century BCE to fifth century)] provide information on *toraṇas,* though from these texts it is not easy to visualize their precise configuration (see Chapter 1). Detailed and technical articulations of the typology, placement, form, proportion, and thematic content of the *toraṇas* is met in the *vāstuśāstras* (architectural treatises), the *āgamas,* and the *saṁhitās* (texts of a ritualistic and technical nature) of medieval times.

A degree of fluidity appears to have prevailed in the application of terms such as *toraṇa, gopura, and pratolī* during the early period.[8] Kauṭilya's *Arthaśāstra* mentions the *toraṇa* and the *pratolī* while discussing the construction of forts.[9] Both occur as architectural members placed at the main entrances punctuating a fortification. The *pratolī,* located between two gate towers or pylons *(dvāra-aṭṭālakas)*,[10] served a defensive purpose, while the *toraṇa* (about which no detail other than its measurement [two cubits] is mentioned)[11] as a part of the gatehouse appears to have had no more than a symbolic and ornamental role. An early example of a *toraṇa* as part of the gatehouse (*pratolī* with gate towers) may be seen in a relief sculpture from Amaravati (Fig. 1.24).

Yet, the differentiation in the usage and meanings of the two terms is not always clear. Destroying the *toraṇa* of a fortified city in order to break into the enemy's territory finds mention in the *Saṁgāmāvacara Jātaka*. Here, the term *toraṇa* appears to have been used loosely for indicating the *gopura* or the *pratolī*, which are not mentioned (see App. 2, *The Jataka...*). In the *Amarakośa*, *Abhidhānaratnamālā*, and later Sanskrit dictionaries, the meaning of *pratolī* is associated with the synonyms *rathyā* and *viśikhā*, which indicate the main street or the carriage road of a city.[12] Perhaps implicit is the association of the city gateway *(pratolī)* leading directly to the main street *(rathyā, viśikhā)* of a city. An even greater merging of boundaries is noticed in case of the terms *pratolī* and *gopura,* which seem to have acquired clearer formalistic differentiation only during the medieval times, as for example, the medieval Dravidian temple *gopuras*. Etymologically, *gopura* (*gup*: to guard, defend, or protect) shares the defence function of the *pratolī*.[13]

The medieval *pratolīs* such as those at Jhinjhuvada (Fig. 4.91; c. 1100-1140 CE) and Dabhoi (Figs. 4.92-4.94; c. 1225-1253 CE) are embellished with *toraṇas* in their upper regions.[14] Such *toraṇas* are designated as *pratolī-toraṇas* and are distinct from other free-standing examples. Yet, the confusion between *pratolīs* and free-standing *toraṇas* resurfaces in the interpretations of medieval texts (such as the *Śilpa Smṛti Vāstuvidyāyām*, the *Prāsādamañjarī* of Sūtradhāra Nāth, the *Kṣīrārṇava*, and the

Dīpārṇava) by traditional practitioners of architecture who describe the five types of free-standing *toraṇas* as *pratolīs* and *pratolyā-toraṇas*.[15] In this study, the term *pratolī* is employed for the main gateways of medieval forts and the term *pratolī-toraṇa* is used to indicate the *toraṇas* gracing the upper regions of the gateways after such references in medieval texts such as the *Samarāṅgaṇasūtradhāra (SS)* and the *Aparājitapṛcchā (Appr.)* (App. 3, nos. 7a and 7b).

The Approach

The *toraṇas*, free-standing or in relief, did not serve a structural or utilitarian purpose in the same manner in which the base, walls, pillars, ceilings, or traceries served in a building. Yet their continued presence attests to the importance given to them in traditional Indian architecture due to their auspicious, symbolic, didactic, narrative, and ornamental implications. They are encountered in association with *stūpas,* cave temples, structural temples, secular buildings, and also some Indo-Islamic structures. The varied creedal and architectural settings and the different regional and temporal frameworks, alongside the growing complexity of India's material culture, seem to have led to several adaptations of the *toraṇa* in relation to the structure in question, its basic formulations, and its thematic content. Within each of these categories too, the *toraṇa* underwent several incarnations. Some of the complex processes of form and transformation of the *toraṇa* found codification in the medieval treatises. Along with the details of terminology, the treatises provide valuable information pertaining to their basic concepts and visual formulations. The reciprocal dialogue between theory and practice and the space for creativity within the textual constructs is highlighted when relating the texts to the actual creations.

The technical terminology employed in this work adheres to that mentioned in the architectural treatises, of southern as well as northern Indian affiliations. Despite criticism against employing technical terms occurring in the treatises in some recent writings, I believe that they play an important role in arriving at a culturally viable framework for an art historical analysis of the Indian temple. There are several terms in Sanskrit that find suitable parallels in the English language; such instances are substituted by English equivalents for purposes of readability and lucidity. Yet this is not always possible. The necessity of using the vocabulary given in the treatises is evident when referring to those aspects which are specific to a culture and which may not be represented authentically by substitute terms belonging to another tradition. In the present case, for instance, the *toraṇa* is not an arch in the sense that the arch is understood in European art history. Nor is it equivalent to a festoon, a garland, a lintel, or a niche-frame by virtue of its varied and changing locations within an architectural setting. The danger of arriving at misleading nomenclatures by studiously avoiding culture-specific terminology is perhaps greater than the effort required to understand the logic of the concepts and the constructs that went hand-in-hand with the architectural exercise. The pertinent focus in Indian art historiography of doing away with colonial mindsets and approaches on the one hand and also abandoning indigenous texts on the other hand, does appear paradoxical. No doubt, the technical treatises do not provide all the answers and are also unintelligible in parts. Yet, when understood in relation to actual practice and in conjunction with other historical sources, they constitute a significant corpus of traditional knowledge. The texts referred to in this study include the *Bṛhat Saṁhitā*, *Viṣṇudharmottara Purāṇa*, *Samarāṅgaṇasūtradhāra*, *Aparājitapṛcchā*, *Mayamata*, *Kāmikāgama*, *Īśānaśivagurudevapaddhati*, *Jinasaṁhitā* of Bhaṭṭāraka Ekasaṁdhī, *Kāśyapaśilpa*, and *Mānasāra,* among others.[16]

One of the main concerns of this study is to understand the shifts in the configuration and context of the *toraṇa* during the ancient and medieval times. The manner in which the *toraṇa* integrates itself in a *stūpa* complex, for example, varies from that of its manifestation in cave architecture, which, in turn, differs from the way it appears in a structural temple. Its articulation on the Dravidian temples of the Pallava period is distinct from its presence on the medieval temples of Karnataka, which, in turn, reveal a repertoire different from that seen on medieval temples in Gujarat and Rajasthan. Within these broad parameters are the subtler alterations in the intent and rendition of *toraṇas.* An attempt to understand the broader shifts as also the subtler developments in the art-historical journey of the *toraṇa* requires a comprehensive approach. Wherever possible, historical records in the form of inscriptions and literary sources of a non-technical nature have also been studied in addition to the actual examples and the technical information given in the treatises. The endeavour here has been to consider 'the text,' 'the image,' and 'the context' as partners.

In arriving at a comprehensive visual database of sites and monuments relevant to a study of *toraṇas*, earlier researches, surveys, reports, documentations, and archival efforts made by organizations such as the Archaeological Survey of India (ASI), the American Institute of Indian Studies (AIIS), Gurgaon, and the Institut Français de Pondichéry, proved indispensable. It is only recently that such comprehensive and comparative works have been made possible, largely due to the documentation and archival efforts made by these organizations. The inclusion of some Southeast and South Asian parallels in the final chapter is intended for understanding the comparative development of this feature in varied yet allied cultural contexts, often leading to visual formulations not encountered in India.

An important concern relates to chronology. No attempt is made here to suggest a date on the basis of the stylistic character of the *toraṇa* alone. A motif or an element with a long life does not always follow a linear path of development. Detailed research on the morphology of Indian architecture is already available to a large extent and the dating here follows the established norms.[17] In Southeast Asia, as for instance in Cambodia, some scholars have attempted to date the monuments on the basis of the evolution of motifs (see Chapter 5). This approach is not wholly reliable; current and future research on Southeast Asian temples geared towards a holistic chronological assessment would perhaps yield more reliable results. For the present purpose, I have of necessity taken the available chronology of Southeast Asian structures as given to us.

The *toraṇas* are often embellished with representations of divinities, narratives, and with varied motifs and symbols such as *kīrttimukhas* (gorgon faces), *makaras* (fantastic crocodile-dolphin creatures), *vyālas* (leonine creatures), *gaṇas* (goblin-dwarfs), *vidyādharas* (angelic semi-divinities), *kinnaras* (bird-men), *nāgas* (serpents), *haṁsas* (geese), *ratnas* (jewels), *puṣpas* (flowers), and *patras* (leafy motifs). Each of these is also found on several other parts of the temple and relates to the conceptual and symbolic basis of the structure with which the *toraṇa* is associated. At some places, I have suggested their symbolic relationship to the *toraṇa*. However, my emphasis throughout is on the visual processes of form and transformation of the *toraṇa* within the framework of its shifting contexts.

The dividing line between the artisan and the artist, fine and decorative art, and, art and craft, is a product of the modern mind and circumstance. In Europe, the Renaissance marked a shift in attitudes towards the visual arts which were till then not considered as exalted as the liberal arts. This shift was reflected in the beginnings of a division between fine art and decorative art that ultimately separated the artist from the artisan. Traditional ornament, which had been an integral part of art and architecture, ran out of favour in the midst of newer intellectual and ideological principles of design and rational aesthetics that advocated "a consciously celebrated poverty of ornament."[18] The resultant design ideologies that spoke of the honesty of structure, function, and material also showed an aversion to traditional ornament,considered to be in "bad taste."[19] Yet, post-modern ideologies began to evince a renewed interest in the past histories of ornament. Though the history of medieval European architectural ornament has received fair attention from scholars, this subject is yet to receive its due share of attention in the Indian context. One offshoot of the present study, it is hoped, shall be to evoke a greater interest in the validity of traditional Indian architectural forms and ornament as integral to the structure, aesthetically significant, and visually evocative, that can offer certain visual criteria and aesthetic principles as a frame of reference to the contemporary world.

Notes & References

[1] Detailed attention to specific architectural elements is found in the works of M.A. Dhaky, who has traced the progression of temple ceilings and traceries as manifestations of an intricate set of inter-relationships between intent, function, form, and cultural contexts. Adam Hardy has addressed the compositional grammar of the Indian temple elements as proliferations and progressions of patterns of inter-relationships between aedicular components, the resultant forms and transformations in turn being inextricably linked to the Indian concept of manifestation. Gerard Foekema has discussed Indian architectural expression as a tradition in which architectural components and smaller shrines form patterns to decorate Indian temples. See Dhaky, *The Indian Temple Traceries*; Nanavati and Dhaky, *The Ceilings in the Temples of Gujarat*; Hardy, *Indian Temple Architecture: Form and Transformation*; and Foekema, *Architecture Decorated with Architecture*.

[2] As per Liṅgayasūrin's *Amarapadavivṛti* in *Amarakośa* [I], p. 205. This meaning is followed in later dictionaries such as Monier, Monier-Williams, *A Sanskrit-English Dictionary*, pp.450, 456.

[3] Monier, Monier-Williams, *A Sanskrit-English Dictionary,* p.454.

[4] *Amarakośa* [I], p. 205:
toraṇostrī bahirdvāraṁ puradvāraṁ tu gopuram/ 2.2.16.
The *Vaijayantīkośa* (c. 10th-11th century) conveys the same interpretation of the *toraṇa*. See *Vaijayantīkośaḥ of Śrī Yadavaprakāśācārya*, p.118:
toraṇostrī bahirdvāraṁ pracchanna dvāramāntaram/ 4.3.42.

[5] *Halāyudhakośaḥ (Abhidhānaratnamālā),* p.36: *budhairvandanamālā tu toraṇaṁ parikīrtyate/*2.301.

[6] *Ibid.* p.339: *dvārāgre nikhātastambhayorupari nibaddhaṁ nānāvastraratnādimayaṁ dhanurākāraṁ yallakṣyaṁ tattoraṇamiti bahavaḥ; upari sragādiyukta stambhādi dvaya nirmita purādi bahirdvāram/*

[7] *Abhidhānacintāmaṇiḥ*
(of Shri Hemacandrācārya), p.248:
pracchannamantaradvāraṁ syād bahirdvāraṁ tu toraṇam/
toraṇordhve tu māṅgalyaṁ dāma vandanamālikā/ 4.73, 74.

[8] Dhar, "Text, Context and Architectural Practice:," pp. 59-66.

[9] *The Arthaśāstra of Kauṭilya,* Vol. I, p. 122, Section 2:3 *(Durga Vidhānam).*

[10] *Ibid.* p. 122: *dvayoraṭṭālakayormadhye saharmya dvitalāmadhyārdhāyāmāṁ pratolīṁ kārayet/*

[11] *Ibid.* p. 125: *dvi hastaṁ toraṇa śiraḥ/*

[12] *Amarakośa [I],* p. 196: *rathyā pratolī viśikhā syāñcayo vapramastriyam/*2.2.3.

[13] Monier, Monier-Williams, *A Sanskrit-English Dictionary*, p.358.

[14] The details pertaining to *pratolīs* and *toraṇas* are also mentioned in the medieval architectural texts. The *Appr.* mentions the different types of *pratolīs (Utsaṅga, Pūrṇabāhu, Hīnabāhu,* and *Pratikāya)* and the placement of *toraṇas* within the *pratolī* structure. See Dhāṅkī (Dhaky) and Sompura, *Bhāratīya Durga Vidhāna,* pp.18-22, 63-66 and Fig. 7.

[15] *Śilpa Smṛti Vāstuvidyāyāṁ*, pp.276-286; *Prāsādamañjarī by Sūtradhāra Nāthjī,* p.11; *Kṣīrārṇava,* p.36; *Dīpārṇava,* pp.42-46. The five textual types of free-standing *toraṇas* are the *Uttuṅga, Mālādhara, Vicitra, Citrarūpaka,* and *Makaradhvaja.*

[16] See Bibliography (Primary Sources). As some of these have not been edited or translated, the relevant portions need to be read and interpreted directly from manuscripts or texts. I would like to acknowledge Prof. M.A. Dhaky's guidance in this regard.

[17] The significant contribution of the *Encyclopaedia of Indian Temple Architecture* (EITA), a project of the AIIS, Gurgaon, is well known. See Bibliography.

[18] Brolin, *Architectural Ornament: Banishment and Return,* p.14.

[19] *Ibid.* pp.91-105.

CHAPTER 1

The Beginnings

1.13

The origin of an architectural form or motif may rest in the shared realm of the utilitarian, the symbolic, and the aesthetic. The early stages of the *toraṇas* may be understood from the material evidence of available free-standing examples, depictions in relief sculpture, as well as the fragments in various museum collections. These are further substantiated with their notices in inscriptions, early literary texts, and a few of the *purāṇas* and *saṁhitās*.

Early Instances

The earliest recorded Indian instance of an arched entrance that bears some affiliation to a *toraṇa* is located at the Lomas Ṛṣi Cave in the

1.1

1.2

Barabar Hills near Gaya in Bihar (Fig. 1.1; c. mid-third century BCE). This stone archway simulates earlier wooden prototypes and presages some of the features seen on later *toraṇas*. The *makaras* at the ends of the arch emit a semicircular band carved with four pairs of elephants interspersed with miniature *stūpas*. The pattern of *makaras* emitting forms and motifs inscribed within an arch is oft repeated on later *toraṇas*. Other rock-cut caves with arched ornamentation at the entrances include those at Udaygiri and Khandagiri (Fig. 1.2; c. first century BCE to first century) in Orissa. These arched entrances are carved with floral and vegetal patterns and animal figures at the ends. Though visually similar to *toraṇas*, such arched entrances derive from the *gavākṣa* (dormer) arch and are not *toraṇas* in the strict architectural sense.[1]

The earliest extant free-standing *toraṇa*, which is presently located at the Indian Museum, Kolkata, belonged to the Bharhut *stūpa* (Fig. 1.3).[2] An inscription on it records that it was erected during the period of the Śuṅgas (c. second to first century BCE) (App. 1, Inscr. 1a). Comprising two pillars with pairs of lions seated on bell capitals, it has three architraves in its upper portion. *Makaras* mark the volute ends of the architraves which bear scenes of worship of the Buddha. The Buddhist wheel *(cakra)* atop a half-lotus *(ardhapadma)* and a palmette crowns the ensemble. Dwarf pillars alternating with *yakṣas* and *yakṣīs* fill the space between the lower and the central architraves. The manner of rendition betrays simulation of wooden prototypes. Two other donatory inscriptions which mention '*toraṇa*' were found at this site (App. 1, Inscr. 1b and 1c).

The well-known Sanchi *toraṇas* are exquisite in their ivory-like finish (Fig. 1.4; c. late first century BCE to first century).[3] Buddhist narratives, aniconic representations of the Buddha and a variety of forms – *makaras, vyālas, kinnaras,* garlands, jewels, vegetal scrolls, flowers, animals, and humans – the spectrum of life itself – fills every inch of their space. They are structurally similar to the one from Bharhut and serve as markers of the passage from secular to sacred space. The narratives and motifs carved on them indicate their religious and didactic functions. The *makaras* at the volute ends of the architraves, noticed earlier at Bharhut, are absent here; the bracket dryad *(śālabhañjikā)* figures between the lower architraves and the pillar uprights are amongst the most celebrated sculptures of the Sanchi *toraṇas*. Miniature *toraṇas* carved in relief are part of architectural settings in the narratives depicted on these *toraṇas*. They offer additional information about

Fig. 1.1 : Arched entrance, Barabar Hills (Gaya), Lomas Ṛṣi Cave, c. mid-third century BCE.

Fig. 1.2 : Arched pattern above doorway, Rani Gumpha, Orissa, c. first century BCE-first century.

Fig. 1.3 : Free-standing *toraṇa*, Bharhut, c. second-first century BCE, Indian Museum, Kolkata.

1.3

1.5

1.6

the context and placement of the *toraṇa* in ancient Indian architecture. In the Sanchi reliefs, *toraṇas* can be noticed in relation to sacred as well as secular structures, as for instance, at the city limits and in front of a *bodhighara* (Figs. 1.5 and 1.6). The presence of a *toraṇa* as part of a city gate is also recorded in the early texts.

Fragments and Inscriptions

1.7

A number of *toraṇa* fragments are part of the collections of different State Museums; some are housed in the museums abroad. These fragments include architraves, pillars, and bracket dryads *(śālabhañjikās)*.[4] As at Sanchi, miniature *toraṇas* carved in relief are also visible on some of these fragments (Fig. 1.7). The size and shape of the fragments reveal that they belonged to the Bharhut-Sanchi type of free-standing *toraṇas,* as may be affirmed by the example of an intact architrave (c. first century, 148 x 19.6 cm) now in the Government Museum, Mathura. This bears the scenes of Indra's visit to Buddha in the Indraśilā Cave and the worship of the *bodhi* tree.[5]

The volute ends of *toraṇa* architraves are often carved with *makaras*, with or without human figures emerging from the jaws.[6] One also encounters other mythical animals at the volute ends such as the fish-tailed winged lion,[7] the '*garuḍa* and serpent' motif,[8] and the winged elephant[9] (Figs. 1.8-1.10). The architraves bear religious narratives as also motifs such as the triton, *nandīpada, swastika,* lotus, and creepers; at times images of divinities are also found.

1.4 : *Toraṇa* (eastern), Sanchi, *Stūpa* I, c. first century BCE-first century.

1.5 : *Toraṇa* at the city limits, relief sculpture, Sanchi *Stūpa* I, c. first century BCE-first century.

1.6 : *Toraṇa* fronting a *bodhighara*, relief sculpture, Sanchi *Stūpa* I, c. first century BCE-first century.

1.7 : *Toraṇa* architrave, Mathura, c. first century, Government Museum, Mathura.

1.8 : *Toraṇa* fragment, Kankali Tila, Lucknow State Museum, c. second-first century BCE.

1.9 : *Toraṇa* fragment, Kankali Tila, Lucknow State Museum, c. second-first century BCE.

1.10 : *Toraṇa* architrave, c. second-first century BCE, Sarnath Museum.

1.8

1.9

1.10

1.4

The fragment of a *toraṇa* architrave from Kausambi (c. first century BCE), for instance, depicts a *makara* at the volute end of the architrave, followed by a triton and a double-knot motif with foliate ends forming a *swastika*.[10] The damaged central portion of the architrave reveals Lakṣmī standing on a lotus and lustrated by elephants (Fig. 1.11). In later temples of Orissa and South India, this goddess is often found at the centre of door-lintels *(lalāṭa-bimba)* and also on *toraṇas* carved over door-lintels.

Donatory references to *toraṇas* are found in early inscriptions. The fragment of an inscribed Jain tablet of homage *(āyāgapaṭṭa)* (c. first to second century) from Kankali Tila pictures the base of a *stūpa* with a *vedikā* (railing) and a *toraṇa*, very similar in arrangement to that seen in the

1.12

1.11 : *Toraṇa* architrave, Kausambi, c. first century BCE, Allahabad Museum.

1.12 : *Āyāgapaṭṭa* depicting *toraṇa*, Mathura, c. first-second century, Lucknow State Museum.

1.13 : *Toraṇa* (relief sculpture, ivory), Begram, Kabul Museum, c. late first century BCE-first century.

1.14 : *Toraṇa* (relief sculpture, ivory), Begram, Kabul Museum, c. late first century BCE-first century.

1.11

Buddhist context at Sanchi (Fig. 1.12) (App. 1, Inscr. 2). A donatory inscription on a doorjamb from Mathura records the erection of a *toraṇa* and a *vedikā* for the temple of Bhāgavata Vāsudeva (App. 1, Inscr. 3). A pillar inscription of Jain affiliation records the dedication of a *toraṇa* by the lay disciple of the ascetics (App. 1, Inscr. 4). Another inscription of Jain dedication on a *toraṇa* architrave from Kankali Tila mentions the gift of a *toraṇa* for a temple (App. 1, Inscr. 5). Two Buddhist inscriptions from Mathura record the dedication of a *toraṇa* for the worship of all Buddhas (App. 1, Inscr. 6 and 7). An inscription on an architectural fragment pronounces imprecation against him who takes away or causes to be taken away the *toraṇa* or the *vedikā* (App. 1, Inscr. 8). The free-standing examples, the relief sculptures, fragments, and inscriptions testify to the wide prevalence of *toraṇas* in association with the Buddhist, Jain, Brahmanical, and secular structures in ancient India.

The North-Western Region

Begram: *Toraṇas* are prominently represented on many of the ivory fragments discovered at Begram in Afghanistan. A rich collection of Begram ivories had been preserved in the Kabul Museum and some are displayed at the MG (Guimet), Paris. They are represented as part of secular settings, often depicting leisurely activities of women. They reveal distinctive Indian traits as well as cross-cultural influences; several of these are dated between the late first century BCE and the early first century.[11] A few instances would suffice to illustrate their extent, form, and context.

In the first example, a *toraṇa* with two pillars and three architraves terminating in volutes, is clearly seen (Fig. 1.13).[12] A part of a *vedikā* is visible on the sides indicating that this is a portal to an enclosed area. Two women, one assisting the other in adorning herself, are shown standing under the *toraṇa*. Their attires and attitudes reveal leisurely preoccupations. The central architrave is decorated with a floral design inscribed within squares. The other two architraves are adorned with undulating creepers and flowers. The spaces between the architraves are filled by *gaṇas* (goblins) and *kinnaras* (half human-half bird creatures). *Makaras* in profile are visible at the intersections of the uprights with the architraves. Auspicious symbols are placed above the top architrave; pine-cones and fruits, suggesting auspiciousness, are hung at the volute ends. *Vyālas* serve as brackets, a feature seen also on the Nasik *Vihāra* 3 *toraṇa* (Fig. 1.19). The arched entrance is adorned with ornamental festoons.

Another ivory from Begram offers a view into a room with two ladies engaged in adorning themselves (Fig. 1.14).[13] The entrance is through a simple *toraṇa* that frames a door. Some Begram ivories are carved with archways that resemble the *caitya* arch-façade of the Lomas Ṛṣi Cave.[14] One of the ivories shows a group of five women, with one of them on a swing suspended from a *toraṇa*; this provides an early instance of the *hiṇḍola-toraṇa*.[15] The recurring portrayals of the *toraṇa* in secular settings indicate its popularity during the early period. Very few instances of free-standing *toraṇas* from this period actually survive today because, presumably, perishable material was employed for their construction. A common type of archway noticed on these ivories has vertical uprights with horizontal crossbars resembling the free-standing *toraṇas* from Bharhut and Sanchi. The second type is ogee-shaped, similar to the one noticed at the entrance to the Lomas Ṛṣi Cave.

1.13

1.14

1.15

Sirkap: As revealed by the 'Shrine of the Double-Headed Eagle' (c. first century BCE to first century) in Block F at Sirkap in the Gandhara region, the *toraṇa* was familiar to this region during the early period (Fig. 1.15).[16] The drum façade of this structure is relieved with three varieties of entryways interspersed by pilasters with Corinthian capitals. Those flanking the central stairway resemble a classical Greek pediment façade. The central archways on either side of the stairs are ogee-shaped, as in several early Buddhist caves, with a double-headed eagle perched on top. A *toraṇa* with an eagle perched over it is shown at each of the two extremities of the drum.[17]

1.16

Butkara: Excavations in the Swat valley situated to the north of the Gandhara region have yielded *toraṇa* representations in a Buddhist context. A fragment relief of grey-green schist from Butkara (c. first century) depicts a male figure passing through a *toraṇa* and dressed in Indian attire, with a relic casket in his hands (Fig. 1.16).[18] The two *toraṇa* architraves terminate in volutes; pine cones are suspended from the lower architraves as at Begram. The architraves are adorned with rosettes; human busts appear between the architraves. A *triratna* symbol is visible atop one of the vertical uprights and a palmette is placed at the apex. The pattern of flowers within squares carved on the *toraṇa* uprights is similar to the one that occurs on several of the Begram ivories. Another fragment from the same site shows a portion of a *toraṇa* at the limits of the city of Kapilavastu in a scene depicting the Great

Departure *(mahā-abhiniṣkramaṇa)* of Prince Siddhārtha (Fig. 1.17).[19] Similar examples are found at Sanchi, Pitalkhora, and Amaravati (Figs. 1.5, 1.18, 1.24 and 1.25).

The Western Deccan

Pitalkhora: The early period (c. second century BCE to second century) witnessed excavations of several Buddhist *caityas* and *vihāras* in the Deccan. In 1958, during a clearance undertaken by the Department of Archaeology (Archaeological Survey of India), the architectural features of the Pitalkhora caves in Maharashtra were more completely revealed.[20] Several detached sculptures (c. second to first century BCE) were found in the debris in front of the forecourt common to Caves 3 and 4, including a square panel carved with the famous scene of the great departure of Prince Siddhārtha (Fig. 1.18).[21] This panel bears a *toraṇa* with two uprights and three architraves terminating in volutes. A horse (Kaṇṭhaka), with decorative trappings indicative of its royal association, is shown galloping out of the *toraṇa*. An attendant holds a parasol over the horse's back, which symbolizes the presence of Prince Siddhārtha. Two *vedikās* (railings), the first in the top portion of the fragment and the second just beneath the *toraṇa* architraves, are visible. This appears to be a device employed by the artist to indicate the inner and outer enclosures. The *toraṇa* appears to mark the place of entry or exit from the outer enclosure at the city limits. The two uprights have an inward taper, a structural expedient usually employed in wood architecture to ensure greater stability.

1.17

1.15 : *Toraṇa*, (relief sculpture), Sirkap, Shrine of Double-headed Eagle, c. first century BCE-first century.

1.16 : *Toraṇa* (relief sculpture), Swat, Butkara, c. first century, IsIAO collection, Museo Nazionale d'Arte Orientale 'G.Tucci', Rome.

1.17 : Relief sculpture depicting the Great Departure, Swat, Butkara, c. first century, IsIAO collection, Museo Nazionale d'Arte Orientale 'G.Tucci', Rome.

1.18 : Relief sculpture depicting the Great Departure, Pitalkhora, c. second-first century BCE, National Museum, New Delhi.

1.18

D.1

1.19

Nasik: The low wall at the entrance to the veranda of *Vihāra* 3 at Nasik (Gautamīputra Cave; c. 125-130 CE) is carved in the manner of a *vedikā* (railing) and the door leading to its interior is framed with a *toraṇa* carved in relief (Fig. 1.19; D.1). This arrangement is analogous to the *vedikā* and *toraṇa* seen in association with the actual as well as the sculptural representations of some early Indian shrines and *stūpas.* The same idea is transferred within a new setting at *Vihāra* 3, Nasik, where *toraṇa* uprights are placed in the position of doorjambs and the architraves are located in the position of the door-lintel. A scene depicting *stūpa, cakra* (wheel), and *vṛkṣa* (tree) worship is rendered between the two architraves. Festoons are suspended from the lower architrave and *vyālas* serve as brackets. The subject matter on the uprights is compartmentalized into six sections, beginning with two *gaṇas* in the lowest section and followed by those of *yakṣīs, mithunas,* etc. Such portrayals are often seen on the *rūpaśākhās* (doorjambs with figural sculpture) of temple doorframes from the fifth century, thus recording further parallels between the *toraṇa* and the *dvāra* (door). The tall *yakṣas* flanking the Nasik *toraṇa* correspond to the *pratīhāras* (attendant or guardian figures) on temple doorframes. The Nasik *toraṇa* thus relates to the earlier Bharhut-Sanchi type of *toraṇas* on the one hand and provides a transitional link with the later temple *dvāra-toraṇas* (*toraṇas* as part of doorways) on the other.

The Bharhut-Sanchi type of *toraṇa* is rarely encountered after the second-third centuries. Instead, one witnesses the post, lintel, and eave-cornice *(kapotapālikā)* type of entryways. Such instances are seen in Amaravati[22] and Nagarjunakonda narratives as well as in the fifth century paintings at Ajanta (Figs. 1.20 and 1.21). From about the fifth century, such an entrance gateway became an integral part of temple doorframes, termed as the *'toraṇabandha.'* Its posts served as pilaster-doorjambs *(stambha-śākhās)* and the eave-cornice integrated with the lintel (Fig. 1.22). As the fifth century *toraṇas* became more akin to contemporaneous temple doorframes, the *toraṇa-śālabhañjikās,* such as those at Sanchi, assumed the role of Gaṅgā and Yamunā figures, at first on L-shaped brackets attached to the upper portions of the doorframe and later in the lower sections *(pedyā)* of the doorframe.[23] The shared intent of the *toraṇa* and the *dvāra* (door) resulted in the transference and integration of several features of the two elements that manifested later as *dvāra-toraṇas.*

1.22

D.1 : *Toraṇa* carved on doorframe, Nasik, *Vihāra* 3, c. 125-130 CE.

1.19 : *Toraṇa* carved on doorframe, Nasik, *Vihāra* 3, c. 125-130 CE.

1.20 : Relief sculpture depicting scenes of Buddha's birth, Nagarjunakonda, c. second century.

1.21 : Post-lintel-cornice type of entryway, Ajanta, Cave 1, c. 462-478 CE.

1.22 : *Toraṇabandha* on the doorframe, Deogarh, Viṣṇu temple, c. late fifth-early sixth century.

1.20

1.21

1.23

The Eastern Deccan

Amaravati: The splendour of the *stūpa* at Amaravati, an important Buddhist site in Andhra Pradesh, is today accessible to us only through careful reconstructions and fragments located in various museums, in particular the BM in London and the Government Museum in Chennai. From the reconstructions, it has been possible to infer the type of entrances that originally existed along the circumference of the outer railing. Unlike Sanchi, there is no evidence of a free-standing *toraṇa* that fronted any of the entrances to the *stūpa*. Yet, *toraṇas* are ubiquitous in sacred and secular settings in the Amaravati narratives.
In Amaravati reliefs, the *toraṇas* are noticed more often in secular contexts, serving as portals to a palace or a residential quarter, at times leading into a courtroom, or in similar circumstance.[24] Two roundels belonging to railing crossbars, both portraying Śuddhodana and Māyā, in the Aśoka grove, offer interesting examples. In the first (Fig. 1.23), the handsome figure of Śuddhodana with his elbow resting on a horse is complemented by the languid Māyā who is surrounded by companions and maids. A part of a building fronted by a *toraṇa* with three architraves is visible in the backdrop. It probably marks an entrance to the grove, or is a portal for the building in the background. The second (not illustrated)[25] shows Śuddhodana and Māyā in a similar attitude, with many accompanying figures. The structure in the backdrop is more clearly visible in this case. On the two sides of the building, one can see *toraṇas* with two architraves and with festoons suspended underneath the lower architrave. In these roundels, *toraṇas* are employed as portals to secular edifices.

A *toraṇa* at the city limits is seen prominently in the depictions of the Great Departure from Amaravati, as at Pitalkhora and Sanchi. Two illustrations of the Great Departure from Amaravati may be mentioned. The first is a dome slab in the BM in which a *toraṇa* is part of an elaborate city gate (Fig. 1.24). This double-storied city-gate of Kapilavastu has thick walls with *gavākṣa*-arches and railings demarcating the upper storey. Below it, and just under the eave-cornice, the entrance is framed by a *toraṇa* made of two vertical uprights and three curved architraves with volute ends. Kaṇṭhaka, the horse, trots out of the city limits through the *toraṇa*. An attendant holds a parasol over the horse's back, indicating Siddhārtha's presence; Chandaka, his loyal attendant, leads the way. The four-petalled floral pattern inscribed in a square on the *toraṇa* uprights is similar to that noticed on the Begram *toraṇas* as well as on the one from Butkara in the Swat valley. A second illustration of the Great Departure from the Amaravati *stūpa* is recorded in a drawing prepared for MacKenzie.[26] The original is now in the Government Museum at Chennai, though not in a good state of preservation (Fig. 1.25). Because of its dimensions, it has been suggested that this must have been originally located behind the *āyaka* pillars at the base of the dome. The slab is divided into three registers, with the scene of the Great Departure placed lowest. Here too, a *toraṇa* appears as part of an elaborate city-gate. A railing in the lower portion of the illustration probably represents the boundary wall of the city.

The Amaravati reliefs discussed so far reveal the placement of *toraṇas* in a secular setting. We also encounter them in a sacred context, though in fewer numbers. Drum pilasters from the Amaravati *stūpa* housed in the BM show Buddha seated on a throne and seen through a *toraṇa* with two crossbars.[27] Another such pilaster from the same collection depicts the *mahāparinirvāṇa* of Buddha in the form of a *stūpa* of the Amaravati type (Fig. 1.26). *Toraṇas* with two uprights and three crossbars, with a lady standing under each *toraṇa*, flank this miniature *stūpa* representation. This is of interest since a reconstruction of the actual Amaravati *stūpa* has not yielded the presence of free-standing *toraṇas*.

1.26

1.24

1.25

1.23 : *Toraṇa* within medallion, Amaravati, c. first-second century, British Museum, London.

1.24 : *Toraṇa* within city-gate, Amaravati, c. first-second century, British Museum, London.

1.25 : *Toraṇa* within city-gate, Amaravati, c. first-second century, Government Museum, Chennai.

1.26 : *Toraṇas* flanking a *stūpa*, Amaravati, c. first-second century, British Museum, London.

D.2 : *Toraṇa*, Amaravati *Stūpa*, c. second century, MacKenzie folio, OIOC, British Library, London.

MacKenzie's folio of drawings of the Amaravati *stūpa* at the British Library in London includes *toraṇas* represented in architectural settings.[28] There are several in which either a couple or a solitary figure is shown in the attitude of adoration *(añjali hasta)*; they are framed within the *toraṇas* flanking the *stūpa*. Two drawings invite special attention. The first is of a lady with elaborate coiffure and ornaments standing under a *toraṇa* (D.2).[29] Her right hand holds a man's severed head pierced with a dagger and in her left hand is another severed head. The second drawing also shows a woman standing beneath a *toraṇa*, holding a weapon in her hand.[30] This drawing is arranged as a pair with the drawing of a *stūpa*.[31] The heights of the slabs depicting the *stūpa* and the *toraṇa* are well-matched. In all probability, the slab with the *toraṇa* flanked the *stūpa* slab and both belonged to the dome of the original Amaravati *stūpa*. However, the significance of the women with severed heads leave some questions unanswered. Does this bear ritualistic significance? Are these women in malevolent attitudes, standing under *toraṇas* and flanking the *stūpa*, guardians of the sacred site?

Eastern India

Free-standing *toraṇas* were also found in the eastern Indian belt during the early period of Indian art, as has been observed in the case of *toraṇa* fragments from Sarnath (Fig. 1.10). Terracotta seals (c. first-second century) with *toraṇas* of the Bharhut-Sanchi type have been found at Chandraketugarh, north-east of Kolkata.[32] On these, a bird is found perching on the upper architrave, as at the Shrine of the Double-headed Eagle at Sirkap. A similar terracotta seal from Tamluk (c. second-first century BCE) is preserved in the Tamralipta Museum and Research Centre, Tamluk.[33] The arches above the entrances to the cells of the Udaygiri-Khandagiri caves in Orissa (c. first century BCE to first century), though essentially originating from the dormer *(gavākṣa)*, are closely affiliated to *toraṇas*. The Kumrahar terracotta plaque (c. second-third century), three inches in diameter, now housed in the Patna Museum, shows a towered temple structure within a railing. A post and lintel type of *toraṇa* fronts this structure.[34]

Early Literary Sources

A reference found in Kauṭilya's *Arthaśāstra* (c. third century BCE to first century) in the section on forts, refers to the measurement of the upper portion of the *toraṇa* placed within the city gate as being of two *hastas* (App. 2). The Sanchi and Amaravati reliefs give us a fair idea of the visual form of such *toraṇas* (Figs. 1.5 and 1.24).[35]

The author of the *Milindapanho* describes the city of Sagala, which was protected by strong towers, gateways, and *toraṇas (varaparava gopura toraṇam)* (App. 2). Here too, the archway is shown as a part of the city-gate. In the same text, the city is compared to the "blessed one's city of righteousness."[36] The various parts of a city are expressed as a metaphor for qualities leading towards the attainment of the final goal. The city-gate (with the *toraṇa*, etc.) is a metaphor for knowledge, leading the way towards the attainment of the final goal and removing the danger of falling into the moat, which is a metaphor for fear of sin. This suggests the symbolism of the *toraṇa* as marking a place for initiation or knowledge and leading towards the desired goal.

The *jātakas* also refer to *toraṇas*. In the *Saṁgāmavacara jātaka*, for instance, the Bodhisattva and the elephant trainer cajole the elephant standing at the gate (here, *toraṇa*) of the city of Varanasi to break the gate and enter the enemy's city (App. 2).[37] In the *Vidhurapaṇḍita jātaka*, Yakkha Punnaka enters the city of Indapatta (Indraprastha) and describes the splendour of a city with many gateways (*toraṇas*) along the ramparts (App. 2).[38]

The *Mṛcchakaṭika* of Śūdraka includes a description of Vasantasenā's mansion, adorned with an ivory *toraṇa* (*dantidanta-toraṇava-bhāsitasya*), with jewels and swinging festoons that conjure the image of an elephant's trunk and beckon the visitor to enter the mansion (App. 2).[39] The placement of *maṅgala kalaśas* (auspicious vases) on the pedestals of the *toraṇa* pillars mentioned there remind one of the *ghaṭapallava* bases of the *toraṇa* pillars seen in the relief sculpture of the period. The city-gate is stated to be impregnable. The *toraṇa* and the gateway thus seem to have served the purposes of ornamentation, auspiciousness, and defence. Aśvaghoṣa's *Buddhacarita* (c. mid-second century) narrates prince Siddhārtha's Great Departure from Kapilavastu, an episode often represented in visual art with a *toraṇa* at the city limits. There is a description of the women of the palace, who were asleep when the prince was preparing to leave the city. The languorous, bow-like stance of one of the slender-bodied women is likened to a *toraṇa śālabhañjikā*, which brings to mind the Sanchi *toraṇa-śālabhañjikās* (App. 2).[40]

The *Rājapraśnīya Sūtra*, a Jain text (c. second-third century) gives a detailed account of life in the city of Āmalakappā, including a detailed account of *toraṇas* (App. 2). A deep, circular moat *(gambhīra khāta-phalihā)* surrounded and defended the city and an enclosure wall *(pāgāra)* punctuated by pylons *(aṭṭālakas)* fortified it. A *toraṇa* at the entrance *(gopura-toraṇa)* was a part of the total gate structure (*sūtra* 1). The upper portions of the doors of a chapel *(caitya)* located to the north-east of Āmalakappā city were ornamented with *toraṇas* of good craftsmanship (*sūtra* 2). The same text mentions gem-studded *toraṇas* with pearl festoons and star-like clusters fronting the stairways of a shrine *(vimāna)* constructed by the *Abhiyogika devas* (*sūtras* 25-28). The bejewelled *toraṇas* gracing a celestial shrine may be an exaggerated version of actual examples from the early period. Some stone *toraṇas* of a later period (c. fifth century onwards) are carved with diamond-shaped and circular gem-like motifs along with pearl festoons. In the medieval architectural treatises, they are termed *ratna-toraṇas* (bejewelled *toraṇas*).

This text further states that the gem-studded *toraṇas* were embellished with *aṣṭamaṅgalas* (eight auspicious symbols) in their upper portion. This feature finds transference on the door-lintels of later stone temples. The upper portions of the *toraṇas* are stated to be adorned with auspicious *cāmara-dhvajas* (fly whisks) of varied colours, *chatras* (parasols), *ghaṇṭas* (bells), and with clusters of pendant lotuses (*sūtra* 29). Some later stone *toraṇas* are carved with a pendant lotus underneath the central portion of the arch.

The same text also mentions a pillared auditorium *(prekṣāgṛha)* embellished with well-structured *vedikās, toraṇas,* and *śālabhañjikās* (*sūtra* 45). The gem-studded pillars were painted with images of animals such as the *ihamṛga* (an imaginary animal), *vṛṣabha* (bull), and *turaṅga* (horse). Each door of the auditorium was adorned with *toraṇas* and sandalwood jars.[41] A detailed description of *toraṇas* made of various types of gems and adorned with *śālabhañjikās* and lotus clusters, as also *toraṇas* flanking the entrance gateway, is found in this text (*sūtra* 132). In an elaborate commentary, sandal paste jars, mirrors, and vessels filled with flowers, condiments, cosmetics, garlands, fragrant oils, rice, water, cloth, fruits, and ornaments are mentioned in association with *toraṇas* to usher good fortune and auspiciousness. Of interest is a simile drawn between the effulgent radiance of the jewelled crown *(ratnakaraṇḍaka)* of the *cakravartin* (king) and the *ratnakaraṇḍaka* of the *toraṇa*. Both are said to light up the *pradeśa* (regions) with their radiance. Another Jain text, the *Jivājivābhigama Sūtra,* also reveals similar information on the *toraṇas* found in early Indian art.[42]

Toraṇas are mentioned several times in the two great epics, the *Mahābhārata* (c. second century BCE to fifth century) (App. 2) and the *Rāmāyaṇa* (c. first century) (App. 2).[43] These notices do not dwell upon the formal characteristics of the *toraṇas* but they do refer to the *prākāra-toraṇas* (*toraṇas* punctuating the city enclosure walls), *dvāra-toraṇas* (*toraṇas* at entrances), and *ratna* or *maṇi toraṇas* (bejewelled *toraṇas*). There is also a reference to a *hema-toraṇa* (golden *toraṇa*) decorating the palace of the Kaurava princes, Duryodhana and Duḥśāsana. The *Matsya-purāṇa* (c. fifth to tenth century) mentions that a *toraṇa* could be made out of brick *(aiṣṭaka),* wood *(daru)*, or stone *(śaila)* (App. 2). The *Vāyu-purāṇa* (c. sixth to seventh century) mentions *prākāra-toraṇas* (see App. 2).

In the *Meghadūta* (c. fifth century), Kālidāsa refers to a rainbow-like *toraṇa* belonging to the *yakṣa's* house (App. 2). In the *Kumārasambhava,* he describes the splendour of the city bedecked with golden *toraṇas* on the occasion of Pārvatī's marriage, conjuring heaven on earth (App. 2). In the *Raghuvaṁśa*, the flight of *sārasa* birds is compared to a *toraṇa* garland. In the same poem, there is a description of a city adorned for marriage celebrations with several rainbow-like *toraṇas*. Kālidāsa also describes the poignant farewell given by the people of Ayodhya to Rāma and Lakṣmaṇa as they departed for the forest. The street they walked was graced by the (genial) glances of the people, as though a series of *toraṇas* were lined along the street (App. 2).

These literary references further testify that *toraṇas* were an integral part of the city: city-gates, streets, shrines, residences, forts, and palaces, and that they conveyed auspicious, symbolic, honorific, celebratory, and ornamental connotations. They find mention in Buddhist, Jain, and Hindu texts. Wood, brick, stone, ivory, gem-studded, and golden *toraṇas* are mentioned. Not much can be made out about their formal traits from the early texts, but their basic configuration can be known from the surviving instances as well as those depicted in relief sculpture.

1.27

1.28

Free-standing *Toraṇas*: c. 300-500 CE

1.27 : *Toraṇa* architrave fragment, Pawaya, c. late fourth-early fifth century, Gwalior Museum.

1.28 : *Toraṇa* pillar fragment, Khilchipura, c. late fifth-early sixth century.

Some instances of free-standing *toraṇa* fragments belonging to the period of Gupta dominance in northern, western, and central India bear witness to the survival of the earlier tradition (Figs. 1.27-1.28).[44] These are noticed at Eran, Pawaya, Nagari, Khilchipura, and Garhwa. They share some traits of the earlier *toraṇas* but are closer to temple doorframes in details. Their pillar uprights resemble the figural doorjambs *(rūpaśākhās)* of temples. The transitional link between the *toraṇas* of the early period and the temple doorframes of a slightly later period has been pointed out while discussing the instance of *Vihāra* 3 at Nasik.

The late fourth-early fifth century example from Pawaya, located south of Gwalior, may have been associated with the brick structure found at Pawaya (Fig. 1.27).[45] This *toraṇa*-lintel has a large sunken square on the surface above the side panel, indicating that an additional member rested above it. Exquisitely carved, it depicts the episode of Viṣṇu as Vāmana humbling the pride of King Bali, and Viṣṇu as Kūrma in the episode of the churning of the ocean. Interestingly, in the section where Bali's sacrifice is portrayed, the upper register shows a *toraṇa* similar to the ones at Sanchi and other early sites. It is likely that the remnants of the Pawaya lintel may have been a part of a similar *toraṇa*.

Whether the two pillars found at Mandor, north of Jodhpur in Rajasthan, belonged to a *toraṇa* or were part of a doorframe, is difficult to assess.[46] Made of red sandstone and carved only on one side, these pillars harbour scenes from Kṛṣṇa's life. The sculptural programme follows the narrative of the *Harivaṁśa*, plausibly the oldest

D.3

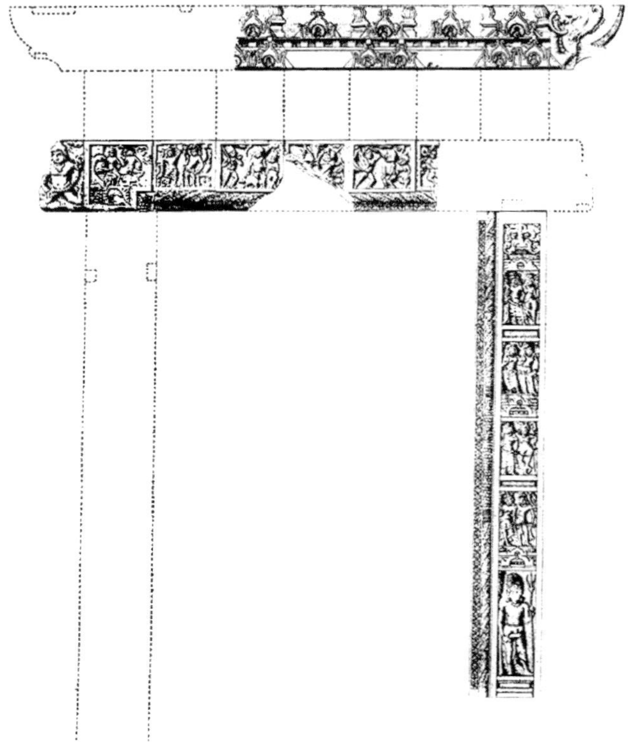

D.4

work dealing with Kṛṣṇa's childhood. Stylistically, and on the basis of the palaeography of an all but effaced inscription, these pillars have been dated to the same period as the Pawaya lintel.

Remains of a free-standing *toraṇa*, dated to the early sixth century on the basis of style, have been found from Nagari near Chittor in Rajasthan. Bhandarkar (1920) has provided a convincing reconstruction of the fragments of this *toraṇa* with two architraves (D.3). A pillar broken into five fragments and portions of two architraves were recovered by him. The sculptures on the lower architrave include a celestial garland-bearer (*mālāvidyādhara*), incarnations of Viṣṇu as Nara-Nārāyaṇa, and narratives such as of *Kirātārjunīya* from Śaiva mythology. The upper architrave is ornamented with miniature dormers *(candraśālikās)* and with a *makara* facing outwards at the extremity of the surviving portion (D.4). Mortices at the top of the upper architrave indicate that the *toraṇa* had some surmounting ornament. The pillars are divided into five panels; the lowermost are carved with a Śaiva guardian on one face and a *śālabhañjikā* on the other. At Khilchipura near Mandasor, the recovery of a tall post that compares with the Nagari fragments suggests that it may have belonged to a *toraṇa* (Fig 1.28).[47] Three other Gupta sites, Eran, Garhwa, and Bilsadh, may be mentioned for having yielded pillar fragments stylistically datable to the sixth century,[48] but there is no clear evidence to suggest that they belonged to *toraṇas*.

D.3 : *Toraṇa* (reconstructed), Nagari, c. early sixth century.

D.4 : *Toraṇa* fragment, Nagari, c. early sixth century.

1.29 : *Candraśālikā,* Darra, c. fifth century (ref. Chp.3).

1.29

Notes and References

[1] The *gavākṣa* (dormer), a functional device in early Indian architecture, later acquires ornamental and symbolic significance. *Makaras* at the extremities of the *gavākṣa* can be seen in fair number in medieval temples and the *toraṇas* deriving from these are termed as *nāsī-toraṇas* in some Dravidian architectural treatises.

[2] Cunningham was of the opinion that originally there were more, probably four such *toraṇas*. See his *The Stūpa of Bharhut,* pp.128-130.

[3] The Sanchi *toraṇas* have been discussed at length by several scholars. The focus here is to view them in their early architectural context.

[4] For instance, *Toraṇa Śālabhañjikā,* Sanchi *Stūpa* I, Gift of Mrs. Tucker, BM, OA 1842.12-10.1.

[5] Vogel, *Catalogue of the Archaeological Museum at Mathura,* pp.162-165 and Plate XXV (M 1).

[6] For a possible explanation of this imagery, see Coomaraswamy, "The Makara," p.144: "From Bhartṛhari's *Nītiśataka*, pt. 4, it is clear that there existed some legendary connection of *makaras* with pearls and that to extract a pearl from a *makara's* jaws was a proverbial example of courage."

[7] Fragment from Kankali Tila, Lucknow State Museum, J 546, c. first century BCE.

[8] *Ibid.* J 547, c. first century BCE, 23 x 55 cm.

[9] Sarnath Museum No. 539, c. second to first century BCE, Chunar sandstone, 43 x 33 cm.

[10] Allahabad Museum No. 65, buff sandstone, 0.260 x 1.40 m, c. first century BCE.

[11] See Jarrige and Cambon, *Afghanistan - les trésors retrouvés..,* pp.244, 247; illus. 200 and 208.

[12] *Ibid.* illus. 208; Begram, site II, chamber 13, 42.7 x 24.6 cm, Musée national d'Afghanistan, MK 04.1.113; Tissot, *Catalogue of the National Museum of Afghanistan,* p.184: KM inv. no. 58-1-65.

[13] Jarrige and Cambon, *Afghanistan - les trésors...,* illus. 200: Begram, site II, chamber 13, ensemble 191h, 8.3 x 15.1 cm, Musée national d'Afghanistan, MK 04.1.68; Tissot, *Catalogue of the National Museum of Afghanistan,* p.234: K.p.Beg. 556.296, KM inv. no. 58-1-139.

[14] Tissot, *Catalogue of the National Museum of Afghanistan,* pp.183, KM inv. no. 58-1-64.

[15] *Ibid.* p.237, KM inv. no. 58-1-158.

[16] Marshall, *Taxila,* Vol. III, Plate 30 a.

[17] Huntington, *The Art of Ancient India,* pp.117-118. Huntington suggests a funerary symbolism for an eagle perched atop an entryway.

[18] For an early publication of this image, see Facenna, *Sculptures from the Sacred Area of Butkara I,* Plate CXLI and p.40. This is part of the IsIAO collections and is housed in the Museo Nazionale d'Arte Orientale 'G.Tucci,' in Rome.

[19] *Ibid.* Plate CLI.

[20] Deshpande, "The Rock-Cut Caves of Pitalkhora...," p.67.

[21] *Ibid.* Plate LV; NM no. 67-183, 55 cm x 55.5 cm x 19.5 cm.

[22] Knox, *Amaravati:,* Plate 40, p.99. A *toraṇabandha* is depicted on a railing stone fragment (BM no. 34).

[23] For instance, the doorframes of the Kankali Devi temple at Tigawa and the Parvati temple at Nachana Kuthara.

[24] See also Burgess, *The Buddhist Stūpas ...,* Plates v.2, xi.2, xii.3, xvi.1, xx.2, xxi.2, xxii.2, xvi.3, xxvii.5, and xxviii.3, and Knox, *Amaravati:,* Plates 9 inner face, 12 inner face, 13 inner face.

[25] Burgess, *The Buddhist Stupas..,* Plate xviii.2.

[26] Knox, *Amaravati:,* p.29, Plate 13.

[27] *Ibid.,* pp.158-161, Plates 85 and 86; BM no.s 84 and 86, c. third century.

[28] *WD 1061, Antiquities at Amaravati 1816-1817,* Drawings W. Cat. ccxxiii 9, OIOC, British Library, London.

[29] *Ibid.* No. 37/ 42, 1; TA 15th February 1817. The dimensions of the slab on which this is carved have been indicated as 3' 11¾" x 1' 2¼"; the slab is broken from the top so that the actual height must have been more than 4'.

[30] *Ibid.* No. 66/ 71 b; T.A. June 1817. The dimensions of this slab are recorded as 5' 10" x 10¼".

[31] This type has been identified by Knox and others as being the dome slabs on the original Amaravati *stūpa*. The dimensions of this latter slab are recorded as 5' 10" x 3' 6¾".

[32] Bandyopadhyay, *Architectural Motifs in Early Mediaeval Art of Eastern India...,* p.7 and Fig. 4.

[33] Tamralipta Museum and Research Centre, Tamluk, Accession No. 583, as mentioned by Bandyopadhyaya, *Architectural...,* p.7.

[34] See Cunningham, *Mahabodhi...*; Spooner, "The Bodh-Gaya Plaque," pp.1-4.

[35] Meister, ed., *Ananda Coomaraswamy: Essays in Early Indian Architecture,* pp.5-13, Plate CXXII, Fig. 3.

[36] *The Questions of Milinda,* p.1: "The Blessed One's City of Righteousness has righteousness for its rampart, and fear of sin for its moat, knowledge for its city gate, zeal for the gate tower, faith for the pillars at its base, mindfulness for the guard, and wisdom for the palace, the *Suttantas* for the market place, the *Abhidhamma* for the public square, the *Vinaya* for its judgement hall, and constant self-possession for its street."

[37] *The Jātaka or Stories of the Buddha's Former Births,* Vol. II, pp.63-65:

"O Elephant, a hero thou, whose home is in the field;
There stands the gate *(toraṇaṁ)* before thee now: why dost thou turn and yield?
"Make haste! Break through the iron bar, and beat the pillars down!
Crash through the gates *(toraṇāni)* made fast for war and enter in the town!

"The elephant listened; one word of advice was enough to turn him. Winding his trunk about the shafts of the pillars, he tore them up like so many toadstools: he beat against the gateway *(toraṇaṁ madditvā)*, broke down the bars, and forcing his way through, entered the city and won it for his king."

[38] *Ibid.* pp.135:

Tr. "Behold created in this jewel a city furnished with solid foundations, with many gateways and walls *(bahupākāratoraṇaṁ),* and with many pleasant spots where four roads meet. Pillars and trenches, bars and bolts, watch towers and gates, behold all created in the jewel.

"See various troops of birds in the roads under the gateways *(toraṇamaggesu)*, geese, herons, peacocks, ruddy geese and ospreys; cuckoos, spotted birds, peacocks, *jīvājīvakas*, birds of every sort, behold gathered together and created in the jewel."

The word *toraṇamaggesu* has been translated by Cowell to mean 'under the gateways'. It has also been interpreted as the street *(mārga)* in which a *toraṇa* is present, *i.e.* the main street of a city. See Meister ed. *Ananda Coomaraswamy: Essays in Early Indian Architecture,* p.5

[39] *Mṛchchhakaṭika of Śūdraka,* p.157:"Oh! How beautiful is this gate of Vasantasenā's mansion! ... It has raised its top to a great height, as if out of curiosity to have a sight of the celestial regions. It is adorned with a string of a huge garland of jasmine flowers which is tossing about and hanging down from it, making one mistake it for the trunk of (Indra's elephant) Airāvata. It is splendidly decked with a lofty arch of ivory *(dantidanta-toraṇa)*. It is decorated with a number of auspicious banners, which look lovely with the lustre of costly jewels, whose finger-like tips are tremulously shaking as they are tossed about by the force of wind, and which thus seem as if it were beckoning me to get in. Both its sides are rendered attractive by auspicious crystal jars, which are kept on the pedestal of the pillars supporting the archway *(toraṇa-dharaṇa-stambha-vedikā)*, and which are charming on account of the green mango leaves placed gracefully therein. Its golden panels are thickly set with diamonds, and are as hard to break open as the chest of a big demon..."

[40] *Aśvaghoṣa's Buddhacarita,* v.52, p.71: "Another lay, leaning against the side of a window with her beautiful necklaces dangling, and seemed with her slender body bent like a bow as if turned into the statue of a *śāla* plucker *(śālabhañjikā)* on a gateway *(toraṇa)*."

[41] It is well-known that the main temple in South India is termed *vimāna.* The auditorium corresponds to the *raṅgamaṇḍapa* of later temples where ritualistic music and dance performances took place. The entrance doors and interiors of the various halls of medieval temples are often embellished with *toraṇas.*

[42] *Jīvājīvābhigama Sūtra [Part I].*

[43] See also Acharya, *A Dictionary of Hindu Architecture,* p.250.

[44] The *Bṛhat Saṁhitā* (c. mid-sixth century) as well as the *Viṣṇudharmottara Purāṇa* (c. late sixth to early seventh century) make several references to *toraṇas* made of wood. See App. 3, nos. 1 and 2.

[45] Dimensions: 195 x 67 x 69 cm; For details, *see* Williams, *The Art of Gupta India.,* pp.52-55, Plates 50-53; and *ASIAR* 1924-25, p.165, Pl. XLII c, d.

[46] The height of the pillars is approximately 12 ft., which is much less than the *toraṇas* from Sanchi and Bharhut, and the pillars appear too thin (20 cms. in cross section) to be *toraṇa* pillars. See Bhandarkar, "Two Sculptures at Mandor," pp.135-140. Bhandarkar mentions that the structure seems to have been intact during the time of Colonel Tod; See Tod, *Annals and Antiquities of Rajasthan,* Vol. I, p.684: "The chief memorials of the Purihara are a gateway and a magnificent *torun*, or triumphal arch, placed towards the south-east angle of the castle." Bhandarkar mentions that the *toraṇa* pillars (?) were found exactly at the spot where Tod's gateway and *torun* stood. See also Marshall and Sahni, "Excavations at Mandor," pp.93-96, Plate XLIV b; Williams, *The Art of Gupta India.,* pp.55-58.

[47] Williams, *The Art of Gupta India.,* p.142.

[48] *Ibid.*, pp.152-155.

CHAPTER 2

The Toraṇa in Treatises

D.54

The Treatises and their Nature

A critical analysis of the technical information recorded in the architectural treatises is seldom met in contemporary writings on Indian architectural history, partly because such an attempt is fraught with difficulties. The texts are written in the form of Sanskrit verses and are cryptic and corrupt at places. Familiarity with the traditional architectural forms alongside knowledge of Sanskrit is crucial to a critical interpretation of these texts. As the codification of the architectural principles was the domain of temple priests or the literate group rather than the architects-sculptors, not all aspects of practice were recorded; conversely, some theoretical extrapolations are not encountered in practice. Even so, the medieval treatises do contain vital information about the practice of traditional Indian architecture. The formal features, types, constituent parts, forms and proportions, architectural settings, thematic content, and significance of the *toraṇas* recorded in these are critically interpreted here to arrive at workable categories for analysis. The following treatises have been consulted in this study:

Śaiva Āgamas
Kāmikāgama (KA) (c. 12th century and later)
Suprabhedāgama (SA) (c. 11th-12th century)

Śaiva Kriyā-grantha
Īśānaśivagurudevapaddhati of Īśānaśivācārya *(ISP)* (c. 12th century)

Jain Saṁhitā
Jinasaṁhitā of Bhaṭṭāraka Ekasaṁdhī *(JS)* (c. late 13th-early 14th century: unpublished)

Vāstuśāstras
Mayamata (MM) (c. 11th century)
Prayogamañjarī
(c. late 11th-early 12th century: unpublished)
Samarāṅgaṇasūtradhāra (SS) (c. 1035-1055 CE)
Kaṭakabhūṣaṇa (c. 12th century: unpublished)
Aparājitapṛcchā (Appr.)
(c. late 12th-early 13th century)
Kāśyapaśilpa (KS) (c. 13th century)
Mānasāra (MS) (c. 15th-16th century)[1]

Other than the *SS* (central Indian text) and the *Appr.* (western Indian text), all the texts mentioned above are from southern India. However, some additional western Indian texts have also been consulted at times for gaining greater clarity. Of these, the *Vāstuśāstra* of Viśvakarmā, the *Vāstuvidyā* of Viśvakarmā, and the *Jayapṛcchādhikāra* are earlier than the *Appr.* and have been assigned to the latter part of the 11th century.[2] In addition, the *Kṣīrārṇava* (c. early 15th century), the *Vṛkṣārṇava* (c. third quarter of 15th century)[3], and the *Rūpamaṇḍana* of Sūtradhāra Maṇḍana (c. mid 15th century) are also taken into account. Given the close affinities between western and central Indian temples, these regions may be treated as a unit while analysing technical treatises for *toraṇas* in relation to practice.[4] A study of the sections on *toraṇas* in the *SS* and the *Appr.* also provides some general guidelines that can be extended to an understanding of parallel traditions in regions beyond western and central India. The larger corpus of texts belongs to southern India and details about *toraṇas* articulated in them are also relevant to the other regions.

Meaning of the Term

The lexicons clarify the meaning of a *toraṇa* as understood during the ancient and medieval periods (see Introduction). The author of the *SS* describes a *toraṇa* as the star-shaped segment of a circle *(tārakākṛti-maṇḍalam)* that links the upper sections of two pillars. It bears two *makara* faces and two half-moon shaped arcs *(ardhacandra-dvayākṛti)* (App. 3, no. 3). Such *toraṇas* are known from the early medieval monuments from diverse regions such as the Sonkansārī temple no. 1 (c. late seventh century) at Ghumli in Gujarat,[5] the Mālegittī Śivālaya at Badami (c. seventh century), the Draupadī Ratha at Mamallapuram (c. mid seventh century), and the Lakṣmaṇa temple (954 CE) at Khajuraho.

Role and Purpose

The literary and archaeological sources of the early period highlight the auspicious, symbolic, didactic, narrative, and ornamental significance of the *toraṇa* (see Chapter 1). The *SS* notes its auspicious significance at the entry and exit points (App. 3, no. 4). This text also devotes an entire chapter to the prayer for peace in the inauspicious event of damage caused to the *toraṇa* (App. 3, no. 5).[6] It discusses the ways in which a *toraṇa* may suffer damage or destruction, the calamities that would befall a nation or a community as a consequence, and the remedial measures that should be undertaken. Though several observations in this chapter reveal prevalent superstitions,[7] they also underline the importance given to the *toraṇa*. Stray references to the ornamental purpose of *toraṇas* are found in many of the medieval treatises. The *ISP* distinguishes between the main *(kāya)* and the subsidiary parts *(anukāya)* of a structure. The base, pillars, walls, etc. form the main body *(kāya)* of a structure, while the *toraṇa* as part of its ancillary limbs *(anukāya)* is meant for embellishment (App. 3, no. 6).

Architectural Setting

Almost all these texts discuss the location of the *toraṇa* in relation to the structure. The *SS* and the *Appr.* mention three sizes: large, medium, and small. They may be constructed in the upper region of the gateway *(pratolī)*, at the entrance to the temple (here, *gaṇḍa*), and in front of the balustrades flanking the stairway of a temple (*śuṇḍikā*) (App. 3, nos. 7a-b).[8] Free-standing *toraṇas* are seen at the entrances to several medieval temples in Gujarat, Rajasthan, and Madhya Pradesh. Those at Asoda in Gujarat (Fig. 4.80) may be cited here as an illustration, while those at Dabhoi and Jhinjhuwada are fine examples of *pratolī toraṇas* (Figs. 4.91-4.94). In practice, the distinction between those in front of the temple balustrades (*śuṇḍikā*) and those fronting the temples is not always spelt out.[9] The *Kṣīrārṇava* (v. 2.22) and the *Dīpārṇava* (vv. 3.23, 3.24) repeat the description, with minor modifications. The *Appr.* states that the *toraṇa* meant for petty rulers is inferior to the lion gate (*siṁhadvāra*) used at the entrance to the king's palace (App. 3, no. 8).

The *toraṇa* should be placed in the (i) *stambha-garbha* (at the centre of the pillar), (ii) *bhitti-garbha* (centre of the wall), (iii) in between the two, or (iv) in the *brahmasthānādi-garbha,* according to the texts (App. 3, no. 9). Though its exact import is obscure, a *toraṇa* placed in the *brahmasthānādi-garbha* may refer to the one framing the image installed in the sanctum *(garbhagṛha)* or to the one at the sanctum's entrance. Several examples of both varieties are found in practice; the one framing Vaikuṇṭha Viṣṇu in the sanctum of the Lakṣmaṇa temple at Khajuraho and another on the door-lintel of the sanctum of the Mahāvīra temple at Ghanerav bear this out (Fig. 4.16). The *toraṇa* in the *bhitti-*

D.5 : *Uttuṅga-toraṇa* (after a drawing of the Siddhapur *toraṇa* by Kinloch Forbes reproduced in Burgess and Cousens, *Architectural...*, Plate XLIV, 2).

D.6a-f : *Āndola-toraṇas.*

garbha probably refers to the one carved in the niche or at the central offset on the temple wall, of which there are numerous examples. The garland *(toraṇamālā)* of the free-standing examples is placed between the pillars and it appears to emerge from the centre of the pillars (*stambha-garbha)*, as at the Limboja Mātā temple at Delmal (Fig. 4.74). The *Kṣīrārṇava* (v. 2.23) and the *Dīpārṇava* (v. 3.26) also give similar accounts.

Dravidian texts such as the *MM* (Chapters 18-22) place the *toraṇas* at entrances to the temple halls, palaces, and other dwellings. In sacred architecture, they should be placed at the *hāra* (parapet of a storied temple) recesses, at the centre of the building's façade, flanking the entrance doors, above the entrance doors, between pilasters, and on the median and corner projections and recesses. The *KS* refers to *toraṇas* located in the centre of temple halls, on the temple walls, parapets, and above the entrances. It refers to the *kuḍya-toraṇa* (wall *toraṇa*), the *dvāra-toraṇa* (*toraṇa* at the entrance), and the *stambha-toraṇa* (pillar *toraṇa*) and draws parallels between them (App. 3, nos. 10, 23). There is also reference to the presence of *toraṇas* on the *nāsīs* (gable-ends) of Dravidian temples (App. 3, no. 11). The *MS* adds that *toraṇas* are also meant for the thrones of gods and kings (App. 3, no. 12). Other Dravidian texts give more or less comparable notices.

The Formal Types

The *toraṇas* may be categorized on the basis of their (i) placement in an architectural setting, (ii) their visual formulations, and (iii) their sculptural embellishment. The first has already been discussed in the previous section. Of the other two, Dravidian texts are more articulate on categories based on sculptural embellishment whereas the *Appr.* explicates basic formal varieties. The latter mentions five types of free-standing *toraṇas*, namely, the *Uttuṅga, Mālādhara, Vicitra, Citrarūpaka,* and *Makaradhvaja* (App. 3, no. 13). Each differs from the other in the number of pillars or other components.

The *Uttuṅga-toraṇa* is described in detail along with the proportionate measurements of its component parts (App. 3, no. 14).[10] It comprises two pillars topped by attic pillars that support a lintel and an undulating pediment *(illikāvalaṇa)* above. A *toraṇa*-garland, known by the name *illikā*[11] (composed of sequential arcs or loops) is placed between the attic pillars, with *makaras* and miniature niche-shrines *(tilakas)* at the extremes. The text states that images of the *purāṇic* triad (Śiva, Brahmā, and Viṣṇu), with Sadāśiva at the centre, should grace the pediment. This variant (D.5), with some adaptations, was very popular in western India;

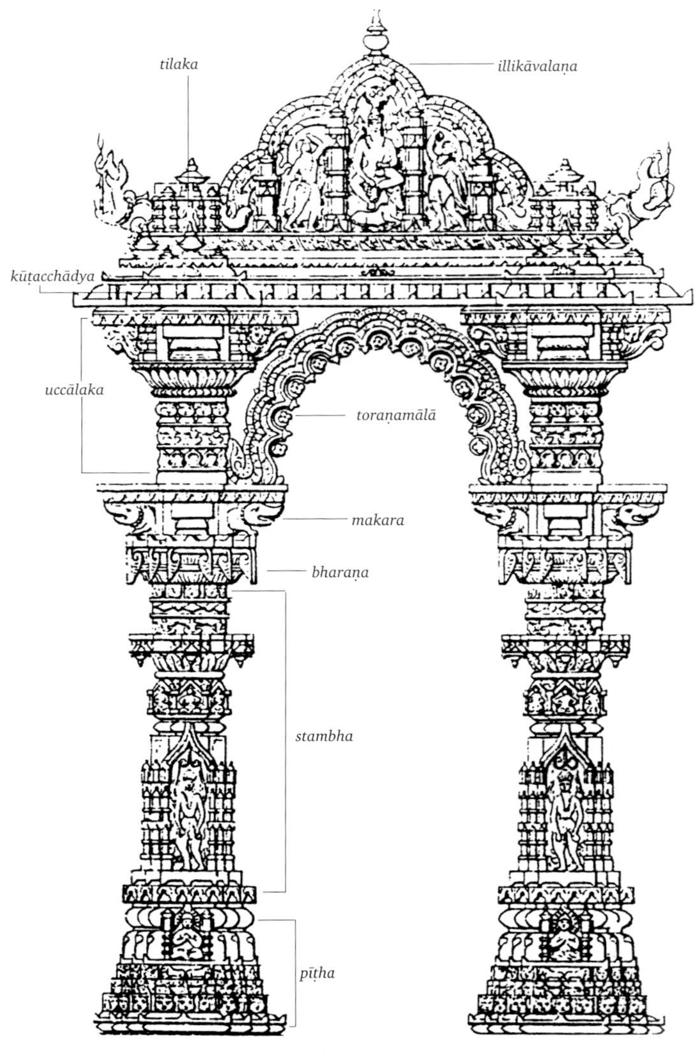

D.5

it is also illustrated in the manuals of the architect-sculptors belonging to the Sompura family. It can be seen, for instance, at the entrance to the Limboja Mātā temple complex at Delmal, at Piludra (Figs. 4.74, 4.81), as also at several other sites. In practice, the deity to whom the main temple is dedicated occupies the central position on the pediment in place of Sadāśiva. For instance, the *toraṇa* at Piludra bears the Sun god; in the Delmal instance, the central image is of a goddess (Limboja Mātā). The *Uttuṅga-toraṇa* is bifacial, meant to be viewed from both sides (when entering the temple and returning from it), so the undulating pediment and the inset figures are often carved identically on the two faces. The pillars, like the temple pillars, are decorated with bracket figures; attic pillars are present only in the larger *toraṇas*.

When two adjacent pillars are added to the *Uttuṅga-toraṇa*, the *Mālādhara-toraṇa* is created (App. 3, no. 15). It is not commonly found in practice, but those at Nagda and Menal fit the description (Figs. 4.66, 4.75). The *toraṇa* with four pillars forming a square and decorated with *illikā* arcs in the four directions is described as the *Vicitra-toraṇa* (App. 3, no. 16). The arrangement between the pillars of the northern porch of the dance hall *(raṅgamaṇḍapa)* of the damaged Rudramahālaya at Siddhapur fits this description (Fig. 4.37). The *Citrarūpaka-toraṇa* is described as one in which balustered dados (*mattavāraṇas*) surround the two sides of the pillars. The *Makaradhvaja-toraṇa* is of a similar nature but comprises six pillars (App. 3, no. 17). There are no exact extant examples of the *Citrarūpaka* and *Makaradhvaja* varieties as described in the *Appr.*, though the instance in the upper reaches of the Mānastambha at Chittor, or those in the front porches of some medieval central Indian temples, could be interpreted as coming close to the *Citrarūpaka* variety (Figs. 4.15, 4.111). The last two textual varieties reflect the tendency in the treatises to extrapolate theoretical types from more established norms and invent complex progressions which are not likely to exist in practice. The five textual types are also described similarly in the *Vāstuvidyā* of Viśvakarmā.[12]

In the manuals of the practising architect-sculptors such as P.O. Sompura,[13] the *toraṇa*-garland is primarily of two types, *āndola* and *illikā* (D.6a-f and D.7a-g). The *illikā* garland

D.6a

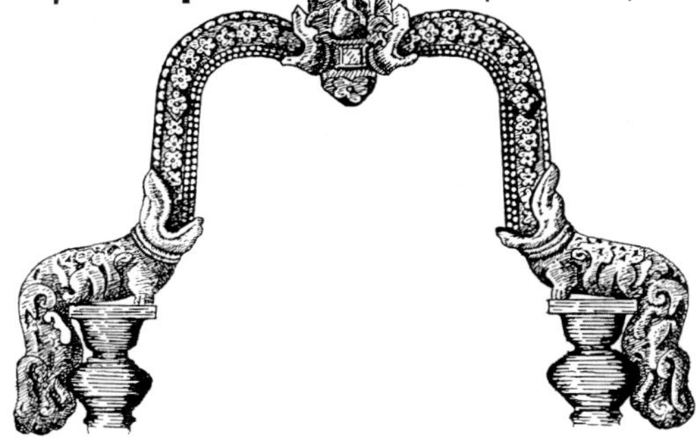
D.6b

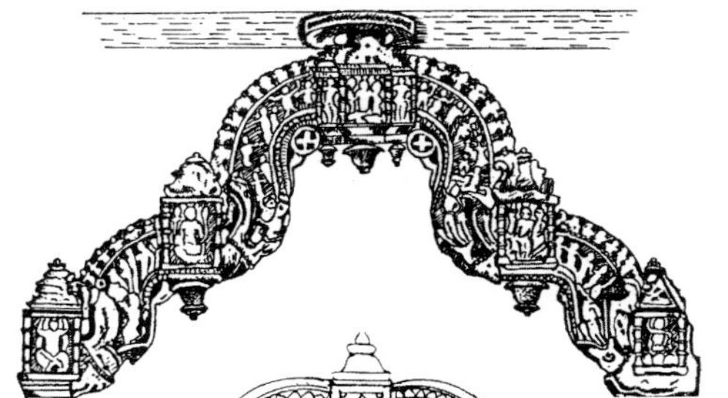
D.6c

D.6d

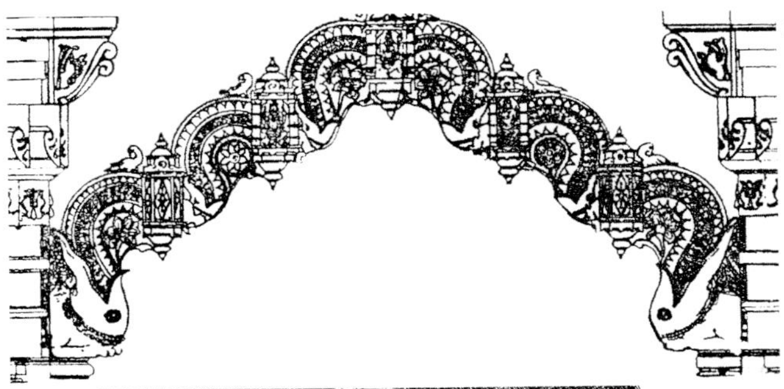
D.6e

D.6f

D.7a-g : *Illikā-toraṇas*

D.7e

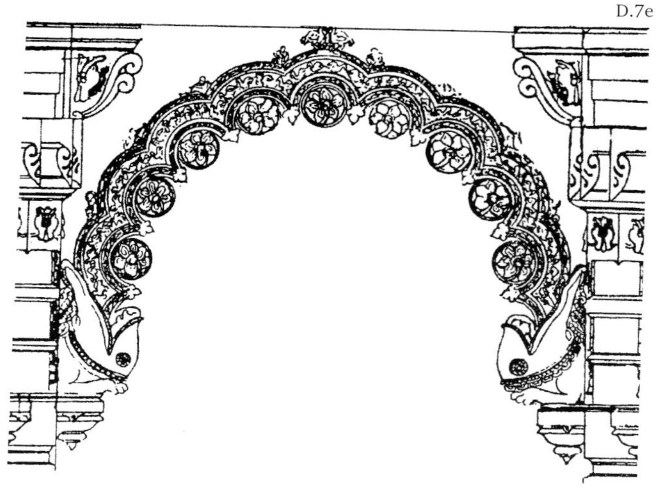

D.7a

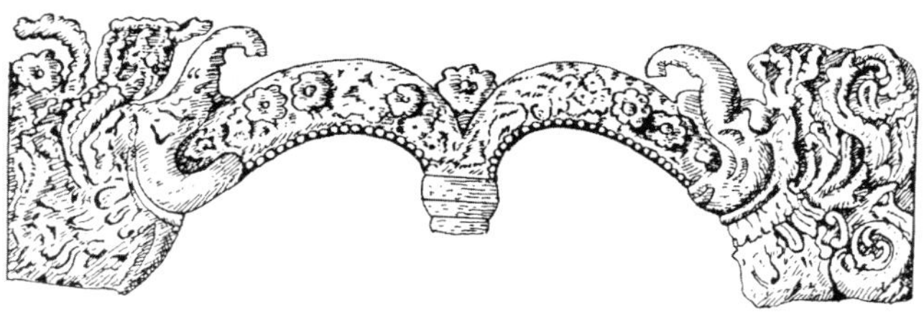

D.7b

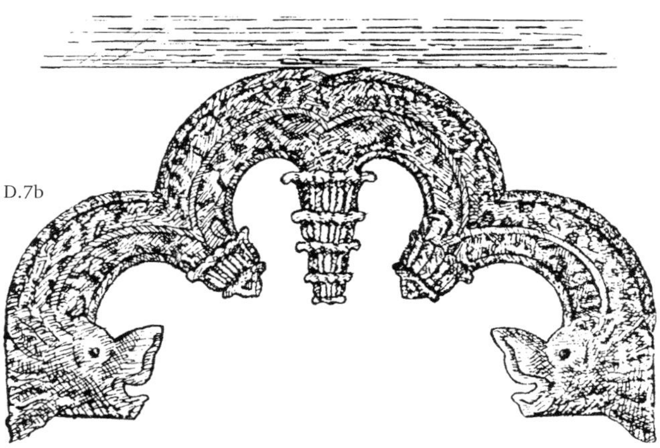

D.7c

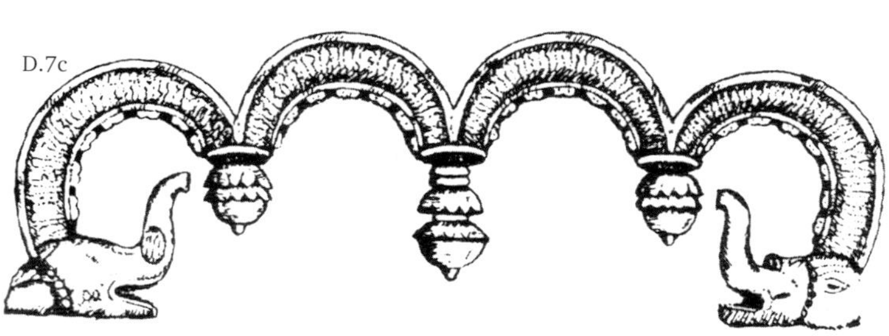

D.7d

derives its name from the gait of a caterpillar and is formed of a succession of semi-circular arcs. The *āndola* garland emulates wave-like undulations and follows a sinusoidal rhythm. Both variations are met in Gujarat, Rajasthan, and Central India; in Karnataka, one encounters prolific, innovative, and luxuriant variants of the *illikā-torana,* distinct from those seen in Gujarat. At times the two basic units, the arc or loop of the *illikā* and the S-shaped unit of the *āndola*, combine to create newer patterns, as in the dance-hall of the Lūṇa Vasahī temple at Mount Abu (D.8; Fig. 4.56).

Unlike the *illikā-toraṇa*, which finds mention in the *SS* and the *Appr.* (App. 3, no.s 14, 27), the *āndola-toraṇa* is rarely mentioned in the treatises although it is seen frequently in practice and is also recorded in the sculptors' manuals. One omnibus manuscript does describe the *āndola-toraṇa* (App. 3, no. 18).[14] There, the components of the *āndola-toraṇa*: *tilaka* (miniature niche-shrine), *lumbī* (pendant motif), *amaragaṇa* (gods), and *grāsa* (gorgon face) are mentioned as also the S-shaped segments *(madalas)* of the *toraṇa,* which should pass through the miniature niches. The author of the *Rūpamaṇḍana* classifies five types of *toraṇas* based on the number of *rathikās* (niches harbouring divinities). These are the *Lalitam, Illikākāram, Valitodaram, Śrīpuñjam,* and *Nandavardhana* (App. 3, no. 19).[15] It refers

D.7f

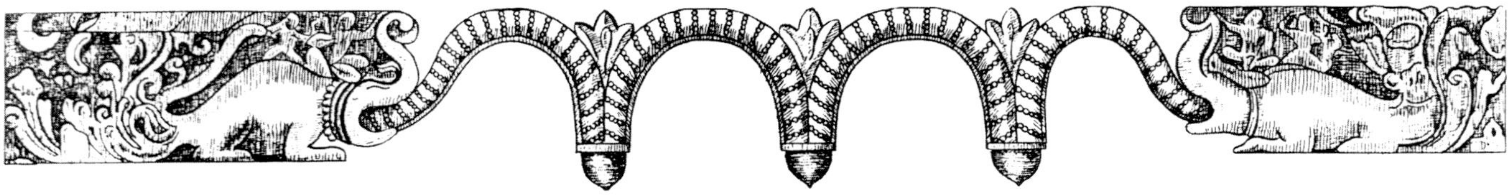

to the *toraṇas* that are carved as image-frames for various divinities. *Lalitam* represents the arch of single curvature and *illikākāram* plausibly refers to the shape of the arcs of the *illikā-toraṇa* explained earlier. *Valitodaram* was *triratha* (with three projections), *Śrīpuñjam* was of five *(pañcarathikā)*, and *Nandavardhana* of seven projections or niches. These seem to indicate the *āndola* (sinusoidal) variety punctuated with the niches *(rathikās)* harbouring various divinities, *grāsas* (gorgon faces), and *makaras*. Corresponding drawings can be seen in a collection of architectural drawings by P.O. Sompura,[16] which clarify the particular interpretation of the Sompura sculptors.

Amongst Dravidian texts, the *MS* is the most explicit on the subject of the configuration of *toraṇas*. The arch may be circular *(vṛttam,* D.9*)*, of three or six sections *(triyugmam)*, in the shape of a half- or crescent-moon *(ardhacandrākṛti* or *bālacandra)*, of these three types *(tridhā)*[17], or bow-shaped *(cāpākāra, dhanurākṛti,* D.10*)*, or any other desired shape (App. 3, no. 20). The methods of construction of various types of arches are also explained. Semi-circular arches were very popular in the Tamil region during the Coḷa period. The crescent- or half-moon shaped arches are mentioned in passing by as many as six of the texts (App. 4).

Sculptural Embellishment and Material

Toraṇas have also been classified on the basis of the material used for their creation and also by the nature of their sculptural embellishments. The *SS* mentions three types: those made of gold (*suvarṇa-toraṇas*), of jewels or precious stones *(maṇi-toraṇas)*, and of flowers *(puṣpa-toraṇas)* (App. 3, no. 21).

Dravidian texts are more articulate in classifying them by the nature of sculptural embellishment (App. 4). The *patra-toraṇa* finds elaboration in seven of them; the *JS* describes a similar type but labels it *bhadra-toraṇa,* most likely an error in spelling.[18] The *makara-toraṇa* and *citra-toraṇa* are treated at some length in eight of the texts.

The *MS* is the only Dravidian text (from those considered here) to take note of the *ratna-toraṇa* and the *puṣpa-toraṇa*. It advocates the depiction of Lakṣmī with various adornments in the central portion of the arch, along with the lotus and the elephants (App. 3, no. 26). An example may be seen on the lintel at the entrance to Sanctuary 1 (a Śiva temple) in the Guḍḍam Wānparthy *tāluk* of Mahboobnagar District (Fig. 3.55). The *MM* refers to three types, *patra-toraṇa, makara-toraṇa,* and *citra-toraṇa* (App. 3, no. 22). The *patra-toraṇa* is stated to be in the shape of a crescent moon, ornamented with foliage. That in which *makaras* are placed at the ends and the arc is filled with creepers of various kinds is called the *makara-toraṇa*. The *citra-toraṇa* is one in which Purin[19] at the centre is flanked by *makaras* which he holds by their trunks. From their jaws pour celestials, dwarfs, leonine creatures, geese, as well as garlands and cascades of jewels. This type is stated to be appropriate for gods and kings.[20] The measurements of these are given in detail. The presence of the eight auspicious symbols *(aṣṭa-maṅgalas)* above the lintel and Pañcavaktra (Śiva) at the centre are prescribed for all varieties of *toraṇas* suitable for gods and others.

D.7g

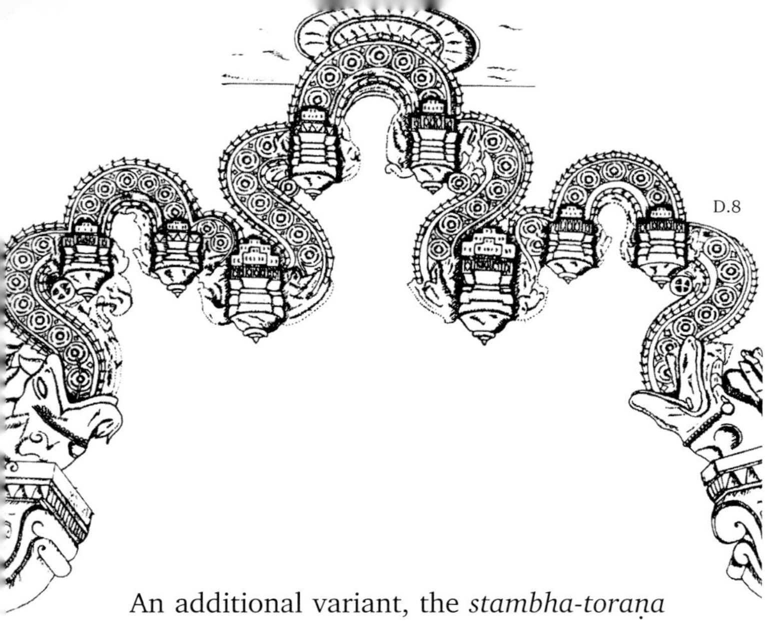

D.8

refer to pillared *toraṇas* placed at the entrances (App. 3, no. 23, v.30). Verses found in the *MM* are frequently repeated in this text also, and a separate discussion on them is therefore not required.[24] Verses from the *KA,* which describe the various types of *toraṇas,* are also comparable to those in the *MM* (App. 3, no. 24).[25] Such borrowings (as also noticed in central and western Indian texts)[26] clearly indicate the extent and scope of dissemination of traditional knowledge as well as the familiarity of the writer of one text with the other texts.

An additional variant, the *stambha-toraṇa* (pillared *toraṇa*), is also included (App. 3, no. 22). This plausibly refers to the free-standing examples or may even be a reference to those crowning the *kuḍya-stambhas* (wall-pilasters) and those carved on pillars (p.273) as seen in medieval Karnataka temples. The *MM* makes several repeated references to *toraṇas* in various parts of the temple, pavilion, house, etc.[21]

The *KS* devotes two chapters to the *toraṇas*.[22] The types and their descriptions are very similar to those given in the *MM,* but there are some minor differences (App. 3, no. 23). For instance, the *makara-toraṇa* is described as the one with the *makaras* at the two sides, with five-faced Śiva (*pañca-vaktra*), with Purim (*kīrttimukha*?)[23] in the centre, with a variety of creepers, fruits, and other ornamentations filling the arch. Such examples may be met on the walls of the Kailāsanātha temple at Kanchipuram. The *KS* also states that the *dvāra-toraṇa* (door or entrance arch) and the *stambha-toraṇa* (pillared arch) are one and the same. This is understandable, because, in practice both these

The *KA,* interestingly enough, relates the archways to the hierarchical structure of social orders (App. 3, no. 24, 55.87-88). Thus, the *makara-toraṇa* is deemed fit to adorn the abodes of gods, brahmins, and kings. The *citra-toraṇa* is considered suitable for the residences of merchants and the *toraṇa* with lotuses for the houses of *śudras*, the lowest in the social hierarchy. The *ISP* also discusses various types of *toraṇas* in a similar vein (App. 3, no. 25).[27]

The different types of *toraṇas* mentioned in the Dravidian texts can be substantiated with examples from ancient and medieval Indian architecture. Their names seem to adhere to the materials of which they were made. The *puṣpa-toraṇa* would have derived from the floral festoons seen to this day on festive occasions in India. The *patra-toraṇa* emulates those made of leaves, whereas the *ratna-toraṇa* appears to derive its name from the arches adorned with precious gems and semi-precious stones, as mentioned in some early texts. All these varieties were later carved in stone to embellish the medieval monuments.

D.9

D.8 : Serpentine *toraṇa*-Lūṇa Vasahī variant.

D.9 : *Vṛttākāra-toraṇa.*

D.10 : *Cāpākāra-toraṇa.*

D.10

Measurements and Proportions

Dravidian texts also provide details about the structural aspects of *toraṇas*. The relative proportions of the pillar with respect to the lintel-arch, the distance between the pillars supporting the arch, the dimensions of the architrave above the pillars supporting the arch, the constituents of the lintel-arch such as the *jhaṣa* (big fish or crocodile, *makara*), and other details are all indicated.[28] These have not been discussed here as they do not deal with criteria relevant to our analysis.[29]

The many elaborations, adaptations, and transformations of the *toraṇa* observed during the ancient and medieval periods have, of course, not all been postulated in the treatises. All the theoretical extrapolations of the texts are also not found in practice. Yet, the textual criteria and norms pertaining to *toraṇas* give insights into its traditional understandings, provide a vocabulary, and suggest some guidelines within which an analysis of the available examples can be attempted. One may add that the manner in which norms and criteria are laid out in the treatises betrays the fluidity and reciprocal relationship to practice that inheres within their seemingly tenacious and rigid framework. To the discerning mind and eye, it reveals the artistic licence that always rested with the architect-sculptors to affect a refreshing range of creative expressions within the framework of tradition.

Notes and References

[1] The dates of the various treatises are based on the consensus of scholars in the case of the edited texts. For some, such as the *MS,* a later date is ascribed, based on the details of architectural elements given in the text in relation to what is observed in practice. I am grateful to Prof. M.A. Dhaky for his guidance in this regard.

[2] See Dhaky, "Genesis and Development ...," pp.125-127.

[3] *Ibid.*

[4] Especially noteworthy is the close link between the central Indian *SS* and the western Indian *Appr.* The former text is earlier by more than a century and a half and appears to have inspired the latter. See Dhaky, "The Influence of *Samarāṅgaṇasūtradhāra...*," pp.226-234.

[5] After the earthquake of 2001, one of the *toraṇas* from the central offset niche on the outer temple wall has been destroyed. See Fig. 4.3 here.

[6] Chapter 46 of the *SS* is devoted to *Toraṇabhaṅgādi śāntika*. This section states that: (*tr.*) If an old or new *toraṇa*, or a half-constructed *toraṇa*, or a *toraṇa* constructed for gods or kings falls down or is damaged..., there could be apprehension of death and draught. (In such an event), the wise should cause the following for (restoring) peace... destruction of a *toraṇa* indicates (prognosticates) the destruction of a nation.

[7] For example, there is a description of the misfortune brought about by the entry of a pigeon, *SS* 46.19-35.

[8] The *SS* mentions *śukāgre* whereas the *Appr.* mentions *śuṇḍikāgre* (*śuṇḍikā,* shape of a she-elephant's trunk). *Śukāgre* (lit. parrot's beak) applies to the *śukanāsa* of the temple.

[9] If the term is taken as *śukāgre,* these would then refer to *toraṇas* carved in relief at the superstructure antefix. Several such instances are encountered in Karnataka.

[10] *(Tr.)* The socle *(pīṭha)* [of the *toraṇa*] should be a little lower than the socle of the temple. The lintel *(paṭṭa)* should correspond to that of the temple. The proportions of the constituent parts (from bottom to top) should be: socle-1.75 parts, pillar base *(kumbhikā)*-1 part, pillar shaft *(stambha)*-5 parts, echinus *(bharaṇa)*-0.5 parts, capital *(śiraḥ)*-0.25 parts, attic pillar *(gadaḍī)*-1.75 parts. The lintel resting upon the attic pillars should be of one part and above that should be the ribbed awning. Miniature niche-shrines *(tilakas)* should be placed at the centre of the pillars *(stambha-garbha)*, and from either side should emerge

makaras. The *illikāvalaṇa* (convoluted caterpillar-like arcs of the *toraṇa* garland) should be of six arcs. The image of Sadāśiva should be placed in the centre, Brahmā to his left, and Viṣṇu to his right. Above this should be the *illikā* (*i.e. illikāvalaṇa* of the pediment) decoration. This type of *toraṇa* is known by the name *Uttuṅga* in the *Appr.* I have not attempted to verify the proportions mentioned in the text.

11 *Illikā* literally means caterpillar, thus drawing an analogy with the arc-like gait of caterpillars.

12 *Śilpa Smṛti Vāstuvidyāyām (Uttarārdha)*, pp.276-278.

13 Sompura, *Album of Architectural Designs*.

14 I am grateful to Professor M.A. Dhaky for drawing my attention to these verses from an omnibus manuscript in his collection, suggested by him to be of the 11th century. But he also mentions that the use of different metres, as is evident from the verses in this manuscript, was resorted to in western Indian *vāstuśāstras* only in the 15th century (through personal communication, May 2005).

15 The text is corrupt, so it is difficult to say if *ca + illikākāram* (and the *illikā* shape) or *ca+iti+ākāram* (and this shape) is intended.

16 Sompura, *Album of Architectural Designs*, p.97.

17 Another interpretation of the word *tridhā* could be 'triangular', as is the case with P.K. Acharya's translation, although triangular ones are rarely met in practice. The *toraṇa* at the entrance to the front porch of the Ghaṭeśvara temple at Badoli resembles a triangle (Fig. 4.22a).

18 This may be a grammatical error as the alphabets *'pa'* and *'bha'* as also *'da'* and *'ta'* share the same script in Tamil. Hence *patra* and *bhadra* would be written similarly in Tamil. When transcribed in Sanskrit, such an error becomes a possibility.

19 It is not clear what the author intends to suggest by the term Purin. The placement indicated is most suitable to its interpretation as *kīrttimukha*. Purin(m) may even stand for a filling element.

20 The three-fold classification of *toraṇas* as belonging to the *patra-*, *makara-* and *citra-toraṇa* types in *MM* differs, in nomenclature and details, from the four-fold classification of *puṣpa-*, *patra-*, *ratna-* and *citra-toraṇas* given in the *MS;* the basic sculptural embellishments, however, remain the same.

21 *Mayamatam,* Vols. I & II, 18.79, 175,19.49, 20.8, 21.20, 22.12, 25.41, 59, 179$^1/_2$, etc.

22 Chapters 12 *(Toraṇalakṣaṇam)* and 14 *(Stambhatoraṇam)*.

23 The simultaneous mention of the names, Purim and Pañcavaktra, clearly indicates that Purim could not stand for Śiva. Further, the description in the *MM* (21.70-72) indicates that it is most likely the *kīrttimukha* that is being referred to. Such representations of the *kīrtttimukha* at the apex of the *toraṇa*, flanked by *makaras* held by the trunks, are also reminiscent of *toraṇas* carved on the lintels of Cambodian temples.

24 Verses 16, 17, 18 and 20 of the 14th chapter of the *KS* almost repeat the verses 74 and 75 of the 21st chapter of *MM.* Again, verses 26-29 of the 14th chapter of *KS* correspond to verses 77-79 of the 21st chapter of *MM.* The *aṣṭamaṅgalas* mentioned here also correspond to another list of *aṣṭamaṅgalas* mentioned in the *MM* (12.34,35). Yet again, the description of the *stambhatoraṇaṁ* in verses 31-34 of the 14th chapter of the *KS* tallies with the same given in the verses 29-33 of the *MM.*

25 The chapter on the methods for the ornamentation of temples *(Prāsādabhūṣaṇavidhi)* in the *KA* includes different types of *toraṇas*. These correspond very closely to verses occurring in *Toraṇādividhāna* in the 21st chapter of the *MM* (21.68-76).

26 See endnote 4.

27 The three-fold classification of the *toraṇas* compares well with the one given in *MM* (21.68-80). *MM* recommends the *citra-toraṇa* for gods and kings (App. 3, no. 22) whereas *ISP* and *KA* suggest the *makara-toraṇa* for the same.

28 See *MM* 20.36-39 and 21.29-33; *KS* 12.1-5; *MS* (XLVI.2-15), in the respective editions mentioned in the Bibliography. See also endnote 10 for the proportionate measurements of an *Uttuṅga-toraṇa*.

29 A comparison of the measurements and proportions with actual examples is not attempted by this author.

3.82

CHAPTER 3

Southern Representations

Maharashtra, Karnataka, Andhra Pradesh, and Tamil Nadu

3.1

The commencement of temple construction in stone at the turn of the fifth century marked a new phase in the history of Indian architectural expressions. Close on its heels came the increased pace of rock-cut excavations in the Deccan. This shift in the nature and material of sacred architecture was accompanied by an assimilation of earlier architectural forms in the new structures. The *toraṇas* were carved more often in relief on the sacred stone structures and were rarely 'free-standing' between the fifth and ninth centuries. From the ninth century, free-standing *toraṇas* again registered their presence in association with sacred architecture. Those seen in relief sculpture from the fifth century stem from a web of generic relationships. Their antecedents are met in:

- the auspicious and ornamental festoons made of jewels, flowers, and leaves at entrances to shrines, palaces, and dwellings, which find mention in some early Indian texts (see Chapter 1);

- the *caitya-gavākṣa* on cave façades, which was at times adorned with an arched pattern, quite often with *makaras* depicted at the lower ends, as at the entrance to the Lomas Ṛṣi Cave (Fig. 1.1; c. third century BCE) or, the *candraśālikās* employed as a motif, as for example, the one from Darra (Fig. 1.29; c. second quarter of fifth century);

- the *toraṇa* architraves, such as those from Bharhut, Sarnath, Begram, Mathura, and other sites (Figs. 1.3, 1.8-1.10, 1.13; c. first two centuries BCE and CE) have representations of the *makara, garuḍa, gaja* (elephant), or *siṁha* (lion) at the volute ends. These also foreshadow some developments of the second phase (post-fifth century).

In the Deccan and South India, *toraṇas* were carved in relief on cave façades, at entrances to cave chambers, and above divinities; some were carved on the entablatures of pillared cells in the cave interiors. From the late sixth to early seventh century, they began to appear on the temple walls.

The Maharashtra Region (c. fifth to seventh centuries)

Ajanta: *Dvāra-toraṇas:* Most of the Mahāyāna caves at Ajanta were excavated between c. 462-478 CE, during Vākāṭaka rule.[1] In some instances, as at the entrance to Cave 6 (lower) (Fig. 3.1), the *toraṇas* are part of doorframes *(dvāra-toraṇas)*. Resting on a pair of pilaster jambs, the arch emerges from the jaws of *makaras*; minor water divinities *(udadhikumāras)* ride the *makaras*. As in a *ratna-toraṇa,* this is made of a bejewelled garland of alternating diamond and oval-shaped gems. A figure is seated in the cross-legged yogic posture *(padmāsana)* under the arch, holding a jar in his hands; he is canopied by a penta-cephalous snake and flanked by attendant figures holding garlands. Pearl festoons are suspended from the underside of the arch; celestial beings and female figures are visible at the upper corners. Such examples from the Deccan and South India appear to have inspired the *toraṇas* noticed on several Southeast Asian door-lintels, particularly those of the Sambor Prei Kuk period from Cambodia, and predate the latter by at least a century and a half (see Chapter 5). Another example of a *toraṇa* integrated with a doorframe may be observed at the doorway to the hall of Cave 20 (Fig. 3.2). Of twin arcs, it is rather unimpressive in the disproportionate rendering of its constituent parts and the lack of detail, except for a well-carved inverted lotus at the intersection of the arcs. A winged figure in *añjali hasta* (hands folded in adoration) is seated atop the inverted lotus. Minor water divinities with swords in their hands ride the *makaras*; a group of four figures is

3.2

visible at the top corners. This example of twin arcs is significant as it provides an early record of the tendency towards the multiplication of arcs.

3.1 : *Ratna-toraṇa (dvāra),* Ajanta, Cave 6 (lower), c. 462-478 CE.

3.2 : *Dvāra-toraṇa,* Ajanta, Cave 20, c. c. 462-478 CE.

3.3 : *Ratna-toraṇa (parikara),*Ajanta, Cave 9, c. c. 462-478 CE.

3.4 : *Ratna-toraṇa (parikara),*Ajanta, Cave 26, c. c. 462-478 CE.

3.5 : *Puṣpa-toraṇa (parikara),* Ajanta, Cave 21, c. c. 462-478 CE.

Parikara-toraṇas: A second type from Ajanta is that which frames images *(parikara-toraṇas)*, such as the *ratna-toraṇa* crowning Buddha on the façade of Cave 9 (Fig. 3.3).[2] Intricate *parikara-ratna-toraṇas* crowning Buddha images in the interior of Cave 26 are reminiscent of the art of woodcarving (Fig. 3.4).[3] An ornate central band of diamond and oval-shaped gems is bordered with a string of pearls. Pearl festoons are hung under the arch; a sequence of lace-like inverted *fleurs-de-lis* *(gagārapaṭṭī)* adorns the top border. *Parikara-toraṇas* also frame divinities on the entablatures above the pillars defining the cave aisles, as in the interior of Cave 21 (Fig. 3.5). These could belong to the *puṣpa-, puṣpa-ratna-, patra-,* or *ratna-toraṇa* varieties as per the details of their embellishment. Barring the one at the entrance to Cave 20, all instances at Ajanta comprise of only a single arc.

3.3

3.5

3.4

3.6

Jogeshvari: The Śaiva cave at Jogeshvari (c. 525 CE) in the Koṅkaṇa region is amongst the earlier Brahmanical caves excavated in the Deccan region. Fresh approaches are observed here, reflecting local predilections and changing creedal affiliations. The portion above the entrance to the cave's outer front hall harbours a dramatic but much-effaced depiction of Rāvaṇa's attempt to lift Mount Kailāsa *(Kailāsottānamūrti).* It is rendered within the arch of a *ratna-toraṇa* with *makaras* at its ends (Fig. 3.6). Even though effaced, it is possible to recognize Śiva and Pārvatī seated on Mount Kailāsa, surrounded by attendants. Gaṇeśa squats to the right of Śiva; Kārttikeya, who expectedly would be to the right of Pārvatī, is no longer visible. The ten-headed Rāvaṇa kneels in a vain attempt to shake Kailāsa with his many arms. Celestials occupy a cloudscape at the top corners. The door-lintel on the western wall of the main front hall that leads to the innermost chamber of this cave is adorned with another *ratna-toraṇa*, the profuse ornamentation on the arch conjuring a *patra-toraṇa* (Fig. 3.7).[4] Lakulīśa and his four disciples are positioned within the arch. Scenes from Śaiva mythology fill the top corners. A trefoil *puṣpa-toraṇa* decorated with rosettes circumscribes an image (Lakulīśa or female deity?) above the sanctum's western door (Fig. 3.8).

3.7

3.8

3.6 : *Ratna-toraṇa (dvāra),* Jogeshvari, Śiva Cave, c. 525 CE

3.7 : *Ratna-toraṇa (dvāra),*Jogeshvari, Śiva Cave, c. 525 CE

3.8 : *Puṣpa-toraṇa (dvāra)*, Jogeshvari, Śiva Cave, c. 525 CE

3.9 : *Citra-toraṇa (parikara),* Magathana, Buddhist cave, c. 575 CE.

3.10 : *Ratna-toraṇa (parikara),* Kanheri, northern subsidiary cave, Cave 3 complex, c. early to mid-sixth century.

3.11 : *Puṣpa-ratna-toraṇa (parikara)*, Kanheri, Cave 90, c. early to mid-sixth century.

At Jogeshvari, all the *toraṇas* circumscribe figures and narratives within the arch; there are only few precedents for this, such as at Cave 6 at Ajanta (Fig. 3.1). This is a distinctive feature, but one that has not merited a separate category in the texts. All are *makara-toraṇas* as also *dvāra-toraṇas* of the *ratna-, patra-,* or *puṣpa-toraṇa* class. Except for the trefoil arch over the western door leading to the sanctum, all the others are bow-shaped (*cāpākara*) arcs. This variant with figures and narratives circumscribed by the arch finds interesting parallels in the seventh-eighth century Cambodian temples.[5]

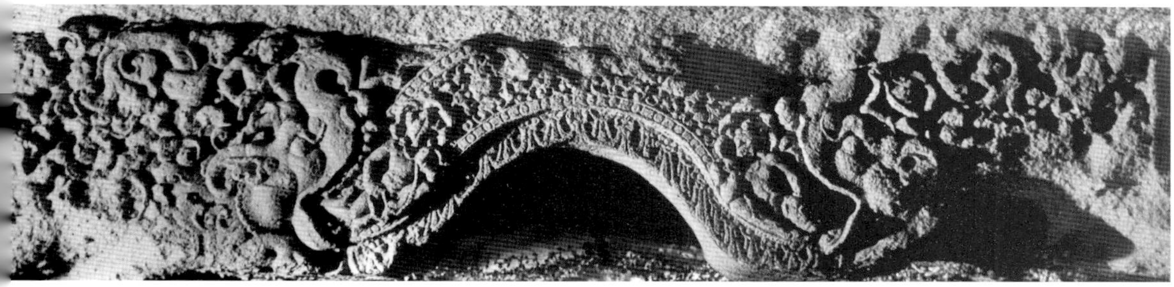

3.9

3.11

Magathana: A small Buddhist cave in Magathana in the Mumbai District of Maharashtra houses what perhaps is the most elegant and intricately carved sixth century *toraṇa* from the Deccan region (Fig. 3.9; c. 575 CE). Registering advancement in sophistication and style, it compares favourably with similar examples in Ajanta Cave 26 (Fig. 3.4). Carved on the back wall in the cave's interior, the Magathana *toraṇa* is placed above an image of Buddha. The tails of the *makaras* are so profusely carved that they assume the character of luxuriant foliate scrolls. Their faces are rendered in a masterly manner with bold, well-defined contours: wide-open jaws, protruding eyes, prominent cheeks, and markedly raised trunk, all contributing to a powerful image brimming with vitality. Minor water divinities *(udadhikumāras)* ride the *makaras*. A garland-bearing figure canopied by a penta-cephalous snake emerges from the jaws of the *makaras*; the rest of the arch is ornamented with floral and jewel motifs *(parikara-citra-toraṇa)* and festoons are suspended from its lower margin. This too has affinities with the seventh century Cambodian examples.

3.10

Kanheri: *Caitya* Cave 3 at Kanheri, excavated during the second century, was extended during the Mahayana phase when Buddhist images were added on either side of the gallery.[6] All the *toraṇas* here are inverted U-shaped and form a canopy over the images *(parikara-toraṇas)*, conveying the impression of a halo (Figs. 3.10-3.12). Those in the veranda of the main *Caitya* Cave 3 are all *patra-toraṇas* (Fig. 3.12), but one is also bejewelled and with a tiny Buddha image placed at the vertex *(citra-toraṇa)*. Those seen in the gallery of the northern subsidiary cave of the Cave 3 complex are by far the clearest examples of *ratna-toraṇas* (Fig. 3.10). A neatly undercut,

3.12

bejewelled chain of diamond and circular shaped motifs laced with strands of pearls forms the central portion of the arch. Those on the west wall of Cave 90 are made of alternating diamond and rosette shaped motifs encased between plain borders (*puṣpa-ratna-toraṇa*) (Fig. 3.11). The placement of a triangular decorative motif at the apex gives it the appearance of a pointed arch.[7]

Ellora (Pre-Rāṣṭrakūṭa Phase): A small *toraṇa* is carved above the figure of Gaṅgā on the northern wall contiguous with the Rameshvara cave (c. 575 CE; not illustrated). Śiva, Pārvatī, and Nandī are depicted within the space inscribed by the arch. A slim *ratna-toraṇa* made up of a line of alternating circular and square motifs is carved above a window on the back wall of the veranda of Cave 27 (Fig. 3.13; Milkmaid's Cave, c. 575 CE). *Parikara-toraṇas* carved in low relief, impressive neither in conception nor in execution, may be observed on the walls of the hall of the Brahmanical Cave 14 (Rāvaṇa kā Khāi, c. early seventh century). *Puṣpa-toraṇas* of twin arcs canopy the figures of Tārā and Mahāmayūrī in the interior of the Buddhist Cave 6 (c. early seventh century). Fairly similar, the one framing Mahāmayūrī on the southern wall is in a better state of preservation (Fig. 3.14). Its twin arcs, made of rosettes lined with beaded borders, meet centrally in a bulbous, pendant lotus. The *makaras* with upturned elephantine trunks and floriated tails are in the tradition observed earlier. These two *toraṇas* register the tendency towards the multiplication of arcs, observed earlier at Ajanta Cave 20.

These examples from Maharashtra are important as early records of the *toraṇas* from the second phase. However, it is in Karnataka, in the region of the early Western Calukyas, that one sees an exuberant vitality and variety in *toraṇa* forms from the early seventh century. One will have occasion also to return to Maharashtra (Ellora), to look at the newer expressions brought about by a renewal of artistic activity in the mid-eighth century during Rāṣṭrakūṭa rule.

3.13

3.14

Karnataka and Andhra Pradesh (c. seventh and eighth centuries)

The artistic language at the important Western Calukyan sites such as Badami, Aihole, and Pattadakal reflects an assimilation and transformation of the influences that interacted and merged with the local vocabulary. The *kuḍya-toraṇas* (wall *toraṇas*) found at Badami and Aihole are amongst the earlier ones seen on southern Indian temples.

Badami: The Upper Śivālaya at Badami must have been a Vaiṣṇava temple originally, as is indicated by the temple's imagery. The niches on the central offsets of the main temple walls are graced with elegant *toraṇas* of twin arcs (Fig. 3.15; c. first half of the seventh century). In the instance cited, *makaras* on either side emit a twisted pearl cable whose twin loops converge at the centre in a lotus with a pendant pearl tassel *(kuḍya-muktā-toraṇa)*. Together with the figures in the niches, these *toraṇas* effect an aesthetic transformation of the outer walls.

The Mālegittī Śivālaya at Badami offers another variant of a *ratna-toraṇa* with dual arcs (Figs. 3.16, 3.17; c. 655-680 CE). Its closed hall *(gūdhamaṇḍapa)* is larger than the main temple and exhibits richer ornamentation. The walls have latticed windows framed by *toraṇas* in the recesses *(salilāntaras)*. The guardian figures in the recesses flanking the doorway on the east are

3.12 : *Patra-toraṇa (parikara)*, Kanheri, main caitya Cave 3, c. early to mid sixth century.

3.13 : *Ratna-toraṇa*, Ellora, Cave 27, c. 575 CE.

3.14 : *Puṣpa-toraṇa (parikara)*, above image of Mahāmayūrī, Ellora Cave 6, c. early seventh century.

3.15 : *Muktā-toraṇa (kuḍya)*, Badami, Upper Śivālaya, c. first half of seventh century.

3.15

crowned with *toraṇas* of twin arcs made of three jewelled bands that issue from the jaws of *makaras* sprawled on pilaster capitals (Fig. 3.16). *Makaras* are also carved on both sides of a central ornament at the intersection of the twin arcs. The sinusoidal form of this *toraṇa* starts at one end from the jaws of the first *makara*, peaks in a crest and enters the jaws of the second one, then passes through the central ornament in a trough to issue forth from the jaws of the third *makara* and peak again before entering the jaws of the fourth. This is a precursor to the later *āndola-toraṇas* where the sinusoidal shape repeats to form a pattern.[8] A similar instance, also from the Mālegittī Śivālaya, has festoons suspended under the arcs (Fig. 3.17).

3.16

3.16 : *Ratna-toraṇa, (kuḍya)*, Badami, Mālegittī Śivālaya, c. 655-680 CE.

3.17 : *Ratna-toraṇa, (kuḍya)*, Badami, Mālegittī Śivālaya, c. 655-680 CE.

3.18 : Carved lintel, Aihole, Buddhist *Vihāra*, c. early seventh century.

3.19 : *Makara-toraṇa* above *jālavātāyana*, Aihole, Durga temple, c. late seventh century.

3.17

3.18

3.19

Aihole: The beams of the oblong veranda *(vīthikā)* of the Buddhist *Vihāra* at Aihole are carved with an ornament that is a close kin of the *makara-toraṇa*, although the arch is missing here (Fig. 3.18; c. early seventh century).[9] Minor figures emerge from the mouths of *makaras* at the corners and meet in the central motif of a gorgon face *(grāsamukha)* emitting pearl strands *(muktāgrāsa)*. In later examples, the central pearl ornament metamorphoses into an arch of varying embellishments emitted by the gorgon at the apex. This kind of *kāla-makara* ornament is also present on the octagonal members of the pillars in Cave 1 at Ajanta (c. 462-478 CE).

The outer wall of the inner ambulatory of the Durga temple at Aihole (c. late seventh century)[10] is punctuated by deities within niches and by latticed windows. Whereas the niche pediments are made of miniature superstructures of varied temple models, the latticed windows are topped by *toraṇas*. The *toraṇa* on the southern side of the ambulatory is especially noteworthy (Fig. 3.19). This arch is formed of the raised, floriated tails of two *makaras*; at the vertex is a vegetal transposition of the gorgon, from which a pearl festoon terminates in a floral pendant. The open jaws of the recumbent outward-facing *makaras* release pearl festoons; water divinities are seated on the *makaras*. The artist's creativity is obvious in the superlative carving and innovative approach exemplified here. It has affinities with those on the Kailāsanātha temple at Kanchipuram (Fig. 3.45) and more remotely with the Javanese *dvāra-toraṇas* such as those on the Dieng Plateau *caṇḍīs* (see Chapter 5). Other instances from Aihole belong to the 10th and 11th centuries and will be discussed at the appropriate chronological juncture.

Pattadakal: The temples at Pattadakal chiefly belong to the period of Calukya Vikramāditya II (c. 733-745 CE) and his successor. Of the three royal foundations built in the Dravidian mode, the Saṅgameśvara is the earliest (c. 733 CE). The ornamental detailing on the walls of this temple remains in an unfinished state but the walls were designed to include *toraṇas* that framed images at the intermediate offsets *(pratirathas)*. A novel inclusion is the *mayūra-toraṇa,* seen on the west wall of the *vimāna* (not illustrated, see Fig. 3.22 for a similar example). The graceful and elongated necks of two peacocks make the twin arcs of this *mayūra-toraṇa*.

On the Virūpākṣa temple at the same site, divinities within niches at the central offsets *(bhadras)* of the sanctum's outer walls are crowned with *toraṇas*. A composite *patra-toraṇa* frames Viṣṇu on the northern wall (Fig. 3.21; c. 743 CE). It has *makaras* with floriated tails rising up in the manner observed in the Deccan trap and Karnataka so far, but also cascading down as noticed in the Tamil region from the seventh century. Powerfully delineated *makaras* dominate the *toraṇa*; the arch itself is composed of a leafy scroll and looks much subdued in comparison. The divine couple, Śiva-Pārvatī, are seated under the arch.

The outer walls of the closed hall *(gūdhamaṇḍapa)* of the Virūpākṣa temple are marked by corner *(karṇa)* and intermediate *(pratibhadra)* projections; the central *(bhadra)* section extends into porches. While miniature temple models crown the corner niches, the intermediate niches are graced with *toraṇas*. The upward swing of the floriated tails of the *makaras* of Deccan affiliation noticed earlier on the *toraṇas* from Ajanta, Badami, and other sites, is replaced here by *makaras* with cascading tails in the Dravidian manner. The tutelary position of Lakṣmī gains in prominence on the *toraṇas*. The *mayūra-toraṇa*, noticed earlier on the Saṅgameśvara *vimāna* wall, embellishes Śiva Liṅgodbhavamūrti on the outer wall of the front porch of this temple (Fig. 3.22). Another that deserves special mention is the one that forms a canopy over an exquisitely rendered image of Umā-Maheśvara on the southern wall of the closed hall (Fig. 3.23). The original elements comprising the *toraṇa* mutate into a vegetal abstraction here. Lakṣmī, seated on a lotus, is carved at the apex. Such a vegetal abstraction finds echoes in the examples of the Kompong Preah style from Cambodia (see Chapter 5).

Sandur: The Pārvatī temple at Sandur (c. 700 CE) in the Bellary District of Karnataka appears to have been a Śiva temple originally, judging by the Śiva images on the outer walls of its sanctum. These are crowned with *toraṇas*. Although the niches on the walls of the attached hall are too shallow to house images, these are cantoned by square pilasters and topped by *toraṇas* similar to those on the main temple. In the cited instance (Fig. 3.20), a *toraṇa* of twin arcs meets at the centre in a pendant bulbous terminal, similar to those in Ellora Cave 6 (Fig. 3.14).

3.20

3.21

3.23

3.20 : *Kuḍya-toraṇa*, Sandur, Pārvatī temple, c. 700 CE.

3.21 : *Patra-toraṇa* (composite) *(kuḍya)*, Pattadakal, Virūpākṣa temple, c. 743 CE.

3.22 : Overleaf.

3.23 : *Patra-toraṇa (kuḍya)*, Pattadakal, Virūpākṣa temple, c. 743 CE.

A *citra-toraṇa* of twin arcs (Fig. 3.24), carved over the vestibule *(antarāla)* doorframe of the Virūpākṣa temple, deserves special mention. *Makaras* with pendant tails, seated on octagonal pilasters, are affiliated to the style noticed in the Tamil region. The basic sinusoidal form of the *toraṇa* resembles those noticed on the walls of the Mālegittī Śivālaya at Badami (Fig. 3.16). The twin arcs harbour musicians and dancers; armed figures emerge from the jaws of *makaras*. The central medallion appears to house Śiva on Nandī. Surviving portions of *toraṇas* may also be seen at the entrances to the double-storied shrines *(dvitala parivārālayas)* surrounding the main temple.

3.22 : *Mayūra-toraṇa (kuḍya)*, Pattadakal, Virūpākṣa temple, c. 743 CE.

3.23 : See p.47

3.24 : *Citra-toraṇa (antarāla)*, Pattadakal, Virūpākṣa temple, c. 743 CE.

3.25 : *Muktā-kinnara-toraṇa (kuḍya)*, Pattadakal, Jambūliṅga temple, c. first half of eighth century.

From this period, the *toraṇas* became ubiquitous. They are observed on the walls of temples such as the Kāḍasiddheśvara, Jambūliṅga, and Mallikārjuna temples (c. mid-eighth century). Their increased presence reveals a variety of experimentations on the basic form, resulting in a range of innovations. At the Jambūliṅga temple, for example, a *muktā-toraṇa* is held aloft by two celestials *(vidyādharas)* above a niche on the main temple wall (Fig. 3.25). Pearl festoons flanked by *vyālas* are suspended from it.[11]

3.24

3.25

3.26

3.27

3.28

3.29

Undavalli: The entrances to the cells of the Anantaśayana rock-cut temple at Undavalli (Fig. 3.26; c. 575-625 CE) in the Guntur District of Andhra Pradesh are carved with *dvāra-toraṇas* of twin arcs. Though effaced, these are comparable to contemporary specimens from Mamallapuram and Dalavanur in the Tamil region and Badami in Karnataka (Figs. 3.16, 3.17, 3.43, 3.44).

Kudaveli Sangameshvara: The *kinnara-toraṇas* on the exterior walls of the reassembled Śiva temple (due to the Śrīśailam dam project) of Kudaveli Sangameshvara in the Mehboobnagar District of Andhra Pradesh form a unique group (Figs. 3.27-3.29). Some of these are almost entirely made up of *kinnaras* (half-human, half-bird); some others are made up of either *haṁsas* (geese) or *makaras*, all pictured with rustic charm. The best among them mirror the innovative skills of their artists. The surviving examples make one wonder at the loss of several other early instances from the region.

Maharashtra (Rāṣṭrakūṭa Phase)

Ellora: During the latter half of the eighth century, Rāṣṭrakūṭa rule stretched from Karnataka and Andhra in the South to regions beyond the Narmada in the North. The most eloquent representative of

3.26 : *Makara-toraṇa (dvāra),* cave temple, Undavalli, c. sixth/seventh century.

3.27 : *Kinnara-toraṇa (kuḍya),* Kudaveli Sangameshvara, Śiva temple, c. seventh century.

3.28 : *Kinnara-toraṇa (kuḍya),* Kudaveli Sangameshvara, Śiva temple, c. seventh century.

3.29 : *Kinnara-toraṇa (kuḍya),* Kudaveli Sangameshvara, Śiva temple, c. seventh century.

3.30 : *Kinnara-toraṇa (kuḍya),* Ellora, Kailāsa, c. third quarter of eighth century.

3.31 (overleaf): *Kuḍya-toraṇas,* Ellora, Kailāsa, c. third quarter of eighth century.

3.32 : *Dvāra-toraṇa,* Ellora, Kailāsa, *Nandī-maṇḍapa,* c. third quarter of eighth century.

3.32

3.30

the heights of artistic excellence scaled under the patronage of the Rāṣṭrakūṭas is the Kailāsa at Ellora. Its tall *vimāna* walls are marked by broad, square pilasters that demarcate the central, intermediate, and corner divisions, with no recessed interventions. The central and corner niches are crowned with gorgeous *toraṇas* bearing *kinnaras, makaras,* and *mayūras* at the extremities, their tails cascading rhythmically in a curled vegetal ornament (Figs. 3.30, 3.31). The exuberantly foliate extremities, not the arched garland of twisted pearl cable, are the most evocative feature of these *toraṇas*. A seated deity is inscribed beneath every arch. As distinct from the Pattadakal *toraṇas*, which have powerfully rendered *makaras* that exude earthiness and strength, the *toraṇas* here convey a delicate lightness that seems to lift the structure out of its naturally sunken position. The scheme of decoration on the exterior walls of the *gūḍhamaṇḍapa* does not include *toraṇas*. The upper storey of the Nandī-*maṇḍapa* has entrances on all four sides *(sarvatobhadra)*. The *dvāra-toraṇa* at the eastern entrance is reminiscent of the one seen on the vestibule *(antarāla)* doorframe of the Virūpākṣa temple at Pattadakal, though the rendition is less forceful here and lacks the vitality of the Calukyan model (compare Figs. 3.24 and 3.32).

3.31

Besides the magnificent Kailāsa, a large number of cave excavations took place at Ellora during this period. New *toraṇa* forms were evolved in these caves during the eighth and ninth centuries. The River Goddess Chapel in the north-western corner of the northern court of the Kailāsa complex has Gaṅgā, Yamunā, and Saraswatī framed by *toraṇas* (Figs. 3.33-3.35; c. 757-773 CE). Elegant and slim arches spring from the mouths of *makaras* seated on the pillar capitals. The inverted U-shaped curvature of

3.33 : *Ratna-toraṇa (parikara)* over image of Saraswatī, Ellora, River Goddess Chapel, Cave 16 (Kailāsa), c. 756-772 CE.

3.34 : *Ratna-toraṇa (parikara)* over image of Gaṅgā, Ellora, River Goddess Chapel, Cave 16 (Kailāsa), c. 756-772 CE.

3.35 : *Ratna-toraṇa (parikara)* over image of Yamunā, Ellora, River Goddess Chapel, Cave 16 (Kailāsa), c. 756-772 CE.

3.36 : *Toraṇa,* Ellora, Cave 15, c. eighth century.

3.37 : *Haṁsa-toraṇa,* Ellora, Cave 15, c. eighth century.

3.38 : *Illikā-toraṇa (parikara)* over image of Gaṅgā, Ellora, Cave 16, Laṅkeśvara section, c. early ninth century.

3.34

3.35

3.33

3.37

3.36

these *ratna-toraṇas* meets in a central ornament with protruding *makara* heads. The one crowning Saraswatī has the *kīrttimukha* carved within a medallion at the vertex of the arch. All the three arches dip subtly at the centre, lending them delicate grace and a gentle wave-like drift. These examples conjure a likely picture of the contemporaneous free-standing *toraṇas* (probably made of perishable materials). An exquisite sinusoidal *āndola-toraṇa* of twin arcs with suspended festoons is noticed in Cave 15 (Fig. 3.36; c. eighth century), which also records an incomplete yet appealing instance of a *haṁsa-toraṇa* (Fig. 3.37).

3.38

The Laṅkeśvara Cave in the Kailāsa complex is located to the north of the main temple and has been stylistically assigned to the end of the eighth or beginning of the ninth century. The doorframe at the entrance to the cave's sanctum is flanked by Gaṅgā to the right and Yamunā to the left, placed within *toraṇas*. The *toraṇa* seen above the nimbus of Gaṅgā offers a fresh variant and adds a distinctly new type, the *illikā-toraṇa,*[12] to the vocabulary of the *toraṇas* from this region (Fig. 3.38). It later transforms into an intricate juxtaposition of several loops and becomes a favourite with the sculptors of the Karnataka and Andhra Pradesh where it invades the temple walls and lintels in rampant profusion.

Illikā-toraṇas frame images of Jain *yakṣas* and *yakṣīs* in the Indra Sabhā (Cave 32) and Jagannātha Sabhā (Cave 33) at Ellora (Fig. 3.39). Typologically, they correspond to the one above river goddess Gaṅgā in the Laṅkeśvara Cave, but those in the Jain caves are rendered with considerable fluidity, revealing assurance and familiarity on the part of the sculptor. A Jina image is placed at the apex of some of these *toraṇas* of four segments; the arch itself gives the impression of a vegetal stalk. The interstices of the arcs are rendered with sophistication and conclude in a combination of the lotus and pendant bud *(kalikā)*. As is evident from the *parikara-toraṇas* gracing the images on the façade wall of Cave 32, *toraṇas* in a range of designs were already in vogue by this period. The single arc, the sinusoidal twin-arc, the elementary *illikā* variety, as well as the four-arc wave-like *āndola* type, are all met at Ellora.

3.39

In some of the Jain caves, the pillars of the vestibule *(antarāla)* support a *toraṇa* (Fig. 3.40). Though the stone has been scooped out from the portion immediately below the arch, this is not true of the section above the arch. The arch is thus not 'free-flying' as in the instances from western and central India, particularly from the tenth century onwards. Some of the *antarāla-toraṇas* from Ellora include the one inside the cave adjacent to Jagannātha Cave as also the one in the upper storey of the cave in the left wing of the Kailāsa. The former is a representative of the quadruple-arc sinusoidal *āndola* type while the latter represents an early *illikā* type (Figs. 3.41, 3.42). While Choṭā Kailāsa may be dated to the late eighth century, the other Jain caves mentioned here appear to be creations of the first half of the ninth century.

3.40

3.39 : *Illikā-toraṇa (parikara)*, Ellora, Cave 32, Indra Sabhā, c. ninth century.

3.40 : *Āndola-toraṇa (antarāla),* Ellora, Cave 31, Jain group, c. ninth century.

3.41 : *Āndola-toraṇa,* Ellora, Cave 32, Indra Sabhā, c. ninth century.

3.42 : *Illikā-toraṇa (antarāla),* Ellora, Cave 16, upper storey, c. 810-880 CE.

3.41

3.42

3.43

The Tamil Region (c. seventh and eighth centuries)

The earliest *toraṇas* in the Tamil country are found in association with the excavated caves[13] and rock-cut temples of the Pallava period (Figs. 3.43, 3.44). These, along with the *toraṇas* from the western and eastern Deccan (c. fifth to seventh centuries), represent the early repertoire of this architectural member in southern India. A composite *ratna-toraṇa* of two undulating arcs, positioned beneath a finely delineated eave cornice (*kapota*) with dormer *motifs (nāsīs)* spans the portion between the brackets *(potikās)* of the two central pillars to affect an aesthetic transformation of the plain cave façade at Dalavanur (Fig. 3.43; c. 610-630 CE; Gingee Taluk, South Arcot District). Reminiscent of those on the outer walls of the Mālegittī Śivālaya at Badami, the Dalavanur instance is anterior by two to three decades. The *makaras* mounted by water divinities release an undulating arch, which dips to pass through a central ornament flanked by outward-facing *makaras*. A figure is seated in a yogic posture *(padmāsana)* above this central ornament; a lotus pendant is placed underneath. Similar *toraṇas* adorned the niches flanking the entrance façade of the Siyamangalam cave (North Arcot District; c. 610-630 CE).[14] Another example crowns Mahiṣāsuramardinī on the Trimūrti cave façade at Mamallapuram (c. second to third quarter of seventh century).[15] The Draupadī Ratha at Mamallapuram belongs to the same period as the Trimūrti Cave and has four similar *makara-toraṇas*, one each above the three niches on the outer walls of the sanctum and a fourth one above the sanctum entrance (Fig. 3.44). The tails of the *makaras* are delineated as waves, accentuating the undulating effect of the *toraṇas*. One

3.44

3.45

3.43 : *Ratna-toraṇa* (composite), Dalavanur, cave temple, c. 610-630 CE.

3.44 : *Ratna-toraṇa* (composite), Mahabalipuram, Draupadī Ratha, c. second-third quarter of seventh century.

3.45 : *Makara-toraṇa, (kuḍya),* Kanchipuram, Kailāsanātha, c. 700-728 CE.

3.46 : *Citra-toraṇa (kuḍya),* Kanchipuram, Kailāsanātha, c. 700-728 CE.

3.46

may surmise from these and other instances[16] that the sinusoidal arch with twin arcs was widely prevalent in the Tamil country during the seventh and the eighth centuries.

The next phase is noticed on the Kailāsanātha temple at Kanchipuram (Figs. 3.45-3.47; c. 700-728 CE). Some of the innovations witnessed on this temple are classified in the Dravidian *vāstu* texts. Of the three main categories found here, the first relates to an arch formed of the tails of outward-facing *makaras* (Fig. 3.45). Their raised and curled tails meet at the apex and their upturned snouts further enhance the curvature and dynamism of the well-defined arch of twin arcs. This is similar in conception to the one met at the Durga temple, Aihole (Fig. 3.19). Such *toraṇas* do not find specific classification in the texts; as such they are grouped under the broad category of *makara-toraṇas*.

The second category seen on the walls of the Kailāsanātha temple appeals for the lavish and variegated figural entourage of which the arch is formed. It is very close to the *citra-toraṇa* of the Dravidian texts (see Chapter 2). This type is met above the image of Dakṣiṇāmūrti in the central niche of the central abutted shrine on the southern side of the Kailāsanātha *vimāna* (Fig. 3.46). Each of the two *makaras* seated on the crossbeam above the cantoning pilasters releases an energetic *vyāla* from its jaws. Gaṇeśa is at the centre and above him is a figure (Purim, as per the texts) that seems to clasp the *vyālas*. From within the luxuriant foliage of the tails of the *makaras*, emerge two additional powerfully wrought *makaras* facing outwards. The total ensemble is a striking representation of the *śāstric citra-toraṇa* variety.

3.47

The third group of *toraṇas* on the Kailāsanātha walls belong to the *vṛttākāra* (circular) or *ardhacandrākāra* (half-moon or semi-circular) variety described in the texts. The one crowning Liṅgodbhavamūrti on the western face of the *vimāna* comprises a semi-circular arch with bands of jewels (Fig. 3.47). A human figure armed with a sword and shield emerges from the jaws of the *makaras* on each side and *vyālas* seem to spring from within the vegetal efflorescence of their tails. *Vyālas* also flank the central image (Śiva?) inscribed within the arch. Similar *vṛttākāra citra-toraṇas* may be seen adorning niches on the main and subsidiary shrines of the Kailāsanātha and other contemporaneous temples.[17] The *vṛttākāra* or *ardhacandrākāra citra-* and *ratna-toraṇas* occur in prolific numbers on the walls of the later Tamilnadu temples.[18]

Karnataka and Andhra Pradesh (c. 9th-10th centuries)

Bhavanasi Sangam: The *vimāna* of the Rūpālā Saṅgameśvara temple (c. second quarter of ninth century) at Bhavanasi Sangam on the banks of river Kṛṣṇā in the Kurnool District of Andhra Pradesh has broad central offsets with deep-set niches canopied by *toraṇas*. The twin-arc-*toraṇa* is experimented with here. A pronounced dip in the central portion at the juncture of the two curvilinear segments of each *toraṇa* is a characteristic feature. Minor water divinities mount the *makaras* whose open jaws are upturned and whose tails cascade in a volley of curled ornament. The one above the latticed window *(jālavātāyana)* on the northern connecting wall *(kapilī)* is particularly well-rendered (Fig. 3.48). The two inverted U-shaped loops of the *toraṇa* meet in a central ornament flanked by *makaras*. Śiva (?) is seated in *ardhaparyaṅkāsana* atop the central ornament which has a lotus pendant. Festoons hang from the arch. Water divinities hold lotus stalks in their hands, as do the *makaras* in their upturned trunks, a trait oft repeated on Later Cālukyan and Hoysaḷa *toraṇas*. The affinity with Pattadakal is far stronger than with Ellora, expected due to shared regional stylistic factors.[19]

The Bhujaṅgeśvara temple at the same site is contemporaneous to the Rūpālā Saṅgameśvara temple. Its *gūdhamaṇḍapa* is destroyed but the central niches of the main temple and the vestibule walls are adorned with *toraṇas*. Each of these arches has a flat, plateau-shaped curve that dips slightly at the vertex where it passes through a central ornament. Below the arch of the northern *bhadra* niche, there are seven inverted knob-like lotuses from which festoons are suspended (not illustrated). This development has a bearing on the later free-standing *toraṇas* from the Andhra region. In the 11th century free-standing *toraṇa* from the Rāmaliṅgeśvara temple at Nandi Kandi, as also the *toraṇa* gateway at Kulpak belonging to the same period, knob-like buds are suspended below the *toraṇa* lintel. Further variations of this feature are seen in the 13th century examples associated with the Sahasraliṅga temple at Warangal, and the Mallikārjuna temple at Ainavolu, also in the Warangal District (Figs. 3.131-3.134).

3.47 : *Citra-ratna-toraṇa (ardhacandrākāra, kuḍya)*, Kanchipuram, Kailāsanātha, c. 700-728 CE.

3.48 : *Citra-toraṇa (kuḍya)*, Bhavanasi Sangam, Rūpālā Sangameśvara temple, c. second quarter of ninth century.

3.48

Kukkanur, Sirval, Hallur, Aihole, Pattadakal, and Mudhol (Late Rāṣṭrakūṭa period)

The architectural style in the Rāṣṭrakūṭa territory from the last quarter of the ninth century to the end of the tenth century registers a departure from its earlier norms. There is a decided preference for architectonic clarity, with plain wall surfaces and minimal ornamentation, which seem to lean towards the Coḷa idiom. Only a few temples are adorned with *toraṇas* on their wall surfaces.

One of the earlier shrines in the Navaliṅga group of temples at Kukkanur (c. late ninth century) registers simple representations of the *kuḍya-toraṇa* at the corner divisions *(karṇas)* of its main temple walls. Simple twin-arc-*toraṇas* formed of two S-shaped segments are emitted by *makaras* and meet centrally in a dormer motif (*nāsī*) (not illustrated). This type of *kuḍya-toraṇa* does not frame a niche or divinity, yet it proliferates on the walls of the medieval Karnataka temples to assume intricate forms in the succeeding centuries.

In the interior of the same temple at Kukkanur, a remarkable *illikā-toraṇa* supported on square *(Brahmakānta)* pilasters is placed in the vestibule *(antarāla)* (Fig. 3.49). Though some of the Ellora *toraṇas* foreshadow this development,[20] the present instance is a remarkable advancement in terms of design, composition, and execution. At the extremities, *makaras* with upturned tails emit *vyālas* and an *illikā* garland of elegant proportions. Composed of four tightly rendered loops of twisted pearl cable, the arch traces a gentle convex curvature. The loops of the arch terminate in shapely lotus buds; celestials *(gandharvas)* flank the upper regions of the arch. This example reveals the innate grace of the *illikā* type and heralds as well as validates its persistent presence in the later temples of Karnataka and Andhra Pradesh.

A comparable example, also from the Navaliṅga group at Kukkanur, belongs to the western shrine (c. mid-tenth century) (Fig. 3.50). The delicate carving and attention to detail observed in the earlier example is replaced here by a bolder rendering. The loops of this *antarāla-toraṇa* are organized linearly and the intersections of

3.49

3.50

3.51

3.52

successive loops terminate in prominent, bulbous lotus pendants. Each looped segment inscribes celestials; the two central ones depict couples, whereas at the corners, each loop harbours a single figure. The pendant lotus terminals serve as seats for divinities.

Situated in the Gulbarga District on the banks of river Bhima, the temple *toraṇas* at Sirval (c. mid-tenth century) are comparable to those at Kukkanur, although qualitatively the latter are superior. In the vestibule *(antarāla)* of Temple 12 at this site, a rampant *vyāla* is inset within each loop of the *toraṇa* (Fig. 3.51). The one in the vestibule of Temple no. 13 at this site is similar (Fig. 3.52).[21] As the temples of this region and period have rather plain exteriors, the best examples are found in their interior. Nevertheless, we do encounter some *toraṇas* on the outer walls and niches.[22]

3.49 : *Illikā-toraṇa (antarāla),* Kukkanur, older shrine, Navaliṅga group of temples, c. late ninth century.

3.50 : *Illikā-toraṇa (antarāla),* Kukkanur, western shrine, Navaliṅga group of temples, c. mid-10th century.

3.51 : *Illikā-toraṇa (antarāla),* Sirval, Temple no. 12, c. mid-10th century.

3.52 : *Illikā-toraṇa (antarāla),* Sirval, Temple no. 13 (Munīśvara), c. early 11th century.

3.53 : *Dvāra-toraṇa,* Aihole, Haḷḷibasappā temple, c. mid-ninth century.

3.54 : *Āndola-toraṇa (dvāra)*, Papanasam, Pāpavināśeśvara temple (no. 3), c. late 10th century.

3.55 : *Āndola-toraṇa (dvāra)*, Beccour, Guḍam Guḍalu group of temples, c. late 10th century.

3.56 : *Citra-toraṇa (kuḍya),* Biccavolu, Goliṅgeśvara temple, c. 806-847 CE.

Two fine examples of *dvāra-toraṇas* are known; one is in the Haḷḷibasappā temple no.11 at Aihole (Fig. 3.53; c. mid-ninth century) and another in the Jain temple at Pattadakal (of the same or slightly later period, not illustrated). In the former, the tails of the *makaras* seated on the capitals of pilaster door-jambs *(stambha-śākhās)* cascade luxuriantly down the greater part of the doorframe's height. The arch is a further elaboration of the type first noticed on the walls of the Mālegittī Śivālaya at Badami; the twin segments of the arch show a further subdivision, each terminating in a bud suspended from the centre of the two semi-circles. It presages the *dvāra-toraṇas* of the Pāpavināśeśvara temple no. 3 at Papanasam and the one seen at the Guḍam Guḍalu group of temples in the Mehboobnagar District (Figs. 3.54, 3.55; c. late 10th century). Of the *toraṇa* at the sanctum doorframe of the Jain temple at Pattadakal, only the *makaras* survive to vouch for the fine workmanship of the lost arch.

3.53

3.54

3.55

Biccavolu and Chebrolu: Eastern Calukyan (c. 9th-10th centuries)

The Biccavolu temples date from the time of the Eastern Calukyan king, Vijayāditya II (c. 806-847 CE). The recessed central sections *(bhadras)* of the Rājarājeśvara *vimāna* walls at this site are decorated with *toraṇas*. These, along with the images that they canopy are the only adornment on the otherwise stark temple walls. The Goliṅgeśvara temple is more ornate in comparison, but there too, only the *bhadra* niches are crowned by *toraṇas* (Fig. 3.56). At Biccavolu, the drooping and floriated tails of the *makaras* acquire a formulaic character, as opposed to the earlier instances at Ellora, Bhavanasi Sangam, and Pattadakal, where one observes greater spontaneity in rendition.

One variety at this site is made up of the twisted pearl cable ornament or the beaded pattern. It rises steeply and meets in the central motif with outward facing *makara* heads. This type of *kuḍya-toraṇa* may be seen on the western and southern *bhadras* of the Candraśekhara *vimāna* and on the western wall of the Rājarājeśvara *vimāna*. A noteworthy example is the one crowning Indra on the southern *bhadra* of the Goliṅgeśvara *vimāna*, with stylized water divinities riding the *makaras* (Fig. 3.56). A *muktāgrāsa* (gorgon with pearl festoons) motif flanked by *vyālas* is positioned above the central ornament of twin *makaras*. Unfortunately, the *toraṇamālā* is partially damaged. A second variety from Biccavolu is encountered on the

3.56

walls of the Nakkulaguḍi and the Vīrabhadra temple; it bears affinities with those on the Bhujaṅgeśvara temple at Bhavanasi Sangam. In this type, the arch is formed of two quarter-circles that meet at the centre; the *makaras* at the ends have shorter tails (Fig. 3.57). While a majority of these are *makara-toraṇas*, the one crowning Viṣṇu on the south wall of the Vīrabhadra *vimāna* is a *mayūra-toraṇa*.[23]

At the Bhīmeśvara temple in Chebrolu, south of the river Krishna in eastern Andhra Pradesh, *makara-toraṇas* crown the niches on the lower outer wall (Fig. 3.58; c. early decades of the 10th century). They bear formal affinities with those from the Rūpālā Saṅgameśvara temple at Bhavanasi Sangam (Fig. 3.48; c. ninth century) and the still earlier cave temple at Undavalli in eastern Andhra Pradesh (Fig. 3.26; c. sixth-seventh century).

3.57

3.58

3.59

3.57 : *Citra-ratna-toraṇa (kuḍya),* Biccavolu, c. 806-847 CE.

3.58 : *Makara-toraṇa (kuḍya),* Chebrolu, Bhīmeśvara temple, c. early 10th century.

3.59 : *Citra-toraṇa (kuḍya),* Kambadahalli, Pañcakūṭa basti, Ādinātha basti, c. 10th century.

Instances from Cālukyan, Gaṅgā, Noḷamba, Śāntara, and other territories

Most of the tenth century temples from western Andhra Pradesh have plain and unadorned walls. *Toraṇas* are generally found on lintels in the hall interiors of the temples. Of the twin shrines in the Pāpavināśeśvara complex at Papanasam, the western shrine has a *toraṇa* carved on the lintel above the vestibule *(antarāla)* pillars (Fig. 3.54).[24] Its basic form shows a slight progression over the one earlier observed at the Haḻḻibasapppā temple no. 11 in Aihole (Fig. 3.53), though the *makaras* are inconsequential in the Papanasam instance. A further elaboration may be seen at the Guḍam Guḍalu group in the Mehboobnagar District of Andhra Pradesh (Fig. 3.55), resulting in a mature *āndola-toraṇa*, rare in Karnataka and Andhra Pradesh.[25]

Tenth century temples built during the period of the Gaṅgās ruling from the Mysore region of Karnataka also have relatively plain exterior walls. None-the-less, the central *(bhadra)* niches of some of the temple walls are adorned with florid *toraṇas*. A *citra-toraṇa,* seen on the southern wall of the western *vimāna* of Ādinātha basti, in the Pañcakūṭa basti complex at Kambadahalli, stands as an example (Fig. 3.59). The *makaras* seated on slabs placed over square pillars release *vyālas* with riders. At the apex, a figure with arms outstretched in combat with the *vyālas,* stands over the central coiled motif. This tree-shaped coiled ornament has precedents in the *kuḍya-toraṇas* from the late ninth century Aihole Temple no. 52 (not illustrated).

The *toraṇas* on the walls of the twin shrines in the Pañcakūṭa basti complex are formed completely of vegetal scrolls, except for the seated Jain images (Figs. 3.60, 3.61). These belong to the *patra-toraṇa* variety noticed on the *gūḍhamaṇḍapa* wall of the Virūpākṣa temple at Pattadakal (Fig. 3.23). The vegetal abstractions are further ornamented with pearl festoons on the underside. Well-rendered *kuḍya-toraṇas* are noticed above the latticed windows *(jālavātāyanas)* of the Bhoganandīśvara temple at Nandi in the eastern part of southern Karnataka, a centre that came to prominence under the Noḷambas of Hemavati (Fig. 3.62). Another elegant *toraṇa* made of a single arc is placed above a sham niche on the northern vestibule wall of Akkāguḍi at Hemavati (Fig. 3.63; c. late 10th century).

The *toraṇa* fragments found at Humacha in western Karnataka were originally parts of the sculptures located in the Pārśvanātha temple. According to Dhaky, two of these *toraṇas* are plausibly from the Sūle basti and Bogāra basti, and the remaining one may have belonged to a temple that has disappeared.[26] One of them is the

3.60

3.61

3.60 : *Patra-toraṇa,* Kambadahalli, Pañcakūṭa basti, twin shrines, *pratolī* niche, c. 10th century.

3.61 : *Patra-toraṇa,* Kambadahalli, Pañcakūṭa basti, twin shrines, *pratolī* niche, c. 10th century.

3.62 : *Makara-toraṇa (kuḍya),* Nandī, Bhoganandīśvara temple, c. late ninth century.

3.63 : *Makara-toraṇa (kuḍya),* Hemavati, Akkāguḍi, c. late 10th century.

3.64 : Lakṣmī *toraṇa*, Humacha, Pañcakūṭa basti, c. 1077 CE.

3.65 : *Toraṇa* fragment, Humacha (found near Pārśvanātha temple), c. 1062 CE.

3.62

3.63

3.64

pediment of a *makara-toraṇa*, harbouring Gajalakṣmī, and placed upon a pair of columns at the entrance hall of the Pañcakūṭa basti from the same site (Fig. 3.64; c. 1077 CE). Though resting atop an architrave, the stone matrix upon which it is carved has been scooped out. This is rare amongst medieval *toraṇas* from southern India. Another *toraṇa* fragment in the precincts of the Pārśvanātha temple at Humacha probably belongs to the one set up by Cāgaḷadevī (consort of the King Vīra Śāntara) (Fig. 3.65; c. 1062 CE).[27] Only the end portion survives, so what one gets to see on this fragment are exquisitely chiselled *makaras* with *vyālas* and three serpentine loops of the *illikā* arch. But these are sufficient to convey the elegance that must have characterised the original. Directional divinities *(dikpālas)* are carved on the upper margin; Jina images housed within miniature shrines *(kūṭas)* are visible underneath the garland. A *vyāla*, with its back touching the upturned tail of the *makara,* is also visible. It is this variant of the *illikā-toraṇa* that invades the Cālukyan and Hoysala temple walls, beginning from the 11th century.

3.65

3.66

Northern Karnataka & Maharashtra (c. 10th-13th centuries)

Antarāla- and Dvāra-toraṇas: Temple Interiors and Entrances

The incipient stages in the development of the *āndola-* and *illikā-toraṇas* were observed at Badami, Ellora, and other sites discussed earlier. The *illikā* was undoubtedly the favoured type in Karnataka. From about the late ninth century, sites such as Kukkanur, Sirval, and Humacha registered further developments. Medieval Karnataka and also Andhra Pradesh contributed a very distinctive, ornate, graceful, and meandering version of the *illikā-toraṇa* discussed in the western Indian treatises. This regional variant struck a leading note in the ornamental inventory of the temple walls of Karnataka. Made up of curvaceous serpentine loops, it transformed into a leitmotif to adorn the walls (*kuḍya-toraṇas*), vestibule lintels (*antarāla-toraṇas*), images of major and minor deities (*parikara-toraṇas*), dormer motifs (*nāsī-toraṇas*), and even the basal mouldings *(adhiṣṭhāna-toraṇas,* Fig. 3.98*)*.

A much-effaced *antarāla-toraṇa* in the Kālguḍi at Ron, south of the erstwhile Western Calukyan heartland of Badami-Aihole-Mahakuta (Fig. 3.66; c. last quarter of 10th century) is distinct from the *illikā-toraṇas* encountered thus far, though it appears to repeat the basic schema of the trefoil arch witnessed at the Śiva Cave, Jogeshvari (Fig. 3.8; c. 525 CE). It comprises three sets of trefoil arches alternating with two miniature shrines, one bearing Gaṇeśa and the other Lakṣmī. Naṭeśa is housed within the central trefoil arch; Brahmā and Viṣṇu, also within trefoil arches, flank him. Tripuruṣa (triad of divinities) representations with Śiva at the centre were extremely popular in medieval Karnataka. The *antarāla* pillars of the Mallikārjuna temple at Sudi (c. early 11th century) also support a tripartite *illikā-toraṇa*.

Antarāla-illikā-toraṇas similar to those at Kukkanur and Sirval (Figs. 3.49-3.52) are also met at Bevur, Kuralgeri, and Nagai (Figs. 3.67-3.70). The *gūḍhamaṇḍapa* nave of the Rāmeśvara temple at Bevur (c. 1055-1060 CE) has a central pit, surrounded by pillars. The pillars surrounding the pit support lintels carved with *illikā-toraṇas* on the inner profile (Fig. 3.68). The loops are made up of twisted pearl cable ornament (seen earlier at Badami, Pattadakal, Ellora, Kukkanur, Sirval, etc.) terminating in three pendant lotus buds beneath which is the *purāṇic* triad with their vehicles *(vāhanas)*: *haṁsa, Nandī,* and *garuḍa*. The *makaras* at the two ends do not rest on the architrave; they appear to be standing instead. Water divinities *(udadhikumāras)* seated in the *ardha-paryaṅk-āsana* ride them. The vestibule pillars of this temple also support an *illikā-toraṇa* (Fig. 3.67); its greater visibility by virtue of its location is accorded due importance and the carving is superior to the other four in the *gūḍhamaṇḍapa* nave. The employment of the *illikā* arch as well as the representation of the Tripuruṣa with Śiva at the centre make these *toraṇas* more in conformity with the western Indian textual prescriptions than with the Dravidian texts.

The Maḍivāḷappaguṇḍu temple at Nagai in the north-eastern sector of Karnataka features a rather plain *antarāla-illikā-toraṇa* of five segments (Fig. 3.69; c. 1055-1058 CE). The pendant bud motifs acquire a mango-like profile here; *garuḍa* and musicians flank the centrally positioned Viṣṇu beneath the arch. The Nāgaliṅgeśvara temple at Kuralgeri in north-eastern Karnataka also displays an *antarāla-*

3.67

3.66 : *Illikā-toraṇa (antarāla),* Ron, Kālguḍi, c. last quarter of 10th century.

3.67 : *Illikā-toraṇa (antarāla),* Bevur, Rāmeśvara temple, c. 1055-1060 CE.

3.68 : *Illikā-toraṇa (gūḍhamaṇḍapa),* Bevur, Rāmeśvara temple, c. 1055-1060 CE.

3.69 : *Illikā-toraṇa (antarāla),* Nagai, Maḍivaḷappaguṇḍu temple, c. 1055-1058 CE.

3.68

3.69

3.70

illikā-toraṇa (Fig. 3.70; c. 1050-1060 CE). This well-proportioned arch marks advancement in conception. Canopied images of the *purāṇic* triad stand on lotus pedestals at the interstices of the arcs. *Kīrttimukhas* are placed at the apex of each arc and celestial beings *(vidyādharas)* fill the spaces under the arcs. *Makaras*, water divinities *(udadhikumāras),* and *vyālas* at the two ends are treated with attention to detail; the ornate figural sculpture complements the plain band of the arch. Each loop meets the next in a boldly rendered pendant bud. Flywhisk-bearers on the *toraṇa* posts make their appearance here, a feature which recurs from now on. The placement of *kīrttimukhas* at the apex of each arc and the celestials inscribed within the four loops matches well with the *illikā-toraṇa* at the entrance to the Kandariyā Mahādeo (c. first half of 11th century) at Khajuraho (compare Figs. 3.70 and 4.29), even though the visual impact and stylistic treatment are decidedly different. In a similar vein, the *antarāla-illikā-toraṇas* from the temples at Kukkanur and Sirval (c. late ninth century) compare with that from Gurgi (c. 10th century) in Madhya Pradesh (compare Figs. 3.49, 3.51, and 4.26).

Similarly styled *illikā-toraṇas* are seen at Lakkundi (Figs. 3.71) as well as Huli (Fig. 3.72). The *antarāla-toraṇa* in the Andhakeśvara temple at Huli (c. 1060-1070 CE) is made of a twisted pearl cable garland of five loops. The central loop is the largest and harbours an image of Śiva Tāṇḍaveśvara. A seated Brahmā playing the *vīṇā* and a three-headed Viṣṇu within the adjoining loops flank Tāṇḍaveśvara. At the apex is a *kīrttimukha* with *makaras*; the space above the arch is filled with a retinue of *dikpālas* with their consorts seated on their vehicles *(vāhanas)*. This *toraṇa* bears allegiance to the type seen in the vestibule of Temple 13 at Sirval (Fig. 3.52).

3.7

Three of the four shrines around the central *maṇḍapa* of the Śrī Basaveśvara temple at Kallur (c. 1050-1060 CE) include intricately carved *antarāla-illikā-toraṇas* of several undulations, spanning a long stretch. These were supported by cylindrical columns (Figs. 3.73, 3.74). The long arch is designed as a central group of five arcs flanked by two smaller *illikā-toraṇas* of four arcs each in Shrine 1 and as a series of five sets of miniature *illikā-toraṇas* of four arcs in Shrine 2. In each case, a profusion of flora, fauna, and divinities fills the entire lintel upon which the arch is carved. Tripuruṣa figures occupy centre space in both cases; *apsarās* and Naṭeśa are prominent on the *toraṇa* of Shrine 1, and Gaṇeśa, Varāha, and Narasiṁha are clearly discernible on the *toraṇa* of Shrine 2, with *kīrttimukhas* and *vyālas* in both instances. The *toraṇa* of Shrine 3 has Naṭeśa in the centre; it also shows narratives in the upper row and the heads of divinities in the lower. The *toraṇa* of Shrine 2 bears some links with the Kālguḍi *antarāla-toraṇa* in the arrangement of successive *illikā* arches in a row (compare Figs. 3.66 and 3.74).[28]

3.70 : *Illikā-toraṇa (antarāla),* Kuralgeri, Nāgaliṅgeśvara temple, c. 1050-1060 CE.

3.71 : *Illikā-toraṇa (antarāla),* Lakkundi Virūpākṣa temple, c. 1000-1010 CE.

3.72 : *Illikā-toraṇa (antarāla),* Huli, Andhakeśvara temple, c. 1060-1070 CE.

3.73 : *Illikā-toraṇa (antarāla),* Kallur, Śrī Basaveśvara temple, Shrine 1, c. 1050-1060 CE.

3.74 : *Illikā-toraṇa (antarāla),* Kallur, Śrī Basaveśvara temple, Shrine 2, c. 1050-1060 CE.

3.71

3.72

3.73

The increased facility of the medieval sculptors in Karnataka was complemented by the usage of soft stone, and the ornamental repertoire of the Later Cālukyan and Hoysaḷa temples grew more complex and elaborate as their construction activity progressed. The *antarāla-toraṇa* of the Mallikārjuna temple at Kuruvatti in the Bellary District (Fig. 3.75; c. 1070-1072 CE) has detailed ornamentation typical of the later Cālukyan monuments. The semi-circular *illikā* arch carved in relief is made up of four S-shaped curls on either side. A *kīrttimukha* is carved at the apex; *makaras* with floriated, upwardly oriented tails rest on the lintel. The main arch inscribes three similarly formed miniature arches that shelter Tripuruṣa images.

Above the doorway of the eastern porch entrance of the Candramaulīśvara at Unkal (c. 1080-1090 CE), is a *dvāra-illikā-toraṇa* raised on a pair of pilasters. The three empty spaces defined by the *illikā* arcs would have harboured Tripuruṣa images. The Rāmeśvara temple at Kamdolli (c. late 11th or early 12th century) possesses an *antarāla-illikā-toraṇa* with Naṭeśa at the centre flanked by Brahmā and Viṣṇu (Fig. 3.76). Compared to those from Kuruvatti and Unkal, this *toraṇa* is relatively simple and unadorned.[29] At Dambal, an important medieval Śaiva site, the Doḍḍābasappa temple (c. end 11th to early 12th century) has an *antarāla-illikā-toraṇa* resting on circular (*Śrīkāra* or so-called lathe-turned) pillars (Fig. 3.77).[30] The space under the arch, where one could expect the Tripuruṣa images, is broken. This gives the *toraṇa* the virtual appearance of being partially free from the stone matrix of the lintel and hence like a "free-flying arch," a type seen often in western but not in southern India. The apical *kīrttimukha* and the corner *makaras* as well as the arch of five loops, except for the pendant buds, are intact.

An *illikā-toraṇa* lintel recovered from Hampi and now displayed in the National Museum, New Delhi,[31] appears to have been a part of an important Later Cālukyan temple of the late 11th or early 12th century (Fig. 3.78). Small-sized *makaras* seated on pillar capitals release a tripartite *toraṇa*. Each segment consists of a trefoil arch, as in the Kālguḍi instance from Ron. The three segments of the arch are partitioned by miniature pillars topped by the motif of twin *makaras* and miniature shrines harbouring seated deities. Each trefoil arch segment passes

3.75

3.77

3.76

through the *makaras* and flows into the next trefoil arch segment. The *toraṇa* is thus a combination of the *illikā* as well as the *āndola*. This is similar in concept (though not so much in appearance) to the composite *toraṇas* at Lūṇa Vasahī in Mount Abu, Rajasthan (Fig. 4.56). The central segment frames Naṭeśa with his retinue; to his left is Viṣṇu with attendants, and to the right, Brahmā is conspicuous by his absence in the now empty space. An undulating creeper ornament made up of curls and counter-curls, typical of the Karṇāṭa idiom and also very prevalent in medieval western Indian architecture, adorns the entire band of the arch. Each small curl is inscribed with a tiny figure engaged in some activity. The trefoils are

3.75 : *Illikā-toraṇa (antarāla)*, Kuruvatti, Mallikārjuna temple, c. 1070-1072 CE.

3.76 : *Illikā-toraṇa (antarāla)*, Kamdolli, Rāmeśvara temple, c. late 11th or early 12th century.

3.77 : *Illikā-toraṇa (antarāla)*, Dambal, Doḍḍābasappā temple, c. end 11th or early 12th century.

3.78 : *Illikā-toraṇa (antarāla?),* Hampi, c. late 11th or early 12th century, now in the National Museum, New Delhi.

3.79 : *Illikā-toraṇa (antarāla),* Niralagi, Siddharāmeśvara temple, c. early 12th century.

3.80 : *Patra-citra-toraṇa (antarāla),* Belagavi, Fort, Jain temple, c. 1204 CE.

crowned with the *kīrttimukhas*; the central one releases a beaded festoon terminating in a bell *(grāsakiṅkiṇikā)*. The top register is packed with *aṣṭadikpālas* (eight directional divinities) and narratives. The lower border of the lintel that supports the *toraṇa* is adorned with an undulating curled creeper; each curl is inscribed with a figure. In one instance, a tiny swan is carved beneath Brahma's empty space.

3.80

3.79

3.78

Amongst other examples,[32] a fine specimen can be seen in the vestibule of the Siddharāmeśvara temple at Niralagi (Fig. 3.79; c. early 12th century). A dancing Viṣṇu occupies the central position beneath the arch, suggesting that the temple was originally dedicated to Viṣṇu. A pearl *illikā* garland of eight segments with dense foliate scrolls is carved between the usual *makaras* at the two ends and a powerful *kīrttimukha* at the apex. Even the array of buds suspended from the loops, as also the lotus buds held aloft by the *makaras*, are adorned with lush foliage. *Makaras* positioned on either side of the *kīrttimukha* at the top release an undulating creeper of curls and counter-curls inscribed with tiny figures. The Jain temple in the Old Fort at Belagavi (c. 1204 CE) has an *antarāla-toraṇa* with a dancing Indra at the centre, between curled foliate ornaments on either side (Fig. 3.80).

3.81 : *Citra-toraṇa,* Kuralgeri, Narasiṁha temple, Sūrya shrine, c. 1060 CE.

3.82 : *Citra-toraṇa (antarāla)*, Sinnar, Īśvara temple, c. mid-11th century.

3.83 : *Illikā-toraṇa (dvāra),* Sedam, Pañcaliṅgeśvara temple complex, c. late 11th century.

3.84 : *Illikā-toraṇa (antarāla),* Umarga, Śiva temple, west shrine, c. end 11th century.

3.81

3.82

3.83

Two *toraṇas* deserve special mention for their conceptualization and striking presence. The first, above the sanctum niche in the Sūrya shrine at the (so-called) Narasiṁha temple, Kuralgeri, is a *citra-toraṇa* dominated by the powerful imagery of Narasiṁha vanquishing Hiraṇyakaśipu, a subject that has given the temple its name (Fig. 3.81).[33] The second is the *antarāla-toraṇa* at the Īśvara temple in Sinnar (Fig. 3.82; c. mid-11th century), built during the early phase of Seuṇa or Yādava rule. It has a perfect half-moon shape *(ardhacandrākāra)* upon which is carved a central row of dancing goblins *(gaṇas)*; the lower row has tiny festoons within which also dancing *gaṇas* are placed. The top margin shows a leafy scroll border. The arch inscribes a dynamic Naṭeśa accompanied by musicians. Foliate tails of the *makaras* at the two ends flare upwards to fill the space above the arch. It has distant affiliations with some early Deccan *toraṇas* such as the one from Magathana (Fig. 3.9) in its formal qualities and with Jogeshvari in the style of figural sculpture.

3.84

The *toraṇas* from the Gulbarga District in Karnataka and those from Later Cālukyan territories in present-day Maharashtra show similarities in conception. The one placed above the vestibule doorframe of the west-facing shrine in the Pañcaliṅgeśvara complex at Sedam in Karnataka is a simple *illikā-toraṇa*, with a towering Tāṇḍaveśvara accompanied by tiny musicians within the arch (Fig. 3.83; c. late 11th century). The sculptor, in a partial attempt to free the images from the stone matrix, has scooped out large portions of the supporting stone. Celestial musicians are shown in the register above the top margins of the arch. A *toraṇa* from the main shrine of the Śiva temple at Umarga in Osmanabad District, Maharashtra (Fig. 3.84; c. end 11th century) is fairly similar to the one from Sedam. In this instance, Naṭeśa is placed in the centre and miniature shrines *(kūṭas)* on either side shelter Brahmā and Viṣṇu. The stone has been scooped out from the area immediately under the loops; garland bearing celestials *(mālāvidyādharas)* occupy the top register.

3.85 : *Illikā-toraṇa (antarāla),* Hottul, Pārvatī temple, c. 12th century.

3.86 : *Illikā-toraṇa (antarāla),* Hottul, Siddheśvara temple, c. 12th century.

3.87 : *Illikā-toraṇa,* Government Museum, Gulbarga, c. 12th century.

3.88 : *Illikā-toraṇa (dvāra),* Kalgi, Mallikārjuna temple, c. 12th century.

3.89 : *Illikā-toraṇa (dvāra),* Bilgi, Gomateśvara temple, Vardhamāna shrine, sanctum doorway, c. 16th century.

3.90 : *Toraṇa* fragment, Narayanpur, Īśvara temple, c. 11th-12th century.

The *antarāla-illikā-toraṇa* in the Pārvatī temple at Hottul in the Nanded District of Maharashtra is ideally proportioned with assured figural carving complemented by restrained ornamentation (Fig. 3.85; c. 12th century). A towering Naṭeśa occupies the centre stage, with a hierarchic gradation in the heights of the other accompanying figures. This arch traverses a serpentine path between the jaws of the *makaras* at the two ends with the *kīrttimukha* placed at the vertex. Miniature shrines housing Brahmā and Viṣṇu are placed in front of the *makaras*.

3.86

3.85

3.87

3.88

Garland-bearing celestials in the top register are distinctly Dravidian. (See also Fig. 3.86, under *Patra-toraṇas,* pp.94-95).

3.89

A restored granite *illikā-toraṇa* in the Government Museum, Gulbarga, shares several features with that at Hottul (compare Figs. 3.85 and 3.87). It is an arch of six loops with five pendant buds, and Naṭeśa with his entourage inscribed within the arch. An ascending sequence of garland-bearing celestials, three on each side, is depicted on the inner margins of the arch. The *vyālas* are positioned above the raised snouts of the *makaras* at the two ends. The example from Mallikārjuna temple at Kalgi is similar but its details have been obliterated by the application of lime plaster (Fig. 3.88). Four centuries later, in the instance from the Gomateśvara temple at Bilgi in the Shimoga District, the earlier composition was schematized and frozen in a *dvāra-illikā-toraṇa* (Fig. 3.89; c. 16th century). It is, never-the-less, of fine proportions and has an austere beauty. Underneath the arch are three miniature Dravidian shrines. In contrast are the profusely carved *toraṇa* fragments from the Īśvara temple, Narayanpur (c. 11th to 12th century). One of the fragments reveals the end of the main arch made up of a meandering pattern of curls and counter-curls, released by a *makara* (Fig. 3.90), with Viṣṇu seated on Garuḍa under a miniature *illikā* arch. This must have been an ornate, florid, and tripartite arch harbouring the Tripuruṣas.

3.90

Southern Karnataka: Hoysaḷas (c. 11th-13th centuries)

***Antarāla- and Dvāra-toraṇas*:**
With the ascent of Vinayaditya to the throne in 1047 CE, the Hoysaḷa dynasty gained significance in southern Karnataka until the early 14th century. Precedents to the Hoysaḷa or southern Karnataka style are largely to be found in the architectural style that prevailed in northern Karnataka, which was ruled by the Cālukyas of Kalyana.[34] Never-the-less, the zenith of the southern Karnataka style was attained at a time when the northern

3.91 : *Illikā-toraṇa (dvāra)*, Belur, Cennakeśava temple, c. 1173-1220 CE.

Karnataka style was losing its prime. Though drawing from the architecture that prevailed under the aegis of the Cālukyas of Kalyana, the Hoysaḷa style offered fresh approaches that resulted in novel creations.

The Hoysaḷa style revelled not so much in the grandiose as in the intricate, the opulent, and the ornate. The *toraṇas* resonate with this predilection and appear on the walls and entrances of the temples in a profusion of filigreed adornment. Even so, as compared to the Cālukyan temples, there appears to be a quantitative reduction in their presence on the temple walls. This is because the Hoysaḷa architects had evolved several other innovative ways to enrich the wall surfaces: with divine and semi-divine figures, and with other adornments such as diamond-, rosette-, and lotus-shaped motifs. This reduced the prominence of the *toraṇas* on their temple walls. However, *toraṇas* placed at the recesses, a pattern earlier noticed on Cālukyan buildings, did continue. The *antarāla-toraṇas* in the interiors, just as the *dvāra-toraṇas* at entrances to the halls, were present mainly in the bigger or royal foundations.

3.91

The *toraṇas* placed at the entrances to the halls and vestibules of the Cennakeśava (c. 1117 CE to late 12th century) and Cennigarāyā temples are amongst the finest representatives of the Hoysaḷa variant (Figs. 3.91, 3.92). Both temples were consecrated during the reign of Hoysaḷa Viṣṇuvardhana and his consort Śāntalādevī. The *dvāra-toraṇas* at the northern, southern, and eastern entrances leading to the *raṅgamaṇḍapa* of the Cennakeśava temple were added during the time of Vīra Ballāla (c. 1173-1220 CE). In tune with the Vaiṣṇava affiliation of the temple, that on the eastern or main entrance shows Viṣṇu-Narasiṁha on Garuḍa circumscribed by a slender and ornate *illikā-toraṇa* with a *kīrttimukha* at the apex (Fig. 3.91). The sculptor has exploited the full potential of the soft stone in carving every millimetre of available space with an unrelenting eye for detail. So enthusiastic is the sculptor's effort at detailing that the frail and fragile beauty of the main *illikā* garland is somewhat lost in the midst of a forest of intricacies. One half of the luxuriant tails of the *makaras* cascade to three-fourths the span of the supporting pilasters; the other half curl upwards in an ornate scroll. The eight directional divinities *(aṣṭadikpālas)* on their vehicles *(vāhanas)* are located immediately above the arch. The *antarāla-toraṇa* in this temple was also added during the time of Vīra Ballāla. An image of Lakṣmī-Nārāyaṇa in the centre and a row of dancers carved in the round on the segment below are the distinguishing features of this elaborate *toraṇa*.

3.92 : *Illikā-toraṇa (antarāla),* Belur, Cennigarāyā temple, c. 1117 CE.

The *antarāla-toraṇa* in the western (main) shrine of the Kappe Cennigarāya temple (consecrated 1117 CE) is a fine instance, though comparatively modest in appearance (Fig. 3.92). It harbours Lakṣmī-Nārāyaṇa framed by a serpentine *illikā-toraṇa* of ten loops, with a *kīrttimukha* at the vertex. A miniature shrine *(kūṭa)* housing a seated deity is placed at the extremity of the arch on either side and partially covers the *makaras*. Directional divinities, four on each side, are positioned in the corners above the arch. Like the Cennakeśava example, this too forms a perfect semi-circle or a half-moon *(ardhcandrākāra)*. Beneath the architrave supporting the *toraṇa,* on the upper portion of the doorframe *(uttaraṅga)*, is an array of festoons inscribed with the bud motif. The supporting pilasters bear large-sized Vaiṣṇava guardians.

At the famous double-shrines of the Hoysaḷeśvara temple at Halebidu (c. 1121 CE), one encounters a complex yet ordered flourish of sculptural ornament on the exterior walls. There is neither room nor occasion for the usual *kuḍya-toraṇas* crowning the *kūṭastambhas* (pilasters topped by miniature shrine models) on the wall recesses. Never-the-less, the arrangement of *toraṇas* in the interior and at entrances (Figs. 3.93, 3.94) is fairly similar to those noticed at the Cennakeśava temple, Belur. The exceptionally detailed and minutely carved *toraṇa* on the southern opening of the southern (Hoysaḷeśvara) shrine's hall is credited to sculptor Kāḷidāsī by an inscription (App. 1, no. 9).[35] Demoje was the author of a doorframe (including the *toraṇa* on the door-lintel?) at the eastern opening, as per another record (App. 1, no. 10).[36] These two *toraṇas* image Tāṇḍaveśvara flanked by Brahmā and Viṣṇu beneath the semi-circular curvature of the *illikā* arch of ten loops. Unlike the Cennakeśava *toraṇa* and similar to the one in Cennigarāyā, the space occupied by the cascading tails of the *makaras* is now usurped by large-sized door guardians. Both, the eastern as well as the southern *toraṇas* in the hall have a border of festoons on the underside of the lintel. The one over the southern door, sculpted by Kālidāsī, reveals a subtle and sensitive balance of structured composition with intricate ornamentation. The *dikpālas* on their *vāhanas*, another recurring theme on Karnataka *toraṇas*, are arranged in a row on the top register on either side of the arch. Though several other instances of *toraṇas* from the southern Karnataka region are available;[37] it suffices our present purposes to have discussed their general characteristics and trends.

3.94

3.93

3.93 : *Illikā-toraṇa,* Halebidu, Hoysaḷeśvara temple, c. 1121 CE.

3.94 : *Illikā-toraṇa,* Halebidu, Hoysaḷeśvara temple, c. 1121 CE.

3.95 : *Illikā-toraṇa (kuḍya)*, Lakkundi, Kāśīviśveśvara temple, c. 1030 CE.

3.96 : *Illikā-toraṇa (kuḍya)*, Dambal, Doḍḍābasappā temple, c. end 11th or early 12th century.

Karnataka: c. 10th-13th centuries

Kuḍya-toraṇas (wall *toraṇas*)

We may distinguish between two types of *kuḍya-toraṇas.* The first are those that crown niche images, sham niches or latticed windows on the temple walls (Figs. 3.48, 3.95, and 3.99); the second are those that do not crown niches or windows, yet adorn the temple walls in generous numbers (Figs. 3.96, 3.97). The first type is first encountered from the late sixth-early seventh century, while the second, a particular favourite in Karnataka, begins to appear from the ninth century.

The *kuḍya-toraṇas* invade the walls of Later Cālukyan temples and also inhabit the Hoysaḷa and Kākatīya temple walls. Their opulent presence in a sense characterizes the ornamental programme of several Later Cālukyan temples. Those adorning the walls of the Kāśīviśveśvara temple at Lakkundi exhibit rare symmetry, balance, proportion, grace, and workmanship (Fig. 3.95; c. 1030 CE). They also embellish the recesses on the exterior walls of the Andhakeśvara and Kalmeśvara temples (c. 1060-1070 CE) at Huli. Those at the central niches and above the *kūṭastambhas* of the Mallikārjuna temple walls at Kuruvatti (c. 1070-1072 CE) appear as though bejewelled, and vie with the creations of a master goldsmith. Against the play of light, these delicately wrought *kuḍya-toraṇas*

3.95

3.98

3.97 : *Illikā-toraṇa (grāsa, kuḍya)*, Ittagi, Mahādeva temple, *vimāna,* c. early 12th century.

3.98 : *Adhiṣṭhāna-toraṇa,* Lakkundi, Kāśīviśveśvara temple, c. 1030 CE.

3.99 : *Illikā-toraṇa (kuḍya)*, Panagal, Paccala Someśvara temple complex, c. late 11th century.

3.100 : *Nāsī-toraṇa,* Ittagi, Mahādeva temple, c. early 12th century.

3.97

exemplify the high standards in architectural ornament set by the medieval Karnataka sculptors, no doubt aided in their endeavours by the manoeuvrable schist-stone used for building these temples. Those on the walls of the Doḍḍā Basappā temple at Dambal, with powerfully wrought *kīrttimukhas* at the apex, are striking (Fig. 3.96). The stellate plan of the main temple and the hall create fan-like divisions of the wall spaces that are ingeniously embellished with bi-facial *kuḍya-toraṇas* at the angles; the recesses also bear *toraṇas* above the *kūṭastambhas*. The frequent placement of *toraṇas* on temple walls leads to newer adaptations. The recesses, as on the Candramaulīśvara temple at Unkal (c. late 11th century), register a new development: *Kuḍya-toraṇas* surround images of deities placed above the *kūṭastambhas*.[38] The subsidiary central offsets of the Rāmeśvara temple at Kamdolli have niches topped by miniature temple superstructures which are enveloped by *toraṇas*. At the Mahādeva temple, Ittagi (c. early 12th century), the outer wall recesses are punctuated by elongated *grāsa-toraṇas* (decorative arches with a prominent gorgon face at the apex) placed above short *kūṭastambhas* (Fig. 3.97). The Tārakeśvara *vimāna* walls at Hanagal (c. 1180 CE) exhibit fine *toraṇas* framing *kūṭastambhas* crowned with miniature temple superstructures in the recesses.

Though less appealing than their northern Karnataka counterparts, the *kuḍya-toraṇas* are also noticed on temples built during the Hoysaḷa period in southern Karnataka. Those on the exterior wall recesses of the Siddheśvara temple, Marale, Śantīśvara basti, Nittur, Amṛteśvara temple, Amritapura (c. 1196 CE), and the Yoga Narasiṁha temple complex at Narasipura (c. first half of 14th century) bear this out.

Karnataka: c. 10th-13th centuries

Nāsī-toraṇas

The Amṛteśvara temple at Annigeri (c. second quarter of 11th century), which has well-crafted *kuḍya-toraṇas,* can also boast of *nasī-toraṇas* at the central projections of its *vimāna's* superstructure. The *nāsī-toraṇas* lend accent and grace to the temple superstructures. Their aesthetic appeal is even more pronounced on the superstructure of the grand Mahādeva temple at Ittagi (Figs. 3.100, 3.101; c. early 12th century). Each serpentine *illikā-toraṇa* emerges from the jaws of a powerfully rendered *kīrttimukha* at the apex and enters the mouths of two tiny *makaras* facing inwards. There is a generic likeness to those seen on *Caṇḍī* Kalasan in Central Java (Fig. 5.40). The Bhīmeśvara temple at Nilagunda (c. late 11th to early 12th century) in the northern Karṇāṭa style, has well-crafted *nāsī-* and *kuḍya-toraṇas*.

3.99

3.100

The Andhra Region: c. 11th-13th centuries

Consequent to the conquest of Hanamkonda by Kākatīya Garuḍa Beṭa I, the Kākatīya dynasty gradually rose to power. The reign of Rudradeva (1158-1195 CE) and Gaṇapatideva (1199-1262 CE) proved to be particularly opportune for the arts. Some of the Kākatīya temples were built of granite, a stone much harder than the schist employed in southern Karnataka. This, in addition to other regional stylistic compulsions in the Andhra region, led to the crystallization of a distinct Teliṅgāna or Kākatīya style of architecture. The temples from this region are fewer in number and more restrained in décor; none-the-less, they are not wanting in fine workmanship. The *toraṇas* too are lesser in number and less ostentatious in appearance, but the finest, such as those from Hanamkonda and Warangal (Figs. 3.102-3.104), vie with the best from the Cālukyan and Hoysaḷa territories. The exterior wall specifications of temples belonging to this style usually include schematised, inverted 'U'-shaped *kuḍya-illikā-toraṇas* above the niches and the *kūṭastambhas*. Some notable examples include those at the Paccala Someśvara temple complex, Panagal (Fig. 3.99; c. late 11th century), Trikūṭa temple, Nagunur (c. early 13th century), and the Caturmukha temple, Manthena (c. early 13th century).

3.101

3.101 : Detail, *Nāsī-toraṇa,* Ittagi, Mahādeva temple, c. early 12th century.

3.102 : *Illikā-toraṇa (antarāla),* Hanamkonda, Veyistambhālaguḍi, western shrine, c. 1163 CE.

In the interiors, the vestibule *(antarāla)* entrance is at times graced by a *toraṇa* supported on pillars with latticed screens on either side, as in the Later Cālukyan and Hoysaḷa temples. Perhaps the finest examples are located inside the *trikūṭa* temple called Veyistambhālaguḍi at Hanamkonda, a royal foundation of Kākatīya Rudradeva (Figs. 3.102, 3.103; c. 1163 CE). The *antarāla* entrances leading from the shared *maṇḍapa* to the three shrines (eastern Sūrya, central Vāsudeva, and western Śiva shrines) have *citrakhaṇḍa* (variegated) pillars flanked by latticed screens and topped by *toraṇas*. Each of these is made up of an *illikā* garland of six serpentine loops with a tiny *kīrttimukha* placed at the apex. The one at the western entrance is sculpted with the figure of Naṭeśa with Nandī and accompanying musicians (Fig. 3.102). The profile of the lintel supporting the *toraṇa* is embellished with festoons and the underside is rendered attractive by nine bud-like knobs *(mukulas)* arranged in a sequence. A second example from the same temple images a

3.103 : *Illikā-toraṇa (antarāla),* Hanamkonda, Veyistambhālaguḍi, c. 1163 CE.

3.104 : *Illikā-toraṇa,* Warangal, now in the National Museum, New Delhi, c. late 12th or early 13th century.

3.105 : *Toraṇa* fragment, Panagal, Paccala Someśvara temple complex, c. late 11th century.

3.106 : *Illikā-toraṇa (antarāla),* Pillalamarrai, Nāmeśvara temple, c. 1195-96 CE.

3.107 : *Toraṇa* lintel, Nandi-Kandi, Rāmaliṅgeśvara temple, c. 1015 CE.

3.105

dancing Indra accompanied by celestial musicians and maidens, and his vehicle, Airāvata (Fig. 3.103). The deeply undercut lines and carefully rendered details doubtless situate these *toraṇas* with the best in any other style.

A *toraṇa* lintel now housed in the National Museum, New Delhi,[39] reveals remarkable allegiance to the Hanamkonda *toraṇas,* and appears to be of the same stock as the remains recovered from the wreckage at the famous site of the Svayambhūliṅgeśvara temple at Warangal (Fig. 3.104; c. late 12th to early 13th century). It was recovered from the temple ruins at this site, and must have belonged to the Svayambhūliṅgeśvara temple originally.[40] Refined craftsmanship, fine proportions, and a judicious balance of the figural and the ornamental characterize this *toraṇa.* At the two ends, tiered

3.104

3.107

3.106

shrine models are placed in front of the *makaras* who emit a slender *illikā* garland of seven loops. Each loop meets the next in a shapely bud motif *(kalikā)* adorned with foliate scrolls. The arch circumscribes a tall Naṭeśa at the centre and smaller dancing images of Brahmā and Viṣṇu along with their vehicles at the sides. Nandī is positioned close to Naṭeśa, a tiny *garuḍa* is seen next to Viṣṇu, and a graceful *haṁsa* sits near Brahmā. The relative sizes of the deities are in harmony with the curvature of the arch. Every detail, the attributes in the hands of the gods, the musicians, and the directional divinities in the top register, is chiselled with sensitivity and clarity. In place of the festoons noticed elsewhere, the lower border of the lintel here is decorated with embossed geometrical motifs; underneath are the *kalikā* knobs. Amongst others,[41] a notable example includes the fragment from the Paccala Someśvara temple group, Panagal (Fig. 3.105; c. late 11th century).

Also of the same time-bracket and region, is the *toraṇa*-lintel from the Rāmaliṅgeśvara temple at Nandi-Kandi (Fig. 3.107) and the vestibule *toraṇa* of the Nāmeśvara temple at Pillalamarrai (Fig. 3.106).

103

Tamilnadu and other Southern Regions: c. 9th-12th centuries

Patra-toraṇas

There are relatively very few examples, in southern as well as northern India, that singularly qualify as *patra-toraṇas*. A plausible explanation for this is found in some of the medieval Dravidian texts, which ascribe *patra-toraṇas* as being apt for (the dwellings of) the *śūdras,* the lowest of the hierarchical social order. In addition, the texts also indicate that the *citra-* and *makara-toraṇas* are fit for gods and nobles (App. 3, nos. 22, 24, 25). The rationale for this textual injunction most likely rests in traditional modes of practice followed in the tying of actual garlands *(toraṇa-mālās)* of leaves, flowers, jewels, etc. A garland of leaves *(patra)* would obviously have been the humblest (as compared to a garland of flowers or jewels) and was thus ascribed for those with the least status and means, the *śūdras*. This offers an explanation for the disfavour accorded to the *patra-toraṇa* in temples. Another possibility is that a particular type such as the *citra-toraṇa* gradually gained in favour with the artists and patrons and became the norm in a major part of the Tamil region.

3.108

3.109

The *toraṇas* framing shallow niches on temple walls from the Pāṇḍya country during the ninth and tenth centuries, however, provide some fine versions of *patra-toraṇas*. These deserve special mention as much for their rare occurrence as for their sound design. The earliest of these are found on the walls of the Manonmanīśvara temple at Vijayanarayanam (c. last quarter of the ninth century). That over a niche on the northern wall of the *vimāna* is completely composed of a scroll-like exuberance (Fig. 3.108). Only a faint semblance to *makaras* can be traced in the abstraction of its form. Miniature pearl festoons are carved on the underside of the arch; the only figural sculpture is that of Nandī, placed within the arch. Another example, from the western wall, which is a *ratna-(makara)-toraṇa*, reveals the blueprint from which the former must have been inspired (Fig. 3.109).

Similar examples of *patra-toraṇas* from Karnataka may also be cited here. An early representative is seen on the Virūpākṣa temple at Pattadakal (Fig. 3.23; c. 743 CE). Those on the walls of the twin shrines of Pañcakūṭa basti at Kambadahalli (Figs. 3.60, 3.61) follow close on the heels of the example from Vijayanarayanam

3.110

3.111

just discussed. *Patra-toraṇas* also adorn the walls of the Kailāsanātha temple at Tirupattur (c. late eighth century, Pallava). The Tālinātha temple (c. 867 CE, Pāṇḍya) at this site reveals scroll-like variants of bejewelled *toraṇas*. Perhaps there was a preference for the foliate arch in the region, as may also be seen on the northern wall of the *ardhamaṇḍapa* of this temple (Fig. 3.110). However, the same example also registers clear affinities with the semi-circular *ratna-* and *citra-toraṇas* in the Coḷa country.

The *vimāna* walls of the main Neliapparswāmī shrine at Tirunelveli sport some gracefully rendered *patra-toraṇas* atop shallow central niches, giving the impression of an expansive wave of foliage with its curls and counter-curls (Fig. 3.111; c. early to mid-10th century). Underneath the arch are tiny representations of Śiva Liṅgodbhavamūrti flanked by Viṣṇu and Brahmā. A differently styled, compact, and schematic *patra-toraṇa* from the Coḷa region graces a niche on the Sundareśvara temple in Melapalluvur, Tiruchinapalli District, Tamilnadu (Fig. 3.112; c. early 11th century). At a later date, a much-depleted repertoire of *patra-toraṇas* is represented on the *vimāna* walls of the mid-12th century Citraratha Vallabha Perumal temple at Kuruvitturai.

The *antarāla-patra-toraṇa* of the Siddharāmeśvara temple at Hottul in the Nanded District of Maharashtra (Fig. 3.86; c. 12th century) is an innovative variant. The span between the *makaras* at the ends and the *kīrttimukha* at the apex is traversed by a meandering, foliate arch. The portion just beneath the arch is occupied by Naṭeśa with musicians, encircled by garland-bearing celestials. The *vyālas* are placed amidst foliage in the top register.

3.112

3.108 : *Patra-toraṇa (kuḍya),* Vijayanarayanam, Manonmanīśvara temple, c. last quarter of ninth century.

3.109 : *Ratna-toraṇa (kuḍya),* Vijayanarayanam, Manonmanīśvara temple, c. last quarter of ninth century.

3.110 : *Patra-ratna-toraṇa (kuḍya),* Tirupattur, Tālinātha temple, c. 867 CE.

3.111 : *Patra-toraṇa (kuḍya),* Tirunelveli, Neliapparswāmī temple, c. early to mid-10th century.

3.112 : *Patra-toraṇa (kuḍya),* Melapalluvur, Sundareśvara temple, c. early 11th century.

3.114

3.113

The Tamil Region: c. 9th-12th centuries

Citra- and *Ratna-toraṇas*

Citra- and *ratna-toraṇas*, prescribed in the Dravidian treatises as appropriate for gods and kings, thrive on the temple walls of Tamilnadu. These may be bow-shaped (*cāpākara, dhanurākṛti*) or semi-circular (*ardhacandrākāra, vṛttākāra*); the latter gains precedence from the 10th century.

Belonging to the early Coḷa period, the Nāgeśvaraswāmī temple at Kumbhakonam has finely carved semi-circular *(ardhacandrākāra) citra-toraṇas* above the central wall niches (Fig. 3.113; c. later half of ninth century). Carved in low relief, these, however, pale into insignificance before the striking sculptures within the niches which they frame. Amongst several such representations, those on the sanctum walls of the Saptarṣīśvara temple (c. 875-898 CE) at Lalgudi in the Tiruchinapalli District are worthy of note (Fig. 3.114). Crowning an image of Ardhanārīśvara on the eastern sanctum wall is a *citra-toraṇa* that is a perfect visual translation of the textual description of this *toraṇa*. The *makaras* with floriated tails bring forth a retinue of riders on animals, a band of jewels, pearl festoons, and a leafy scroll-like ornament, all of which converge in the central ornament of a medallion inscribed with a *kīrttimukha* and outward-facing *makaras*. At the apex, the arch dips subtly, conjuring the shape of a bow *(cāpākāra)*. These and other such early Coḷa examples[42] seem to have been codified in Dravidian texts such as the *Mayamata*.

Amongst many contenders, those seen on the Koraṅganātha temple at Srinivasanallur (c. 927

CE) deserve special notice. The hand of a master sculptor is evident on the one above the central niche on the western wall (Fig. 3.115). This *cāpākāra-citra-toraṇa* is carved with precision and attention to detail. The *vyālas* with riders emerge from the jaws of *makaras* and constitute the central band of the arch, which is laced on the upper margin with a leafy scroll. As at the Saptarṣīśvara temple, two *makaras* and a *kīrttimukha* form the central ornament of the arch. Tiny representations of elementals *(bhūtas),* goblins *(gaṇas),* and Nandī, amid delicate floral festoons, adorn the underside of the arch. These surround a miniature image of Varāha and Bhūdevī within the central circular cavity *(gāḍha)* under the arch.

Citra-toraṇas circumscribing divinities are placed above the central niches on the walls of the Pipileśvara (Tiruverumbiyūr Aḷvar) temple at Tiruverumbur (Fig. 3.116; c. 950 CE). The one with Yogapaṭṭa Narasiṁha in the central cavity is placed above an image of Brahmā on the western niche of the sanctum wall.[43] As many of the temples are covered with lime, some of the finer details are obliterated. The ornamentation follows the well-established vocabulary of the *citra-toraṇa* of this region: *makaras* at the two ends release *vyālas* with riders in the central band, foliate scrolls occupy the upper margin, and festoons are suspended from the lower margin; the whole converges in the apical ornament of outward-facing *makaras* topped by a *kīrttimukha*. Similar *citra-toraṇas* are noticed on several other contemporaneous temples in the region.[44]

3.113 : *Citra-toraṇa (kuḍya),* Kumbhakonam, Nāgeśvaraswāmī temple, c. later half of ninth century.

3.114 : *Citra-toraṇa (kuḍya),* Lalgudi, Saptarṣīśvara temple, c. 875-898 CE.

3.115 : *Citra-toraṇa (kuḍya),* Srinivasanallur, Koraṅganātha temple, c. 927 CE.

3.116 : *Citra-toraṇa (kuḍya),* Tiruverumbur, Tiruverumbiyūr Aḷvar temple, c. 950 CE.

3.116

3.115

The Mayarcindeśvara temple in Tirumiyaccur (c. last decades of the 10th century) registers some shifts in the manner of rendering *citra-toraṇas*. Figural sculpture receives greater emphasis: there is an increase in the space reserved for the central cavity *(gāḍha)* to inscribe images, an additional row of celestials *(vidyādharas)* is added above that of the *vyālas,* and a divinity is placed at the apex in place of the *kīrttimukha*. The *makaras* at the ends are now pushed further to the corners, the lower margin of festoons is given summary treatment, and the arch assumes a more definitive semi-circular shape. The central cavity *(gāḍha)* of the one over an image of Brahmā on the northern wall is filled with a multi-armed image of Narasiṁha ripping Hiraṇyakaśyapu (Fig. 3.117); Naṭeśa is placed at the apex. Two sequences, one of *vidyādharas* and the other of *vyālas* are organized along the curved band of the arch; a figure emerges from the *makara's* jaws on each side. A niche on the southern vestibule wall of this temple harbours Kalyāṇasundara Śiva with Umā in the *gāḍha*; Ardhanārīśvara is appropriately placed at the vertex (Fig. 3.118).

3.117

3.119

Madathukovil in Pudukottai possesses another innovative and refreshing variant of the *citra-toraṇa* (Fig. 3.119). A prominent *kīrttimukha,* carved as in the *mahānāsīs* of Coḷa temples, is placed at the apex of this well-proportioned *cāpākāra-toraṇa*. The *kīrttimukha* releases *makaras* from his jaws, who in turn emit a triple band of *vyālas, haṁsas* (geese), and *patras* (foliage) which yet again flow into the jaws of *makaras*. Seated images of Gaṇeśa, Lakṣmī, and Devī are placed beneath the arch.

3.117 : *Citra-toraṇa (kuḍya),* Tirumiyaccur, Mayarcindeśvara temple, c. last decades of the 10th century.

3.118 : *Citra-toraṇa (kuḍya),* Tirumiyaccur, Mayarcindeśvara temple, c. last decades of the 10th century.

3.119 : *Citra-toraṇa,* Pudukottai, Madathukovil, c. late 10th century.

3.118

3.120

The central wall niches of the two surviving *vimānas* of the quaint Mūvarkovil temple complex in Kodumbalur are carved with *toraṇas* of a composite class (*citra-ratna-toraṇas*) (Fig. 3.120; c. 880 CE). The Agastīśvara (c. 884 CE) and the Coḷīśvara (c. 884 CE) temples at Kilaiyur in Tiruchirapalli District also reveal deftly carved *citra-toraṇas* above the central niches of the *vimānas'* walls.[45] The one crowning Dakṣiṇāmūrti on the southern wall of the Agastīśvara *vimāna* bears a multi-armed Śiva dancing to the musical accompaniment of *gaṇas* and a *kinnara*, with celestials *(vidyādharas)* as witnesses (Fig. 3.121). The central band of the arch displays *vyālas* with riders and *gaṇas*. A majority of the *vṛttākāra-citra-toraṇas* on the walls of the Thañjāvūr Bṛhadīśvara *vimāna* inscribe images of Śiva under the arch (Fig. 3.122). Several are incomplete, reflecting that artistic activity was interrupted before the completion of details. The tradition of carving *citra-toraṇas* continued through the major part of the medieval period (Fig. 3.123).[46]

3.123

3.122

3.121

3.120 : *Ratna-citra-toraṇa, (kuḍya),* Kodumbalur, Mūvarkovil, c. 880 CE.

3.121 : *Citra-toraṇa (kuḍya),* Kilaiyur, Agastīśvara temple, c. 884 CE.

3.122 : *Citra-toraṇa (kuḍya),* Thanjāvūr, Bṛhadīśvara temple, c. 1003-1010 CE.

3.123 : *Citra-toraṇa (kuḍya),* Pattishvaram, Ramanāthan kovil, c. 1025 CE.

3.124 : Lotus Mahal from south,
modern positive (2007) from
waxed-paper negative (1856), ACP.

3.124

Late Southern Indian *Toraṇas* c. post-13th century

The rise of the Vijayanagara Empire in c. 1336 CE ensured continuity in the patronage accorded to temples. At its height, the empire spanned a vast region, controlling territories that earlier were ruled by powerful dynasties of the Deccan and South India. With regard to the *toraṇas*, there was hardly any significant development during this period. The Lower Dravidian trend of the earlier period continued but the *toraṇas* acquired a very schematic, formulaic, and metallic look. The *parikara-toraṇas* in metal as well as in stone continued to prevail. On some structures, such as the Lotus Mahal at Hampi, one observes the adaptation of the *toraṇa* (with the *kīrttimukha* at the apex) on the cusped and staggered arches of a mixed affiliation. More significantly, an earlier image of this structure reveals "free-flying" *illikā-toraṇas* under the cusped and staggered arches (Fig. 3.124).[47] Instances that merge Islamic architectural traditions with the local practices abound in Indo-Islamic architecture of the Bahmānī and Ādil Shāhī periods, as for instance, the central archway of the Jāmī Masjid façade at Bijapur in

3.125

Karnataka (c. 1576 CE). Component elements from the *toraṇa* repertoire were at times adapted to newer purposes, as in the combination of the S-shaped segment *(madala)* and the bud motif *(kalikā),* which is employed under the eaves of Indo-Islamic structures. At Gol Gumbaz in Bijapur (c. 1656 CE), for instance, the eave that runs through the building has brackets shaped like a series of S-shaped segments *(madalas)* and the bud motifs *(kalikās)* seen on *toraṇas*.[48] In some cases, the same *madala-kalikā* ornament is placed between successive brackets under the eave, conjuring the *toraṇa* form, as is visible in the Ibrahim Rauza at Bijapur (Fig. 3.125; c. 1627-28 CE).

Free-standing *Toraṇas*

Fewer free-standing *toraṇas* are available from the southern region as compared to medieval western India. However, several inscriptions testify to the prevalence of free-standing and portable *toraṇas* in southern India (App. 1). Those from Aihole (c. first half of the 11th to early 12th century) and Warangal (c. early 13th century) are the best known. Very few of the free-standing examples show elaboration or complexity in design; their basic form comprises two vertical posts and one or two crossbars. The *toraṇa* garlands, unlike their western and central Indian counterparts, are sculpted in relief on the lintels. This excludes the play of light upon their otherwise well-carved forms.

Among the free-standing examples prior to the 10th century, is the one at Ittagi (Fig. 3.126; c. 676-699 CE). Its crossbeam rests on two square pillars with tapering necks and square but curved cushion capitals. The crossbeam bears sixteen auspicious symbols.[49] Gajalakṣmī is placed at the centre on both faces of the lintel. Although *makaras* are not seen on the lintel, they are found on the die below it. The auspicious symbols on the northern and southern faces include *nidhi* (treasure), *pūrṇakumbha* (vase of plenty), *siṁhāsana* (lion throne) with *śaṅkha* (conch) and *cakra* (disc), *darpaṇa* (mirror), *siṁha* (lion), *varāha* (boar), Gajalakṣmī, crossed *cāmara* (whisk) under *chatra* (parasol), couchant Nandī, and *mīna-yugala* (a pair of fish). An elongated eave with miniature shrines *(kūṭas* and *śālās)* makes the coping of the lintel; a lotus is carved on its soffit and brackets carved with foliate scrolls are seen at the ends. Another pre-10th century instance (c. eighth century) is located between Temples 1 and 2 of the Kontiguḍi group. It has four pillars in a rectangular arrangement with the *vyālas* acting as brackets between the pillars and the roof.

Two *toraṇas* from Aihole, one fronting the Mallikārjuna temple, and another associated with the Veṇṇiyavar group, belong to the early 11th century.[50] The two supporting pillars of the Mallikārjuna instance have fluted sections above square shafts (Fig. 3.127). This is followed by inverted bell-shaped shoulder elements *(laśunas)*, topped by capitals and brackets carved with flowers. The lintel bears an undulating *toraṇa* garland, similar to that noticed on the *antarāla-toraṇa* of the western shrine at the Pāpavināśeśvara complex at Papanasam (Fig. 3.54). The corner arcs frame leonine figures; female figures are placed under the two central arcs. The *toraṇa* pillars of the Veṇṇiyavar group

3.126

3.125 : Ibrahim Rauza, façade, underside of eave, Bijapur, c. 1627-28 CE.

3.126 : Free-standing *toraṇa,* Ittagi, c. 676-699 CE.

3.127 : *Toraṇa,* Aihole, in front of Mallikārjuna temple, c. first half of 11th century.

127

3.128

3.128 : *Toraṇa,* Aihole, Veṇṇiyavar group, c. first half of 11th century.

3.129 : *Toraṇa,* Aihole, Gaḷaganātha group, c. late 11th century.

Fig. 3.130 : *Toraṇa,* Alampur, c. 11th century.

Fig. 3.131 : *Toraṇa,* Nandi-Kandi, in front of Rāmeśvara temple, c. early 11th century.

3.130

include additional features such as the presence of the *pīpal* leaf on the curved portion (Fig. 3.128). The profile of the lintel is graced by an *illikā* garland made of five loops of twisted pearl cable. The *vyālas* are positioned underneath the corner loops and the Tripuruṣas are housed within the three central loops. The third free-standing *toraṇa* at Aihole, associated with the Gaḷaganātha group (c. late 11th century), is refined in appearance (Fig. 3.129). The two lower segments of its pillars resemble the 'vase and foliage' *(ghaṭapallava)* pillars of central Indian affiliation. Above these are the gorgon bands *(grāsapaṭṭikā)* and the shoulder sections *(laśuna)* carved with the dormer motif *(candraśālikā* or *nāsī)*. The lintel, resting upon the pillar capitals and brackets, is carved with an *illikā* garland of four inverted U-shaped loops of pearl cable which terminate in bud motifs. Casually rendered images of Lakṣmī and Gaṇeśa are sheltered under the two central loops; the soffit of the lintel bears three lotuses. The fourth instance of a free-standing *toraṇa* from Aihole (c. 11th century) is located near the Rāmaliṅga group of temples.

3.131

Among other examples, the one at Alampur is made up of two *citrakhaṇḍa* (of variegated cylindrical and cubical sections) pillars that support a crossbeam (Fig. 3.130; c. 11th century). The lower square shaft of the pillar has guardian figures.[51] A simple *toraṇa* gateway is found to the east of the Rāmeśvara temple at Nandi-Kandi in Andhra Pradesh (Fig. 3.131; c. early 11th century). Two square posts, carved sparingly in shallow relief, support a lintel with tiny *makaras* at the ends. Gajalakṣmī at the centre and vase-finials *(stūpīs)* at the corners crown a plain cornice. The lintel's soffit is adorned with a row of seven buds *(kalikās)*.

3.129

The four Warangal *toraṇas* (Fig. 3.132; c. first half of the 13th century) are intact *in situ* at what must have been the grand Svayambhūliṅgeśvara temple complex. The architectural fragments recovered from this site and those re-used in Tugluq structures bear this out.[52] The near-identical granite *toraṇas* at the cardinal points of this complex define an area of c. 460' x 450'. Their survival, despite the complete desecration of the Svayambhūliṅga temple has been attributed to the significance of their alignment within the cosmographical organization of the medieval city of Warangal.[53] Apart from a few insignificant representations of animals, goblins, etc., these *toraṇas* have almost no figural embellishment; as such they are also in tune with the Islamic sensibilities. Each of the four pairs of the *toraṇa* pillars have chamfered square bases and support an architrave resting on S-shaped *(madala)* brackets at the ends. Above each bracket, an ornate *haṁsa* (goose) was placed, as seen at one end of the northern *toraṇa*. The profile of the architrave is embellished with festoons; the soffit

3.132 : *Toraṇa,* Warangal, Svayambhūliṅgeśvara temple complex, c. first half of 13th century.

3.133 : *Toraṇa,* Ainavolu, Mallikārjuna temple complex, c. first quarter of 13th century.

3.134 : *Toraṇa,* Kulpak, Nalagonda District, c. 11th century CE.

3.135 : *Toraṇa,* Dichpalli, in front of the Office of Deparment of Archaeology, Hyderabad, Vijayanagar period (pillars appear older than the arch).

3.132

3.134

3.133

is graced with seven buds. Storied shrines and *makaras* in profile at the ends flank an *illikā* arch of seven loops and five pendant buds.

The three *toraṇas* added to the Mallikārjuna temple at Ainavolu are modest versions of the Warangal instances (Fig. 3.133; c. first quarter of 13th century). The free-standing example of an earlier period from Kulpak (Fig. 3.134) is typical of the region. The *toraṇa* arch of another example from Dichpalli belongs to the Vijayanagara period (Fig. 3.135). It resembles the schematized *parikara*-frames that accompany the divine images of the period from the 14th century onwards. The pillars appear to be of a slightly earlier date. Free-standing *toraṇas* with a lintel resting on pillars continued to be seen after the 13th century also, as for example, the *Tulābhāra toraṇa* at Hampi (Vijayanagara period). It is believed to have been used as a balance for weighing gold, grains, and other things equivalent to the weight of the king, for distribution amongst deserving persons.[54]

3.135

Notes and References

[1] See Spink, *Ajanta: History and Development,* Vol. I, for chronological details of the Ajanta caves.

[2] Though the cave was excavated during Sātavāhana rule, this sculpture was carved during the Vākāṭaka period.

[3] According to Walter Spink, evidence of the early beginnings of Cave 26 (c. 462 CE) "is masked by its overlay of typically late forms" (c. 475-478 CE). See Spink, *Ajanta: History and Development,* Vol. 5, pp.311-342.

[4] The doorframe of the main front hall of this cave is damaged but the presence of a *toraṇa* is evident. The image of a dancing Śiva surrounded by *gaṇas* is framed within the bow-shaped *(cāpākāra)* space defined by the faintly visible *toraṇa*.

[5] The lintels on the eastern and western faces of Sanctuary S 1 at Sambor Prei Kuk, to mention two instances.

[6] An inscription found at Kanheri states that a donation to the Buddhist monastery was made during the augmenting kingdom of the Traikūṭakas: Kanheri copper plate inscription (494 CE). See Stevenson, "Historical Names and Facts contained in the Kānherī (Kenery) Inscriptions.," p.33.

[7] Another *ratna-toraṇa,* on the front wall in the interior of the antechamber to Cave 34, is only faintly visible.

[8] The most elegant and mature instances of *āndola toraṇas* are seen on the temples of early medieval Gujarat and Rajasthan.

[9] On the basis of the characters of the inscription found on one of the pillars on the ground floor as also the advancement in sculptural motifs and style. See *EITA* Vol. I, Part 2, pp.20-22.

[10] *EITA* Vol. I, Part 2, pp.49-52; Tarr, "Chronology and Development..," pp.155-184.

[11] Yet another type, above a niche on the outer south wall of the main Kāḍasiddheśvara temple, frames Viṣṇu and is much-effaced. Here, festoons are suspended directly from the underside of a *muktā-makara-toraṇa*. The space between the arch and the upper margin of the niche is carved with a *kīrttimukha* placed above a square central ornament with protruding *makara* heads.

[12] The term *illikā* is used in western Indian treatises to indicate a variety of *toraṇas.* The name derives from the curvaceous gait of the caterpillar, which such an arch appears to emulate.

[13] Srinivasan, *Cave Temples of the Pallavas,* pp.37-43, 71-79, 89-94.

[14] See Dubreuil, *Pallava Antiquities,* Vol. I: Plate XVI, A, for a photograph of the Dalavanur *toraṇa*, and Plate XVIII for a line drawing of the Siyamangalam *toraṇa.*

[15] Srinivasan, *Cave Temples of the Pallavas,* Plate XLIX.

[16] The one above the central niche on the eastern wall of the Northern Piḍari Ratha at Mamallapuram (c. late seventh to early eighth century), though incomplete, is clearly visible. So also is the one on the southern wall of the Valaiyānkuṭṭai Ratha at Mamallapuram. Two other instances may be cited: Śankaranayinār kovil, Malaiyadikkurici, Tirunelveli District; and Tirukkolakkudi, Tirupaṭṭur Taluk, Ramnad District.

[17] For instance, those gracing the niches with *Sandhyā-tāṇḍava-mūrti* and *Ūrdhva-tāṇḍava-mūrti* on this temple, as also those on the walls of the Iravātaneśvara temple at Kanchipuram.

[18] Those on the walls of the Kailāsanātha temple, Tirupattur, c. latter half of the eighth century; Sundaravarada-perumāl temple, Uttaramerur, c. 805 CE; Tiruvīrattaneśvara temple, Tiruvadigai, c. 854-880 CE; and Vīrattaneśvara temple, Tiruttani, c. last quarter of ninth century, to mention a few.

[19] The *gūdhamaṇḍapa* walls of this temple bear variants of the *patra-*, *citra-* and *makara-toraṇas* crowning niches that flank the balcony or window at the central offsets on the northern and southern sides.

[20] At Ellora, the *toraṇa* is flung between the pillars of the vestibule, with the matrix of the stone removed from underneath the arch. This accords greater possibility for the play of light on them. The early medieval Karnataka *toraṇas*, on the other hand, are usually carved in relief on the profiles of lintels, where the impact of light is much reduced.

[21] The Munīśvara temple is datable to the early 11th century and belongs to the post-Rāṣṭrakūṭa/ Later Cālukya phase. Yet another example of an *antarāla-toraṇa* may be spotted between two ornamented pillars inside the mid-10th century Kalleśvara temple at Bagli. This *toraṇa* showcases meditating male figures within the side loops and images of Naṭeśa and Gajāntaka in the central loops.

[22] For example, those canopying images of Pārśvanātha and Bāhubalī on the central offsets of the *gūḍhamaṇḍapa* of the Melguḍi Jain temple at Hallur. Only the outlines are visible; work on them appears to have been abandoned midway. The central offsets of the *vimāna* of Temple 52 from the Gaḷaganātha group of temples at Aihole, as also the corner offsets of the *gūḍhamaṇḍapa* of the Siddheśvara temple at Mudhol, are adorned with *toraṇas*.

[23] Spaces earmarked for *toraṇas* on the walls of Kāñcanaguḍi at this site have not been carved; one notices instead *toraṇa* bosses that were meant to be completed.

[24] A rare Cālukyan instance (c. 11th century, granite) comes fairly close in its basic form to the Pāpavināśeśvara *toraṇa*. It is now housed in the Bijapur Museum, and is likely to have belonged to the vestibule of a temple in the region.

[25] Some other examples of *toraṇas* from the region may also be documented. *Makara-toraṇa* lintels can be seen resting above the façade pilasters of some temples from the Someśvara group at Somasil (to the north-east of Papanasam in western Andhra Pradesh, on the banks of river Krishna), datable to the late 10th-early 11th century. Inverted U-shaped *makara-, mayūra-,* and *patra-toraṇas* adorn the narrow niches on the walls of the 10th century subsidiary Gaṇeśa shrine at Ullala, south of Mangalore.

[26] *EITA* Vol. I, Part 2, p.224.

[27] *EITA* Vol. I, Part 3, pp.281-284.

[28] Another *toraṇa* fragment from Tansua in Karnataka, showing two serpentine *illikā* loops and a *kīrttimukha,* is now housed in the Kannada Research Institute, Dharwad.

[29] *EITA,* Vol. I, Part 3, pp.187-189. An undated inscription on the soffit of the vestibule's *toraṇa* has been dated between late 11th and early 13th century on the basis of palaeography. Stylistically the *toraṇa* as well as the pillars appear to be of the late 11th century.

[30] For an early illustration of this *toraṇa, see* Cousens, *The Calukyan Architecture of the Kanarese Districts,* Plate CXXVI. The central portion is already broken in this illustration.

[31] NM 59.159/3, Granite, Hampi, Bellary District.

[32] Other examples from the region include the *antarāla-toraṇa* at the Kṛṣṇa temple, Huvinahadagalli (c. end 11th to early 12th century), which, like several other Cālukyan instances, has Tripuruṣa figures within an *illikā* arch. The Gaḷageśvara temple *raṅgamaṇḍapa* at Galaganatha (c. 1040-1050 CE) houses a fragment of a Vaiṣṇava *illikā-toraṇa* with a seated image of Viṣṇu flanked by Devīs, each beneath trefoil *illikā* canopies. The vestibule of Temple 1 at Balambidu (c. 1050-1070 CE) displays an *illikā-toraṇa* above the entrance, with the oft-repeated Tripuruṣa representations. For visuals of some Later Cālukyan *toraṇas* not illustrated here, see *EITA* Vol. I Part 3, Plates 170 (Narasiṁha temple, Kuralgeri), 437 (Candramaulīśvara temple, Unkal), 616 (Kṛṣṇa temple, Huvinahadagalli), 668 (Gaḷageśvara temple, Galaganatha), and 673 (Temple 1, Balambidu).

[33] The niche pedestal, however, clearly shows the seven horses of the Sun god, revealing the identity of the deity that was originally housed within it.

[34] Several sculptors and architects are known to have travelled from the Cālukyan territory to the Hoysaḷanāḍu, particularly in the first quarter of the 12th century. See, Settar, *The Hoysaḷa Temples,* Vol. I, pp.97-122.

[35] Also Settar, *The Hoysaḷa Temples,* Vol. I, pp.97-122 and Vol. II Plates 85 a and 86 a.

[36] Dhaky mentions Demoje as the author of the eastern one. See *EITA* Vol. I, Part 3, pp.393-395.

[37] For more Hoysaḷa *toraṇas*, see Settar, *Hoysaḷa Sculptures in the National Museum, Copenhagen,* Plates XVIII D.a.7, XIX D.a.808, VII D.a.789, and pp.71-72. Also Settar, *The Hoysaḷa Temples*, Vol. II, Plates 7, 46a, 83, 84, 85 a, b, 86 a, b, and 112. Some others that may be mentioned in passing include the *dvāra-toraṇas* in the two porches leading to the elongated hall of the Pañcaliṅgeśvara temple at Govindanahalli (c. 13th century).

[38] Similar instances may be seen on the walls of Lakṣmeśvara at Kundagol, as well as at the Purdheśvara temple, Saundatti (c. late 11th century).

[39] NM 4154, .970 x 3.620 m, Warangal, c. 12th century, Granite.

[40] A picture of this *toraṇa* amongst the ruins at the Svayambhūliṅgeśvara temple site is also available. See *ARADH* 1934-35, Plate VI a.

[41] Plain *antarāla-toraṇas* of scant aesthetic appeal are found above the vestibule doorways of the three shrines of the Trikūṭa Śiva temple, Kothapalli (c. late 12th century). Beneath the arch is a female dancer accompanied by female musicians, plausibly a representation of temple dancers and musicians. At each end, a *Bhūmija* shrine is placed in front of the *makaras* in profile.

[42] For example, those on the Vedapurīśvara *vimāna* at Tiruvedikudi (c. 890 CE), Kailāsanātha at Alambakkam (c. 910 CE) and Brahmapurīśvara temple at Pullamangai (c. 910 CE), in the early Coḷa style.

[43] The one on the northern wall of the *ardhamaṇḍapa* has a seated Lakṣmī. Geese in varied attitudes are placed within the lower festoons.

[44] The *citra-toraṇas* at Cadaiyār kovil (c. 920 CE), Tiruccenampundi, are in low relief; some are effaced and incomplete. The northern and southern *ardhamaṇḍapa* walls of the Umā-Maheśvara temple (period: Gandaradittam, c. 974 CE) at

Konerirajapuram display better preserved *citra-toraṇas* above each of the three sculptures within niches. Of the same category but hardly discernible through the lime plaster, are the niche *toraṇas* from the Acaleśvara temple at Tiruvarur (c. 991 CE).

[45] The *ardhamaṇḍapa* walls of the Tirukkodikaval temple (c. 980 CE) in Tirukoteshvara also have *citra-toraṇas* above the three niches on the northern and southern faces.

[46] Some other medieval instances include those on the Kāyārohaṇa temple (c. 1010 CE) at Nagapattinam in Thanjavur District, Rāmanāthan kovil in Pattishvaram (c. 1025 CE), the apsidal Vyāghrapurīśvara in Tirupullivanam (c. latter half of 11th century), as also amongst others, the Kampahareśvara temple at Tribhuvanam (c. 1178-1216 CE). From the end of the 10th century, one observes schematic rendition lacking the vitality and spontaneity of the earlier period.

[47] Lotus Mahal from South, Image by Alexander Greenlaw, modern positive (2007) from waxed-paper negative (1856), from the Alkazi Collection of Photography. See also Michell, ed. *Vijayanagara: Splendour in Ruins...* (Royal Centre 107).

[48] Cousens, *Bijapur and its Architectural Remains,* Plate XCI and Fig. 23 on p.102. See also Plate XLIV for the ornament under the eave on the façade of Ibrahim Rauza.

[49] Carol Radcliffe Bolon has described this *toraṇa*. See *EITA* Vol. I, Part 2, pp.65-66.

[50] *EITA* Vol. I, Part 3, pp.56-58 & 202-203.

[51] Another of about the same period from Mudhol may be mentioned here; square pillar shafts with inverted shoulder moulding *(laśuna)*, and with brackets carved with Gaṇeśa on one and an effaced image on another, are topped by an eave decorated with Gajalakṣmī in the centre, miniature dormers and elephants. Another instance is from Kulpak in the Nalagonda District of Andhra Pradesh (c. 11th century). Square pillars support a lintel adorned with a schematized *illikā* garland interspersed with *grāsamukhas*. Seven bud-knobs are placed along the lintel's soffit.

[52] See *ARADH* 1925-26, Plate XVI, and "Excavations," *ARADH* 1934–35, pp.6-10, Plate V a.

[53] Wagoner and Rice, "From Delhi to Deccan: Newly Discovered Tugluq Monuments..," pp.77-116.

[54] Another instance belonging to the Vijayanagara period is seen in association with the Sampige Siddheśvara temple (c. 15th-16th century) at Chitradurga in Karnataka.

CHAPTER 4

Northern Representations

Gujarat, Rajasthan, Madhya Pradesh, Chattisgarh, Uttar Pradesh, Orissa, Bihar, and Bengal

4.34

Western and Central India

In the western and central Indian tract,[1] beginning from the sixth century, *toraṇas* appeared on temple walls and in the temple interiors. Free-standing *toraṇas* from this region are known from an earlier period, as at Bharhut and Sanchi, and continued to be in evidence until the fifth-sixth centuries, as at Pawaya and Nagari (see Chapter 1).

The architectural language of the contiguous regions of Gujarat and Rajasthan, and also of central India, reveals several commonalities in the formal articulation of elements, the dynamics of their inter-relationships, and the proportionate arrangement of their parts. Despite the various styles and sub-styles that flourished in this vast geographical expanse, their shared denominators justify as well as necessitate a closely correlated and integrated discussion here.

Some basic features pertaining to the architectural setting, form, and treatment set apart the central and western Indian *toraṇas* from their southern Indian counterparts. The occurrence of free-standing instances is more frequent in western and central India as compared to southern India, where a few relatively austere examples, particularly from Andhra Pradesh and Karnataka, have been noted earlier. Again, as distinct from the southern tract, the presence of *toraṇas* on temple walls is comparatively limited and largely restricted to the earlier phase here. This is because the exterior wall definitions of the medieval temples in these regions considerably differ from those of the southern ones, where the walls are given a vertical accent by intervening pilasters. As the preferred ornament crowning the niches on the exterior walls of the western and central Indian temples is the triangular pediment *(udgama)*, the occasion for the presence of a *toraṇa* seldom arises except when it is placed underneath the *udgama*-pediment.

The western and central Indian *toraṇas* unfurling between the pillars in the temple interiors (as also in the free-standing examples) are 'free-flying,' that is, the arch is freed from the surrounding matrix of the stone upon which it was carved. This singular feature alters the appearance of the arches, with their graceful contours and delicately rendered masses shown to advantage in the elusive play of light and shade. The viewer thus experiences them in varied dispositions, now casting shadows in response to the rays of the sun, at other times, often in the interior of the temple's halls, subtly unfolding in a symphony of curves. This is at variance with their southern counterparts, which are usually carved in relief on the exterior walls or on the door and vestibule lintels. Even when portions of the surrounding matrix of stone are scooped out, the southern Indian *toraṇa* is almost always integrated with the lintel upon which it rests. In the western and central Indian region, the sinusoidal *āndola-toraṇa* was as popular as the serpentine *illikā* variety. The latter was the decided preference of the Karnataka and Andhra sculptors, who experimented with its basic form to create ingenious innovations.

Several subtler differences as well as correspondences may also be observed, but these would gradually reveal themselves during the course of the discussion. The central and western Indian architectural texts, though explicit about the basic visual formulations, are less articulate than their Dravidian counterparts in the matter of classifications based on sculptural embellishments and architectural settings. At times, therefore, the Dravidian texts offer a viable alternative in arriving at taxonomies for western and central Indian *toraṇas*. A combined pool of terminology drawn from both textual traditions will be employed, while opting in favour of western and central Indian terms wherever available. A parallel approach was adopted in the case of the southern *toraṇas* also.

Early Representations c. sixth to ninth centuries

A few of the sixth-seventh century temples from this region have *toraṇas* carved in relief that frame niches on the central salient of their exterior walls. The form is very simple at this stage: two pilasters support the *makaras* that release S-shaped arcs, which meet in a pendant motif at the centre. Parallel instances are known from southern India also. A simpler variation, with a single continuous arc between two pilasters, as seen on the sanctum doorframe of the Kālikāmātā temple in Chittorgarh (c. second half of seventh century), occurs less frequently.

The Devarānī (Śiva) temple at Tala near Bilaspur in central India (c. third quarter of sixth century) has plain *toraṇas* of twin arcs, placed above shallow and empty wall niches on its median offsets (Fig. 4.1). Excavations at Sirpur in Chattisgarh have yielded a late sixth century fragment of a lintel with a *makara* seated on the capital of a pilaster at one end; this is followed by flying celestials and a seated divinity (Fig. 4.2). It bears close affinities with the Vākāṭaka style and may have been part of a *toraṇa* on the door-lintel.[2]

Better integrated with the temple and also of finer proportions than those at Tala, were the *toraṇas* that (until the Gujarat earthquake in the year 2001) had graced the median wall niches of Sonkansārī Temple no. 1 (Fig. 4.3; c. third quarter of seventh century) at Ghumli in the Saurashtra sector of Gujarat. The earliest surviving temples in Gujarat are from Saurashtra and these are austere in adornment. This explains the absence of a non-utilitarian feature such as the *toraṇa* on them. This particular temple, however, had been modestly but suitably embellished. As may be observed from

4.1

4.2

4.3

4.1 : *Kuḍya-toraṇa*, Tala, Devarānī temple, c. third quarter of sixth century

4.2 : *Dvāra-toraṇa* (?) fragment, Sirpur, c. late sixth century

4.3 : *Kuḍya-toraṇa*, Ghumli, Sonkansārī Temple no. 1, c. third quarter of seventh century

4.4

earlier photographs, the northern niche had a simple yet elegant *toraṇa*, with pilasters supporting *makaras* that released two S-shaped arcs to meet in a pendant *fleur-de-lis (gagāraka)* motif at the centre. It is a miniature representation of a free-standing *toraṇa,* contemporaneous instances of which are unavailable from this region. That on the western wall of the same temple had a similar contour and was raised on square pilasters of modest embellishment.

Of the seventh century instances from Rajasthan, the one that canopies a dancing Gaṇeśa at Rampol in the Chittor District is amongst the finest specimens of this period (D.11; c. late seventh century).[3] Made of twin arcs that meet at the centre in a foliate motif, its chiselled lines and graceful proportions are a fine example of the predilection towards adornment that Rajasthan is justly famous for. The shafts of old pillars (c. 650-700 CE) re-used in the *gūḍhamaṇḍapa* of the Kumbhaśyāma temple at Chittorgarh bear exquisite *muktā-toraṇas* (arches carved with pearl patterns). On some pillars, these *toraṇas* canopy images of guardians and celestial maidens; on others, they are placed above the vine-and-foliage pattern. Also at Chittorgarh, a *muktā-toraṇa* crowns a guardian figure on a doorjamb datable to early eighth century but built into the early 10th century Temple no. 2, north of Samidheśvara.[4] The Kālikāmātā (Sūrya) temple at the same site (c. second half of seventh century) has Sūrya within a *parikara-toraṇa* at the centre of the sanctum's door-lintel *(lalāṭa-bimba)*. Miniature arches framing dancing images are also placed on either side of this door-lintel. Fragments in the Chittorgarh State Museum bear *toraṇas*; one frames a standing image of Sūrya.[5] More examples of this period have been found from the Śiva temple at Kusuma in the Sirohi District of Rajasthan (Fig. 4.4; c. 636 CE).

D.11

Some niche fragments from the ruined Harṣatamātā temple complex at Abaneri (south of Alvar) in Rajasthan have deities bracketed between tiny pilasters. Celestials seated atop these pilasters hold the ends of the garland that forms the central band of these unusual *vidyādhara-* or *mālādhara-toraṇas* (Fig. 4.5; c. 800-825 CE). Other courses on the arch include lotus leaves and half-diamonds *(ardha-ratnas)*. Eccentric but exquisite, such *toraṇas* are rare; this combination of ornament is in fact more akin to that seen on the halos *(prabhā-maṇḍalas)* of deities in central India from the fifth century onwards. Those located in the well at Abaneri (Fig. 4.6; c. 800-825 CE) are important because they are placed above miniature models of temple superstructures, a position often accorded

D.11 : *Parikara-toraṇa*, Rampol, Chittorgarh, c. seventh century.

4.4 : *Parikara-toraṇa*, Kusuma, near Śiva temple site, c. 636 CE.

4.5 : *Vidyādhara-toraṇa (ratna-puṣpa)*, Abaneri, Harṣatamātā temple complex, c. 800-825 CE.

4.6 : *Toraṇa* above miniature *śikhara*, Abaneri, *kuṇḍa*, c. 800-825 CE.

4.7 : *Muktā-toraṇa (parikara)*, Karvana, c. early ninth century.

4.8 : *Patra-toraṇa (parikara)*, Deogarh, western shrine of Temple 15, c. third quarter of eighth century.

4.5

to the *toraṇas* in Karnataka, but seldom in western India. On the sumptuously carved doorjambs from Karvana, south of Vadodara in Gujarat, the twin arcs of the *muktā-toraṇas* meet in a clasped *fleur-de-lis (gagāraka)* motif and crown guardian figures and deities (Fig. 4.7; c. early ninth century).

A *patra-toraṇa* of single arc is found in the sanctum of the western shrine of Temple 15 at Deogarh in Uttar Pradesh (Fig. 4.8; c. third quarter of eighth century). Flying celestials and garland-bearers are depicted underneath the arch. The instances cited are seen on pillars, doorframes, and niches, and also canopy the main image in the sanctum (as at Deogarh). No free-standing instances of the seventh and eighth centuries are known from here.

C. 10th Century

The 10th century witnessed an onrush of *toraṇa* forms embellished with a variety of motifs. To facilitate a better understanding of their form and context, the available examples need to be streamlined chronologically and typologically. The *toraṇas* are first met at the entrances to the temple halls and a little later, between the

4.6

4.8

4.7

4.9 : *Kuḍya-toraṇa*, Kaleshvari-ni-nal, Kaḷeśvarī temple, c. mid-10th century.

4.10 : *Kuḍya-toraṇa*, Kaleshvari-ni-nal, Kaḷeśvarī temple, c. mid-10th century.

4.11 : *Kuḍya-toraṇa*, Nagda, Sās temple, c. last quarter of 10th century.

4.12 : *Kuḍya-toraṇa*, Vadhavan, Rāṇakdevī temple, c. 915 CE.

4.13 : *Parikara-toraṇa*, Nagda, Sās temple, c. last quarter of 10th century.

4.14 : *Dvāra-toraṇa*, Kakoni, main temple, c. early 10th century.

4.12

4.9

4.10

pillars in the hall interiors. Occasionally, they are also noticed on the temple walls.

The niches on the outer walls of the 10th century temples from this region are usually framed by pilasters topped by an eave *(daṇḍacchādya)* and a pediment *(udgama)*. There are few exceptions, however. On the outer sanctum walls of the Kaḷeśvarī temple at Kaleshvari-ni-nal (north-east of Ahmedabad), *toraṇas* have replaced the customary *udgama*-pediments at the niches on the intermediate offsets (Fig. 4.9; c. mid-10th century). The two segments of the arch rise steeply and meet in a *fleur-de-lis (gagāraka)* motif topped by a prominent *kīrttimukha*. The *toraṇas* also crown divinities that originally belonged to the median offsets of the same temple, as for example, the one noticed above Caṇḍikā (Fig. 4.10). At the Sās temple, Nagda (Fig. 4.11; c. last quarter of 10th century), a delicate *toraṇa* is carved underneath the eave and pediment. On the wall niches of the Rāṇakdevī temple at Vadhvan, *toraṇas* are placed under miniature shrine superstructures (Fig. 4.12; c. 915 CE). During this period, a *parikara-toraṇa* was also standardized (Fig. 4.13). It has a flaming scroll-like ornament at the top, at times a row of celestials *(vidyādharas)* beneath it, and a garland on the lower margins, released by *makaras* attached to minor niches *(tilakas)* above the pilasters.

The *toraṇas* carved on lintels, prolific in Karnataka and Andhra, are rare in this region. After a few initial attempts at Kakoni, Ghanerav, and Shamalaji, this was given up.[6] The earliest of its kind is found at the entrance to the hall of the main temple at Kakoni in the Kota District of Rajasthan (Fig. 4.14; c. early tenth century). It resembles the early examples with twin arcs, as seen at Ghumli (Fig. 4.3). At Kakoni, the arch on the lintel is adorned with an undulating creeper, classified as the *dvāra*- and *patra-toraṇa* by the treatises. A *kīrttimukha* at the vertex releases a bell and chain ornament *(grāsakinkiṇikā)* flanked by curled scrolls. Beneath each arc, an elephant is carved.

4.14

4.13

4.11

4.15 : *Citra-toraṇa (dvāra)*, Khajuraho, Lakṣmaṇa temple, 954 CE.

4.16 : *Dvāra-toraṇa*, Ghanerav, Mahāvīra temple, c. 950 CE.

4.17 : *Kuḍya-toraṇa*, Ghanerav, Mahāvīra temple, c. 950 CE.

4.18 : *Citra-toraṇa*, Nagda, Sās temple, *gūḍhamaṇḍapa*, southern side, c. last quarter of 10th century.

4.19 (overleaf) : *Patra-toraṇa* (composite), Āṭha Khambhā, c. 982 CE.

At Khajuraho, a *toraṇa* of twin arcs spans the distance between the dwarf pillars in the front porch *(mukhamaṇḍapa)* of the Lakṣmaṇa temple (Fig. 4.15; 954 CE). This delicately rendered arch is free of the supporting stone matrix. A bevy of celestials *(vidyādharas)* fill the upper margins and a row of *fleurs-de-lis (gagārakas)* laces the lower hem. Two goblins *(pramathas)* engage a *makara* in combat on the viewer's right; on the left, only the upper one partially survives. A *kīrttimukha* at the apex and a prominent pendant *gagāraka* completes the arch. Though retaining the shape of the Tala and Ghumli instances, the manner of rendition registers a greater degree of sophistication in this case and fits the description given in the *SS* (App. 3, no. 3).[7] It heralds two developments that become the norm in medieval western and central Indian *toraṇas:* one, the 'free-flying' status of the arch and another, the presence of creatures such as celestials and goblins along its curvature.

A further elaboration can be seen at the Mahāvīra temple near Ghanerav in the Mewar region of Rajasthan. The *toraṇa* at the sanctum door-lintel is composed of four segments (Fig. 4.16; c. 950 CE), as in the ninth century instances from Ellora (Figs. 3.39, 3.42). The S-shaped curves at the sides evolve into two

4.16

4.15

4.17

central *illikā* loops, with pendant *fleurs-de-lis (gagārakas)* at the intersection of successive segments. Auspicious conches are placed at the top corners. The *toraṇa* is ornamented with a band of flowers and jewels and circumscribes Śaṅkhapāla flanked by garland bearers. Similar examples shelter musicians under the arch; they are carved like a tracery on the balconied windows of the main temple (Fig. 4.17). This appealing variance in the placement of *toraṇas*, a result of the peculiar arrangement of the mouldings and architectural members on the walls of this temple, is not repeated elsewhere.

The four-lobed *toraṇa* seen at Ghanerav is found a little later in the interior of the Sās temple at Nagda in Rajasthan (Fig. 4.18; c. last quarter of 10th century) and the Āṭha Khambā at Gyaraspur in the Vidisha District of Madhya Pradesh (Fig. 4.19; c. 982 CE). Both reveal greater sophistication and are quite independent of the supporting matrix of the parent stone. The one carved in the vestibule of the Āṭha Khambhā is made up of lush scrolls and a deeply undercut chain of diamonds and rosettes. The *kīrttimukhas* placed at the interstices of successive lobes of the *toraṇa* seem to merge with the ample foliage. Its most distinguishing feature is the transposition of Nandī's head at each intersection of the segments of the arch. Symbolic of the Śaiva dedication of the temple, the Nandī heads are masterful abstractions that skilfully merge animal and vegetal forms.

4.18

4.19

4.20

4.21

An exquisite *toraṇa* fragment was found at the Garḥ *Gaccha* at Atru in the Kota District of Rajasthan (Fig. 4.20; c. late 10th century). It is laced on one margin with a diamond and rosette pattern between pearl strings, as noticed earlier at the Āṭha Khambhā. The rest of the arch is deeply undercut, filled with a meandering leafy scroll. In a corner above the arch, partly damaged *vidyādharas* and the seated figure of a woman are visible. One of the *toraṇa* fragments that belonged to the ruined Harṣanātha temple at Harshagiri in the Shekhavati region of northern Rajasthan is an arc carved with *vidyādharas*; another shows a *makara* with a weapon-bearing figure emerging from its mouth (Fig. 4.21; 973 CE). A dated inscription from here eulogises a beautiful *toraṇa* which harboured all the divinities and appeared like a portion of heaven sculpted by the creator himself (App. 1, no. 11b).

4.22

The front hall *(mukhamaṇḍapa)* of the Ghaṭeśvara temple at Badoli, 30 miles south of Kota in Rajasthan, is graced with a simple but unique *toraṇa* (Figs. 4.22, 4.22a; c. mid 10th century). The arch traverses the distance between the *makaras* above the pilaster capitals and a *kīrttimukha* at the apex. The upper band of the arch is sculpted with *vidyādhara* couples in varied stances. Two celestial flautists *(gandharvas)* flank the *kīrttimukha*; beneath this is a band of leafy scroll bordered by buds and diamonds. The drooping ornament at the centre, released by the *kīrttimukha*, is damaged on this *citra-toraṇa*.

The Sās temple at Nagda in the Udaipur District (c. last quarter of 10th century) and the Viṣṇu

4.22a

4.20 : *Patra-toraṇa* (composite, fragment), Atru, Gaṛh *Gaccha*, c. late 10th century.

4.21 : *Toraṇa* fragment, Harshagiri, Harṣanātha temple, 973 CE.

4.22 and 4.22a : *Citra-toraṇa (dvāra)*, Badoli, Ghaṭeśvara temple, *mukhamaṇḍapa*, c. mid-10th century.

4.23 : *Āndola-citra-toraṇa* (eastern & western), Nagda, Sās temple, *gūḍhamaṇḍapa*, c. last quarter of 10th century.

temple at Kiradu in the Barmer District of Rajasthan (c. 975-985 CE) introduce a novel spatial arrangement of *toraṇas* in the temple halls. This feature becomes the hallmark of Maru-Gurjara dance halls *(raṅgamaṇḍapas)*, beginning from the 11th century. At Nagda, the four *toraṇas* hung between the composite *(miśraka)* pillars forming the square nave of the closed hall *(gūḍhamaṇḍapa)* have transformed the interior of the Sās temple (Figs. 4.18, 4.23, and 4.24). In the eastern and western ones, *makaras* attached to the miniature shrine-like niches *(tilakas)* release S-shaped segments *(madalas)* of the *toraṇa* (Fig. 4.23). Each segment appears to pass through the succeeding niche and re-emerge from the jaws of another *makara* attached to it. The waves of these *āndola-toraṇas* rise to a crescendo to meet in the shrine-like niche *(tilaka)* at the apex. These sinusoidal arches are ornamented with two rows of tightly juxtaposed *vidyādharas*. The niches harbour seated divinities and are adorned with a knob-like bud *(mukula)* at the bottom.

4.23

The undulating *āndola* arch on the northern side emanates from the jaws of the *makaras* to meet the *tilaka* at the apex without passing through any niches (Fig. 4.24). An ornamental band borders the central array of *vidyādharas* and *kirttimukhas* that form the main body of the

4.24 : *Āndola-citra-toraṇa*, Nagda, Sās temple, *gūḍhamaṇḍapa* (north side), c. last quarter of 10th century.

4.25 and 4.25a : *Āndola-citra-toraṇas*, Kiradu, Viṣṇu temple, *raṅgmaṇḍapa*, c. 975-985 CE.

4.24

arch. Yet another row of *vidyādharas* forms the upper margins; the space immediately below the arch is occupied by adoring celestials and those that play music. Groups of three celestials are also carved at the top corners of the arch.

The contour of the southern *toraṇa* (Fig. 4.18) resembles those noticed at the Mahāvīra temple, Ghanerav (Figs. 4.16, 4.17). The S-shaped sections of the arch further evolve into two central *illikā* loops. The *kīrttimukhas* at the junction of the successive loops merge with the *vidyādharas* along the curvature of the arch. Celestials occupy the space below the arch in a manner that foreshadows their portrayal in the 11th century Kandariyā Mahādeo temple at Khajuraho (Fig. 4.29). Of refined proportions, delicate grace, and sumptuous embellishment, these *toraṇas* register marked advancement in conception as well as articulation.

The dance halls *(raṅgamaṇḍapas)* of the Caulukyan (Solankī) temples are characterized by an octagonal arrangement of pillars in the middle. These composite pillars support profusely carved ceilings and *toraṇas*, of which the Viṣṇu temple at Kiradu in the Barmer District of Rajasthan (c. 975-985 CE) provides an early example. It registers advances when compared to the *gūḍhamaṇḍapa* of the Sās temple at Nagda. At Kiradu, the presence of attic pillars above the main pillars lend height to the octagonal space defined in the *raṅgamaṇḍapa*. The eight *toraṇas*, of which only two are intact, occupied the intermediary spaces between the attic pillars (Fig. 4.25). The temple is much damaged; the ceiling, superstructure, and the outer walls of the *raṅgamaṇḍapa*, as also the peripheral pillars of its interior are lost. Due to this, the central *raṅgamaṇḍapa* pillars and two surviving *toraṇas* are now completely exposed. Together with the ones at Nagda, they are the earliest available mature representations of the *āndola-toraṇa*. The *makaras* at the base of the attic pillars release a figure along with the sinusoidal arch (Fig. 4.25a). Each S-shaped segment *(madala)* of the

4.25

arch passes through an incipient niche *(tilaka)* and each niche along the course of the arch shelters a dancing figure. The undersides of the niches reveal mortises to append the knob-like buds that can also be seen at Nagda and in the 11th century examples. Small *makara* heads are carved to the right and left of each niche. The *kīrttimukhas,* placed on the outer margins at the union of the *toraṇa* segments, are damaged. The *vidyādharas* in varied poses, some with swords in their hands, define the central band of the arch. The underside is covered by a stencilled undulating creeper, bordered with lotus leaves. On the outer margins, a twisted pearl-cable is lined by the flame-like foliage typical of western India. Except for the missing knob-like buds, no part of the niche was designed to project out of the arch. Though their octagonal arrangement within the hall is pleasing, these *āndola-toraṇas* are not as well proportioned as the ones at Nagda.[8]

4.25a

4.26 : *Illikā-toraṇamālā,* Gurgi, now in front of Rewa Mahārāja's palace, c. 10th century.

4.27 : *Toraṇa* fragment, Gurgi, now in Rewa *(koṭwālī)*, c. 10th century.

4.28 : *Toraṇa* fragment, Gurgi, now in Rewa *(koṭwālī)*, c. 10th century.

4.29 : *Illikā-toraṇa,* Khajuraho, Kandariyā Mahādeo, *mukhacatuṣkī,* c. late 11th century.

The lintel of the Gurgi *toraṇa*, relocated in front of the Mahārājā's palace in Rewa in Madhya Pradesh (Fig. 4.26; c. 10th century), attests to the presence of the Karnataka type of *illikā-toraṇa* in central India. Built during the period of the Kālacuris of Tripuri, who had alliances with the Rāṣṭrakūṭas, it shows an interesting blend of influences.[9] It is closely affiliated to those noted at Kukkanur and Sirval (Figs. 3.49-3.52), yet betrays allegiance to the local style. The *illikā* arch is carved on the lintel and has four loops terminating in pendant buds at the interstices, quite like the late Rāṣṭrakūṭa *toraṇas* in Karnataka. The female figures with attendants positioned at the two ends of the arched segment are reminiscent of the Deccan mode in terms of placement, though not stylistically. The lower margin below the gorgon and pearl *(muktāgrāsa)* band has a delicately carved row of buds, again conceptually but not stylistically similar to those in south-western India. Yet, several other features distance this *toraṇa* from its southern counterparts. *Fleurs-de-lis (gagārakas)* lace the lower margins of the arcs and an intricate leafy scroll dresses the arch in ornate finery. The arch does not emerge from the jaws of the *makaras;* instead, *vyālas* race outwards from their jaws and the arch springs from above the heads of *makaras*. Fragments of another *illikā-toraṇa* from the same site are also now in Rewa (Kotwālī);

these appear to be of a date slightly later than the one in front of the Rewa Palace. There is greater figural ornament on these fragments; one of them shows pot-bellied creatures within a band of lush scrolls, with part of a *kīrttimukha* and seated figures at the top (Fig. 4.27); another shows the bust of a woman. Yet another fragment reveals a pendant ornament very similar to the one on the Kandariyā Mahādeo *toraṇa* (Figs. 4.28, 4.29).[10]

4.29

C. 11th-12th Centuries

The grandest in western and central Indian temple architecture belongs to the 11th and 12th centuries, when the Caulukyas dominated the politics of western India. Their power catalyzed the infiltration of cross-cultural influences from the neighbouring regions of Rajasthan and Malava into Gujarat. As a result, the region experienced an intense intermix of ideas and practices. While the late 10th century saw the early phase of this process of assimilation, the 11th and 12th centuries witnessed its zenith. Temples received patronage from the rulers, nobility, ministers, merchants, and the collective faith of the people. The sheer magnificence of the Sun temple at Modhera, the delicate beauty and filigree-like craftsmanship of the medieval Jain temples at Delwara and Kumbhariya, the commanding presence of the Rudramahalaya at Siddhapur, and the majesty of temples such as the Viśvanātha and Kandariyā Mahādeo at Khajuraho are all products of this glorious age. The *toraṇas* from this period lend

4.28

4.30 : *Illikā-toraṇa,* Khajuraho, Javārī temple, *mukhacatuṣkī,* c. late 11th century.

4.31 : *Illikā-toraṇa,* Panna, Siddhanātha temple, c. 12th-13th century.

4.30

infinite grace and elegance to temples. Following the 10th century instance from Gurgi, the *illikā-toraṇa* registers its presence more definitely from the 11th century and receives favour particularly in Gujarat, even as the *āndola-toraṇa* continues to prevail. The best examples of the free-standing *toraṇas* also belong to this period.

***Illikā-toraṇas*:** The Karnataka and Andhra sculptors excelled in transforming the simple *illikā-toraṇa* into intricate, varied, delicate, and graceful forms. These pervaded their temple walls, entrances, interiors, and even pillars, doorframes, bases, as well as superstructures. Their central and western Indian counterparts retained the simplicity of its basic form, used it with restraint, carved the arch with crisply rendered details, and released it from the bondage of the stone matrix to accord it a 'free-flying' status.

The *illikā-toraṇas* placed at the entrance porch *(mukhacatuṣkī)* and adjoining hall[11] of the Kandariyā Mahādeo (Fig. 4.29) and the entrance porch of the Javārī temple at Khajuraho (Fig. 4.30; c. late 11th century) are liberated from the bondage of being carved in relief. The links with the 10th century Gurgi *toraṇa* and also the *toraṇa* fragments from the same site are obvious. That at the entrance porch of the Kandariyā Mahādeo is a fine blend of assured form and graceful adornment. Elongated pendants made up of neat rows of petals are placed at the intersection of successive arcs to affirm the contours of its well-defined form. As at Gurgi, the arch does not spring from the jaws of the *makaras* but begins from above their heads. As per convention, the *kīrttimukhas* are placed at the interstices of successive loops and are aligned with *vidyādharas* on the top margin. A thin defining band separates the array of *vidyādharas* from the finely chiselled and deeply undercut leafy scroll base. A kneeling celestial *(gandharva)* with a delightful twist of the body is visible on the proboscis of the *makara* to the viewer's left. The artist had most likely carved flying celestial couples with garlands *(mālādharas)* under each loop but the right half of the arch has lost this embellishment. Niches at the ends harbour images of Hara-Gaurī. This *toraṇa* is the best-preserved representative of the central Indian *illikā* variant. A similar one, but more damaged than the Kandariyā instance, is encountered in the front porch of the Javārī temple (Fig. 4.30). Khajuraho had more *toraṇas* that are now in an

4.31

extremely fragmentary state.[12] The newly discovered Siddhanātha temple at Panna in Madhya Pradesh, stylistically of the 12th or 13th century, is also adorned with a similar *illikā-toraṇa* at its entrance porch (Fig. 4.31).

In western India, a significant part of medieval architectural heritage has been destroyed either by natural disasters or by other events during the course of history. Ruins from sites like Sikar (Harshagiri) and Kiradu amongst others provide incontrovertible evidence of a vibrant phase of medieval temple architecture. The available 10th century examples reveal that, unlike the *āndola* variety, the *illikā-toraṇa* was only incipient at this stage. It is noticed at the Mahāvīra temple, Ghanerav, as also in the *gūḍhamaṇḍapa* (southern *toraṇa*) of the Sās temple at Nagda (Figs. 4.16-4.18). The only clear instance of an *illikā* arch of the 10th century from northern India is the one at Gurgi. What the shape of the fragmented *toraṇa* from Harshagiri was like or for that matter the one that existed in the pilgrim's hall *(āsthāna maṇḍapa)* of the Ambikā temple at Jagat, to quote two examples, are questions that remain unanswered.

The *raṅgamaṇḍapa* of the much damaged Someśvara temple at Kiradu (c. 1020 CE) was once adorned with eight *toraṇas* placed between the pillars of the central octagon, as can be made out from the barely surviving portions of the arch released by *makaras*. Not even one exists *in situ*

4.32 : *Illikā-toraṇa* (reassembled fragments), Kiradu, now in VAM, London, c. early 11th century.

4.33 : *Āndola-citra-toraṇa* (fragment) Kiradu, c. late 10th century.

4.34 : *Illikā-toraṇa*, Modhera, Sun temple, c. 1066-1094 CE.

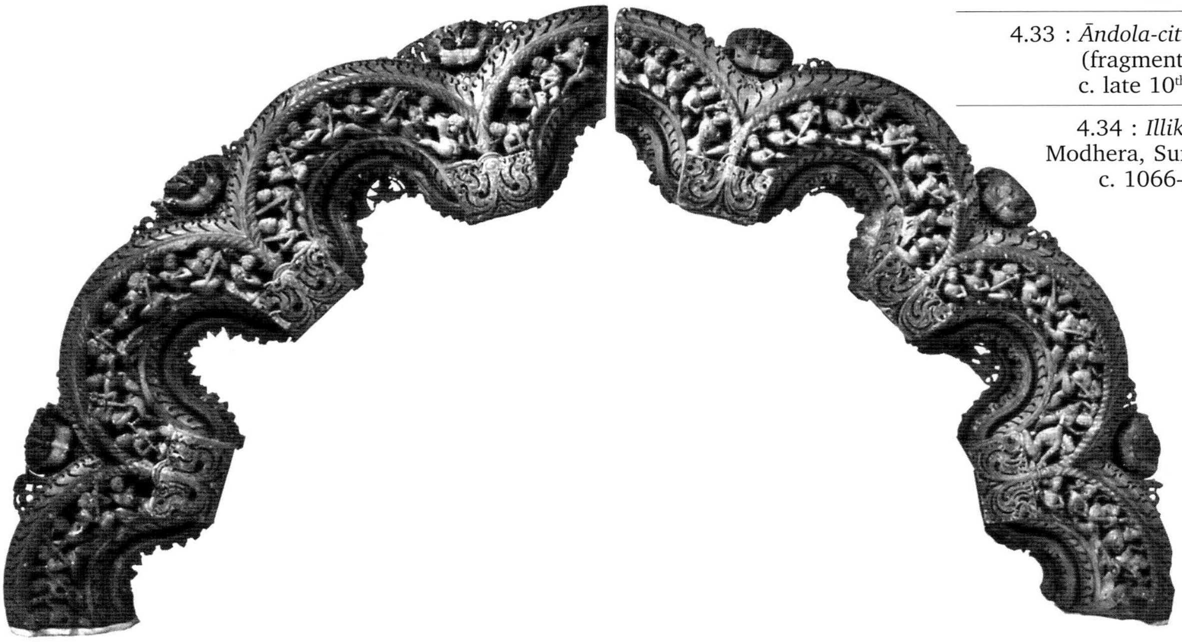

4.32

now. Judging by the qualitative excellence of the Someśvara temple, the missing arches must have been amongst the finest of their times. Interestingly, fragments of an *illikā-toraṇa,* pieced together and displayed in the Nehru Gallery of Art at the VAM in London, bear strong affinities with the craftsmanship and style observed at Kiradu (Fig. 4.32).[13] Although the provenance of this reassembled *illikā-toraṇa* in VAM's records is stated as 'Shatrunjaya, Palitana,' it reveals several features that indicate its allegiance to Kiradu.[14] Several of its traits closely correspond to the two surviving in the *raṅgamaṇḍapa* of the Viṣṇu temple at Kiradu (Figs. 4.25, 4.25a). The style of carving the *vidyādharas* in a variety of poses, with delightful twists and near-impossible contortions of the torsos, is very similar in the two instances. What is more, their physiognomy and other facial features also tally. In both cases, a twisted pearl cable topped by the typical flame-like ornamental band adorns the *toraṇa* above the row of *vidyādharas*. The stencilled lotus leaves below bear remarkable resemblance to each other as do the *kīrttimukhas* placed at the junction of consecutive arcs. What is more, the stone too, is of the same type.

But some features on the VAM *toraṇa* fragments (for instance, a greater degree of finesse in chiselling as well as some additional embellishments) indicate a date slightly later than that of the Viṣṇu temple at Kiradu. This tallies with the date ascribed to the VAM *toraṇa* and also conforms to the date of the Someśvara temple at Kiradu (c. 1020 CE). Importantly, the Viṣṇu temple *toraṇas* belong to the *āndola* class whereas the VAM *toraṇa* is the western Indian variant of the *illikā-toraṇa*. The latter appears to have gained popularity in western India only from the 11th century. In the VAM example, a delicate sequence of *fleurs-de-lis (gagāramālā)* hangs from the underside. This is visible in the fragmentary ends of the *toraṇas* attached to the octagonal pillars of the Someśvara temple, but is missing in those at the Viṣṇu temple. Also, an ornamental scroll motif at the lower intersections of the successive *illikā* arcs of the VAM *toraṇa* is similar to the workmanship and motifs carved on the Someśvara temple. The VAM fragments appear to fit the missing *toraṇa* spaces in the Someśvara temple hall in a very specific manner. In all likelihood, the VAM fragments originally belonged to the Someśvara temple at Kiradu and are not from Śatruñjaya in Palitana as mentioned in the VAM records.[15] Two fragments of the *āndola* type are also part of the collections of the VAM, London (Fig. 4.33). These are also stylistically affiliated to the Kiradu temples, but the *fleurs-de-lis* sequence *(gagāramālā)* at the lower margin is absent in them.[16] They appear to belong to a different temple, though from the same site.

Beginning from the 11th century, *illikā-toraṇas* gain favour and continue to flourish for the next two centuries, particularly in Gujarat. Eleventh century sites such as Modhera, Kumbhariya, and Mount Abu (Vimala Vasahī), and the 12th century examples at Girnar, Delmal, Asoda, Vadnagar, and Siddhapur attest to this development. Gujarat perfects her own *illikā*-variant, which standardizes and repeats itself at temple entrances and in the interiors tenaciously and somewhat monotonously. Seen at its finest during the 11th and 12th centuries, the western Indian *illikā-toraṇa* is made up of semi-circular or crescent-shaped arcs that vary from seven *(sapta-candrabhāgā)*[17] and nine *(nava-candrabhāgā)* to eleven *(ekādaśa-candrabhāgā)* in number. This geometry of the individual arcs is reaffirmed in the total contour of the arch, which traces a semi-circular path. More often than not, the arch bears two rows of tightly juxtaposed *vidyādharas*, punctuated at the interstices of the arcs with *kīrttimukhas* and pendant buds *(mukulas)*. The upper margins of the arch are fringed with the typical flame-like foliage and lotus leaves are stencilled on the lower margins; both these appear in medieval western Indian temples frequently. The underside of each arc is carved with a serrated course *(karṇadardarikā)* between a delicate *fleurs-de-lis* lace. Adorned with symbolic and auspicious motifs, this variant of the *illikā* arch unfurls between the *raṅgamaṇḍapa* pillars, at the entrance porches, and is a part of the free-standing *toraṇas*. This is the preferred arrangement on *toraṇas* from sites such as Modhera, Siddhapur, Vadnagar, and Delmal. Those in the interiors of the Jain temples at Delwara, the Mahāvīra temple at Kumbhariya, the Neminātha temple at Girnar, and the Jasmalnāthajī temple at Asoda register minor variations.

4.34

4.33

The main temple to the Sun god at Modhera is ascribed to 1027 CE, whereas its *raṅgamaṇḍapa* was added later (c. 1066-1094 CE).[18] An *illikā-toraṇa* of eights arcs *(aṣṭa-candrabhāgā)* survives at the southern entrance to its *raṅgamaṇḍapa*. The eastern entrance to the *gūḍhamaṇḍapa* is graced with another *illikā-toraṇa* (Figs. 4.34, 4.34a). Stylistically, the frontal pillars and the *toraṇa* on the eastern face of the *gūḍhamaṇḍapa* are more akin to that of the *raṅgamaṇḍapa* (c. 1066 -1094 CE).[19] The *toraṇas* also unfold between the attic pillars of central octagon of the *raṅgamaṇḍapa* (Fig. 4.35). *Āndola-toraṇas* placed at the angles alternate with *illikā-toraṇas* in the cardinal directions.

4.34a : *Illikā-toraṇa*, Modhera, Sun temple, c. 1066-1094 CE.

4.35 : *Toraṇas,* Modhera, Sun temple, *raṅgmaṇḍapa*, c. 1066-1094 CE.

4.36 : *Illikā-toraṇamālā,* Delmal, Limboja Mātā temple complex, c. third quarter of 11th century.

4.37 : *Illikā-toraṇa*, Siddhapur, Rudramahālaya, c. 1140 CE.

4.35

4.34a

4.36

The free-standing *toraṇa* at the entrance to the Limboja Mātā temple-complex at Delmal in the Mehsana District of Gujarat is embellished with an *illikā* garland between the attic pillars (Fig. 4.36; c. third quarter of 11th century). It has nine arcs *(nava-candrabhāgā)*, of which one is broken. The central portion is carved with a row of figures in varied stances. Some of them are in the attitude of dancing. Much of the carving on the southern face has been defaced. It is stylistically allied to the Modhera *toraṇas*.

The eastern and northern porches from the colossal ruins of the Rudramahālaya at Siddhapur have delicately rendered *illikā-toraṇas* on three sides (Fig. 4.37; c. 1140 CE). The figural carvings on the central band as well as the decorative elements on the margins of their nine semi-circular arcs *(nava-candrabhāgā)* testify to high standards of workmanship. The extant free-standing *Uttuṅga-toraṇa* from this complex also had an *illikā* arch as can be known from an earlier illustration (D.5, p.30).[20] All these follow the Modhera *toraṇas*; at Siddhapur, as at Delmal, there is a single row of figures in the central band in place of the double row noticed at Modhera. Of the two grand (*jyeṣṭha* in the treatises) *Uttuṅga-toraṇas* at Vadnagar, one stands on a high platform; fragments of the other one now lie in the vicinity. Included in these fragments is an intricately carved *illikā* arch of 11 arcs *(ekādaśa-candrabhāgā)* (Fig. 4.38; c. 1135-1145 CE). An earlier illustration of the Vadnagar *toraṇa* reveals an intact *illikā* arch.[21]

4.37

4.38

The *gūḍhamaṇḍapa* of the Neminātha temple at Girnar, a revered Jain pilgrim centre, has entrance porches adorned with *illikā-toraṇas* in the northern and southern directions (Fig. 4.39). The one at the southern porch, with six arcs, is in a fine state of preservation. Carved with an appealing mix of figures, it beautifully exemplifies the description of the *citra-toraṇa* mentioned in the Dravidian treatises. A Jina in meditation is shown in the centre. Flanking him are garland-bearers, followed by musicians and dancers. At the sides are monkeys, cavalry men, and elephants. Similar *toraṇas* are also placed between attic pillars in the *gūḍhamaṇḍapa*. The *toraṇas* are synchronous with the older portion of this temple, datable to c. 1129 CE.[22]

At the entrance porch attached to the main Jasmalnāthji Mahādeo temple's *raṅgamaṇḍapa* at Asoda, an *illikā-toraṇa* of seven arcs is released by *makaras* resting on *vyalās* attached to dwarf pillars (Fig. 4.40; c. second quarter of 12th century). The figural band on this arch is interspersed with a *kīrttimukha* motif at the meeting points of successive arcs *(citra-toraṇa)*. The semi-circular arcs are tentatively articulated and the arch as a whole does not convey the crispness of the Modhera and Siddhapur examples.

4.39

4.38 : *Illikā-toraṇamālā* with other fragments of *toraṇa*, Vadnagar, c. 1135-1145 CE.

4.39 : *Illikā-toraṇa*, Girnar, Neminātha temple, c. 1129 CE.

4.40 : *Illikā-toraṇa*, Asoda, Jasmalnāthjī Mahādeo temple, c. second quarter of 12th century.

4.40

A free-standing *toraṇa* in dark stone is placed in front of the elephant hall *(hastiśālā)* attached to the Vimala Vasahī temple at Mount Abu (Fig. 4.71; c. 1032 CE or slightly later). Brackets supporting *vyālas* project from the centre of the pillar shaft and *makaras* placed above them release an *illikā* arch of eight arcs. Two rows of seated Jina figures, in lieu of the usual *vidyādharas,* are carved in close succession on this arch. A *kīrttimukha* is placed at the intersection of successive arcs, which also show hanging knob-like buds *(mukula)*. The portion beneath the arcs is filled by devotees with hands folded in adoration *(añjali hasta)*. The *trika* (columnar vestibule with three bays) of the Mahāvīra temple at Kumbhariya has two *illikā-toraṇas* (Fig. 4.41; c. 1061 CE)[23]. The six arcs of the arch end in knob-like buds *(mukula)*; a figural frieze is carved delicately along the central band.

4.41 : *Illikā-toraṇa*, Kumbhariya, Mahāvīra temple, *trika*, c. 1061 CE.

4.42 : *Āndola-toraṇas*, Khor, Navatoraṇa, c. 11th century.

4.41

4.42

Āndola-toraṇas: Mature *āndola-toraṇas* belonging to the later part of the 10th century have been noticed at Nagda and Kiradu. Through the 11th and 12th centuries also, the *āndola-toraṇa* survived despite the favour accorded to the *illikā-toraṇa* and, thereafter, was prolific in the temples of the high medieval period.

A unique congress of *āndola-toraṇas* meets the eye at a ruined temple called Navatoraṇa in a small village near Khor in the Mandsor District of Madhya Pradesh (Fig. 4.42; c. 11th century). Ten *āndola-toraṇas* are aligned in two perpendicular rows, six along the north-south axis and four along the east-west axis, between the pillars of the hall. Each sinusoidal arch has six S-shaped segments *(madalas)* and five miniature niches *(tilakas)*. These niches are crowned by miniature Nāgara *śikharas*. A row of garland bearing celestials *(mālā-vidyādharas)* is sculpted in the central portion of the arch. Much damaged, these *toraṇas* are now supported by iron clamps.

An *āndola-toraṇa* of six S-shaped segments *(madalas)* and five miniature shrines *(tilakas)* is placed at the southern entrance to the hall of the Sūrya temple at Jhalarapatan in Jhalawar District (Fig. 4.43; c. 1075 CE). The Unḍeśvara temple in Bijolia (Fig. 4.44; c. late 12th century) has *āndola-toraṇas* in its hall. Apart from the images enshrined in the miniature niches, the latter do not bear any figural carving on them. A schematic leafy scroll occupies the central register of the arch.

4.43

4.44

4.43 : *Āndola-toraṇa,* Jhalarapatan, Sūrya temple, c. 1075 CE.

4.44 : *Āndola-toraṇa*, Bijolia, Uṇḍeśvara temple c. late 12th century.

4.45 : *Citra-toraṇa* fragment, Deogarh, c. late 12th century.

4.45

Fragments of a well-crafted *citra-toraṇa* were housed in a shed in front of Temple 12 at Deogarh in Uttar Pradesh (Fig. 4.45; c. late 12th century). One of the fragments reveals the profile of a *makara* releasing a portion of an arch carved with two rows of men and women seated in varied poses, some playing musical instruments. A thin defining band underlines each row; underneath the lower band is a scroll ornament.[24] Another fragment of a *parikara-toraṇa* from Uttar Pradesh, now in the Indian Museum, Kolkata, deserves special mention (Fig. 4.46; c. 11th century).[25] It must have framed a Buddhist image, as may be inferred from its thematic content and dimensions. The *makaras* attached to the inner margins of tiered pyramidal aediculae *(phaṁsa-kūṭas)* release a trefoil arch formed of a beaded row sandwiched between stencilled and deeply undercut lotus leaves. The interstices of successive arcs have pendant foliate *gagārakas*. A centrally placed aedicule depicts the scene of Buddha's *mahāparinirvāṇa*. The space beneath the arch is packed with partially damaged narrative registers. A peripheral row of garland-bearers on the outer margin completes the imagery.[26]

4.46

As observed earlier, the octagonal arrangement of *raṅgamaṇḍapa* pillars in the Sun temple at Modhera is embellished with *āndola-toraṇas* at the corners alternating with *illikā-toraṇas* placed in the cardinal directions (Fig. 4.47; c. 1075 CE). Due to the narrow space between the corner pillars, the wavy *āndola-toraṇas* soar steeply. Each arch has four niches *(tilakas)* articulated within the confines of the arch; the usual niche at the apex is absent. Knob-like buds *(mukulas)* are suspended underneath the niches. Two rows of *vidyādharas* in tight sequence adorn the arch; its inner edge is bordered with a saw-tooth course and the upper margin with the flame-like ornament.

The *raṅgamaṇḍapa* of the Mahāvīra temple at Kumbhariya was originally graced with *āndola-toraṇas* at the cardinal points; only the eastern one has survived (Fig. 4.48; c. 1062 CE).[27] The attic pillars are absent and the finely proportioned arch is made up of six S-shaped segments punctuated by seven niches that enshrine deities of the Jain pantheon. A figural band sandwiched between saw-tooth courses runs through the entire length of the arch.[28] A sinusoidal *parikara-toraṇa* is placed at the (now closed) entrance of the *Samavasaraṇa* chapel near the eastern opening of the Mahāvīra temple *jagatī* (Fig. 4.49; c. 1157 CE). It is believed to have been originally set up for the cult image in the main temple.[29] Stylistically, it is distinct from the 11th century instances in the *raṅgamaṇḍapa*. Decorative motifs replace figural carvings on the

4.48

4.46 : *Āndola-toraṇa (parikara* fragment), Uttar Pradesh, now in Indian Museum, Kolkata, c. 11th century.

4.47 : *Toraṇas,* Modhera, Sun temple *raṅgmaṇḍapa*, c. 1075 CE.

4.48 : *Āndola-toraṇa,* Kumbhariya, Mahāvīra temple, *raṅgmaṇḍapa*, c. 1062 CE.

4.49 : *Āndola-toraṇa (parikara),* Kumbhariya, *Samavasaraṇa* chapel near Mahāvīra temple, c. 1157 CE.

4.47

4.49

4.51

arch; star-shaped floral motifs are inscribed in a circle and encased between strands of buds. The outer margin is edged with a row of geese *(haṁsamālā)*. The six intervening niches along the arch are rather slender and each of them enshrines a seated Jain deity. The ornamentation resembles delicate filigree work.

In the *raṅgamaṇḍapa* of the Śāntinātha temple at Kumbhariya, the *toraṇa* placed between the western attic pillars is the sole one to survive (Fig. 4.50; c. 1082 CE).[30] It is very similar to the one in the *raṅgamaṇḍapa* of the Mahāvīra temple; in this case a row of buds replaces the saw-tooth course and the upper margin is edged with a row of geese *(haṁsamālā)*. A chapel with a depiction of the *Aṣṭapada* mythical mountain is located at the southern end of the eastern wing of this temple's *paṭṭaśālā*. Jina images crowned by a series of trefoil arches occupy the body of the mountain (dated 1206 CE).

4.50

4.53

4.50 : *Āndola-toraṇa*, Kumbhariya, Śāntinātha temple, *raṅgmaṇḍapa*, c. 1082 CE.

4.51 : *Āndola-toraṇa*, Kumbhariya, Pārśvanātha temple, c. 1100 CE.

4.52 : *Āndola-toraṇa (parikara)*, Kumbhariya, Pārśvanātha temple, *devakulikā*, 1231 CE (inscribed).

4.53 : *Āndola-toraṇa*, Kumbhariya, Neminātha temple, c. late 13th century.

In the Pārśvanātha temple at the same site, the front porch of the *trika* (columnar vestibule with three bays) is embellished with an *āndola-toraṇa* (Fig. 4.51; c. 1100 CE) similar to those in the Mahāvīra and Śāntinātha temples. The Neminātha temple is the largest of all temples at Kumbhariya; the main temple is datable to c. 1134 CE. The front porch of the *balānaka* attached to this temple is crowned with an *āndola-toraṇa* carved with a row of *vidyādharas* and made of eight S-shaped segments *(madalas)* and seven niches (Fig. 4.53). The temple underwent large scale renovations and additions in the early years of this decade, when a series of new *āndola-toraṇas* were also added.

4.52

Two dated inscriptions refer to the *toraṇas* at Kumbhariya. One of 1125 CE from the Mahāvīra temple (originally from the main sanctuary of the Pārśvanātha temple) mentions that it was erected by a *śrāvaka* (App. 1, no. 12); another on a *parikara-toraṇa* in a subsidiary shrine *(devakulikā)* of the Pārśvanātha temple refers that it was set up to accrue merit for the donor's mother (Fig. 4.52; 1231 CE) (App. 1, no. 13). Five *parikara-toraṇas* have been observed at Kumbhariya.[31]

The interior of the Vimala Vasahī temple at Mount Abu is adorned with *āndola-toraṇas,* notably between the *raṅgamaṇḍapa* attic-pillars (Fig. 4.54; c. 1150 CE). The central portion of the arch comprises eight S-shaped segments and is embellished with celestials; this is interspersed with seven miniature niches harbouring Jain

4.54 : *Āndola-toraṇa*, Mount Abu, Vimala Vasahī, c. 1150 CE.

4.55 : *Āndola-toraṇa*, Jhadoli, Pārśvanātha temple, c. early 12th century.

divinities. The top margin has an immaculately carved saw-tooth course. Though the carving is more intricate in the Mount Abu examples, proportions are more satisfactory at Kumbhariya. Of about the same period are the *āndola-toraṇas* which unfurl in the hall of the Pārśvanātha temple at Jhadoli (Fig. 4.55; c. early 12th century) in the Sirohi District of Rajasthan. From this point onwards, the *āndola-toraṇa* gains prominence across Gujarat and Rajasthan, "like some beautiful creeper running wild between pillar and pillar in cusps and curves."[32]

4.55

C. 13th Century

Lūṇa Vasahī: The dawn of the 13th century saw Bhīma II ascend the throne of a much depleted Caulukya empire.[33] Bhīma II was then a minor and Vāghelā nobles controlled the administration on his behalf with the help of the ministers, Vāstupāla and Tejapāla. The Lūṇa Vasahī at Mount Abu (c. 1232-40 CE) belongs to this period, though some restoration took place during the first quarter of the 14th century. The most remarkable part of this temple is its *raṅgamaṇḍapa* which conjures a shell-like translucence with its leisurely rendition of detail in the interior. One witnesses a new *toraṇa* variant in this temple's *raṅgamaṇḍapa* (Fig. 4.56; D.8, p.34), credited to *sūtradhāra* Śobhanadeva, the chief architect of the Lūṇa Vasahī.[34] In the *āndola-toraṇa*, the S-shaped *madala* passing

4.57

through the niche is the basic unit, while in the *illikā* type, the half-moon shaped arc following a hemi-cyclic course sets the pattern. In the composite *toraṇa* at Lūṇa Vasahī, one encounters an imaginative permutation of the S-shaped *madala* of *āndola* derivation with the semi-circular arc of *illikā* derivation, which are interspersed with miniature niches to create an arch that meanders through a serpentine course. This Lūṇa Vasahī variant remains unparalleled, although similarities may be drawn with some *illikā-toraṇas* from Karnataka that proceed in a series of trefoil arches (Figs. 3.66, 3.74, 3.78). A poor duplication is attempted at the gatehouse of the 15th century Shamalaji temple in Gujarat (Fig. 4.57).[35]

4.56

The *āndola-toraṇas* in the Lūṇa Vasahī *raṅgamaṇḍapa* are slightly later than those at Vimala Vasahī, Mount Abu. A different type of *illikā-toraṇa* is also encountered in the Lūṇa Vasahī *raṅgamaṇḍapa*. It comprises a series of ornamental, radially arranged floral motifs that resemble the ceiling's cusped courses *(kolas)* (Fig. 4.58, rear). In the Lūṇa Vasahī *toraṇas*, figural representations are conspicuous by their absence, except for the presence of Jina figures enshrined within the niches of the *āndola-toraṇas*. The predominance of ornamental motifs and the lack of figural sculpture becomes the norm on arches of the later period.

4.58

4.56 : Serpentine *toraṇa*, Mount Abu, Lūṇa Vasahī, c. 1232-40 CE.

4.57 : Serpentine *toraṇa*, Shamalaji, *pratolī*, c. third quarter of 15th century.

4.58 : *Āndola-toraṇa* (front) and *Puṣpa-illikā-toraṇa* (rear), Mount Abu, Lūṇa Vasahī, c. 1232-40 CE.

Free-standing *Toraṇas*

The *SS* alludes to the significance of a free-standing *toraṇa* as a marker of the prestige and honour of a kingdom and devotes an entire chapter to the remedial measures to be undertaken in case of its unfortunate destruction.[36] Inscriptional (App. 1, no. 15) and textual (App. 2, *The Jataka...*) evidence also alludes to the *toraṇa* as a signifier of the kingdom's glory and honour. In battle, the *toraṇa* at the city limits would be captured or destroyed by the enemy to indicate his supremacy over the conquered kingdom. The extant free-standing *toraṇas* are, however, usually those which have been built in association with a religious structure; *pratolī-toraṇas* such as those at Jhinjhuvada and Dabhoi are of course part of the entrance gateways punctuating the city-ramparts (Figs. 4.91-4.97). Free-standing *toraṇas* associated with temples served as passages of initiation into a sacred space and have been carved with figural and ornamental sculpture replete with symbols and motifs such as *kīrttimukhas, makaras, vyālas, surasundarīs, vidyādharas, ratnas,* and *aṣṭamaṅgalas* conveying auspiciousness, fertility, and other benevolent attributes. Some of the figural sculptures on these *toraṇas* also signify the creedal and sectarian affiliation of the structures with which they are associated. In secular as well as religious contexts, they were also employed as *hinḍola-toraṇas*[37] and *tulābhāra-toraṇas*[38] .

4.59

C. 9th-10th Centuries

Central India

Badoh: The Badoh *toraṇa* stands on the northern extension of a tall *jagati* and must, at one time, have provided an imposing passageway to the Gadarmal (Śakti) temple. Today, the *toraṇa* is in a damaged condition; only the supporting pillars survive (Fig. 4.59; c. second quarter of ninth century). Rising from moulded bases, the fluted shafts of the pillars are adorned with the bell and chain ornament and are sandwiched between the vase and foliage *(ghaṭapallava)* motif placed above and below. The attic pillar survives only on one of the pillars. It bears the *vyāla* and *apsarā* bracket figures and a *makara* emitting an arch of which only a very fragmentary portion survives. This would have otherwise given an idea of the ninth century arches from the region, of which there are no other surviving examples. Judging by the 10th century examples from Āṭha Khambhā and Cār Khambhā at Gyaraspur, this is a significant loss. A majestic lion crowns the segment above the attic pillar of the Badoh *toraṇa*, perhaps a clue to its Śākta affiliation.

Gyaraspur: Known locally as the *Hiṇḍola-toraṇa*, this free-standing example from Gyaraspur belongs to a ruined Viṣṇu temple, now called Cār Khambhā after the four surviving pillars of its hall (Fig. 4.60; c. early 10th century). The temple faced east but the *toraṇa* is along the north-south axis and must have once provided access to the temple from the southern direction. The square *(bhadraka)* pillars of the *toraṇa* rest on a lotus-socle *(padmapīṭha)* and base *(kumbhaka)*. The shafts have niches sheltering incarnations of Viṣṇu, signalling the temple's religious affiliation. On the eastern pillar, Matsya and Kūrma on the northern side, Varāha to the west, Narasiṁha in the southern niche, and Vāmana to the east are clearly discernible. On the western pillar, Paraśurāma in the southern niche, Balarāma (?) in the western one, Śrī Rāma (?) and Kalkī in the northern niche, and an effaced Kṛṣṇa (?) in the eastern one are noticeable. Above these, there are two registers with *mithunas*, dancers, and musicians; a narrow recessed band of diamonds separates the two registers. Next, an ornament comprising the vase and foliage *(ghaṭapallava)* above entwined serpents *(nāgapāśa)* is topped by the *kīrttimukha* and *vyālas,* and a half-diamond *(ardharatna)* with surrounding scroll ornament. Further up is the fluted portion *(bharaṇa)* and next, atlantid *(kumāra)* and *vyāla* brackets. Upon these rest the attic pillars with *āmalaka* capitals and brackets supporting architraves with leafy scrolls emanating from a *kīrttimukha* at the centre. Above this, a row of deities in niches alternates with devotees and is topped by an upper row of figures with an overhanging *gagāraka* lacing. The crowning pediment is unfortunately lost but the *toraṇa* shows several features in common with the Terahi *toraṇa*. It is possible that the pediment of the Gyaraspur *toraṇa* resembled that at Terahi (Fig. 4.61). A miniature Nāgara shrine was placed at some later date as the crowning member and looks rather incongruous. The *makaras* seated on the inner brackets of the main pillars release an arch of twin arcs clasped at the centre to meet the lower horizontal beam of scrolled ornament. These are carved with garland-bearing celestials on the southern face and an undulating creeper juxtaposed with figural ornament on the northern one.

4.60

4.59 : *Toraṇa*, Badoh, (in front of) Gadarmal temple, c. second quarter of ninth century.

4.60 : *Toraṇa*, Gyaraspur, Cār Khambā complex, c. early 10th century.

4.61

4.61 : *Toraṇa,* Terahi,
Mohajamātā temple complex,
c. 10th century.

Terahi: Recovered and resurrected,[39] the *toraṇa* fronting the Mohajamātā temple at Terahi (Fig. 4.61; c. 10th century) in the Shivpuri District of Madhya Pradesh is stylistically affiliated to the one at Gyaraspur. The temple at Terahi is dedicated to Kālī and bears several images of female power *(śakti),* as also ghouls (*vetālas*) on its walls. The square and faceted *toraṇa* pillars rise from a lotus socle *(padmapīṭha)*, knife-edged arris *(karṇikā)*, and next, the pillar base *(kumbhaka* comprising *khura-kumbha, kalaśa, antarapaṭṭa,* and *kapotālī* mouldings) faced with niches in the cardinal directions. Tiered pyramidal *(phaṁsanā)* shrines harbouring divinities like Brahmā, Bhū-Varāha, Balarāma, Gaṇeśa, Lakṣmī, and Umā are found on the lower sections of the pillar shafts. The chamfered corners of the pillars at the same level house serpents *(nāgas)*, goblins *(pramathas)*, and celestials *(gandharvas)*. The square register above this course shows musicians and dancers, the god of wealth, Kubera, etc. Next comes the vase and foliage *(ghaṭapallava)* ornament sandwiched between *kīrttimukhas* above and below. At this level, a projection in four directions may have earlier supported bracket figures (at present there are none). Luxuriantly carved half-medallions and medallions are capped by a ribbed segment *(bharaṇa)* that carries square projecting brackets dressed with ornamental motifs. These brackets support niches housing deities, including an exquisitely carved Varāhī. The *makaras,* resting on the inner brackets, release a delicate arch that has a *kīrttimukha* at the apex; it is adorned with a row of garland-bearers *(mālādharas)* underlined by stencilled lotus leaves. A pendant *fleur-de-lis (gagāraka)* below the *kīrttimukha* is attached to another ornament which is now broken. The architrave above includes a row of figures engaged in music and dance, flanking a centrally seated female figure. Next is the *kīrttimukha* emanating a leafy scroll, topped by another figural band. Above this is a miniature *kakṣāsana* (seat-back member on the walls of a temple's open hall) segment revealing dancers, musicians, and *mithunas* through the balconied openings. A row of figures is placed above this segment; the central one on the eastern face is Sūrya with seven horses and the western one is Viṣṇu, both flanked by attendant figures. A triple-tiered pyramidal shrine *(phaṁsa-kūṭa)* survives as the crowning member. There may have been two additional tiers topped by a bell, *āmalaka* (crowning 'myrobolan' member) and vase finial.[40] This is also corroborated by the presence of similar superstructures above the niches in the lower portions of the pillar shafts. If this were the case, the aesthetic impact of this well-proportioned *toraṇa* would be even more striking.

4.62

Gurgi: The octagonal pillar shafts of the Gurgi *toraṇa*, now relocated in front of the Rewa Mahārājā's palace, are sumptuously carved with divine and semi-divine beings (Fig. 4.62; c. 10th century). This *toraṇa* must have belonged to one of the two Śiva temples built in Gurgi under the patronage of the Kalacuris. The base of the pillar *(kumbhikā)* bears figures in niches with *udgama*-pediments, on each of its eight facets.[41] The rest of the pillar is divided into five zones of figural representations punctuated by four rows of atlantids *(bhāraputrakas)*. The lowest row of atlantids upholds the three lower figural registers. The lowest figural zone has *apsarās* in languorous poses housed in tiered pyramidal shrines *(phaṁsa-kūṭas)*. Two shorter figural registers above this house men, women, and *mithunas*. Next is a row of atlantids supporting *apsarās* alternating with rampant *vyālas*. Further up, an intervening row of atlantids supports divine images under trees carved with remarkable attention to detail, including the portrayal of monkeys and birds. Amongst the divinities, Brahmāṇī, Varāhī, Cāmuṇḍā, and Gaṇeśa can be identified. The *illikā* arch carved on the lintel has been discussed earlier (Fig. 4.26). The crowning member depicts the marriage of Śiva and Pārvatī; above this is a row of semi-divine and divine beings (not illustrated). Though thematically and stylistically aligned to the rest, this apparently is not the original crowning member of the *toraṇa*.[42]

4.62 : *Toraṇa,* Gurgi (now in front of Rewa Palace), c. 10th century.

4.63 : *Toraṇa,* Medta-Phalodi, Brahmāṇīmātā temple complex, c. 875-900 CE.

4.63

Rajasthan

Medta-Phalodi: The *toraṇa* in front of the Brahmāṇīmātā temple at Medta-Phalodi (Fig. 4.63; c. 875-900 CE) suggests links with the earlier art of Abaneri (c. 800-825 CE). It flaunts a florid and lush, yet not excessively ornamental repertoire, and is earlier than even the oldest portions of the Brahmāṇīmātā temple which it fronts.[43] The reconstructed and therefore plain lower halves of the square *toraṇa* pillars spring from a broad base of which three mouldings (*kumbha, antarapaṭṭa,* and *kapotālī*) are visible. The upper halves of the pillars are luxuriantly carved with medallions harbouring Gaṇeśa, Kubera, *kinnaras, mithunas,* etc. Other courses include a band of scroll and a vase *(pūrṇakalaśa)* carved with a projecting member shaped like a lotus, which must have upheld the now missing bracket figures. Next is a row of *vyālas* emanating pearl festoons and then a fluted section topped by a band of leaf-drops; next, a *kīrttimukha* is capped by an upturned cyma *(ūrdhvacippikā)* with lotus leaves. A fluted portion *(bharaṇa)* and foliate roll brackets with an upper padding faced with half-diamonds completes the portion below the attic section. The attic pillars consist of an octagonal shaft that graduates into a fluted section with 32 facets and then a circular section. This is crowned with a deftly chiselled scroll and half-diamond, and next, the fluted portions surmounted by roll-brackets. The pillars thrive in ebullient and vivacious foliate patterns which shelter creatures such as a pair of geese with their necks entwined, horses, parakeets, a camel, and even wrestlers. An architrave with five deep-cut lotuses on its soffit rests on these pillars. The eastern and western profiles of the architrave are sculpted with niches laced on the lower margins with a neatly arranged row of festoons terminating in buds alternating with half-diamonds. On the eastern face, the central niche contains Viṣṇu flanked by personified attributes *(āyudhapuruṣas)*; Śiva occupies the northern niche and Brahmā the southern one. The western face has Gaurī flanked by female attendants at the centre; Viṣṇu occupies the southern niche and the northern niche houses a deity difficult to identify. The arch, possibly displaced from its original position, rests between the attic pillars. The *makaras* at the ends release the arch that is all but completely destroyed. Fragmentary courses that include a band of half-diamonds and a chain of buds are reminiscent of the Abaneri pieces with similar courses (Fig. 4.5). *Ṛṣis* can be seen in the surviving corner portions of the Medta-Phalodi *toraṇa* tympanum. A seated deity at the centre is now too damaged for identification.[44] This piece possibly was the pediment that crowned the entire *toraṇa*.

Harshagiri: The fragments of a free-standing *toraṇa* (Fig. 4.64; c. 956-973 CE) from the ruined Harṣanātha temple at Harshagiri (Sikar) include the base, lower pillar shafts, and roll-brackets (along with the *makara* fragment and portions of the arch discussed earlier in this chapter (Fig. 4.21 and App. 1, nos. 11a-b). The base mouldings of the faceted square *(bhadraka)* pillars include an inverted cyma recta *(jāḍyakumbha)* with elegant lotus petals and scrollwork, followed by arris *(karṇaka)*, a recessed band *(antarapaṭṭa)*, and half lotuses *(ardhapadmas)*. The shaft has figural sculpture on the faceted corners, while the central faces show shallow and empty niches framed between square vase and foliage *(ghaṭapallava)* pilasters. Roll-brackets of fine proportions and craftsmanship have now been placed above this portion. The temple ruins reveal such artistic wealth that the loss can only be suffered.

Badoli: The *toraṇa* pillars, south-east of the Trimūrti temple at Badoli in Rajasthan, perhaps belonged to a temple whose sanctum floor with a Śivaliṅga *in situ* survives to their east (Fig. 4.65; c. mid-10th century).[45] The portion above the fluted upper part *(bharaṇa)* is missing. The pillars are in the Malava style; the base and shaft spring from an octagonal moulding carved with a gorgon frieze *(grāsapaṭṭī)*. Each pillar is adorned with four figures, three female and one male, with several of them in the gesture of adoration *(añjali hasta)*.[46] Above this, is a 16-sided fluted shaft with the chain and bell ornament typical of this region. Next is the circular portion of the shaft dressed with the gorgon and bells *(grāsakiṅkiṇikā)* band capped by a ribbed upper part *(bharaṇa)*. These pillars bear a striking resemblance to the front pillars of the entrance porch *(mukhamaṇḍapa)* of the Ghaṭeśvara temple at Badoli; some idea of the missing *torana* garland may be had from the arch adorning the entrance to the Ghaṭeśvara temple (Figs. 4.22, 4.22a).

Nagda: The free-standing *toraṇa* fronting the stairway of the *jagatī* of the Bahu temple at Nagda in the Mewar region of Rajasthan is a rare example of the *Mālādhara-toraṇa* described in the western Indian architectural treatises (Fig. 4.66; c. late 10th to early 11th century). Atlantids supporting brackets are placed over the capitals of four polymorphic pillars. Whereas the outer pillars support a plain architrave, attic-pillars are placed above the two central pillars. The

4.64

4.64 : *Toraṇa* remains, Harshagiri, Harṣanātha temple, c. 956-973 CE.

4.65 : *Toraṇa* pillars, Badoli, south-east of Trimūrti temple, c. mid-10th century.

4.65

4.66

pediment is missing. Niches harbouring dancing figures are placed above the inner brackets of the central pillars. An arch of four segments occupies the space between the attic-pillars. Garland-bearers are placed beneath the two central loops of the arch and flying celestials are located at the outer corners of the arch. The arch is carved with an undulating creeper pattern of curls and counter-curls, each inscribing a person, a bird, etc. Knob-like buds *(mukulas)* are suspended at the interstices of the segments of the arch.

Gujarat

Shamalaji: Gujarat, which is home to several grand and imposing medieval free-standing *toraṇas*, has no examples to offer prior to the 10th century. The earliest extant free-standing example from this part of the country is the one at Shamalaji.[47] A *toraṇa* (Fig. 4.67; c. mid-10th century) is erected in front of a temple that goes by the name of Hariścandra-nī-caurī (c. early ninth century). It is made of two square *(bhadraka)* pillars, with the arch springing from above the fluted section *(bharaṇa)*. The pillar bases rise from an elevated platform and include the aggregate of five mouldings *(khura-kumbha-kalaśa-antarapaṭṭa-kapotālī)*, faced with niches in the four directions. The lower regions of the pillar shafts are adorned with finely sculpted images, most of which have been damaged. These are framed by square pilasters and sheltered by an awning and a pediment between two miniature Nāgara spires at the corners. Next follow the usual courses of the medallion, vase, and gorgon band, with foliate scrolls in the interspaces. Above this is the ribbed portion that upholds small brackets supporting the lion on elephant motif (*gajakrānta-siṁhas*) at the outer faces. The *makaras* emitting an arch of twin arcs on the inner faces of the pillars are placed at this level. The arch is carved on the lintel and only portions of the surrounding stone from the lower slab have been scooped out. In western and central India, this is a rare occurrence and is not seen after the 10th-11th centuries. The arch is embellished with an undulating, inhabited creeper pattern, with a *kīrttimukha* at the apex; the pendant *(gagāraka?)* motif is now broken. Celestial couples engaged in music and dance fill the space beneath the arcs, as at the Sās temple, Nagda, and some 10th century temple sites in Karnataka. No clear indication of the dedicatory affiliation of this *toraṇa* is available, possibly because the structure surmounting the lintel, which may have carried a clue, is missing. The soffit of the lintel bears a lotus and a stencilled creeper which have the characteristic clean lines of the Mahā-Gurjara style.

4.66 : *Mālādhara-toraṇa*, Nagda, Sās-Bahu temple complex, c. late 10th- early 11th century.

4.67 : *Toraṇa*, Shamalaji, in front of Hariścandra-nī-caurī, c. mid-10th century.

4.67

4.68

Free-standing *Toraṇas* c. 11th century onwards

From the 11th century, the *Uttuṅga-toraṇa* described in the *Appr.* (App. 3, no. 14; D.5, p.30) finds translation in actual examples scattered over Gujarat and Rajasthan. The square *(bhadraka)* *toraṇa* pillars of the preceding period give way to composite *(miśraka)* pillars.

Osian: The *toraṇa* that originally stood in front of the Mahāvīra temple at Osian in Rajasthan, subsequently collapsed and its pillars were placed in the cloistered corridor of this temple (Fig. 4.68).[48] There is a difference of opinion in reading the date of its installation, as recorded in the inscription on one of the pillars of the *toraṇa* (978 or 1018 CE? App. 1, no. 14). The pillars, however, are affiliated to the style prevailing in the region during the first half of the 11th century. These had earlier stood on a tall plinth with several additional mouldings, typical of the medieval Maru-Gurjara style, with seated Jina images in niches carved on four sides of the *kumbha* (moulding with curved shoulder) of the base (D.12).[49] Above this are figures of Jīvantaswāmī Mahāvīra enshrined in niches on the four sides of the shaft, followed by another figural row at the octagonal section of the shaft, with eight niches housing seated Jina figures. Next is the crisply carved row of flaming leaves

D.12

4.69

4.70

with a *vidyādhara* bracket in four directions. The circular section of the pillar has a figural belt, a vine pattern, and a gorgon band. The portion above this has been severed from the pillars, but is known from Dhaky's description and the accompanying visual to have consisted of a ribbed abacus *(bharaṇī)* and roll-bracket *(taraṅga-śīrṣa)*, with the lintel above featuring a vine design and a band of half-lotuses. The awning and the pediment appear to be of a later date, stylistically of the 15th century, and seem to have been added above the original pillars at some point of time. As seen in the visual, minor niches *(tilakas)* are placed at the two ends of the pediment above the lintel and a central *tilaka* images a Jina. Peacocks, straining their necks to look back, are placed near the *tilakas*. This motif gained currency in Gujarat and Rajasthan from about the 15th century. The entire ensemble is crowned with a sinusoidal *(āndola)* arch.

Modhera: The pillars of a *toraṇa* belonging to a ruined temple in the Sun temple complex at Modhera are next in the time-frame (Fig. 4.69; c. 1030 CE). On these, the section above the second figural band is missing. The configuration of sculptures on these *miśraka* pillars is similar to that on the *toraṇa* pillars placed near the eastern entrance of the Sun temple's *raṅgamaṇḍapa*, constructed about four to five decades later (Fig. 4.70).[50] The base and a major portion of the shaft of both the pillars are intact, but the capitals, brackets, attic pillars, and the arch are lost. The bases of these *toraṇa* pillars are faceted by fine chamfering and they gradually taper upwards. The

4.68 : *Toraṇa* pillars, Osian, Mahāvīra temple, 978 or 1018 CE (inscribed).

4.69 : *Toraṇa* pillars, Modhera, southeast of Sun temple, c. 1030 CE.

4.70 : *Toraṇa* pillars, Modhera, Sun temple, c. 1066-1094 CE.

D.12 : *Toraṇa* in front of the Mahāvīra temple at Osian, 978 or 1018 CE (pillars), c. 15th century (pediment).

decorative mouldings consist of inverted cyma recta *(jāḍyakumbha)*, knife-edged arris *(karṇikā)*, a recessed band *(antarapaṭṭa)*, and next, the gorgon *(grāsapaṭṭikā)*, elephant *(gajapīṭha)*, and the human *(narapīṭha)* courses. Above this, deities are represented on the main faces while female figures are shown on the lateral facets, each in a niche. This is topped by a torus, recessed band, cyma cornice, and gorgon band. The first figural frieze is placed above these and is adorned with hanging leaves between the crowning pediments of its niches. A cushion moulding *(maśūraka)* separates it from the second figural frieze, which is followed by a diminutive third figural frieze. These composite medieval western Indian pillars are at times referred to as the pillars of the 'Modhera order'. Fragments of a third *toraṇa* were also found in the vicinity.[51]

Mount Abu: The Vimala Vasahī *toraṇa* in Mount Abu almost touches the temple's elephant hall *(hastiśālā)*. Its pillars are equal in height to the squat *hastiśālā* and lack the attic section (Fig. 4.71; c. 1032 CE or slightly later). Above the brackets, a ribbed awning is crowned by the convolving pediment *(illikāvalaṇa)*, which has minor niches *(tilakas)* with *makaras* projecting outwards. Most of the images once set within the convolving pediment have been destroyed. An *illikā* arch unfolds between the pillars; it has *makaras* placed above *vyālas* at the ends.

4.72

Chandravati: Chandravati was the erstwhile capital of the Paramaras of Abu. The European writers such as James Tod, Gustav Le Bon, and Mrs Colonel Williams Hunter-Blair have reported its destruction at different periods of history. Metropolitan centres such as Patan Anhilvada and Chandravati must have attracted the most accomplished of artists to create the religious and regal structures of their ruler-patrons. *Toraṇas* are imaged in two of the earlier illustrations from Chandravati. A solitary marble *toraṇa* pillar stands desolate amongst the ruins in one of these,[52] much the same as it appears in our photograph (Fig. 4.72; c. 11th century). Its mouldings are organized in the usual manner noticed on the composite medieval western Indian (Maru-Gurjara) pillars.[53] The *toraṇa* in the second illustration[54] appears to be the one that has been re-erected in front of the Madhusūdana temple at Mungathala (Fig. 4.73; c. late 11th century). The *miśraka* pillars with three figural courses support attic-pillars on which rests the architrave and the ribbed awning. The portion above this has been pieced together from available fragments. The arch between the attic-pillars is missing, but the *makaras* above the roll-brackets of the main pillars, from whose jaws it must have issued forth, survive.

4.71

4.71 : *Uttuṅga-toraṇa*, Mount Abu, Vimala Vasahī, c. 1032 CE (or slightly later).

4.72 : *Toraṇa*-pillar, Chandravati, c. 11th century.

4.73 : *Toraṇa* re-erected in front of Madhusūdana temple at Mungathala (originally from Chandravati), c. late 11th century.

4.73

Delmal: The *toraṇa* at the entrance to the Limboja mātā temple complex at Delmal (Fig. 4.74; c. third quarter of 11th century) is a fine representation of the *Uttuṅga-toraṇa* described in the *Appr.* (App. 3, no. 14). The shafts of the composite pillars resting on typical Maru-Gurjara mouldings are decorated with two figural courses and successive bands of foliage *(parṇapaṭṭī)*, diamonds *(ratnapaṭṭī)*, and gorgons *(grāsapaṭṭī)*, followed by a fluted part *(bharaṇī)*, and wave-brackets *(taraṅga-śīrṣa)*. The attic pillars bear bracket figures of maidens with exaggerated bends and twists of their bodies. A ribbed awning and a row of figures topped by the *illikāvalaṇa* constitute the pediment. The central image of the goddess flanked by fly-whisk bearers, inset within the convolving pediment on the southern face, indicates the dedicatory affiliation of the *toraṇa* and the temple it fronts. On the northern face, the central image on the pediment is that of Śiva in the *padmāsana,* flanked by a fly-whisk bearer and a dancing Gaṇeśa. An *illikā* arch of nine arcs *(nava-candrabhāgā)* springs from *makara* brackets above the fluted part of the lower pillars. The pediment is bordered with a row of geese *(haṁsamālā)*; parrots are perched on the crests of the *illikāvalaṇa*.

4.74

Menal: A rare instance of the textual *Mālādhara-toraṇa* (also observed at Nagda) is encountered in the Mahānaladeva temple complex at Menal in the Chittor District of Rajasthan (Fig. 4.75; c. 12th century).

Eklingji: A free-standing Vaiṣṇava *Uttuṅga-toraṇa* found near the Ekliṅgjī temple complex, which probably belonged to a temple at Nagda or Eklingji, now stands in the vicinity, in front of the Principal's room of the Rājakīya Mādhyamik Vidyālaya, Kailashpuri (Fig. 4.76; c. late 12th-13th century). A major portion of the convolving pediment *(illikāvalaṇa)* and the central image of the seated deity on the lintel of this *toraṇa* are now lost.

4.76

4.74 : *Uttuṅga-toraṇa*, Delmal, Limboja Mātā temple complex, c. third quarter of 11th century.

4.75 : *Mālādhara-toraṇa*, Menal, Mahānaladeva temple complex, c. 12th century.

4.76 : *Uttuṅga-toraṇa*, Eklingji, re-erected in front of Rājakīya Mādhyamik Vidyālaya, Kailashpuri, c. late 12th or early 13th century.

4.75

4.77 : *Uttuṅga-toraṇa*, Lodrava, Pārśvanātha temple complex, pillars, c. late 10th or early 11th century; *toraṇamālā* and *illikāvalaṇa,* c. 17th century.

4.78 : *Uttuṅga-toraṇa*, Siddhapur, Rudramahālaya temple complex, c. 1140 CE.

4.77

Lodrava: The pillars of the *toraṇa* belonging to the Pārśvanātha temple at Lodrava in the Jaisalmer District of Rajasthan are of the late 10th or early 11th century, but the arch and the pediment with the seated image of Pārśvanātha stylistically appear to be of the 17th century, when the temple was refurbished (Fig. 4.77). The lower portions of the pillars are defaced. Traces of an earlier arch peep out of the jaws of the *makaras* just above the fluted top portion *(bharaṇī)* of the pillars. Between the attic-pillars, a newer arch consisting of ornamental motifs was added sometime later.

Siddhapur: The 12th century was a witness to the grand *toraṇas* at Siddhapur and Vadnagar. Amidst the ruins of the once imposing Rudramahālaya at Siddhapur, is a *jyeṣṭha* or *uttama Uttuṅga-toraṇa* described in the technical manuals (Chapter 2; App. 3, nos. 7a-b, 14).[55] It is situated north of the front (eastern) porch of the *raṅgamaṇḍapa* (Fig. 4.78; c. 1140 CE). The presence of two more *toraṇas*, one located south of the eastern porch and the other between the Nandī pavilion and the river (as per the original plan of the Rudramahālaya), have been suggested.[56] In the surviving example, the *illikā* arch as well as the pediment sculptures are missing and the lower portions of the pillars are defaced.[57] Never-the-less, this ornate *toraṇa* mirrors the high standards of craftsmanship that prevailed during the mature phase of the Caulukya rule in Gujarat. At the apex, the convolving pediment frames Nandī who supports a full-blown lotus on his back. The missing deity who would have been seated on the lotus appears to have been Śiva, as is warranted by Nandī's presence as well as the temple's dedication. The convolving pediment is bordered with a row of well-carved celestial figures.

Vadnagar: Grander in scale and magnificence are the Vadnagar *toraṇas* (Fig. 4.79; c. 1135-1140 CE), about 20 miles to the south-east of Siddhapur. Originally there were two, of which only one is upright now; the fragments of the second one lie in the vicinity (Fig. 4.38). A line drawing of the first one showcases an intact *ekādaśa-candrabhāgā* arch, which is now broken.[58] The two *toraṇas* were identical in style and size and may have belonged to a very large temple complex at one time. Their bases are of considerable dimensions, a device adopted to lend stability to the tall pillars. The decorative veneer and mouldings of the socle and pillar have been executed with great care. The socle has a simple decoration of lozenges, followed by cyma *(jāḍyakumbha)*, arris *(karṇaka)*, followed by a succession of bands bearing a series of gorgons *(grāsapaṭṭī)*, elephants *(gajapīṭha)*, and humans *(narapīṭha)*, and a *kumbhī* (high basal moulding with curved shoulder) with figures carved on it. Above this is the torus, next a 'drip' projection, and then a gorgon band. The portion above this harbours a standing figure on each face of the pillar, placed under a richly carved canopy. An octagonal band carved with figures is followed by

4.78

4.79

corbelled projections upholding maidens, of whom some have disappeared. The fluted portion *(bharaṇī)* with overhanging leaves is similar to that seen on the Siddhapur and Delmal *toraṇas*. The attic-pillars above are encircled by brackets in the shape of *vyalās* on the inner face and maidens on the other three faces. Above this, are the ribbed awning and the convolving pediment, at the centre of which is the figure of Śiva.

Asoda: Two sets of *toraṇa* pillars are found at the *pañcāyatana* temple complex at Asoda in northern Gujarat. One belongs to the main temple (Fig. 4.80) and the other to the subsidiary shrine located in the north-eastern corner. These pillars have plain bases, except for the gorgon band and niches housing figures on each face of the tall basal moulding *(kumbhī)*. The two figural courses on the shaft are similar to the ones at Modhera, though qualitatively not at par. Above this, are the typical Maru-Gurjara decorative bands, topped by a fluted section *(bharaṇī)* with overhanging leaves, and followed by projections for brackets. The overhanging leaves are absent on the fluted portions of the pillars in front of the eastern subsidiary shrine. A portion of the attic-pillar survives on the northern *toraṇa* pillar of the main shrine.

4.81

Piludra: The *toraṇa* at Piludra probably belonged to a Sun temple, as may be inferred from the images of Sūrya at the centre on the two faces of its pediment (Fig. 4.81; c. 12th century).[59] The configuration is similar to the Siddhapur and Vadnagar *toraṇas*. The arched garland is missing and the convolving pediment is damaged. The images of Sūrya have been damaged, but two lotuses in his hands are visible on the eastern face, as is the surviving lotus on the western one. The pillar mouldings below the gorgon band are plain, as is the top part of the pillar *(bharaṇī)*.

4.79 : *Uttuṅga-toraṇa (jyeṣṭha),* Vadnagar, c. 1135-1140 CE.

4.80 : *Toraṇa* pillars, Asoda, Jasmalnāthjī Mahādeo temple complex, c. second quarter of 12th century.

4.81 : *Uttuṅga-toraṇa*, Piludra, c. 12th century.

4.80

4.82 : *Uttuṅga-toraṇa*, Kapadvanj, c. 13th century.

4.83 : Pillars in front of Deogarh Temple no. 18, c. 1064 CE.

4.82

4.83

Kapadvanj: The Kapadvanj *toraṇa* in the Kheda District of Gujarat is located on the eastern side of a big tank or *kuṇḍa* (Fig. 4.82). It is adorned with the typical western Indian mouldings and motifs, but belongs to a period slightly later than those discussed earlier and is smaller than the ones at Siddhapur and Vadnagar.[60] The lower bracket figures have all disappeared but an *āndola* arch between the attic pillars is intact. The *makaras*, however, are absent. Above this is the lintel and a ribbed awning. A sinusoidal convolving pediment with inscribed figures images a dancing Śiva flanked by drummers.

4.84

Some other instances: Two well-proportioned pillars, embellished with the 'vase and foliage' *(ghaṭapallava)* motif at the bottom and vertical bands of ornamental motifs along the shaft, are placed in front of Temple no. 18 of the Jain group at Deogarh (Fig. 4.83; 1064 CE). In their upper regions, they bear seated Jina images in niches. Of the Śaśibhūṣaṇa temple example at Prabhas Patan, only the *toraṇa*-bases survive (c. 1170 CE). Likewise, only the basal mouldings (up to the elephant band, *gajapīṭha*) remain from the Navalakhā temple *toraṇa* at Ghumli in the Jamnagar District of Gujarat (Fig. 4.84; c. 1175-1200 CE). A fragment of an *illikāvalaṇa* from Somanatha Phase III is now housed in the Prabhas Patan Museum (Fig. 4.85; c. 1169 CE). Amongst others,[61] the *Uttuṅga-toraṇa* fronting the Rateśvara Mahādeva temple at Ratanpur, Panchamahal, deserves mention (Fig. 4.86; c. first quarter of 13th century). It is in a fair state of preservation although the bracket figures and the arched garland have disappeared. The *illikāvalaṇa* reveals Naṭeśa flanked by drummers and dancers.

4.85

4.86

4.84 : *Toraṇa* pillar bases, Ghumli, Navalakhā temple, c. 1175-1200 CE.

4.85 : *Illikāvalaṇa*, Somanatha Phase 3, now in Prabhas Patan Museum, c.1169 CE.

4.86 : *Uttuṅga-toraṇa*, Ratanpur, Rateśvara Mahādeva temple, c. first quarter of 13th century.

4.87

4.88

4.89

4.87 : *Uttuṅga-toraṇa*, Jaisalmer, Pārśvanātha Jinālaya, c. 1417 CE.

4.88 : *Toraṇa,* Abhapur (Polo), Śiva Pañcāyatana complex, c. third quarter of 15th century.

4.89 : *Toraṇa* pillar, Darol, Lakṣmī-Nārāyaṇa temple, c. 15th century.

There are some instances of post-13th century free-standing temple *toraṇas*. The one fronting the Pārśvanātha temple at Lodrava has been discussed earlier (Fig. 4.77). The ornate *Uttuṅga-toraṇa* in front of the Pārśvanātha temple at Jaisalmer was carved during the early 15th century when a revival in temple building activity had taken place (Fig. 4.87; c. 1417 CE). The base of this *toraṇa* is decorated with a band of half-lotuses, topped by a section decorated with half-diamonds at intervals. Above this, is the inverted cyma recta *(jāḍyakumbha)* embellished with delicate scroll-like carvings. Further upwards are the basal mouldings topped by figural and decorative courses. On each pillar, three maidens serve as bracket figures in addition to a *vyāla* bracket on its inner face. Above the shaft is the fluted part *(bharaṇī)* and pillar brackets. The attic-pillars sport maidens as bracket figures in three directions; an *āndola* arch with eight S-shaped *madalas* and seven *tilakas* is hung between these pillars. A plain crossbar under the arch seems to have been added later to lend support. The lintel above is topped by the awning *(kūṭacchādya)* and convolving pediment *(illikāvalaṇa)*. At Abhapur (Polo) in the Sabarkantha District, the pillars and a crossbar of a free-standing *toraṇa* associated with the Śiva Pañcāyatana temple survive (Fig. 4.88; c. third quarter of 15th century). Also of the same time-frame and from the same district, are the *toraṇa* pillars associated with the Lakṣmī-Nārāyaṇa temple at Darol (Fig. 4.89).

4.90

A free-standing *toraṇa* attached to the Jagat Śiromaṇi temple at Amber in the Jaipur District of Rajasthan shows an interesting mix of the Rajput-Mughal style with the earlier Maru-Gurjara style that prevailed in the region (Fig. 4.90; c. 16th century). The pillar shafts above the plain basal mouldings are divided into three sections by means of two awning *(kūṭacchādya)* courses, an adaptation also noticed on the Mānastambha at Chittor (Fig. 4.111). Drawing parallels with the typical Maru-Gurjara temple mouldings from which it is inspired, it appears as though three tiers of the wall and awning courses have been raised one above the other. The convolving pediment and arch of the earlier period are dispensed with. Over the lintel topped by the awning *(kūṭacchādya)*, a miniature Nāgara spire is placed above each pillar. A central *chatrī* of Rajput derivation, which may have housed the presiding deity of the temple, is now empty. There is a reduction in the importance given to figural sculpture. This interesting mix of influences completes the discussion on the medieval free-standing *toraṇas* of western and central India.[62]

Pratolī Toraṇas

A *pratolī* is an entrance gateway, usually at the cardinals of the ramparts of a city, fort, or citadel. The term is also applied to a gate punctuating the enclosure walls of a temple-complex or even of a well *(vāpī)*. Situated at the ramparts of a fort or a city, it includes a gate-house with towers, pillars, pilasters, lintels, doors, and latches.[63] Constructed for defence purposes, it provided selective access to a fort or a city; it also signified the honour and grandeur of the fort or city that it guarded. The inclusion of the *toraṇa* as part of the overall *pratolī* structure was an ingenious expedient by which the various purposes of the latter were integrated into a single architectural creation that was at once structurally viable, functionally apt, and aesthetically significant.

Representations of the *toraṇas* integrated with *pratolī* structures are encountered in early Indian sculpture (Figs. 1.24, 1.25) and also find mention in early texts (App. 2, no.1). During this period (c. second century BCE to third century), terms such as *dvāra-koṭṭhaka*, *gopura*, and *pratolī* appear to have been used interchangeably (see pp.1-3). Later, these acquired specialized characteristics that distinguished them from each other. The *gopuras,* for instance, became synonymous with the temple gateways of medieval South India.

As regards the medieval *pratolīs,* some of the surviving city fortifications such as those at Jhinjhuvada and Dabhoi in Gujarat (Figs. 4.91-4.94) are exemplary in the integration of their defence, symbolic, and ornamental purposes.[64] In addition to the pillars, lintel, towers, and doors that are fundamental for defence, the symbolic, aesthetic, and honorific functions of the *pratolī* are nurtured through the inclusion of *toraṇas* in its upper reaches *(pratolyagre ca toraṇam)* (App. 3, nos. 7a-b). The component elements of these *pratolī-toraṇas* were derived from the prevalent *toraṇa* repertoire. It is in the rearrangement of the parts as also in the integration of the *toraṇas* within the *pratolī* that their distinctiveness is admirably reflected.

4.90 : *Toraṇa*, Amber, Jagat Śiromaṇi temple, c. 16th century.

4.91 : *Pratolī toraṇas,* Jhinjhuvada, c. 1100-1140 CE.

4.91

4.92

4.92 : *Pratolī toraṇas,* Dabhoi, Māhūdī gate, c. 1225-1253 CE.

4.93 : *Pratolī toraṇas,* Dabhoi, c. 1225-1253 CE.

4.94 : *Pratolī toraṇa,* Dabhoi, Baroḍā gate (detail), c. 1225-1253 CE.

4.93

The ramparts encircling a medieval fort or city were constructed purposefully to have substantial width. It is only to be expected that the gate towers flanking the *pratolī* entrance were of impressive dimensions. The *pratolī* passage was thus of considerable depth and the placement of a single pair of pilasters supporting a lintel was inadequate for such a massive structure. A minimum of two pairs of pilasters topped by architraves, one facing the inner city or fort and the other facing the outer limits, were felt necessary. At Jhinjhuvada (Fig. 4.91; c. 1100-1140 CE) and Dabhoi (Figs. 4.92-4.94; c. 1225-1253 CE), one witnesses a series of pilaster pairs placed along the passage of the gatehouse. The *toraṇas* placed between each of the pilasters and the architraves generate a visually enticing and rhythmic pattern in the upper regions of the *pratolī*. Of the same time-frame as the Jhinjhuvada *pratolī-toraṇas* are those at the Sūraj gate at Mandhata in the Khandwa region of Madhya Pradesh (Fig. 4.95). In the latter, the ornamental impact of the *toraṇa* is much subdued.[65]

The instances at Jhinjhuvada and Dabhoi correspond well with the notices on *pratolī-toraṇas* made in the medieval treatises, particularly the *Jayapṛcchā* and the *Appr.* from western India. The *Jayapṛcchā*, for instance, comments that the *toraṇa* must spring from two-thirds of the total height of the pilaster.[66] The constituents of the *toraṇa* in this case include the S-shaped segment *(madala)*, the pillarette *(stambhī)*, and the horizontal salient *(nirvyūha)*

4.94

4.95 : *Pratolī toraṇas*, Mandhata, Sūraj gate, c. 12th century.

4.96 : *Pratolī toraṇas*, Gwalior Fort, Telī-kā-Mandir, (pillars, c. 10th century, rest : high medieval period).

4.97 : *Pratolī toraṇas*, Mān Mandir entranceway, c. early 16th century.

in juxtaposition, as also *makaras*.[67] Beyond textual correlation, these *pratolī-toraṇas* are also profusely sculpted. Of the four gates at Dabhoi – Baroda, Hira, Nanded, and Mahudi – the six pairs of *toraṇas* of the first gate are the most intricately carved (Fig. 4.94). The portion between the S-shaped *madalas* and the pillarettes are embellished with hybrid *gajavyālas* with riders. Images of Devīs, Bhairava, etc., are carved in the spaces between the pillarettes. The top band is carved with an armed procession of elephants and horses with riders. The imagery is well suited to the defensive role of the *pratolī*.

4.96

4.95

A series of *madalas* gradually project inwards and upwards from the pilasters on the two sides of the *pratolī* passage and leave only a narrow space to be bridged by the lintel at the top. Those of the Uparkot (old fort) *pratolī* in Junagarh almost meet at the apex and the brackets formed of a series of *madalas* create the appearance of a triangular arch.[68] This is true also of the *pratolī-toraṇa* at Telī-kā-Mandir, Gwalior Fort (Fig. 4.96). Those at the Mān Mandir are in the Rajput-Mughal style and consist of corbelled brackets adorned with decorative motifs (Fig. 4.97; c. early 16th century). In the interior of the Jahāngīrī Mahal at Agra Fort, the *madala* brackets are in a sequence of four pairs and each opposing pair almost meets at the apex, conjuring the desired impact of the *toraṇa* arches (Fig. 4.98; c. 1570 CE). In technical terms, these *pratolī-toraṇas* are actually ornamental brackets placed between the pilasters and architraves of the gatehouse.

4.97

Later Developments

In the last decade of the 13th century, with Delhi as the seat of power, a large part of northern India gradually came under the rule of the five successive Sultanates. The period also marked a turning point in the history of medieval Indian architecture. From the 14th century, Gujarat was successively ruled by the Khaljī and Tughluq governors, the Ahmed Shāhī Sultanate of Gujarat, and the Mughal governors for over four centuries. In Rajasthan, the two important principalities of Mewar and Marwar retained their independence. Three kinds of architectural enterprises are evident during these centuries: building of mosques, mausoleums, forts, and palaces patronized by the Muslim rulers; construction of forts and palaces by the Rajput rulers and their elite; and revival of temple building activity by the Jain and Brahmanical communities from the 15th century. The *toraṇas* register their presence in all these architectural creations, adapting to the shifts in creedal, functional, and social needs, and consequently in the appearance of the structures that they embellished.

The *Toraṇas* in Medieval Indo-Islamic Monuments and Secular Structures

The Sultans favoured visible architectural symbols that mirrored their theological and cultural ideology, power, and authority. In India, they saw a long-standing and rich living tradition of architecture and skilled craftsmen who could be directed to fulfil their purposes and projects. The resultant dialectic between the local building traditions and the ideals and techniques newly introduced by the patrons resulted in the emergence of new architectural forms. Our purpose here is to understand the manner in which the *toraṇa* was assimilated within this changing architectural environment.

4.98 : *Toraṇas*, Agra Fort, interior of Jahāngīrī Mahal, c. 1570 CE.

The *toraṇa* as an architectural device is not utilitarian in the same way as the pillars, ceilings, doorframes, and even lattices are to a building. Though functionally dispensable, its potential to embellish an architectural creation was well-known to the local sculptors and architects who found ingenious ways of employing it in the Indo-Islamic structures. On some early Sultanate monuments such as the façade arcade of Aḍhāi-din-kā-jhoṁprā in Ajmer (c. 1211-1236 CE) and the *mihrābs* of mosques associated with the tombs of Shamsuddin Iltutmish (c. 1234 CE) and

4.102

4.99 : Cusped arch, Sultan Gharī, *mihrāb* of mosque associated with tomb of Naseeruddin Mahmud, c. 1231 CE.

4.100 : *Mihrāb*, Patan, Gumdā Masjid, c. 14th century.

4.101 : *Illikā-toraṇas*, Bayana, Ukhā Masjid, c. 1316-1320 CE.

4.102 : *Illikā-toraṇa*, Ahmedabad, Jāmī Masjid , completed c. 1423 CE.

4.101

4.100

Naseeruddin Mahmud in Delhi (Fig. 4.99; c. 1231 CE), the cusped arches reflect the fusion of Islamic traditions with the *illikā-toraṇa*. The *mihrāb* pediments in several of the Gujarat mosques emulate the *āndola-toraṇas* or the *illikāvalaṇas* of Maru-Gurjara architecture, which are adapted to suit newer purposes by doing away with all figural embellishments and retaining only the abstract ornamental motifs drawn from the local craftsmen's repertoire (Fig. 4.100).

The free-flying *illikā-toraṇa* is also found in some mosques. The re-used ones in the interior of the Ukha Masjid at Bayana in Rajasthan are stylistically akin to those found in the 12th century temples (Fig. 4.101; c. 1316-1320 CE). In the Jāmī Masjid in Ahmedabad (Fig. 4.102; completed 1423 CE), an attenuated *illikā-toraṇa* of nine semi-circular arcs *(nava-candrabhāgā)* is delicately balanced between two frontal pillars of the mosque, in perfect alignment with the archway of the central façade. Transformed through the sculptor's creativity into an arch of fragile and emaciated beauty, it is ideally suited to the abstraction inherent in Islamic aesthetics. Such an attenuation of form is also noticed in *āndola-toraṇas* at Ranījī-kī-bāorī, Bundi (Fig. 4.103; c. 16th century). The mosque of Hilāl Khān Qāzi at Dholka (c. 1333 CE) has an engrailed arch. The *toraṇa* also recurs on some of the Rajput and Mughal architectural creations, as may be observed on the outer walls and entrances of Mān Singh's Palace, Gwalior (Fig. 4.104; c. end 15th century) and in the famous Fatehpur Sikrī complex of the Akbarī period (Fig. 4.105).

4.103

4.104

4.105

4.106

The *Toraṇas* on Later Temples

The 15th century witnessed Brahmanical and Jain revival in western India. During this period, wherever Rajput states had survived, the task of building religious establishments was resumed. Several Jain temples were built in Jaisalmer. The three *āndola-toraṇas* in the front hall *(mukhamaṇḍapa)* and eight in the *raṅgamaṇḍapa* (pillared hall) of the Pārśvanātha temple are well proportioned (Fig. 4.106). The Candraprabhā temple, with the grandest of the interiors amongst the medieval Jain temples at Jaisalmer, also has *toraṇas* (Fig. 4.107; 1453 CE) in the *meghamaṇḍapa* (hall), decorated with a band of alternating jewels and rosettes *(maṇibandha)* and a saw-tooth course. Whereas those in the Pārśvanātha temple have Jina images within niches, these are replaced by diamond motifs in the Candraprabhā temple. The decorative motifs are rendered with meticulous attention to detail and carry the stamp of woodcraft prevalent during this period. The trend is towards carefully crafted, ornate, and visually pleasing forms, which replaces the vigour and animation of the 11th-12th century *toraṇas* carved with symbolic figural motifs.

4.103 : *Āndola-toraṇas*, Bundi, Ranījī-kī-bāorī, c.16th century.

4.104 : *Āndola-toraṇas*, outer wall, Mān Singh's palace, Gwalior.

4.105 : *Āndola-toraṇas*, Fatehpur Sikrī, Astrologer's seat, pavilion, c. 1571-1575 CE.

4.106 : *Āndola-toraṇas*, Jaisalmer, Pārśvanātha temple *maṇḍapa*, c. 1417 CE.

4.107 (overleaf): *Āndola-toraṇas,* Jaisalmer, Candraprabhā temple, c.1453 CE.

4.107

4.110 : *Āndola-toraṇa*, Chittor, Kumbhaśyāma temple, entrance porch (restored), c. 15th century.

4.111 : *Āndola-toraṇas*, Chittor, Mānastambha, c. 1485 CE.

4.112 : *Āndola-toraṇas*, Sirohi, Ajitanātha temple, c. 1588 CE.

4.109

4.108 : *Āndola-toraṇas*, Ranakpur, Dharaṇavihāra, c. 15th century.

4.109 : *Āndola-toraṇas*, Dungarpur, Deo Somanāth temple, *raṅgamaṇḍapa,* c. 15th-16th century.

4.108

4.110

4.112

The Dharaṇavihāra at Ranakpur is a *sarvatobhadra* Jain temple with *raṅgamaṇḍapas* (open pillared halls) attached to the four sides of the sanctum. According to Jñyānavimala of the Tapā sect, there were 32 *toraṇas* on each of the four sides at Dharaṇavihāra.[69] The vestibule that connects the sanctum to the western *raṅgamaṇḍapa* has an *āndola-toraṇa* with ornamental motifs. The minor niches along the arch enshrine Jain deities. Figural sculpture on the attic-pillars flanking the *toraṇa* is stiff and lifeless. The *toraṇas* in this *raṅgamaṇḍapa's* western and eastern sides are intact and are made of yellow sandstone (Jaisalmer stone?), different from that used in the rest of the temple (Fig. 4.108). These *toraṇas* are stylistically akin to those seen in the Jain temples at Jaisalmer.

The *āndola-toraṇas* in the *raṅgamaṇḍapa* of the Deo Somnāth temple at Dungarpur are similar to those observed earlier at Jaisalmer and Ranakpur (Fig. 4.109; c. 15th-16th century). The Kumbhaśyāma (Fig. 4.110; restored in 15th century) and the Satbīsī (c. mid-15th century) temples at Chittor have *āndola-toraṇas* at the entrance porches; the Mānastambha at Chittor has four in the pavilion on its upper reaches (Fig. 4.111). The symmetrical and well-proportioned *naucaukī toraṇas* of the Ajitanātha temple at Sirohi (Fig. 4.112; 1588 CE) are adorned with a band of buds, an undulating floral vine, and a saw-tooth course. Jina images are inset in minor niches and parrots are placed at the intersection of successive segments.[70]

4.111

4.113 : *Āndola-toraṇa,* Dwaraka, Dwārakādhīśa temple, *raṅgamaṇḍapa*, c. 16th century.

4.114 : *Āndola-toraṇa*, Veraval, Mosque, c. 15th century.

4.115 : *Āndola-toraṇa*, Prabhas Patan, Aṣṭapada temple, c. late 16th century.

4.116 : *Āndola-toraṇa,* Porbandar, Gopāl Lāl's temple, c. 1640 CE.

4.114

The four S-shaped *madalas* interspersed with five niches on the *raṅgamaṇḍapa toraṇa* in the Dwārakādhīśa temple at Dwaraka in Saurashtra (Fig. 4.113; c. 16th century) conjure a gracefully undulating arch. It is carved with a band of pearls in the centre and two rows of saw-tooth courses on either side. The intervening niches are carved with the diamond motif. A similar 15th century instance can be seen at Veraval (now inside a mosque) (Fig. 4.114). The well-crafted sanctum *toraṇa* belonging to the Aṣṭapada temple at Prabhas Patan (Fig. 4.115; c. late 16th century) is punctuated with three niches, each adorned with three diamond motifs. The *toraṇa* in the *raṅgamaṇḍapa* of Gopāl Lāl's temple at Porbandar is embellished with a creeper between two rows of the saw-tooth pattern on either side (Fig. 4.116; c. 1640 CE). The niches are placed along the crests of this undulating arch in a manner reminiscent of the *āndola-toraṇas* in the open hall of the Sun temple at Modhera. The Garuḍa *maṇḍapikā* (hall) of the Jagat Śiromaṇi temple at Amber in Rajasthan is adorned with sinusoidal *hasti-toraṇas* (Fig. 4.117; c. 16th century). Their form, proportion, balance, and craftsmanship are of admirable standards.

4.113

4.115

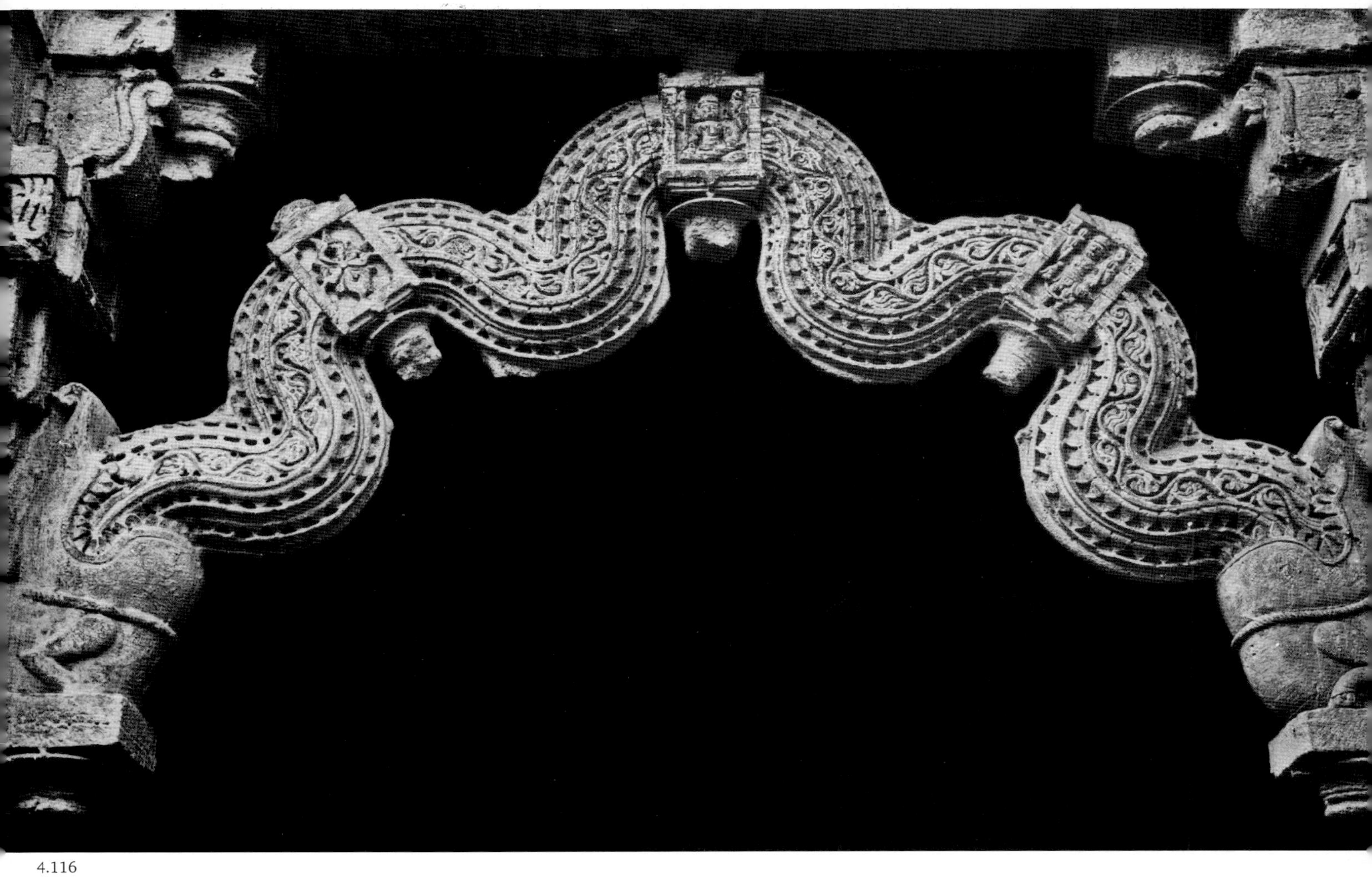

4.116

4.117

4.117 (previous page): *Āndola-toraṇa (hasti),* Amber, Jagat Śiromaṇi temple, c. 16th century.

4.118 : *Āndola toraṇa*, Shatrunjaya, Śreyaṁsanātha temple, c. 1324-1325 CE.

4.119 : *Āndola-toraṇa* within engaged *illikā* arch, Shatrunjaya, Ādīśvara ṭuk, c. 1585 CE.

4.118

4.119

The temples at Shatrunjaya can boast of some of the finest *toraṇas* belonging to the late medieval period. An *āndola-toraṇa* adorns the entrance to the Śreyaṁsanātha temple on the northern peak (Fig. 4.118). The intervening niches are adorned with diamonds and half-diamonds. The motif of the parrot with neck strained backwards is seen near the niches on the upper margins of the arch. At Shatrunjaya, the *āndola-toraṇa* is also placed under a cusped arch,[71] as for instance at the Ādīśvara ṭuk on the southern peak (Fig. 4.119; c. 1585 CE).[72] A creeper pattern edged by saw-tooth courses and a row of buds fill the space between niches adorned with diamonds and half-diamonds. A similar instance may be seen in the Sammeta Śikhara temple (Fig. 4.120; c. early 17th century). The façade of the temple of Ratan Chand Ghūs in Modī's ṭuk is adorned with three *āndola-toraṇas* (Fig. 4.121; c. 19th century).

4.121

4.120 : *Āndola-toraṇa* within engaged *illikā* arch, Shatrunjaya, Sammeta Śikhara temple, c. early 17th century.

4.121 : *Āndola-toraṇas*, Shatrunjaya, Modī's tuk, temple of Ratan Chand Ghūs, c. 19th century.

.120

4.122

The late 19th-early 20th century instances at Mundra (Śītalānātha, 1860 CE; Amijherā Pārśvanātha, 1901 CE) in the Kutch region of Gujarat are well-proportioned but the decorative patterns and the figural sculpture are lack-lustre. However, the *āndola-toraṇa* under a cusped arch in the Śāntinātha temple at Kothara, also in the Kutch region, is refreshingly well-executed with intricate patterns carved on it (Fig. 4.122; 1862 CE). Only the stiff figural sculpture surrounding it makes evident the exhaustion of vitality in the overall arrangement. Even so, until the 20th century, the tradition continued to reappear with renewed vigour, as is testified by the exquisite *āndola-toraṇa* in Mahātmā Gāndhī's Kīrttimandira at Porbandar, and in the porches of the many Jain and Swāmīnārāyaṇa temples in Gujarat, built after independence.

Later *Illikā-toraṇas*

Great favour was accorded to the *illikā-toraṇa* during the 11th and 12th centuries, which witnessed its best examples at Modhera, Siddhapur, Vadnagar, and Delmal. From the 13th century, there are but only sporadic representations of this variety. The *illikā-toraṇa* of seven arcs on the northern side of the *raṅgamaṇḍapa* of Lūṇa Vasahī at Mount Abu is adorned with non-traditional floral motifs, similar to the cusped ceiling courses (Fig. 4.58, rear; c. 1232-1240 CE). Three sides of the entrance hall of the Pārśvanātha Jain temple at Varkana in the Mewar region are graced with *illikā-toraṇas* (Fig. 4.123; c. 15th-16th century) composed of nine arcs and emerging from the mouths of hybrid elephantine creatures. The outer margin of the arch has a saw-tooth course

4.122 : *Āndola-toraṇa* within engaged *illikā* arch, Kothara, Śāntinātha temple, c. 1862 CE.

4.123 : *Illikā-toraṇa*, Varkana, Pārśvanātha Jinālaya, c. 15th-16th century.

4.12

followed by two decorative bands. Underneath each arc is an ornamental leaf-like motif. Gradually receding in significance,[73] the *illikā toraṇa* nevertheless makes a lasting contribution to the secular as well as religious architecture of western and central India. The famous and prolific cusped arches seen in the palatial homes of the rich, in mosques, in Rajput and Mughal forts and palaces, and in the Kṛṣṇa temples of the Vallabha Sampradāya, are composite adaptations of *illikā-toraṇas* of western India and the cusped arches of Islamic affiliation. In its new incarnation as an engaged cusped arch, the *illikā-toraṇa* reappears in many of the late medieval monuments (Fig. 4.124).

4.124 : Engaged cusped arches, Bhuj, Chatrī no.1, interior, c. late 19th century.

4.124

Eastern Indian Representations

Quite distinct from the western, central, and southern Indian regions, free-standing *toraṇas* were hardly part of the standard architectural repertoire in eastern India, although engaged *toraṇa* forms were relatively more frequent. Even so, eastern Indian *toraṇa* representations in sculpture and in manuscript paintings have had an appreciable impact on the development of the *toraṇa* motif in other South and Southeast Asian regions. For this reason, the last mentioned examples would be considered along with a discussion on Southeast Asian parallels in the next chapter.

4.125

4.125 : *Torana,* Mahābodhi temple, Bodhgaya, c. 770-810 CE.

Free-standing Instances

The early appearance of this architectural member at Sarnath, Chandraketugarh, Tamluk, and Kumrahar has been discussed earlier (Chapter 1). Separated in time from these instances by about six centuries, is the plain but imposing granite *toraṇa* located to the east of the Mahābodhi temple at Bodhgaya (Fig. 4.125). It has been assigned to the time of the Pāla king, Dharmapāla (c. 770-810 CE).[74] In the Kumrahar terracotta plaque (c. second-third century), a *toraṇa* is placed in front of a towered temple, which is similar in appearance to that in the reconstructed Mahābodhi temple.

The Mahābodhi *toraṇa* as it is seen today consists of a lintel supported on two pillars of square and octagonal cross-sections, topped by a circular vase *(ghaṭa)*. The southern pillar is relatively better preserved than the northern one. The upper part of the square section of the former bears the 'gorgon and bell' *(grāsakiṅkiṇikā)* ornament, and half-medallions inset with Kubera, *dharmacakra* with deer, and a hybrid dolphin-elephant creature *(karimakara)*. The succeeding sections bear the 'gorgon and bell' band and half and full lotuses. Next, is the gorgon face with vegetal forms. Above this are the vase portion, abacus, and corbels. The lintel placed over the pillars is carved with five trifoliate dormer patterns *(śūrasenakas)* of which the central one and those at the ends are embellished with *stūpas* in the dormer cavity. This *toraṇa* is a rare free-standing example from eastern India.

4.126

A remarkable instance of a free-standing *toraṇa* from Orissa fronts the entrance to the Mukteśvara temple (c. 950 CE) in Bhubaneshvara.[75] It is quite distinct in conception and form from any seen so far (Figs. 4.126, 4.127).[76] Placed before the entrance to the temple enclosure, it stands on a low platform. Two squat pillars of substantial cross-section support a semi-circular arch.[77] The square bases of the pillars bear shrines on all faces except the inner one. The shrines house a female figure flanked by outward-facing rampant lions. 'Lion on elephant' motifs *(gajakrānta-siṁhas)* are depicted at the four upper corners of the square base. The 16-sided shafts have shallow flutes and their upper regions are carved with a 'gorgon and bell' *(grāsakiṅkiṇikā)* band, followed by a thin floral scroll *(vasantapaṭṭī)*. Above this is a compressed shoulder portion from which project four elaborately carved hemispherical bracket-bases, which plausibly supported maidens *(kumārikās)*. This is surmounted by the ribbed member *(āmalaka)*, lotus, *hīraka*-roll, and the dish-shaped *(pāli)* echinus *(maṇḍi)*.[78] In the cardinal directions, it has mortises to accommodate the tenons meant to hold the bracket figures. Above this springs the generously proportioned semi-circular arch with a meandering scroll *(vasantapaṭṭī)*, an ornate frame with dormer motifs *(mukhapaṭṭī)*, and a floral band *(puṣpapaṭṭī)*. The *mukhapaṭṭī* terminates in chamfered mouldings *(khura-kumbha)* at the two ends; it is embellished with figural sculpture within dormer motifs and reclining maidens *(kumārikās)* appropriately placed along the curve of the arch. The upper margin of the arch is adorned with an exquisite vine creeper *(kalpavallī)*. A vase *(kalaśa)* is placed at the apex. At the lateral ends of the arch are outward-facing *makaras*, typical of the *toraṇa* representations from this region.

4.126 : *Toraṇa,* Bhubaneshvara, Mukteśvara temple, c. 950 CE.

4.127 : *Toraṇa,* Bhubaneshvara, Muktеśvara temple, c. 950 CE.

4.128: *Bhadragavākṣa* framed by *toraṇabandha*, Beyalisbati, Gaṅgeśvarī temple, *jagamohana*, north wall detail, c. second half of 13th century.

Another surviving free-standing *toraṇa* from Bhubaneshvara, situated just south of the Vaitāl Deul, is of relatively later date.[79] In form, it follows the Mukteśvara *toraṇa*, but the surmounting arch is cusped and has a pair of *nāgas* carved at the base, with their intertwined tails forming a border. Donaldson has suggested that the Mukteśvara *toraṇa* as well as the one near the Vaitāl Deul, may have served as *hiṇḍola-*

4.127

4.128

toraṇas for swinging the divine image during the *ḍolā-yātrā* ceremony. However, this had been disregarded on the ground that this ceremony was observed by the Vaiṣṇavas and not Śaivas.[80] Though such a ceremony was prevalent in Orissa, it was observed on portable wooden *toraṇas,* which were better suited to *ḍolā yātrās*.[81]

A *toraṇa* made of black stone, dated to the 11th-12th century, is now in the collection of the BM, London.[82] According to tradition, divine images were initially swung from a *toraṇa* in the Jagannātha temple compound at a site to the south-east of the temple (outside the enclosure), but after the frame broke down in the 16th century, the site was changed to the north-east corner where a *toraṇa* was erected on a stone platform.[83] Fragments of *toraṇas* have also been noticed at Ganeshvarpur, Madhava, Sadansa, and in the Yameshvara compound, as well as those framing the doors of the Birañcī Nārāyaṇa temple at Palia, all of which are later in time.[84]

Engaged *Toraṇas* on Temple Walls

The *toraṇas* engaged to wall surfaces are seen on Orissan temples. Those on the central offsets of the Gaṅgeśvarī temple at Beyalisbati are well-preserved (Figs. 4.128-4.130; c. 1260 CE). Their basic form, with a trefoil arch, is an elaboration of the Mukteśvara free-standing instance; it is similar to the one in the BM collection,[85] as also to those depicted as image-frames *(parikara-toraṇas)* and for the purpose of the swing festivals, as seen in medieval sculptures and paintings from the region. A triangular multi-cusped arch is also placed within the sanctum of the Gaṅgeśvarī temple at Beyalisbati (Fig. 4.131).

4.130

4.129

4.131

4.129 and 4.130 : *Bhadragavākṣa* framed by *toraṇabandha*, Beyalisbati, Gaṅgeśvarī temple, *jagamohana*, north wall detail, c. second half of 13th century.

4.131 : *Toraṇa* inside *garbhagṛha*, Beyalisbati, Gaṅgeśvarī temple.

4.133

4.132 : King Narasiṁhadeva on *hiṇḍola-toraṇa*, Surya Deul, Konark, now in NM, New Delhi.

4.133 : Architectural drawing of a *toraṇa* for *ḍolā-yātrā*, painted c. 1816-1822 CE, VAM, London.

4.132

Depictions in Sculpture and Painting

A sculpture of King Narasiṁhadeva I of the Gaṅgā dynasty swinging on a *hiṇḍola-toraṇa*, originally from the Sūrya Deul at Konark and now housed in the NM, New Delhi, is of significance (Fig. 4.132). A *ḍolā yātrā* scene is recorded in an early 19th century drawing, now preserved in the VAM, London. It shows a *hiṇḍola-toraṇa* with Vaiṣṇava deities swinging on a throne suspended from the arch by chains (Fig. 4.133).[86] The *vajra mastaka* ornament with a *kīrttimukha* at the apex and *makaras* at the lateral ends seen on Orissan temples also bears affinities to the *toraṇa* form.

Later Examples from West Bengal

Representations of the *toraṇa* can be noticed at the Adinā Mosque (Fig. 4.134; c. 1364-1374 CE) near Malda in West Bengal. The form is trifoliate and engaged, as has also been observed in the Orissan examples. The symbolic motif of the *kīrttimukha* at the apex has transformed into an ornate abstraction here. The arch rests on tapering *ghaṭapallava* pilasters and is made up of an inner band of rosettes and diamonds bordered by a leafy scroll. This engaged arch is placed in front of a miniature five-storied tiered pyramidal shrine structure. Such trifoliate *toraṇas,* oft noticed in eastern Indian sculpture, are also at times seen as image-frames for deities placed on the temple door-lintels. One such example, a 12th century lintel from Gaur in West Bengal, has Brahmā at the centre and is presently located at the Indian Museum in Kolkata (Fig. 4.135).

4.134

4.134 Engaged trifoliate *toraṇa*, Adinā Mosque (near Malda), West Bengal, c. 1364-1374 CE.

4.135 *Toraṇas* framing deities on a lintel, Gaur, West Bengal, c. 12th century, now in Indian Museum, Kolkata.

4.135

The grave of Major General Charles Stuart (Hindu Stuart; 1758-1828 CE) at the cemetery on Park Street in Kolkata is graced with a trifoliate *toraṇa*, providing us with a rare example from the 19th-20th century in which this architectural member is employed as a memorial to the dead (Fig. 4.136). However, we have several examples of *toraṇas* employed in the context of *stūpas* from the ancient period, which are known to have housed relics. In the Park Street example, a lotus is placed at the vertex of the arch. The presence of ghoulish skeletal figures at the sides is appropriate to its specific setting.

The *toraṇa* forms depicted in eastern Indian art and architecture have had an impact on affiliated forms seen in some South and Southeast Asian regions.

4.136

4.136 : Engaged trifoliate *toraṇa*, Grave of Major General Charles (Hindu) Stuart, Park Street Cemetery, Kolkata, c. 19th century.

Notes and References

[1] Western India in this case includes Gujarat and Rajasthan, but not Maharashtra and Karnataka, which have been covered under southern India. Central India includes Madhya Pradesh, Chattisgarh, and Uttar Pradesh.

[2] This photograph was kindly provided by Dr. A.K. Sharma, former Superintending Archaeologist, ASI, in charge of excavations at Sirpur and Mansar.

[3] The image and the *toraṇa* are now embedded in the 15th century gatehouse at this site.

[4] *EITA,* Vol. II, Part 2, *Text,* pp.284-285.

[5] State Museum No. 319, 0.45 x 0.40 m.

[6] The *toraṇas* carved on the sanctum door-lintel and the over-door of the seventh century Kālikāmātā temple at Chittorgarh are early precedents, which in turn have affinities with those in the Deccan.

[7] See Chapter 2. As per Dravidian textual terminology, it is a *citra-toraṇa*.

[8] Also from Kiradu and now in the Rājakīya Sangrahālaya at Mandor, is a fragment of a *parikara-toraṇa* (c. late 10th century), which is stylistically similar to those in the Viṣṇu temple, Kiradu.

[9] Other *toraṇa* fragments from Gurgi belong to the latter half of the 10th century. See *EITA,* Vol. II, Part 3, pp.36-41 and 53-54.

[10] The fragments may belong to two different *toraṇas* because one has a flame-like ornament in the top-most register whereas the other two show an array of figures. A fragment of a *parikara-illikā-toraṇa* of six loops, seemingly of a slightly later period, was also recovered from this site and is now housed in the Allahabad Museum.

[11] This is barely noticed because of the wired mesh placed before it.

[12] The famous Viśvanātha temple at this site once had a *toraṇa* in its *gūḍhamaṇḍapa* of which only the springers of the arch are in evidence now. Fragments of a *toraṇa* found from this site and now in the site museum reveal exquisitely carved *makaras*. The *parikara-toraṇas* in the sanctum of the Lakṣmaṇa and Jawārī temples are noteworthy.

[13] IM 1916.53-55, VAM, London.

[14] These fragments are part of a larger group gifted by Sir Bartle Frere to the Architectural Association, London, who presented them to the VAM, London, in 1916.

[15] Several other pieces belonging to this group of architectural fragments in the VAM, London, which I photographed and measured, enrich this argument.

[16] VAM, IM 1916.56 & 57. See also Shah, "Some Medieval Sculptures from Gujarat and Rajasthan," plate XXXI, Fig.4.

[17] *Candra-bhāgā* literally means part of the moon, referring to the crescent-shaped segment.

[18] Dhaky, "The Date of the Dancing Hall of the Sun Temple at Moḍherā," pp.211-222.

[19] *Ibid.*

[20] Burgess and Cousens, *Architectural Antiquities of Northern Gujarat.*, Plate XLIV, 2.

[21] *Ibid.* Plates LVII, LIX.

[22] Dhāṅkī (Dhaky), *Mahātīrtha Ujjayantagiri (Girnār tīrtha).*

[23] On the basis of the date recorded on the main deity's pedestal. See Dhaky and Moorti, *The Temples in Kumbhāriyā,* p.24.

[24] The *makaras* from the Deogarh *toraṇa* fragments are comparable to those found at Khajuraho, which are now in the Sri Sadu Shanti Prasad Jain Art Museum, Khajuraho (K 1186 & K 121).

[25] Indian Museum, Kolkata, A 24178/6951, 0.535 x 1.150m, c. 11th century, sandstone.

[26] Another fragment of the same period, belonging to Chandpur in Uttar Pradesh, is housed in the Rani Lakshmibai Palace Collecion in Jhansi (Number 421, 0.580 x 0.405 m, buff sandstone). It depicts a *makara* attached dorsally to an elephant.

[27] Dhaky and Moorti, *The Temples in Kumbhāriyā,* p.59.

[28] This variety of *āndola-toraṇa* was also prevalent during the 15th century with the difference that figural sculpture was replaced by ornamental patterns.

[29] *Ibid.* pp.62-63.

[30] Bhandarkar, *Progress Report of the Archaeological Survey of India, Western Circle.,* pp.40-46. Originally there were four *toraṇas* in the *raṅgamaṇḍapa*.

[31] Dhaky and Moorti, *The Temples in Kumbhāriyā,* p.90; ".. one connected with the Mahāvīra temple, the other originally before the cult image in the main sanctuary in Pārśvanātha, two more also installed in the *devakulikās* of the Pārśvanātha temple, and an

instance that was connected with one of the three very large images, either in the main sanctuary (Neminātha) or in one of the two *bhadraprāsādas* but discarded and removed to the backyard."

[32] Cousens, *The Architectural Antiquities of Western India,* p.37.

[33] In the last quarter of the 12th century, the invasions of Muiz-ud-dīn of Ghazni (c. 1178 CE) and Qutb-ud-dīn, the general of Muhammad Ghorī (1195 & 1197 CE), had shaken Caulukya authority. At about this time, Malava was also wrested from Gujarat by the Paramārs. The kingdom was divided among powerful provincial governors and ministers. The Vāghelās, who had earlier won the favour of Kumārapāla in fighting the chiefs of Mewar and Chandravati, rose to prominence.

[34] Dhāṅkī (Dhaky), *Kalādhām Delvāḍā,* p.21.

[35] The Candraprabhā temple at Prabhas Patan (1610 CE) also has faint echoes of the serpentine *toraṇa*. See Dhāṅkī (Dhaky), *"Gujarāt nī toraṇa samṛddhi,"* pp.298-308.

[36] *"Toraṇaṁ bhajyate ced tad rāṣṭra bhaṅgaṁ vinirdiśet."* App.3, no. 5.

[37] The *toraṇas* used to suspend swings that carry the image of a deity or a king.

[38] The *toraṇas* acting as scales to weigh an equivalent amount of grain or gold against the king's weight for distribution to the subjects.

[39] The *toraṇa* had collapsed sometime in 1971. See *EITA* Vol. II, Part 3, pp.27-29.

[40] *Ibid.* There may have been two more tiers topped by a bell, *āmalaka,* and vase.

[41] Most of these images are damaged, but two figures on the right pillar give the impression of being *vasus*. It is possible that the eight *vasus* were depicted, one on each of the eight facets of the pillar's base.

[42] *EITA* Vol. II, Part 3, pp.53-54.

[43] The organization of ornament on the pillars, some details of the motifs, as well as the half-diamond and bud courses on the surviving portions of the Medta-Phalodi arch bear affiliations with corresponding members of the Harṣatamātā temple at Abaneri. See also *EITA,* Vol. II, Part 2, pp.268-269.

[44] Meister suggests that judging by the presence of *ṛṣis*, the deity may have been Lakulīśa.

[45] Tripathi, *The Temples of Baroli,* p.43.

[46] *Ibid.,* pp.93-94, for a detailed description of the figures.

[47] A likely cause for this could be that very few temples prior to the eighth century survive in northern and central Gujarat. A *toraṇa* associated with the Roda temple complex and placed in front of the Sūrya temple, has been reported. See Dhāṅkī (Dhaky), *"Gujarāt nī toraṇa samṛddhi,"* pp.298-308. However, most of the available ancient free-standing *toraṇas* belong to the Central Indian belt, as is exemplified by sites such as Bharhut, Sanchi, Pawaya, and Eran. Rajasthan is next in the list with the Nagari *toraṇa* (Chapter 1).

[48] Dhaky, "Some Early Jaina Temples in Western India", *Shri Mahāvīra Jaina Vidyālaya...,* pp.312-318 & Fig.4, where he describes the *toraṇa* and provides a photograph with the intact pillars and an added pediment, located before the temple. Handa reports the collapsed *toraṇa*. See Handa, *Osian: History, Archaeology...,* pp.42-47.

[49] Dhaky. "Some Early Jaina Temples in Western India," p.318: "*mahāpīṭha* of the traditional western Indian sequence of mouldings current during the medieval period... after the *bhitta*, the *chajjikā* (rooflet), *jāḍyakumbha* (inverted cyma recta), once more a *chajjikā*, followed by a *grāsapaṭṭikā, gajapīṭha,* and *narapīṭha.* The *kumbha* of the *kumbhikā* of the shaft shows seated and niched Jina figures on all [of] its four faces."

[50] The *toraṇa* pillars are placed extremely close to the *raṅgamaṇḍapa* due to shortage of space. This occurred because the *raṅgamaṇḍapa* and the *toraṇa* were not part of the first phase of construction. See Dhaky, "The Date of the Dancing Hall of the Sun Temple at Moḍherā," pp.211-222.

[51] Lobo, *The Sun Temple at Modhera,* p.47.

[52] Prepared by Mrs. Hunter-Blair and reproduced by Burgess and Cousens for the ASI. See Burgess and Cousens, *Architectural Antiquities of Northern Gujarat,* pp.96-99, Plate IX.

[53] The base mouldings include the *jāḍyakumbha, karṇaka, antarapaṭṭa, chādyakī, grāsapaṭṭī, gajapīṭha,* and *narapīṭha.* The *kumbhaka* above it is faced with images in niches on the four sides; the pillar shaft transforms from an 8- to a 16- and then a 32-sided column, and shows three rows of figural sculpture. Above this is the leaf-course with four projections meant to hold bracket figures. This is topped by bands of celestials and jewels, above which the pillar is broken.

[54] Burgess and Cousens, *Architectural Antiquities of Northern Gujarat,* pp.96-99 and Fig. 9.

[55] *Toraṇas* have been classified on the basis of their size and proportions as *uttama* or *jyeṣṭha* (big), *madhyama* (medium), and *kaniṣṭha* (small).

[56] In the mid-19th century, Kinloch Forbes made a drawing of one of these, then intact. Burgess and Cousens, *Architectural...,* p.67 & Plate XLIV, 2.

[57] *Ibid;* p.67. The height of the *toraṇa* from the ground to the architrave is noted as 24 ft. and the pediment rose 8 ft. above this, making a total height of 32 ft.

[58] *Ibid.* Plate LIX. Also see pp.82-86, where a photograph of both the intact *toraṇas* is reproduced. In 1903, the second *toraṇa* (which has now collapsed) was reported to have been in a fragile state of preservation. The height of the better preserved one is 35 ft. 6 inches.

[59] See also Sankalia, *Archaeology of Gujarat (including Kathiawar)*, p.99 ff.

[60] Burgess and Cousens, *Architectural...,* p.85. This *toraṇa* is reported as being 23 ft. high.

[61] A plain *toraṇa* fronting the Dakṣiṇa Pārśvanātha temple at Chittorgarh has a sinusoidal arch of the late medieval period. A free-standing *toraṇa* is attached to the mid-15th century Sās (Cārbhujā) temple in Chittorgarh. At Arthuna in the Banswara District, a *toraṇa* pillar associated with Śiva temple 1 (c. early 12th century) was found.

[62] See Dhāṅkī (Dhaky), "*Gujarāt nī toraṇa samṛddhi,*" pp.298-308. Dhaky mentions some free-standing *toraṇas,* which are no longer extant. Some others are in a fragmentary state now. One belonging to the period of Karṇadeva existed in front of the huge well erected by Rājamātā Udayamitā at Anhilvad Patan. Another was located in front of the Sūrya temple at Roda from where fragments of the pillars and the *illikāvalaṇa* were found later. A few *toraṇas* were erected at Prabhas during the 12th century. One was constructed in 1169 CE in front of the northern door of the *gūḍhamaṇḍapa* of the temple at Somanath. A fragment of the same is now in the Prabhas Patan Museum (Fig. 4.85). Another existed in front of Śaśibhūṣaṇa Śiva temple at Prabhas. Of the same period are two *toraṇa* pillars in the Liwān of the Jāmā Masjid at Prabhas. At Ghumli, there was a *toraṇa* on the platform of the Navalakhā temple, and yet another in front of a smaller Śiva temple, of which the pillars along with the base are in the Watson Museum at Rajkot. On the Shatrunjaya hills, minister Vāstupāla had erected a Lakṣmī-*toraṇa* in front of the great temple of Ādinātha, before 1232 CE.

[63] *See* Dhaky and Sompura, *Bhāratīya Durga Vidhāna,* for an account of *pratolīs* in medieval western Indian fortifications.

[64] *Pratolīs* at the fortifications in the erstwhile capital of the Caulukyas at Anhilvada Patan, presumably would have been the grandest of all, but unfortunately none survive.

[65] Although the most mature instances belong to Gujarat, the early development of this feature may be observed in Rajasthan. A damaged early precedent can be seen in the interior of the well *(vāpī)* (c. second half of the ninth century) near the Harṣanātha temple at Harsha in the Jetaran region in Marwar. Another early instance of a *vāpī-pratolī-toraṇa* from Rajasthan belongs to the Lahiṇi *vāpī* at Vasantgarh in the Abu region (c. 960 CE).

[66] At Jhinjhuvada, the *toraṇas* spring from two-thirds the total height of the pilasters; at Dabhoi, they spring from about half the total height of the pilasters. For an analysis and correlation of textual types with archaeological representations, see Dhaky and Sompura, *Bhāratīya Durga Vidhāna,* Fig. 7; pp.18-22 and 63-66.

[67] *Ibid.* The pillarette *(stambhī)* comprises *kumbhī, bharaṇa, ghaṭapallava, hīragrahaṇa,* and *śīrṣa.*

[68] Sankalia, *The Archaeology of Gujarat,* p.68.

[69] Dhāṅkī (Dhaky), *Tribhuvana Tilaka Śrī Rāṇakpur Tīrtha*, p.5. While this is most likely a poetic exaggeration, it speaks of the grandeur of Dharaṇavihāra.

[70] The *āndola-toraṇas* between the pillars of the north and south *bhadraprāsāda* of the Ādīśvara temple at Sirohi (1665 CE) are similar to the *toraṇas* in the Ajitanātha temple.

[71] This was very popular in the palatial houses of the rich of the period.

[72] The different portions of the Ādinātha temple in Ādīśvara ṭuk belong to different time periods. In 1585, the *gūḍhamaṇḍapa caukīs* and *śikhara* were redone by Tejaḥpāla Sonī from Khambat.

[73] A late example of the *illikā-toraṇa* can be seen in the *balāṇaka* of the Svamīnārāyaṇa temple (c. 19th century) at Ahmedabad. The front hall of the Śāntinātha temple at Kothara (1862 CE) is embellished with an ornate and well-crafted *illikā-toraṇa* emerging from the mouths of *ihamṛgas*. The principal decorative motif is an undulating creeper.

[74] Asher, *The Art of Eastern India,* and *EITA* Vol. II, Part 2, Text, pp.400-401.

[75] Panigrahi has mentioned *toraṇa* fragments found in the paddy fields near the Brahmeśvara temple, which were earlier than the one at Mukteśvara. See Panigrahi, *Archaeological Remains at Bhubaneswar,* p.89.

[76] Donaldson and Dhaky have both described this *toraṇa*. Donaldson, *Hindu Temple Art of Orissa,* Vol. I, pp.307-308; *EITA* Vol II, Part 3, pp.389-391.

[77] The dimensions as mentioned in *EITA* Vol. II, Part 3, are over 2 ft. 6 inches square at the base, and about 8 ft. 10 inches high. See pp.389-397.

[78] See *EITA* Vol. II, Part 3, pp.389-391. Dhaky further mentions that the *pāli* form with the very prominent *hīraka* ending is a feature perhaps borrowed from Tamilnadu where it was common in the Pallava period.

[79] Donaldson, *Hindu Temple Art of Orissa,* Vol. II, pp.833-834.

[80] Srivastava, "*Toraṇa* in Art and Architecture of Orissa," in Das, Tripathy and Rath eds., *Kṛṣṇa Pratibha: Studies in Indology.,* pp.83-88.

[81] Donaldson, *Hindu Temple Art of Orissa,* Vol. II, pp.833-834.

[82] BM No. OA 1872.7-1.72.

[83] Donaldson, *Hindu Temple Art of Orissa,* Vol. II, pp.833-834. Panigrahi has reported that the interior of the *naṭamandira* of the Liṅgarāja temple had arrangements made for the swing festival, but the practice was discontinued. See Panigrahi, *Archaeological Remains at Bhubaneswar,* p.258.

[84] *Ibid.*

[85] See Endnote 82.

[86] VAM, London, Accession No. IM 194-1920. The entry register reads as follows: "Architectural Drawing executed in watercolours and Indian ink on paper. A page from a large portfolio of drawings of Indian buildings prepared by native draughtsmen from Delhi in the Office of the East India Company's Superintendent, Col. Pownoll Phipps, K.C., the father of the donor, between the years 1816-1822. H. 20 1/8 in., W. 17 3/8 in. Given by Col. Ramsay W. Phipps, (late RA)." It is further mentioned that such rituals were part of the *Holī* festival in the month of *Phālguna* (Feb.-March).

CHAPTER 5

Southeast and South Asian Parallels

Cambodia, Thailand, Champa, Indonesia, Myanmar, Nepal, and Sri Lanka

5.48

Together with India, in other South and Southeast Asian regions too, the intent and form of the *toraṇa* find parallel expressions. A range of novel forms that bear kinship with the Indian representations are noticed in these parts. It is hence of value to expand the orbit of enquiry to understand the presence of this architectural member in regions beyond India.

Terminological Concerns

Several architectural terms that were used in ancient and medieval India are encountered in Southeast and South Asian inscriptions. Inscriptions written in Sanskrit as well as Old Javanese languages record their usage in Indonesia.[1] The term *toraṇa*, for instance, is employed to describe a golden, gem-studded arch in an Indonesian inscription (App. 1, no. 27). The Tanjore inscription of Rajendra Coḷa refers to his conquest of Śrīviṣaya (Śrīvijaya) and alludes to the capture of the *vidyādhara-toraṇa* at the "war-gate" of the enemy (App. 1, no. 15). In Nepal and Sri Lanka, inscriptions and living traditions indicate that the same term is also in use locally to describe this architectural feature in these regions (App. 1, no.s 28-30).

Unlike India, treatises specific to Southeast Asian architecture are unavailable and the prospect of a codified terminology or structured architectural vocabulary specific to Southeast Asian monuments awaits further research. What is encountered so far are some substitute terms for the parts of a building, employed in the local language. As an intermediate solution, a suitable vocabulary may be derived from the architectural treatises belonging to the Indian tradition, with which Southeast Asian monuments bear allegiance, as European terminology is often inadequate in qualifying the subtler details of their intent and form. In the present case, for instance, the *toraṇa* is represented on different architectural members such as lintels, pillars, walls, and niches, but is not in itself a lintel, or by analogy, a pillar, a wall, or a niche, by virtue of its presence on these parts of a structure. The term *toraṇa* is far more apt than the French term *linteau* (lintel) employed by scholars researching on Cambodian structures. Far from being a mere nomenclatural obligation, the usage of appropriate terminology places the architectural member in its specific cultural context and architectural setting. Thus, it is the *dvāra-toraṇa* that finds its specific cultural expression on the Cambodian door-lintels, while the lintel or *linteau* as an architectural construct is quite independent of the presence or absence of the *toraṇa*.

Cambodia

Cambodia registers the most numerous and varied forms of *toraṇas* outside of India. The earliest examples are from about the late sixth or early seventh century.[2] Those of the pre-Angkorian period bear kinship with Indian counterparts of the fifth century and later. The *toraṇa* is found on the door-lintels *(dvāra-toraṇas)* and also in a miniature version, framing niches or miniature shrines on the walls *(parikara-* or *kuḍya-toraṇas)* of temples, a feature in common with Dravidian temples. Some motifs on the *toraṇas* bear allegiance to those seen in eastern India.

French scholars have, over the past several decades, systematically researched the formal progression of Cambodian lintels by splitting the "complex motif" of the *linteau* (here, *toraṇa*) into constituent parts (extremities, arch, areas above and below the arch, etc.).[3] Drawing from this corpus of material on Cambodian lintels and relating it to Indian *toraṇas*, it is now possible to attempt a meaningful comparative analysis. Our discussion focuses on the pre-Angkorian period, as parallels with Indian counterparts are more marked during this period. The reign of Jayavarman II in 802 CE sets the upper limit. A few representative examples have also been selected to indicate the general trends after 802 CE. These later examples serve to underline the individualistic expressions in Cambodia and also to illustrate parallels with some of the Later Cālukyan, Hoysaḷa, and Kākatīya *toraṇas* from India.

D.14

D.13 : *Toraṇa*,
Sambor Prei Kuk (SPK), S 7,
c. first half of seventh century.

D.14 : *Toraṇa*, Prei Kmeng (PK),
PK style, c. seventh century.

D.13

A brief historiographical sketch of the research undertaken by the French on the pre-Angkorian Cambodian lintels *(toraṇas)* may help to register the major trends. Lunet de Lajonquiere[4] isolated two varieties and grouped these into preliminary formalistic types without reference to their chronology. He categorized the lintels with *makaras* at the extremities and a central arched band bearing three medallions with figures as 'Type I'. 'Type II' included lintels of similar disposition but the *makaras* were replaced by vegetation and the medallions were often bereft of figures. His other classifications included lintels with scenic depictions or narratives and lintels made completely of vegetal scrolls.

H. Parmentier,[5] for the first time, characterized and dated what is now known as 'Pre-Angkorian art.' He extended Lajonquiere's classification by adding a new category called 'II intermediate,' in which the arc is replaced by a vegetal scroll. This category came close to Lajonquiere's 'lintels made of vegetal scrolls.' Parmentier was the first to formulate a theory of the decorative evolution of Pre-Angkorian lintels in a chronological perspective. G. de Coral Remusat[6] and Phillipe Stern[7] classified three Pre-Angkorian styles: 1) The Sambor Prei Kuk (SPK) style, which corresponded to 'Type I' of Lajonquiere, 2) the Prei Kmeng (PK) style, which corresponded to 'Type II' of Lajonquiere, and 3) the Kompong Preah (KP) style, which corresponded to 'Type II intermediate' of Parmentier. R. Dalet,[8] and importantly, Pierre Dupont[9] developed this theme further. The latter has presented a detailed analysis of their stage-by-stage progression. Mireille Benisti[10] succinctly analyzed these researches in the light of her own research. The three pre-Angkorian styles of lintels *(toraṇas)* may briefly be re-examined:

• Sambor Prei Kuk style (c. first half of seventh century, D.13): The arch usually comprises four arcs (at times single, dual, or eight arcs) punctuated by medallions at the intersection of successive arcs. Often, festoons *(vandanamālikās)* are suspended from the arch which is emitted by the *makaras* placed at the extremities. The latter are quite often accompanied by a *vyāla* or a human figure and with water divinities *(udadhikumāras)* riding them. The site of Sambor Prei Kuk in Cambodia, where such examples are found, lends the style its name.

• Prei Kmeng style (from the second quarter of seventh to the beginning of eighth century, D.14): The four arcs seen in the SPK style straighten into a single continuous arc with a plateau-like top. This arch does not usually bear

D.16

makaras at the extremities; symbolic forms such as *gajasiṁhas* (lion with elephant head) and foliate motifs substitute *makaras*. Festoons are found underneath the arch. Several instances where the arcs of the SPK style are reduced in emphasis represent the transitional phase from the SPK to the PK style.

• Kompong Preah style (c. eighth century, D.15): In this style, the entire arch is transformed into a lush vegetal efflorescence. The symbolic forms on the *toraṇa* such as the *makara, haṁsa* (goose), *gaja* (elephant), and *kinnara* (half man-half bird), the arch itself, and its festoons are subsumed by this vegetal exuberance which retains only the faint recollection of an arch.

D.15

D.15 : *Patra-toraṇa*, Kompong Preah (KP), KP style, c. eighth century.

D.16 : *Toraṇa*, Sambor on Mekong, c. seventh century.

D.17 : *Dvāra-toraṇa*, Preah Theat Kuk, east entrance, c. seventh century.

D.18 : *Dvāra-toraṇa*, Ashram Maha Rishi, north entrance, c. seventh century.

D.19 : *Toraṇa*, Thala Borivat type, Wat Phu Museum, c. sixth-seventh century.

The Sambor Prei Kuk Style

The earliest *toraṇas* encountered on the door lintels *(dvāra-toraṇas)* and wall niches *(kuḍya-toraṇas)* of Cambodian temples are noticed from about the early seventh century. As in India, here too, these early examples already exhibit a range of well-developed forms, pointing to the probable existence of earlier prototypes, perhaps in perishable materials such as wood. This style presents four variations in relation to the number of arcs on the *toraṇa*:

• The single-arc *toraṇa*, which is rare during the first three quarters of the seventh century. One such instance is from Sambor on Mekong (D.16).

• The dual-arc variant, of which more examples are available, includes the 'Thala Borivat variant,' as well as some others (Figs. 5.1, 5.2; D.17-19).[11]

• The four-arc type, which is abundant, represents the style prevalent during the first three quarters of the seventh century (Figs. 5.3-5.6; D.13, D.20-21).

• The eight-arc variant, which may also include narratives or figural sculpture underneath the arch, is rare. The one from Theat Ba Deum may be cited as an example (D.22).[12]

The Cambodian *toraṇas* with single and dual arcs bear the closest affinity to those from Ajanta, Jogeshvari, Magathana, Ellora, Badami, Mamallapuram, Dalavanur, Siyamangalam, Tirukkodikaval, Kudala Sangameshvara, and Undavalli in India (Figs. 3.1-3.19, 3.43-3.44; c. fifth to seventh centuries). Indian *toraṇas* of the

D.18

D.17

5.1 : Thala Borivat style, Wat Phu Museum, c. sixth-seventh century.

5.2 : *Kuḍya-toraṇa,* Sambor Prei Kuk (SPK) style, SPK, c. seventh century.

D.19

Bharhut-Sanchi type, which belong to a still earlier period, foreshadow some of the later developments (Figs. 1.3-1.12; c. second century BCE to second century). The *toraṇas* with dual arcs have been found at sites such as Kuk Prah Theat, Ashram Moha Rosei (Ashram Maha Rishi), Thala Borivat, Prasat Khtop, Stung Treng, and N 15, N 22, and S 10 at Sambor Prei Kuk (Figs. 5.1 & 5.2; D.17-19).[13]

5.1

5.2

The most characteristic of this style is the four-arc variant,[14] which technically qualifies as the *illikā-toraṇa* mentioned in the western Indian treatises. The arch of this *toraṇa* is adorned with diamonds *(ratna-toraṇa),* flowers *(puṣpa-toraṇa),* or leaves *(patra-toraṇa)*, with or without the *makaras* ridden by water divinities at the extremities. Medallions at the points of inflection of the arcs are inscribed with divine figures, *'garuḍa-nāgas'*, *kinnaras*, or floral and vegetal motifs. The *vyālas* or human figures often emerge from the mouths of the *makaras*. Garlands, flowers, and festoons hung from the arch are extremely ornate and rendered assertively. The subject matter and vocabulary of motifs are shared by the Indian and Southeast Asian sculptors, but some motifs such as the *'garuḍa-nāgas'* are more prolific in Cambodia.

5.4

5.3

D.20

D.21

D.20 : *Dvāra-toraṇa*, Sambor Prei Kuk, S 1, eastern door, c. seventh century.

D.21 : *Dvāra-toraṇa*, Sambor Prei Kuk, S 1, western door, c. seventh century.

D.22 : *Toraṇa*, Theat Ba Deum, now in Phnom Penh Museum, c. late seventh century.

5.3 : *Dvāra-toraṇa,* SPK style, SPK, S 7, c. seventh century, MG.

5.4 : *Dvāra-toraṇa,* SPK style, SPK, storage at site, c. seventh century.

5.5 : *Dvāra-toraṇa,* SPK style, Parmentier's N 21, SPK, c. seventh century.

5.6 : *Dvāra-toraṇa*, SPK style, SPK, storage at site, c. seventh century.

In any case, the visual rendition is very different in the two regions. There is a difference of opinion amongst French scholars regarding the relative chronology of the SPK variant with four arcs and the Thala Borivat variant with twin arcs. Whereas Dupont and Coral Remusat held the opinion that the former predates the latter, Dalet and Benisti maintained that the Thala Borivat variant antedates the four-arc SPK variant.[15]

A unique *toraṇa* from Sambor on Mekong merits special attention (D.16). Like the Thala Borivat variant, it is very close to Indian counterparts from the Deccan and South India. The rendition of the *makaras* and the human figures that emerge from their jaws in the gesture of adoration *(añjali-hasta),* with frontal torsos and legs in three-fourths profile, are of southern Indian affiliation. The central medallion encircled by flaming leaves harbours Śrī-Lakṣmī. The upper portion of the stone matrix is carved with water lilies. Underneath the arch is a vegetal efflorescence.

The *toraṇa* found at SPK (and labelled N 21 by Parmentier)[16] has four shallow arcs emerging from the *makaras* seated atop lotuses at both ends (Fig. 5.5). Water divinities *(udadhikumāras)* ride the *makaras* who release a *vyāla* each along with the arch. Two series of garlands are juxtaposed beneath the arch. The central medallion harbours a seated deity with a hair knot *(jaṭā)*, absorbed in meditation *(dhyānamudrā, padmāsana)*. Benisti has identified this deity as Śiva Yogīśvara.[17] *Kīrttimukhas* are carved at the interstices of successive arcs at the sides. Small flaming leaves lace the central medallion and the upper margins of the arch. It exhibits a more flattened contour than the usual SPK variant with four arcs.

Variants with narrative or figural sculpture beneath a flattened arch are also found in this style, as at the main sanctuary, S 1, in the southern complex at SPK. It appears to belong to a slightly different time bracket as compared to the other sanctuaries in the southern group.[18] The distinct nature of relief carvings noticed on the *dvāra-toraṇas* at S 1 deserve special mention (D.20, D.21).[19] The one carved on the eastern door lintel reveals the undulating body of a serpent placed beneath four shallow arcs of the *toraṇa* (D.20). The right end of the arch is effaced beyond recognition but the left end presents the raised hood of a pentacephalous serpent. At the extreme end is a sword-wielding figure, seated atop an animal, as though in combat with the serpent. Six figures are carved in high relief underneath the body of the serpent. The central figure is that of Indra with the thunderbolt *(vajra)*. To his right are serpents in adoration and to his left are two ladies (devotees?), one of them holding a casket. Anthropomorphic figures in high relief are placed at the interstices of successive arcs.

The *toraṇa* from the western entrance of S 1 at SPK (now relocated) (D.21) circumscribes six ascetics *(ṛṣis)*, each with matted locks *(jaṭā)*, sacred thread *(yajñopavīta)*, and beard. The gestures of the two central figures suggest a religious dialectic or discourse. The worn-out ends of the arch seem to depict the oft repeated combat of a *garuḍa* with a *nāga*. Figures in high relief, *garuḍa* clasping *nāgas* (centre), and rampant *vyālas* (sides) are carved at the interstices of the arcs. The floral and geometric patterns on the arch are reminiscent of the Indian counterparts noticed on the Deccan monuments of the sixth and seventh centuries. The *kīrttimukhas* are found on pilaster capitals that support the lintel.[20] The eastern and western *toraṇas* from S 1 are amongst the earliest to show figural or narrative reliefs under the arch. This and some other characteristics (such as the reduced depth of the arcs and some similarities with the Prei Kmeng style) led Benisti to deduce that the S 1 lintels belonged to the end of the SPK style. The S 1 monument itself lacks inscriptions.

The Prei Kmeng Style

In the PK style, the SPK variant with four arcs irons out into a flattened and continuous arch. The *makaras* at the ends are usually absent but the three medallions along the length of the arch, seen in the earlier style, continue to be present. The gradual transition from the four-arc SPK variant to a rectilinear arch of the PK style has been noted by Dupont.[21] In the latter style, the ends of the arch tend to turn inwards, there is a progression towards vegetal décor, and the *makaras* at the ends are replaced by foliate forms or anthropomorphic figures.

Two possibilities may be observed in this trend towards a flattened arch. The first is the transition of the semi-circular arcs into shallower undulations, as seen in the *toraṇas* from Theat Ba Deum, Vat Eng Khna, and SPK (Figs. 5.5 and 5.6; D.22).[22] The three medallions or inflections at the interstices of the arcs in the SPK style are retained and carried forward to the PK style. The second possibility (suggested by Dupont but refuted by Benisti) is the derivation of the PK arch via the Thala Borivat variant. Due to factors

5.5

5.6

D.22

5.7 : *Dvāra-toraṇa*, SPK style, from SPK, storage at site, c. seventh century.

5.8 : *Dvāra-toraṇa*, PK style, PK, c. seventh century, MG.

5.9 : *Dvāra-toraṇa*, PK style, storage at SPK, c. seventh century.

5.7

5.8

5.9

listed earlier (Endnote 15) and also because of the retention of the three medallions in the PK style (which is not so in the Thala Borivat variant, Fig. 5.1), the second possibility fails to convince.

The mature PK *toraṇas* reflect two variants.[23] The first type has figures at the ends, such as at Kuk Roka, Vat Khnat, and Prei Kmeng (Figs. 5.8, 5.9; D.14). The second has foliate or ornamental medallions at the lateral ends, such as at Svay Preahm. Dupont has opined (and Benisti has concurred) that the general trend during this period being *"l'envahissement progressif du feuillage"* (the progressive invasion of foliage), the type with figural carvings at the ends gives way to ornamental and foliate medallions, which reaches culmination in the vegetal abstraction of the Kompong Preah (KP) style.

The Kompong Preah Style

Figural depictions seen in the PK style are gradually abandoned in favour of vegetal abstraction in the KP style (D.23-D.26).[24] The successive stages are briefly recorded here:

• The rectilinear PK arch, which turns inwards and has pendant lotuses alternating with festoons inscribed with leaves beneath the arch (D.14), undergoes gradual transformation during the second half of the PK style.

• The ends of the arch assume the form of leaves, at first small (as at Trapeang Totung Thnay and Svay Preahm), and large and volute-shaped (as at Vat Preah Neang, Ampil Rolum and Prasat Ko) later. The beaded garlands gradually assume less significance and the carved leaves transform into big scrolls (Vat Prasat, D.23).

• The main arch loses its diamond-shaped motifs and beaded borders to transform into a striated stalk of vegetation (D.23, D.24).

• The fleurons at the ends make way for an outward and upward turn of the arch, which completes the characteristic features of the KP style (Vat Prasat, Prasat Khleang, Prasat Phum Prasat, Kompong Preah) (D.15, D.23-D.26).

Such a gradual transformation[25] is unique to Pre-Angkorian Cambodia and has no parallel in the Indian context. The KP variant is classified in Dravidian treatises as the *patra-toraṇa*. In India, *patra-toraṇas* are seen, for example, at the Virūpākṣa temple at Pattadakal (Fig. 3.23; c. 743 CE), above the niches of the late ninth century Neliappar temple in Tirunelveli, and the outer wall niches of the late 10th century Jain temples at Kambadahalli (Figs. 3.60, 3.61, 3.111). However, unlike Cambodia, these do not represent an important style in India.

D.26

D.24

D.23 : *Patra-toraṇa*, Vat Prasat, western entrance, transition from PK to KP style.

D.24 : *Patra-toraṇa*, Prasat Phum Prasat, eastern entrance, KP style.

D.25 : *Patra-toraṇa*, Sophas, KP style.

D.26 : *Patra-toraṇa*, Prasat Trapeang Phong (Roluoh) KP style, c. eighth century.

D.25

D.23

Later styles

At the end of the KP style, Cambodian *toraṇas* assumed complex and varied forms, rich in iconographic content. This is evident in the succeeding styles such as the Kulen, Preah Ko, Bakheng, Pre Rup, Baphuon, and Bayon styles (Figs. 5.10-5.26; D.27-D.36), which are quite distinct from the Indian examples. Lavish attention to detail, with the addition of several figural and iconographic representations within dense foliate carvings, are the chief characteristics of the Kulen and Preah Ko styles belonging to the major part of the ninth century. The trend continues in the 10th century monuments as may be observed at Koh Ker (Prasat Thom, c. 928-940 CE), on the temples at Eastern Mebon (Fig. 5.15; c. 953 CE), and at Pre Rup (c. 961 CE). Those at the Banteay Srei sanctuaries (Figs. 5.19-5.20; D.31, D.33; c. 967 CE) are superlative in creative imagination, their compositions rich in iconographic and mythological details just as in architectural ornamentation.

5.13

5.10

5.11

5.12

5.14

5.10 : *Dvāra-toraṇa*, Kulen style, c. first three quarters of ninth century, MG.

5.11 : *Dvāra-toraṇa*, Preah Ko style, c. last quarter of ninth century, MG.

5.12 : *Dvāra-toraṇa*, Preah Ko style, Preah Ko, c. 880 CE.

5.13 : *Dvāra-toraṇa*, Bakheng style, Bakheng, c. late ninth-early tenth century.

5.14 : *Dvāra-toraṇa*, c. first half of 10th century, MG.

5.15 : *Dvāra-toraṇa,* Eastern Mebon, c. 953 CE.

5.16 : *Dvāra-toraṇa,* Pre Rup style, c. third quarter of 10th century, MG.

5.17 : *Dvāra-toraṇa,* Lolei, c. third quarter of 10th century.

5.18 : *Dvāra-toraṇa*, Pre Rup, c. 961 CE.

5.18

5.16

5.15

5.17

5.19

5.19 : *Dvāra-toraṇa,* Banteay Srei, c. 967 CE.

5.20 : *Dvāra-toraṇa,* Banteay Srei, c. 967 CE.

5.21 : *Dvāra-toraṇa,* Baphuon style, c. 11th century, MG.

5.22 : Overleaf.

5.23 : *Dvāra-toraṇa,* Bayon style, c. late 12th-early 13th century MG.

5.24 : *Dvāra-toraṇa,* Bayon, c. late 12th-early 13th century.

5.25 : *Dvāra-toraṇa,* Bayon style, Preaḥ Khan, c. late 12th-early 13th century.

5.26 : *Dvāra-toraṇa*, Wat Phu.

5.21

5.23

5.20

5.25

5.24

5.26

5.22

5.22 : *Dvāra-toraṇa,* Angkor Wat, c. early 12th century.

Indian and Cambodian *Toraṇas*: Comparative References

Evidently, the Cambodian *toraṇas* in the SPK and PK styles share several features with the fifth and sixth century examples at Ajanta, Magathana, and Jogeshvari, and the seventh century instances at Badami, Aihole, Ellora, Mahabalipuram, and Dalavanur (Figs. 3.1-3.19; 3.43-3.44).

The twin-arc SPK style *toraṇas* correspond to the Indian *toraṇas* (c. fifth to seventh centuries) in the following respects:

- Twin arcs with a central depression and embellishment with figural and/or ornamental motifs.
- Prominently rendered *makaras* with thick proboscis at the extremities; the arch emanates from the jaws of *makaras*.
- The ornamentation on the arch comprises diamond, floral, and leaf-scroll motifs, thus qualifying them as the *ratna*, *puṣpa*, and *patra toraṇas* mentioned in Dravidian treatises.
- Occasional presence of water divinities *(udadhikumāras)* riding on the *makaras*.
- Garlands and festoons suspended from the *toraṇa*, with a pendant lotus motif at the centre.

Yet, the twin-arc Cambodian *toraṇas* also register differences from those of India:

- The central medallion of the 'Thala Borivat variant' usually bears the *garuḍa-nāgas* motif (Fig. 5.1; D.19).
- The rendition of festoons and pendant flowers beneath the arch as also the flaming leaves on the top margins are a few steps away from Indian versions.

The *toraṇa* as a complex motif in Cambodia, even at this early stage, appears to have been inspired not merely by Indian *toraṇas*, but also by other motifs found in ancient and early medieval Indian architecture. For example, the particular arrangement of festoons underneath the Cambodian *toraṇas* is not as assertively encountered on Indian *toraṇas*. Never-the-less, a similar arrangement of festoons is found on the pillars from the Deccan, for example, at Ajanta (c. fifth century). The flaming leaves at the top margins are distinctly Cambodian in character and are quite removed from the leafy margins seen on some Indian *toraṇas* from Andhra Pradesh (Biccavolu) and Tamil Nadu. In fact, such Indian versions are later than the Cambodian examples.

The *toraṇas* with four arcs are rarely encountered in India before the ninth century. However, the possibility of their existence cannot be ruled out completely.[26] In India, one observes a tendency towards a progressive increase in the number of arcs of the *toraṇa*, resulting in two basic types, the *āndola* and *illikā toraṇas*. From the ninth century, these basic types find myriad expressions in different parts of India. In Cambodia, on the other hand, the earliest available examples from sites such as SPK, Ashram Maha Rishi, and Kuk Prah Theat usually have two, four, or even eight arcs. With time, there is a reduction in the number of arcs, from an arch with plural arcs in the SPK style, to a single flattened arch of the PK style, and further, a vegetal abstraction of the arch in the KP style. After this, the rendition of foliate and animate motifs once again gets more and more detailed and complex. A keen aptitude for design, pattern, elaboration, and ornamental detailing seems to guide the Cambodian artist. By the end of the eighth century, the *toraṇa* assumes a distinct identity in Cambodia, related yet remarkably different from the Indian examples.

The thematic content of the *toraṇa* also presents an interesting picture. In India, one encounters the *makara* (most prevalent), *kinnara* (Kudaveli Sangameshvara-Andhra, Kailāsa-Ellora, Jambūliṅga-Pattadakal), *hasti* (Sarnath), *garuḍa* (Kankali Tila), *siṁha* (Kankali Tila), *mayūra* (Kailāsa-Ellora), and *haṁsa* (Sangameśvara and Virūpākṣa-Pattadakal) at the extremities of the *toraṇas* (Figs. 1.8-1.10; 3.27-3.30). Rarely does the arch spring forth directly from the die of the capital, though this is encountered more often during the later medieval period.[27] In Cambodia, one notices the *makara* (SPK, Prasat Preah Theat, Thala Borivat, Dambang Dek, etc.), *gajasiṁha* (PK), ornamental medallion (Svay Preahm, Trapeang Totum, etc.) and a figure inset in a floral pattern (Vat Khnat). At times, anthropomorphic figures are also seen at the extremities on Cambodian *toraṇas*. They may be devotees in the gesture of adoration *(añjali hasta)* (Udong, Kuk Roka), or standing anthropomorphic *garuḍas* with *nāgas* in the hands, similar to the triton motif (Kuk Roka and Vat Tang Kasang).

Most of the hyrid animals depicted at the extremities of Indian *toraṇas* derive from an earlier period of Indian art (c. third century BCE to fourth century). *Makaras* in Indian art symbolize water, the principle of life.[28] Often, a human figure (at times in combat) or a *vyāla* is shown emerging from the jaws of the *makara*,[29] accompanied by vegetal scrolls and/or jewels. The symbolic significance attached to the *makara* in early Indian art is carried forward to the *toraṇas* also. This symbolism finds its echoes in Cambodia too, but the *makara* loses its dominant status at the extremities of the arch to other symbolic and figural embellishments such as the *garuḍa-nāgas*. In Cambodia, the *mahoraga* (triton), *garuḍa-nāgas*, *gajasiṁha,* and *kīrttimukha* motifs, found at the apex and also at the extremities of *toraṇas*, receive favoured treatment and undergo several transformations. The motif of *garuḍa-nāgas* recurs frequently on Cambodian *toraṇas*. In the Thala Borivat and SPK variants, it is found on the medallions at the inflections of the *toraṇa* arcs. At S 1 in SPK, the undulating body of a serpent underlines the arch at the eastern entrance (D.20), whereas a *garuḍa*

D.27

D.30

in combat with a *nāga* is shown at the ends of the arch that belonged to the western entrance (D.21). In the PK style, the anthropomorphic form of *nāgas* (shown as devotees), as also the anthropomorphic *garuḍa* clutching two *nāgas* (in a triton-like manner) recurs. The privileged position accorded to this motif is subordinated by vegetal efflorescence in the KP style. However, it resurfaces most magnificently to occupy centre stage on Cambodian *toraṇas* from the late ninth century (Figs. 5.11, 5.14; D.29).[30] The *kīrttimukha* and *makaras* seen on Indian and Indonesian *toraṇas* are often replaced by the *garuḍa-nāgas* combination in Cambodia. The *kīrttimukha-makara* combination is also in evidence in Cambodia, but in the post-KP period, the *makaras* or *gajasiṁhas* at the ends are shown facing outwards (Figs. 5.10, 5.12; D.27, D.28).

Benisti's observations that "These (Indian) arches are always associated with *makaras*"[31] and that "...the dissociation of the arch from the *makara* marks a Khmer innovation"[32] are not valid in the light of the evidence and observations made in the foregoing. Further, her observation that "A personage or rearing animal sometimes issues from the mouth of Indian *makaras* although this is very rare,"[33] needs to be re-examined. Indian *toraṇas* with human figures or *vyālas* emerging from the *makara's* jaws are fewer prior to the seventh century. Even so, a few instances (Magathana, Fig. 3.9; also Kankali Tila, c. second century, not illustrated) are well-known. Soon after the seventh century, there are several such representations on Indian *toraṇas*.[34] Importantly, references to such imagery in literary sources such as Bhartṛhari's *Nītiśataka* are also known.[35] As Benisti herself states, the imagery was well known in India from an early period.

In India, the stone *toraṇas* are carved with jewels, leaves, flowers, etc., following the cultural practice of tying floral *(puṣpa)*, leafy *(patra)*, and bejewelled *(ratna)* garlands at entrances, which also find mention in some early Indian texts such as the *Rājapraśnīya Sūtra* and *Jīvājīvābhigama Sūtra* (Chapter 1; App. 2). These acquire the nomenclature of *ratna, patra,* and

D.27 : *Toraṇa*, Kulen style, first three quarters of ninth century.

D.28 : *Toraṇa*, Preah Ko, north-west tower, eastern side, c. 880 CE.

D.29 : *Toraṇa*, Prasat Kok Po A, Angkor (Siem Reap), Preah Ko style, c. last quarter of ninth century.

D.30 : *Toraṇa*, Pre-Rup style, c. third quarter of 10th century.

D.29

D.28

D.31 : *Toraṇa*, Banteay Srei, c. 967 CE.

D.32 : *Kuḍya-parikara-toraṇa*, north *dvārapālikā,* east face, north-west sanctuary, Lolei (Roluoh), c. 893 CE.

D.33 : *Kuḍya-parikara-toraṇa*, east *dvārapāla*, south face, middle sanctuary, Banteay Srei, c. 967 CE.

D.34 : Overleaf.

D.35 : *Toraṇa*, Baphuon style, c. 11th century.

puṣpa toraṇas in later treatises, of southern India to be precise. Those with figural and miscellaneous depictions are termed *citra-toraṇas*. The sculptural embellishment on the Cambodian *toraṇas* is very closely affiliated to Indian prototypes. Yet, geographical distance coupled with local predilections leads the arch to acquire unique, individualistic traits, markedly Cambodian and not Indian. The same holds true for the garlands, floral pendants, and pearl festoons beneath the arch. These are present in association with Indian *toraṇas* too (eg. Figs. 1.12, 3.1, 3.4, 3.9, 3.25, and 3.36), but their rendition is far more assertive and their presence ubiquitous in Cambodia. As regards narrative or figural representations under the arch, instances

D.31

D.35

D.32

D.33

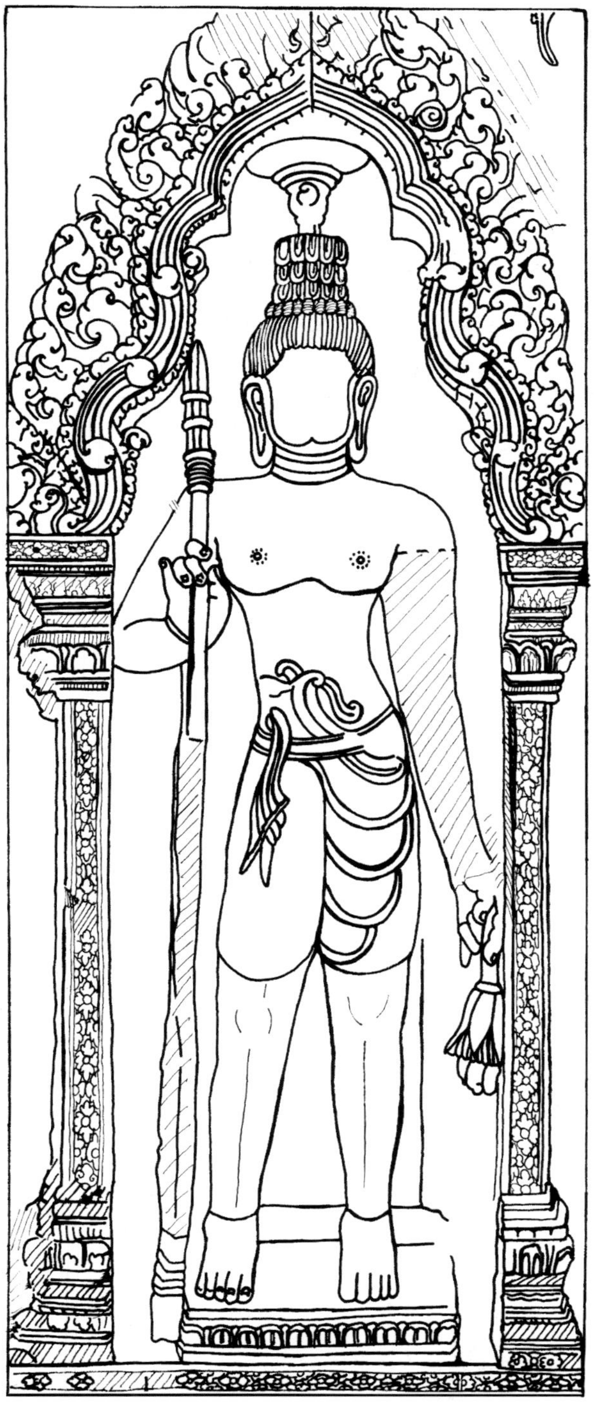

are available beginning from the fifth and sixth centuries in India (Figs. 3.1 and 3.6) and from the seventh century in Cambodia (D.20, D.21, Vat Eng Khna, etc.).

While interpreting the processes of form and transformation with regard to Indian and Cambodian *toraṇas*, one may surmise that the latter are inspired and influenced by the former atleast in their initial phase. But the modes of assimilation as well as the nature of transformation in Cambodia also reveals distinct characteristic traits, leading this architectural feature to trace parallel but individualistic paths.

D.36

D.34 : *Toraṇa,* Lolei,
c. third quarter of 10th century.

D.36 : *Toraṇa*, Bayon style,
c. late 12th-early 13th century.

D.34

Thailand

Present-day Cambodia and Thailand were politically, historically, and culturally linked through a shared Khmer legacy, beginning from the sixth-seventh centuries and persisting in varying degrees until the first half of the 15th century, when the kingdom of Ayutthya was freed of Khmer control in 1431 CE. This shared history is reflected in the Khmer-style architecture of the eastern and north-eastern regions of Thailand, to the north of the Dangrek mountain range which geographically separates Cambodia from Thailand (the Surin Province), and to the west of Cambodia's western border (the Prachinburi region). Some other sites in Thailand that host Khmer temples include Sukothai and Sri Satchanalai in the north, Lopburi in the Chao Phraya valley, Phetchaburi and Ratchaburi in the south-west, and Kanchanaburi towards the west.

The earliest surviving Khmer monument in Thailand in a fair state of preservation is Prasat Phum Phon in the Surin Province, built in the Prei Kmeng (PK) style during the seventh century. A *toraṇa* carved on a lintel found from this site is now housed in the Bangkok Museum.[36] It stylistically belongs to a period of transition between the SPK and PK styles earlier observed in the context of Cambodia. Four shallow arcs with three medallions at the inflexions are visible on the effaced surface of this *toraṇa*. The medallions consist of vegetal ornament; *makaras* of the Sambor style have been replaced by foliate medallions. Pendant flowers fill the space underneath the arch. It has been suggested that some architectural features and motifs seen in the Cambodian heartland appeared in Thailand after a time lag.[37] This was probably due the physical distance of the Thai sites from the Cambodian heartland.

The Cambodian Thala Borivat type of twin-arc *toraṇa* is also encountered in Thailand. The one from Vat Thong Thua in the Chantaboun region is now in the Bangkok Museum.[38] Yet another example of a Thala Borivat type of *toraṇa* found in Thailand, but with the exact provenance unknown, has been housed at Wat Supatnaram, Ubon Ratchathani Province (D.37).[39] Its central medallion is occupied by a lion.

From Prasat Khao Noi, we have examples of SPK style *toraṇas*, datable to the seventh century.[40] Prasat Khao Noi is situated in Wat Khao Noi Si Chomphu, Tambon Khlong Nam Sai, in eastern Thailand near the Cambodian border. The southern and northern *dvāra-toraṇas* from the northern *prang* as well as the one which was reused on the middle *prang*, are remarkably similar to the SPK style *toraṇas*. While the northern *toraṇa* from the northern *prang* (D.38) bears Indra riding Airāvata on the central medallion, with Aśvins on horses in the lateral medallions, the southern *toraṇa* has geese within the medallions. The reused *toraṇa*-lintel from the central *prang* reveals the vehicles of the gods, Airāvata in the centre and horses at the sides, symbolizing the presence of Indra and the Aśvins. The two central arcs of this last-mentioned instance are bigger than the lateral ones. Two of the *toraṇa*-lintels from the northern prang at Prasat Khao Noi, the eastern and the western, are carved in the PK style. *Makaras* are replaced by devotees on the eastern *toraṇa* (D.39) and by incompletely carved figures on the western one.

A rare example of the KP style in Thailand is carved on a lintel of unknown provenance (D.40). It is broken into three pieces, of which the central piece is missing.[41] Other more complex examples of *toraṇas* from Thailand correspond to the Kulen, Bakheng, Pre-Rup, Baphuon, and other Khmer architectural styles noticed in Cambodia (D.41-D.45).[42] The spread and influence of the Khmer empire was also felt in Laos, as for example, at Wat Phu Champasak built in the Angkorian style where, too, one finds the *toraṇa* as seen in the accompanying visual (Fig. 5.26).

D.37

D.38

D.39

D.40

D.37 : *Toraṇa*, Thala Borivat style, (now at) Wat Supatnaram, Ubon Ratchathani province, c. early seventh century.

D.38 : *Toraṇa*, SPK style, Prasat Khao Noi, northern *prang*, northern lintel, c. seventh century.

D.39 : *Toraṇa*, PK style, Prasat Khao Noi, northern *prang*, eastern lintel, c. seventh century.

D.40 : *Toraṇa*, unknown provenance, Thailand, KP style, c. eighth century.

D.41

D.42

D.41 : *Toraṇa*, Koh Ker style, Muang Khaek, c. end ninth century , Phimai Museum.

D.42 : *Toraṇa*, Prachinburi, Pre Rup period, c. mid-10th century.

D.43 : *Toraṇa*, Preah Ko style, National Museum, Bangkok.

D.44 : *Toraṇa*, Baphuon period, Prasat Pako, Nakhon Ratchasima province, c. 11th century.

D.45 : *Toraṇa*, Bakheng style, Prasat Phnom Wan, c. early 11th century , Phimai Museum, Khorat.

D.45

D.44

D.43

D.46

D.46 : *Toraṇa*-pediment, (originally at) entrance to Mi Son E 1 temple, now in Da Nang Museum, Vietnam, c. middle of seventh century.

D.47 : *Parikara-toraṇa*, detail of *liṅga*-pedestal from Mi Son E 1, c. middle of seventh century.

D.48 : *Kuḍya-toraṇa* (flaming leaves type), Khuong My, c. early 10th century.

D.47

Champa

Vestiges of art and architecture from this region, which has a tragic history of war and destruction, have often been neglected in favour of the more substantial remains from Cambodia, Indonesia, and Thailand. The archaeology of Champa also suffers from fragmentary documentary records. Available records are unclear regarding the precise time when a Hinduized kingdom began to exist in the region. With the accounts of the Chinese forces that invaded Champa in 605 CE, Cham history gains more clarity. The Vo Canh inscription, which dates from the third-fourth centuries, is the earliest to show the use of Sanskrit here. Indianization, as evidence seems to indicate, began from the southern shores and gradually spread northwards. Sanskrit and Cham co-existed as spoken and written languages, but the court, which was the political, social, and economic nerve centre, was composed of an elite aristocracy steeped in Sanskrit culture. Cham art is a unique, individualistic expression that assimilates several external influences and imbues them with a strong local character. There is evidence also of the reciprocal influence of the art of Champa in Thailand, Laos, and Cambodia.[43]

Type 1

In the remains of the Cham civilization, five types of *toraṇas* are encountered. The first type belongs to the the sacred structures from Mi Son E 1 and is strongly aligned to the Cambodian PK style.[44] An elegant *dvāra-toraṇa* that originally belonged to the Mi Son E 1 temple is carved in the Cambodian PK manner and depicts Anantaśāyī Viṣṇu and the birth of Brahmā, a subject shown frequently on Cambodian *toraṇas*[45] but rarely in Cham art (D.46).[46] Presently located in the Da Nang Museum of Cham Sculpture,[47] it is stylistically datable to the third quarter of the seventh century. An anthropomorphic *garuḍa* clasping *nāgas*, with affinities to the Mon art of Dvaravati, is located at each end of the *toraṇa*. The flattened, rectilinear arch is relatively unadorned, lending it a dignified and restrained beauty. Although the mythology and iconography relate to India, the style of rendition and Viṣṇu's physiognomy are typically Cham. Viṣṇu holds the lotus stalk that emerges from his navel. Brahmā is seated on the lotus at the centre, just above the limits of the main arch. In lieu of the lateral medallions of the PK style, one notices floral bosses that are prominent due to the plainness of the arch. A bearded ascetic *(ṛṣi)* with matted locks *(jaṭā)* is seated next to Viṣṇu.

Similar arches frame niches carved on the *liṅga* pedestal of the Mi Son E 1 shrine (D.47).[48] The northern and southern niches of this pedestal are fairly similar. An ascetic-musician is seated between a pair of square pilasters from which springs an arch of the Mi Son E 1 (Cambodian PK) style. The northern niche shelters an ascetic-flautist whereas the southern one houses an ascetic-harpist. The arch extends both inwards and outwards, such as those mentioned earlier in the context of the transition between the PK and KP styles (D.23 and D.24). But the ends in this case consist of hybrid animal creatures in place of the vegetal efflorescence of the later PK and KP styles. Each outward and upward extension is carved with a *makara* from whose jaws emerges an exquisite horned animal (deer? *vyāla?*). The inward projections also terminate in animals *(nāgas?)*, reflecting the Cham artist's unsurpassable skill in the portrayal of fantastic mythical creatures. In Indian architectural terminology, the *toraṇas* from Mi Son E 1 just discussed would be categorized as *cāpākāra-dvāra-toraṇas* when found on door-lintels, and *cāpākāra-parikara-toraṇas* when crowning images in niches. They belong to the middle of the seventh century and are comtemporaneous with the PK period in Cambodia.

Type 2

The second type comes to view at first on the Hoa Lai structures belonging to the late eighth-ninth century, situated in the southern regions of Cham.[49] An undulating *(āndola)*, foliate *(patra)*, and inverted 'U'-shaped arch (*toraṇa*) springs from a pair of pilasters and crowns the shallow niches on the walls of the central and northern *kalāns* at Hoa Lai. These may be read as Cham versions of wall arches or *kuḍya-toraṇas* of the *patra* and *āndola* sub-categories mentioned in Indian treatises. This type was also present in the late ninth-early tenth century Dong Duong style, as seen in an earlier documentation.[50] The *toraṇa* is more elaborate and convoluted and ends in the serpent motif on the walls of the central tower at Dong Duong. On the *kalāns* at Khuong My (c. early 10th century) to the south-east of Mi Son, this type of arch finds refinement (D.48).[51] The Khuong My type of *toraṇas*

D.48

continue to be executed during the Mi Son A 1 style that prevailed during the 10th century in Champa. They reflect the assimilation of Khmer and Javanese influences alongside the local. The vegetal motifs on the arches assume flame-like forms. Such undulating flame-like arches are seen in abundance as pediments (frontons) of Cambodian temples from the middle of the ninth century; some of the finest instances being at the Banteay Srei temple (Fig. 5.19; c. 967 CE). Miniature replicas of the same motif frame niche-images on the walls of Cambodian and Cham temples (D.32, D.33, and D.48).

Type 3

The third type of *toraṇa* also belongs to the Mi Son A 1 shrine and has obvious affiliations to the Central Javanese ones. This is the *kāla-makara-toraṇa*, ubiquitous on Javanese *Caṇḍīs*. At Mi Son A 1, the *kāla-makara-toraṇa* crowned devotees in *añjali hasta* on the blind storeys of its superstructure (D.49; c. 10th century).[52] From the 11th century, Cham architectural remains have been grouped under the Binh Dinh or the Thap Mam styles. The ornamental arches on the walls of the late 11th-early 12th century central temple of Bahn It (Silver Towers) at Binh Dinh are constructed in many tiers and show intricate foliate carvings emerging from the jaws of the *kālamukha*.[53]

D.49

D.49 : *Kāla-makara-toraṇa* framing devotee in a niche, Mi Son A 1, c. 10th century.

D.50 : *Toraṇa*, Doung Long (Ivory Towers), c. 12th-13th century.

D.50

Type 4

On the late 12th-early 13th century northern *kalān* of Duong Long (Ivory Towers), where a strong Khmer influence is in evidence, one observes the fourth type of *toraṇa* found in the Cham region.[54] The arcs crowning the false doors assume the form of the gorgon *(kīrttimukha)* emitting an arch that comprises a serpent's body and terminates in the upraised hoods of pentacephalous serpents (D.50).

Type 5

In 1963, Boisselier published the Thap Mam examples, of which four show a *kālamukha* at the centre emitting undulating or curled foliage with mythical animals placed at the two ends.[55] The fifth shows lions and geese in circular medallions. All five are ornamented with what has been labelled as the 'Thap Mam motif'. This is a curled leaf pattern carved in high relief that repeats itself in profusion as an ornamental motif typical of this style (c. 12th-13th centuries).

Indonesia

The major centres of early Indonesian art are found on the western Indonesian islands of Java, Sumatra, Bali, and Kalimantan. During the eighth and ninth centuries, the kings of Central Java patronized numerous Brahmanical and Buddhist structures. From the 10th century, the focus shifted to Eastern Java. The generic affiliation of the Central Javanese *Caṇḍīs* with Indian temples is difficult to doubt, although Indonesian creative genius has brought forth distinctive artistic manifestations and created a style that is unique to the region. The ornamental repertoire seen on the Indonesian monuments is particularly noteworthy and is different from that encountered in India.

The Central Javanese *Caṇḍīs* Architectural Setting of the *Toraṇas*

The Central Javanese *Caṇḍīs* are surrounded by subsidiary shrines arranged in concentric squares, often within enclosure walls (eg. *Caṇḍī* Sewu, *Caṇḍī* Lārā Jonggrang). The base mouldings of these temples resemble those found in the Deccan and South India, but are more closely allied to the mouldings on the pedestals of southern Indian bronzes. Perhaps such portable divine images and miniature shrines brought from India may have had an impact on the building traditions of this land.[56] The horizontal assertion of the base mouldings, the plain wall surfaces, and the well-articulated storeys of the superstructure give the Javanese *Caṇḍīs* their clean geometry. This offers an ideal surface for ornamentation, an opportunity exploited to great heights by the Javanese craftsman-sculptor. The *kāla-makara-toraṇas* on these *Caṇḍīs*, a distinctive Indonesian expression, are found at the entrances (*dvāra toraṇas*) and wall-niches of the various storeys of the monument (*kuḍya* or *parikara toraṇas*).

Kālamukha on Javanese *Toraṇas*

The *kālamukha* enjoys greater prominence on Javanese *toraṇas* than the *kīrttimukha* does on Indian *toraṇas*.[57] The motif finds antecedents and parallels in many cultures. In China, it is known as Tao-T'ieh and is encountered on ritualistic bronzes from the second millennium BCE. In Greek art, the gorgon registers its presence from the archaic period, whereas in medieval English churches it appears as the 'Green Man'. In Cambodia, it is known as the head of Rāhu, in Java and eastern India (Assam) as *banaspati*, and as *boma* in Bali. The three most frequently used synonyms for the *kīrttimukha* in India are *grāsa*, Rāhu and *kālamukha* – all three signify the devourer; it is also interpreted as the devourer of evil and the forbearer of auspiciousness.[58] In appearance, the *kāla* or *banaspati* (*vanaspati*, lord of the woods) is reborn in Java as a fearsome leonine face with flame-like locks, bulging eyes, and protruding fangs and teeth. It is prominently placed at the apex of the *toraṇas*.

Its philosophical underpinnings and accompanying descriptive imagery have been traced to the Ṛg Vedic Vṛtra, who had no hands or feet, whose lower jaw was smitten by Indra's bolt and who brought forth manifestation at the time of his death.[59] However, this is separated by over 1800 years in time before the earliest available visual representations of the *kīrttimukha* appear in Indian art. A later narration from the *Skanda-purāṇa* images the *kīrttimukha* as devouring his own body and also indicates his position on the door of Śiva temples.[60] In art, he is shown with just his face or in some images (as in a Gupta period *kālamukha* from Sarnath), with his hands at his jaw, presumably in the process of devouring himself.[61] Images of the *kāla* devouring his hands and body are often seen on Javanese *Caṇḍīs* and Cambodian temples.

The *kālamukha* has been interpreted as a symbol of the uranic or celestial element in creation and is complemented by *makaras* or *nāgas* which represent the watery and chthonic element.[62] It has been suggested that in Chinese art, it had an apotropaic function and was used with the idea of terrifying malignant spirits. The powerfully rendered Javanese *kāla* or *banaspati,* in all likelihood, bears these various associated meanings to an even greater degree.

Chronology and Links with India

From the sophisticated nature of early artistic remains at sites such as the Dieng Plateau in Java, one may assume the existence of an earlier tradition in more ephemeral materials. Unlike Cambodia however, where French scholars have accomplished a detailed stylistic analysis of motifs, the rich vocabulary of Indonesian motifs has not as yet been systematically analysed. Available inscriptional data is insufficient to evolve a comprehensive chronology of Javanese monuments. Rebuilding and renovation of structures coupled with non-linear patterns of development of architectural motifs have complicated attempts at chronological assessments based on style. However, a combination of inscriptional, literary, and stylistic data has enabled scholars of Indonesian art to arrive at a broad consensus on their chronology.[63]

Indonesian contacts with India were not restricted to a single geographic zone. The network of communications included different regions in southern, eastern, and western India. As in Cambodia, the development of the *toraṇa* motif in Java also exhibits sporadic borrowings of ideas and forms from India.[64] No direct prototypes are met, yet close correspondences with eastern[65] and southern India[66] are evident.

5.28

5.27 : *Kuḍya-toraṇa, Caṇḍī* Ghaṭotkacha, Dieng Plateau, c. late eighth century.

5.28 : *Parikara-toraṇa*, Jain bronze, Karnataka.

Central Javanese *Kāla-makara-toraṇas*: Affiliations with India

***Prabhāvalī Toraṇas*:** The most popular *toraṇas* encountered in Java are those framing the entrances *(dvāra-toraṇas)* and wall-niches *(kuḍya-toraṇas)* of the *Caṇḍīs*. Amongst the earliest of these are noticed on the Dieng Plateau (c. late eighth-early ninth century) in the north-western part of Central Java. These structures are of Śaiva affiliation although several of them are named after the Pāṇḍavas.

Rectangular *dvāra* and *parikara kuḍya toraṇas* grace the *Caṇḍīs* that are known by the names of Ghaṭotkacha, Arjuna, Bhīma (Fig. 5.29), and Puntadeva (Pañcadeva). Those found on *Caṇḍī* Ghaṭotkacha (Fig. 5.27) and *Caṇḍī* Arjuna are the most modestly ornamented. The pride of place, at the apex, is accorded to the *kālamukha (kīrttimukha* or gorgon*)*. A flame-like ornament, emitted by the *kāla*, falls vertically along the entire length of the door or the niche on either side. This terminates in what may be described as vegetal abstractions of *makaras* facing outwards; only the bare outlines of the paws and the trunk identify them as *makaras*. The fangs of the flame-like décor are sparsely arranged on *Caṇḍī* Ghaṭotkacha, which conveys the impression that it may be earlier than most other surviving *Caṇḍīs* on the Dieng Plateau. In this instance, the *makaras* rest at the edges of the lotus seat meant for the missing niche-image. At *Caṇḍī* Puntadeva, the *toraṇa* is more embellished; the flame-like fangs earlier noticed

5.27

on *Caṇḍī* Ghaṭotkacha are now closely juxtaposed and conjure the appearance of a stylised flame pattern (Figs. 5.30, 5.31; D.52). The outlines of the *makaras* subsumed in a vegetal profusion are difficult to recognize. These *kāla-makara-toraṇas*, with their flame-like protuberances, bear similarities with the aureoles *(prabhāvalīs)* around the divine bronzes from India and Indonesia (Fig. 5.28; D.51). In fact, these *toraṇas* framed the wall-niches of the *Caṇḍīs* and thus served as an aureole for the image housed in the niche. Even the outward-facing *makaras* at the lower ends are in common with some of the bronze aureoles, such as the one framing Bodhisattva Avalokiteśvara (c. eighth-ninth century) from Sragen in Central

D.52

D.51

Java (D.51).[67] Such outward-facing *makaras* are also noticed on the aureoles of some Jain sculptures from medieval Karnataka (Fig. 5.28) and are often seen in Orissan architecture, as for example, on the Mukteśvara *toraṇa* (Fig. 4.127). At *Caṇḍī* Kalasan, a similar inverted U-shaped arch inside the wall-niche was probably meant as a halo for the niche-image (Fig. 5.40). It lends further credence to the observation that such *(parikara) kāla-makara-toraṇas* were intended to serve as aureoles *(prabhāvalīs)*. When placed at entrance doors, they, in a sense, served as an aureole for the image in the sanctum which could be seen through the doorway.

The *prabhāvalī* or *makara-toraṇa-tiruvātci* (aureole) that encircles the divine bronzes (such as the famous Naṭarāja bronzes of southern India) are similar in concept to the *prabhāvalī toraṇas* just discussed, although the *makaras* in the former case release the aureole, which may be oblong (usually before the 10th century) or circular (usually from the 11th century). *Prabhāvalī toraṇas* are often noticed on the eastern Indian sculptures of the Pāla-Sena period. All these represent a particular type of *parikara-toraṇas*.

The *prabhāvalī* (or horse-shoe or inverted U-shaped) *toraṇas* seen on Javanese *Caṇḍīs* receive elaboration and attain finesse on monuments of the Gedong Sanga complex on Mount Ungaran (Figs. 5.32 and 5.33; c. ninth century) and *Caṇḍī* Pringapus (c. mid ninth century). On Temple II from this group, the *kālamukha* placed under a bow-shaped canopy is more ornate and sophisticated than those seen on the Dieng Plateau. The flame-like pattern falling along the longitudinal edges of the niche has a floral creeper on its inner margins, similar to that seen in Indian art from the second century BCE.[68] The *makaras* at the lower ends of the *toraṇa* are carved with greater clarity and assertion, reminiscent of those seen in the Ajanta caves (c. fifth century).

Caṇḍī Badut (c. late ninth century), though an early East Javanese monument, shares several features in common with Central Javanese

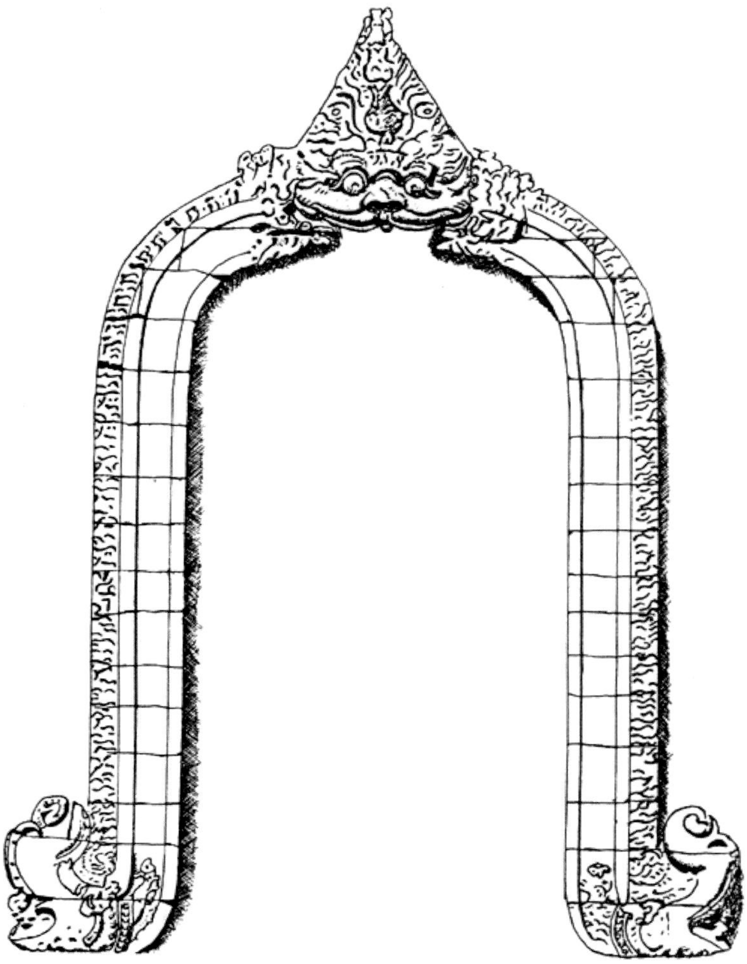

D.53

D.51 : Bodhisattva Avalokiteśvara, Sragen, Central Java, Central Javanese period (c. 732-928 CE), National Museum, Jakarta.

D.52 : *Kuḍya-toraṇa, Caṇḍī* Punṭadeva (Pañcadeva), Dieng Plateau.

D.53 : *Toraṇa* at entrance to the third gallery, Barabudur, c. 800-835 CE.

5.29 : *Kuḍya-toraṇa (parikara), Caṇḍī* Bhīma, Dieng Plateau, c. late eighth century.

5.29

structures and is also adorned with similar *toraṇas*. Its *dvāra-toraṇa*, though not well preserved, is an example of the influence exerted by the Central Javanese style in eastern Java during the ninth century (Fig. 5.34). The *kālamukha* on the *dvāra-toraṇa* at the entrance to *Caṇḍī* Pringapus (Fig. 5.35) marks a transition towards those seen in the succeeding century in eastern Java. It now acquires a more potent and fearsome visage; its lower jaw is clearly visible, as also the claws on either side. From this period, the affiliation with the Indian *kīrttimukha* becomes more remote.

At *Caṇḍī* Bhīma on the Dieng Plateau, the introduction of a curvature on the upper edges offsets the stark linearity of the rectangular *toraṇa*, now shaped as an inverted U (Fig. 5.29). Serpents, another symbol of water cosmology

5.30

5.32

5.33

5.31

5.30 : *Kuḍya-toraṇas (parikara), Caṇḍī* Punṭadeva (Pañcadeva), Dieng Plateau, c. late eighth century.

5.31 : *Kuḍya-toraṇa (parikara), Caṇḍī* Punṭadeva (Pañcadeva), Dieng Plateau, c. late eighth century.

5.32 : *Dvāra-toraṇa, Caṇḍī* Gedong Sanga temple I, Mt. Ungaran, c. late eighth century.

5.33 : *Kuḍya-toraṇa, Caṇḍī* Gedong Sanga temple II, Mt. Ungaran, c. late eighth century.

and fertility, are placed beneath the *makaras*. Instances of this variant may also be noticed at other sites, notably the temple complex at *Caṇḍī* Plaosan (Figs. 5.36, 5.37). On the southern main shrine of the *Caṇḍī* Plaosan complex, a floral pendant dropping from the jaws of the *kālamukha* creates a central depression at the apex of the arch. At the entrances to the Barabudur galleries, this variant attains its zenith (Figs. 5.38, 5.39; D.53; c. 800-835 CE). The arch rises upwards steeply and curves at the top in an inverted 'U' or horse-shoe shape. On one of these (Fig. 5.39), the space beneath the *kālamukha* is filled with flowers, festoons, and pearl garlands amidst which stands an ascetic *(ṛṣi)* on either side, holding a sacred object. On yet another (Fig. 5.38), the ascetics are substituted by three birds with human heads *(kinnaras)* on each side. The proportionate rendering of the parts and the whole in relation to the monument, lend the Barabudur *dvāra-toraṇas* a special place in the history of architectural ornamentation.

5.34 : *Dvāra-toraṇa* from west, *Caṇḍī* Badut, late ninth-early tenth century.

5.35 : *Dvāra-toraṇa*, *Caṇḍī* Pringapus, c. ninth century.

5.34

5.35

Although individual motifs and patterns on Indonesian *toraṇas* echo earlier manifestations of Indian art, there is no equivalent of the Indonesian *kāla-makara-toraṇa* in India. The Indonesian artist doubtless has been inspired by Indian ideas, motifs, and forms. Yet the manner in which these have been employed, the vocabulary of expression which characterizes them, and the layers of artistic consciousness revealed through these creations are distinctly Indonesian. In the development of the Central Javanese artistic expression, India provides some of the alphabets, even words and phrases, yet the language is essentially Indonesian.

5.37

5.39

5.36 : *Kuḍya-toraṇa*, southern main shrine, *Caṇḍī* Plaosan complex, c. 850 CE.

5.37 : Small temple to the west of *Caṇḍī* Plaosan, c. mid-ninth century.

5.38 : *Dvāra-toraṇa*, Barabudur, fourth gallery, c. 800-835 CE.

5.39 : *Dvāra-toraṇas* at entrances to the galleries, Barabudur, c. 800-835 CE.

5.36

5.38

D.54

The *Caṇḍī* Kalasan Variant: *Gavākṣa* or *Nāsī Toraṇas*[69]

The gorgeous and intricately crafted, jewel-like *toraṇas* of *Caṇḍī* Kalasan (c. mid-ninth century)[70] are closer to the art of the goldsmith than of the sculptor. The *toraṇas* on this *Caṇḍī,* situated between Jogjakarta and Prambanan, rise from pilaster capitals and crown niches and entrances. In the cited example, a smaller *toraṇa,* shaped as a dormer *(gavākṣa* or *nāsī),* is enveloped within a bigger 'horse-shoe or inverted U-shaped' *toraṇa* (D.54). On the smaller one, the *kālamukha* is replaced by a floriate motif at the apex, which develops into triangular flame-like adornments oft noticed in Javanese architecture. The arch is supported by load-bearing dwarfs *(bhāraputrakas)*. Enveloping this is the bigger *toraṇa,* in which a *kālamukha* with prominent teeth and fangs, with a delicately rendered triangular crown of vegetal adornment, and with creatures emerging out of the corners of his mouth, is placed at the apex. The group of celestial musicians *(gandharvas)* ensconced within a cloudscape along the margins of the *kāla's* triangular crown is an impressive detail. Immediately beneath the *kāla's* upper jaw are floral pendants. A thin border of flame-like ornament descends vertically to terminate in *makaras* at the lower ends of the door. The arrangement of two *toraṇas,* one framing the other, is a picture of rhythmic balance and harmonious proportions and spells the characteristic decorative tone of the building. Several participating elements and details such as celestials within the cloudscape,[71] besides the recurrent motifs discussed earlier, have precedents in Indian art. Yet, in the totality of conception and rendition, the *Caṇḍī* Kalasan *toraṇa* is unique, the aesthetic impact of the whole being far greater than the sum of its parts.

The niche *toraṇas* on *Caṇḍī* Kalasan are styled as ovoid versions of a dormer *(gavākṣa)* (Fig. 5.40). They are placed at entrances to miniature representations of temples carved on the walls of the *Caṇḍī*. A *kālamukha* is carved at the apex of the *gavākṣa-toraṇa;* outward-facing *makaras* offset those facing inwards at the ends. A faint inverted U-shaped arch inscribed within the niche was probably intended as a halo for the niche-image. The fine detailing of architectural ornament on *Caṇḍī* Kalasan was possible to achieve because the monument was covered with plaster and some of the intricate work was added

5.40

5.40 : *Kuḍya-toraṇa (parikara)*, *Caṇḍī* Kalasan.

D.54 : *Kuḍya-toraṇa,* detail of southern façade, *Caṇḍī* Kalasan.

at the plaster stage. The closest Indian parallels to this Javanese variant are noticed in the *nāsī-toraṇas* (also shaped as dormers) on the superstructures of some medieval Karnataka temples (Figs. 3.100, 3.101).

The *toraṇas* at *Caṇḍī* Sāri,[72] situated in the neighbourhood of *Caṇḍī* Kalasan and belonging to the same time frame, are also *gavākṣa*-shaped, although they do not possess the same finesse. They appear as niche *toraṇas* above divinities in the panels between the windows and also on the eastern and western sides of the roof. The inverted U-shaped variant is also noticed on this *Caṇḍī*, as for instance, on its northern roof niches. The *kālamukha* merges with the leafy ornament carved above and below it and the arch appears to begin from the sides of *kāla's* eyes rather than from its jaws. The flame-like ornament on the sides of the arch looks like a leafy scroll; *makaras* are prominent.

The Bow-shaped Variant: *Cāpākāra Toraṇa*

At *Caṇḍī* Pawon (Fig. 5.41) and *Caṇḍī* Sewu, *cāpākāra dvāra-toraṇas* are placed at the entrance door-lintels. They are characterized by a prominent *kālamukha* at the apex that releases an elegant bow-shaped arch with outward-facing *makaras* at the ends. In the *Caṇḍī* Pawon and *Caṇḍī* Sewu examples, the *toraṇa* is in fact a sort of pediment or fronton above the door-lintel. The space beneath the *Caṇḍī* Pawon arch is filled with garlands of pearls and flowers, with bearded figures releasing treasures from their bags. This imagery suggests that Pawon was dedicated to Kubera, the god of wealth. In a similar instance from *Caṇḍī* Sewu, the space beneath the arch is filled with garlands and garland-bearing celestials. Another variant from *Caṇḍī* Pawon that deserves to be noted is located on the outer wall and acts as a *parikara kuḍya-toraṇa* (Fig. 5.42). Two *cāpākāra toraṇas* from Barabudur are discussed in the next section.

Parikara and *Kuḍya Toraṇas* at Barabudur

Although this category overlaps with some others discussed earlier, a few notable instances found at Barabudur deserve special mention. A *kālamukha*, with a shapely triangular flame-like crowning element and a lotus beneath its upper jaw, conjures the contours of a conch shell on a *cāpākāra toraṇa* from Barabudur (Fig. 5.43). The arch terminates in *makaras*, facing outwards, with pendant bells emerging from their jaws.[73] It fronts a miniature shrine carved in relief, simulating actual structures in all likelihood.

5.41

5.42

5.41 : *Dvāra-toraṇa*, *Caṇḍī* Pawon, Brijnalan, c. eighth century.

5.42 : *Kuḍya-toraṇa (parikara)*, *Caṇḍī* Pawon, Brijnalan, c. eighth century.

5.43 : *Kuḍya-toraṇa (parikara)*, Barabudur, c. 800-835 CE.

5.43

Perhaps the finest example of a multi-arc *toraṇa* from the region is placed at the entrance to a miniature shrine carved in relief at Barabudur (Fig. 5.44). The *toraṇa* of seven arcs is placed in front of the shrine which houses Samantabhadra. Such arches are of a composite class and can be categorized as *kuḍya-, dvāra-, or parikara-toraṇas.* Similar representations are often found in Buddhist manuscript paintings from eastern India and it is very likely that such manuscripts reached Indonesia and inspired parallel representations. Unfortunately, several of the vast quantities of Pāla-Sena manuscripts produced in eastern India, particularly those belonging to the early Pāla period, have been destroyed.[74] Divine images placed within shrines fronted by these kind of *toraṇas* are abundant in eastern Indian sculpture, beginning from about the ninth century. The late 13th century

5.44 : *Toraṇa,* relief no. 36 (Homage to Sāmantabhadra), c. 800-835 CE

5.44

5.45

Gaṅgeśvarī temple at Beyalisbati in Orissa has *toraṇas*, one each on the northern and southern central offsets and another on the western entry to the hall (Fig. 4.128-4.130). Such representations in relief sculpture and paintings seem to present a *toraṇa* at the entrance to a sacred structure and the image in the sanctum as viewed through it. A trefoil *toraṇa* (Fig. 5.45) and another bow-shaped variant that fronts a miniature shrine and is topped by a tiny four-arc arch (Fig. 5.46), both from Barabudur, are also illustrated here. Yet another, from the same site, which has only scrolls *(patra-toraṇa)*, may also be mentioned here (Fig. 5.47). *Cāpākāra toraṇas* also adorn several Buddha images along the walls of the processional path at Barabudur (Figs. 5.48, 5.49).

5.46

5.47

5.45 : *Toraṇa,* Barabudur, c. 800-835 CE.

5.46 : *Toraṇa,* Barabudur, c. 800-835 CE.

5.47 : *Toraṇa,* Barabudur, main wall niche, c. 800-835 CE.

5.48

5.49

5.48 : *Toraṇa,* Barabudur, main wall niche c. 800-835 CE.

5.49 : *Toraṇas* crowing Buddha images, Barabudur, c. 800-835 CE.

5.50 : *Toraṇa,* southern main shrine, *Caṇḍī* Plaosan complex, c. 850 CE.

5.51 : *Cāpākāra-toraṇa,* Barabudur, c. 800-835 CE.

Two further varieties of *toraṇas* from Java deserve notice. The first resembles those seen on *Caṇḍī* Sāri, with some modifications (Fig. 5.50). The *kālamukha* is absent; a lotus flanked by bells forms the central pendant motif; convergent *makaras* also release bells at the ends. The second is sinusoidal with twin arcs such as those seen in India from the fifth century (Fig. 5.51). The *makaras* at the ends release pearl strings. The delicate and fragile arch and supporting pilasters subtly define the enclosed space.

5.51

5.50

5.52

5.52 : *Kuḍya-toraṇa,* Central Javanese style.

Some other instances

The minor cellas of the main structure at *Caṇḍī* Sewu have a row of niches shaped like pointed arches (not illustrated). This variety is rare on Javanese *Caṇḍīs* and spells utmost simplicity. The familiar flame-like scroll on the upper margins of each pointed arch suggests a *patra-toraṇa*. The arches, more akin to those found in Islamic architecture, rest on pilasters with capitals carved with *kālamukhas*.

5.53 : *Kālamukha*, *Caṇḍī* Angka Tahun, *Caṇḍī* Panataran complex, Eastern Javanese style.

D.55 : *Toraṇa* crowning window on south side of Kubyauk-gyi, Myinkaba, Pagan, c. 1113 CE.

5.53

Eastern Javanese Style

The *kālamukha* is more fierce and forceful on the Eastern Javanese *Caṇḍīs*, most of which were constructed between the 10th and 15th centuries. Whereas the *kālamukha* gains in prominence on the doorways and niches, the *makaras* diminish in importance. The *kāla-makara-toraṇa* ornament is thus gradually replaced in favour of representations of the *kālamukha* in isolation, as may be observed at *Caṇḍī* Kidal, Rejokidal, where *makaras* are insignificant, and at *Caṇḍī* Angka Tahun in the *Caṇḍī* Panataran complex, where they are altogether absent (Fig. 5.53).

Myanmar

In Myanmar, the *toraṇa* has a limited range yet recurrent presence. Early representations of the *toraṇa* are seen in relief sculpture of the fifth to seventh century.[75] The ancient city of Pagan in Myanmar has yielded an impressive number of *stūpas* and temples dating from the 11th to 13th centuries. Pagan's geographical location between India and the rest of Southeast Asia made it an important centre at the crossroads of culture. Contacts were maintained with north-eastern and eastern India, with Tibet, and with Sri Lanka.

On the Pagan monuments, a decorative arch frequently appears in the position of a pediment above the doorways, windows, and niches of sanctuaries. It takes the form of an inverted V-shaped undulating arch with flame-like protuberances on the top margins and becomes one of the most characteristic features of Burmese architecture. There is no convincing parallel of this pediment-*toraṇa* on Indian *stūpas* or temples but it does have Cambodian, Thai, and Cham parallels. A representation of this type of arch can be seen above the latticed windows on the outer walls of shrines such as Myinkaba Kubyauk-gyi (D.55; c. 1113 CE).[76] The outer walls of this shrine have exquisite stucco patterns which were fashioned from metal moulds. Above each latticed window is the superstructure of a miniature shrine that is faced by an arch of multiple arcs. As in the case of Central Java, these may have been inspired by similar illustrations in the Pāla period manuscripts from eastern India. In Cambodia too, such portrayals frame standing figures of divine and semi-divine beings on temple walls (D.32 and D.33).

5.54 : Gilded *toraṇa* intended for a throne, Nepal, c. 17th-18th century, VAM.

5.55 : Golden *dyo-toraṇa* with Taleju Bhawānī, Kathmandu, Bhaktapur Durbar Square, c. 17th-18th century.

5.56

5.54

The Cambodian *toraṇas* are carved on lintels and therefore are rectangular in shape, whereas Newari *toraṇas* trace a deep semi-circular pediment-like space. They are rich in iconographic content and, as in the Indian instances, often relate to the deity enshrined within the temple.[78] In the Cārnārāyaṇa temple at the Mangal Bazar in Patan (c. 1565 CE), for example, the deities represented on the *toraṇas* include Viṣṇu (south), Kṛṣṇa Kāliyādamana (east), Mahālakṣmī (west), and Narasiṁha (north).[79]

Newari *toraṇas* have been classified into three categories, based on their location:[80]

• *Jhal-toraṇa*: These are placed above windows. The gilded *toraṇas* with *kālamakara* and deities above the windows at Bhaktapur Durbar (Fig. 5.56) bear this out;

• *Dyo-toraṇa*: These are placed above the doors of a temple. The *toraṇas* above the doorways at the Cārnārāyaṇa temple and the one depicting Taleju Bhawānī at Bhaktapur Durbar square (Fig. 5.55) illustrate this;

• *Dalān-toraṇa*: These are placed between pillars. Those between pillars at the Harihara temple, Patan stand as examples (not illustrated).

An exquisite 17th-18th century Newari *toraṇa*, intended for the throne of a divinity, is now in the VAM in London (Fig. 5.54).[81] Made in three parts of gilt copper, it is repoussé chased and inset with turquoise and imitation gems backed with silver foil. The *toraṇa* is crafted in full relief and some details are painted in black pigment. It shows the typical '*garuḍa-nāga*' motif surrounded by the rich foliage peculiar to Newari *toraṇas*. These and several such examples from Nepal represent the golden *(hema-* or *suvarṇa-) toraṇa* mentioned in the Indian texts.

Some South Asian Parallels

A few examples from some Nepal and Sri Lanka are briefly surveyed here with the limited purpose of sampling parallel progressions of the *toraṇa* form.

Nepal

The most recurrent theme on the Newari (Nepalese) *toraṇas* is that of the *garuḍa* in combat with *nāgas,* seen in profusion in wood, gilded metal, and stone. The *garuḍa-nāga* theme links with Cambodian *toraṇas*; however, the portrayal differs. While a *garuḍa* placed at the apex of the *toraṇa* clasps the body of the serpents with his hands in the Cambodian representations, the *garuḍa's* upraised arms seem to indicate triumph over the serpent whom he clutches with his claws, in that of the Nepalese. Vegetal efflorescence and ornamental motifs are subordinated to figural sculpture, as the latter plays a dominant role on Newari *toraṇas*. Often, the serpents are shown in anthropomorphic form and appropriate iconographic imagery occupies the tympanum. The *kīrttimukha* (Newari: *chepu*) and *makara* (Newari: *hitimanga*) are also seen on these *toraṇas*, and at times *kinnaras* (half human-half bird figures) appear at the ends.[77]

5.56 : *Jhal-toraṇas*, Kathmandu, Bhaktapur Durbar Square, c. 17th-18th century.

5.57 : Inscribed Pañcarakṣā *toraṇa* (wooden) from the Hāratī temple, Svayambhūnāth, now in the Svayambhū Museum, dated 1802 CE.

5.57

5.55

5.58

5.58 : *Citra-makara-toraṇa (parikara)* Anuradhapura, guard stone at entrance to Ratanapāsāda showing Nāgarāja, c. ninth century.

5.59 : *Parikara-toraṇa* framing Buddha, Polonnaruva, Galavihāra, c. 12th century.

An inscription engraved on the door-lintel of the temple of Avalokiteśvara at Bungamati in Nepal records the placement of a golden door and *toraṇa* in the temple of Lokanātha (App. 1, no. 28). It is made of gilt brass and the arch circumscribes Lokeśvara. A wooden Pañcarakṣā *toraṇa* with a dedicatory inscription (dated 1802 CE) that belonged to the Hāratī temple, Svayambhūnāth, is now in the Svayambhū Museum at the same site (Fig. 5. 57; App. 1, no. 29).[82] Another inscribed (gilt) Pañcarakṣā *toraṇa* (dated 1828-29 CE) above the main entrance on the southern side of the same temple is very similar to the one in the site museum (App. 1, no. 30). Both Pañcarakṣā *toraṇas*, as also a third one of a recent date at the same temple, harbour images of Vajrasattva (missing on the wooden *toraṇa*) and the pentad of *rakṣā* goddesses at the centre.[83] The typical Newari *garuḍa-nāga* motif is placed at the apex of the outer band and outward-facing *kari-makaras* occupy the ends.

Sri Lanka

While the *garuḍa-nāga* motif is favoured on Newari *toraṇas*, the *kīrttimukha-makara* motif dominates in Sri Lankan instances. As in India, these are called *makara-toraṇas*. The Sri Lankan representations are closely allied to South Indian *toraṇas* from the Andhra and Tamil regions, though the eastern Indian influence is also in evidence. The practice of constructing *toraṇas* in wood, characteristic of street and gateway decorations for festive occasions, has also been known to prevail in Sri Lanka.[84] Sri Lankan *makara-toraṇas* in stone, metal, and also in medieval Sinhalese paintings are fairly well-known.

At Anuradhapura, the entrance stairway leading to an edifice was singled out for detailed sculptural ornamentation. Guard stones sculpted with guardian figures were placed on either side of the flight of steps at the entrance to a building. One such guard stone at Ratanapāsāda in the Abhayagiri grounds at Anuradhapura (c. ninth century) shows the figure of Nāgarāja between two plain pilasters from which springs forth an elaborately carved *citra-makara-toraṇa* (Fig. 5.58). The *makaras* emit *vyālas,* celestial couples, and garland-bearers, reminiscent of the *toraṇas* at the Pallavan Kailāsanātha temple at Kanchipuram (c. eighth century) in Tamil Nadu. The *makara-toraṇa* also finds representation around a (ritualistic or toilet?) stone seat at Anuradhapura (D.56).

A *toraṇa* framing a seated Buddha from Gal Vihāra at Polonnaruva (c. 12th century) shows an arch springing from vertical uprights and encircling Buddha's halo (Fig. 5.59). The vertical uprights are intersected by three crossbars akin to the ancient Indian examples from Bharhut and Sanchi. The *makaras* at the extremities of the architraves face outwards. The *toraṇa* fronts a miniature shrine representation, in all probability imitating actual or original structures. This method of portraying a *dvāra-toraṇa* fronting a miniature shrine is noticed in the eastern Indian manuscipt tradition and in sculptures.

Two Sinhalese *makara-toraṇas* in metal have been reported from Cleveland.[85] The first springs from uprights placed on an image pedestal. A *kīrttimukha* (Sinhalese *kibihi*) located at the apex releases a schematic arch that in turn flows into the jaws of the *makaras* at the two ends. The imagery of the figures with upraised arms holding a weapon is thematically similar but different in rendition from the southern Indian *parikara makara-toraṇas*. The *toraṇa* has been dated to the eighth century by the author, but appears to belong to a later period. The second example from Cleveland is even more stylised than the first. It may have framed a seated Buddha, judging by the shape of the space created by the inner margins of the arch and by the presence of Buddhist monks in the attitude of adoration on the vertical sections of the *toraṇa*.

5.59

D.56 : *Makara-toraṇa* around stone seat, Anuradhapura, c. ninth century.

D.57 : *Toraṇa* at main entrance to *Vihāra* 3 at Dambulla: wood engraving by Andrew Nicholl, 1860.

D.56

The links with India are remote in this example, which belongs to a period later than the one earlier discussed. A third representation of a *makara-toraṇa*, also in Cleveland, is seen on a Kandyan painting (c. 18th century) on paper.[86] This *makara-toraṇa* is typical of Kandyan art of the 18th century, and resembles the painted version of a *makara-toraṇa* placed above the image of Buddha in the interior of the Kandyan Lankātilaka *Vihāra*.[87] A *makara-toraṇa* embellishes the entrance to the Devarāja *Vihāra* at Dambulla, which also has Buddha images framed by *parikara-toraṇas* resembling those from the Tamil region of South India. A wood engraving of 1860 CE shows a *makara-toraṇa* at the main entrance to the *Vihāra* 3 at Dambulla (D.57).[88]

The cult of Pattini in Sri Lanka, prevalent to this day, offers an interesting example of the ritualistic and ceremonial role played by the *toraṇa*.[89] Pattini is a popular folk deity of the Sinhalese population, who relates to Kaṇṇaki in the *Cilappatikāram*, the great work of Tamil literature. The *toraṇa* serves as the Pattini-altar, in front of which several rituals are performed to the accompaniment of acts such as dancing and lighting of the lamp. The *toraṇa-yāgaya* or the ritual of the *toraṇa*-arch is an integral component of ritual worship to Pattini. Recitation of ritual texts on *toraṇa-yāgaya*, in a mixed dialect of Pali, Sanskrit, and Sinhala, praise the golden *toraṇa*, which is compared to Brahmā's beauty and power (Brahmā-Sahampati of Buddhism and Mahā-Brahmā of pre-Buddhist Brahmanism).[90] The comparison of the *toraṇa* to Brahmā's ocean and person lend it grandeur, dignity, and a ceremonial or ritual presence that is integral to the cult of Pattini. Another, of the set of 35 ritual texts in Pattini worship, describe four types of *toraṇas* - a golden one for the royal clan *(kula)*, one of gems for the Brahman caste, a cloth-*toraṇa* for the merchant caste and a *rãmba-toraṇa* for the farmer caste.[91] The *rãmba-toraṇa* is made of plantain trunks, with the outer bark peeled off so that the glistening trunk is displayed. Usually this is the *toraṇa* of the *gammaḍuva* rituals in the Pattini cult. It may be recalled here that some Indian texts and inscriptions also assign honorific, ceremonial, and ritualistic roles to *toraṇas* (App. 1-3).

During the ancient and medieval periods, the *toraṇa* assumed prominence as a symbolic and ornamental architectural member throughout the South and Southeast Asian regions. In the East Asian region of Japan too, one finds the concept of the *toraṇa* paralleled in the Japanese *torii*, which is an entryway with vertical posts and horizontal beam(s) of refined and restrained proportions, symbolizing the rite of passage. The idea as well as the form of the *toraṇa* took on newer shades of meaning and fresher expressions, reflecting shared and parallel developments in the South and Southeast Asian regions.

D.57

Notes and References

[1] H.I.R. Hinzler, "Inscriptions: Terms for buildings and temples,": "There are a number of inscriptions in Sanskrit, a few in Old Malay, but the majority uses Old Javanese in which Sanskrit loan words as well as indigenous terms for buildings and building material can be found. The word-list in which all the terms and references to the inscriptions in which they are used are contained may help to investigate the preference for either Sanskrit or indigenous terms for certain buildings." I am grateful to Dr. Hinzler for sharing this information.

[2] These are to be found in association with the earliest Pre-Angkorian monuments such as Ashram Maha Rishi, Kuk Prah Theat, Thala Borivat, and the SPK structures.

[3] With specific reference to the study of Cambodian lintels, significant research has been conducted by Lunet de Lajonquiere, H. Parmentier, P. Dupont, G. de Coral Remusat, Ph. Stern, Mireille Benisti and others. Benisti had considerably brought forward the research of her predecessors. See Bibliography.

[4] Lajonquiere, *Inventaire descriptif des monuments du Cambodge*.

[5] Parmentier, *L'art Khmer Primitif.*

[6] Remusat, "De l'origine commune des linteaux de l'Inde Pallava et des linteaux Khmers preangkoriens," pp.242-250; Also *L'art Khmer, les grand etapes de son evolution.*

[7] Stern, "Evolution du linteau Khmer," pp.251-256, Figs. 1-20.

[8] Dalet, "Notes sur les styles de Sambor Prei Kuk, de Prei Kmeng, de Kompong Preah et du Kulen," (page no.s were unfortunately unavailable at the time of sending this manuscript to press).

[9] Dupont, "Les linteaux Khmers du VIIe siecle," pp.30-83.

[10] Benisti, "Recherches sur le premier art Khmer. I – Les linteaux de Thala Borivat," pp.85-96; *Stylistics of Khmer Art.* See Bibliography for more references.

[11] See also Benisti, *Stylistcs...* Figs. 285-290, 295, 297; Dupont, "Les Linteaux...," Figs. 15-20.

[12] The Theat Ba Deum instance has been placed by Dupont in the SPK period and by Benisti in the PK style. Benisti, *Stylistcs...,* Fig. 450; Dupont, "Les Linteaux...," Fig. 9. The *toraṇa*-lintel is now in the Phnom Penh Museum.

[13] See also Benisti, *Stylistcs.,* Figs. 74, 75, 297, etc.

[14] Sambor Prei Kuk *toraṇas* with four arcs have been found from SPK Sanctuary N 7 (east face), the structure to the south-east of S 7, S 1 (western entryway and false door on west), N 15 (east face), Dambang Dek, Vat Eng Khna, Han Chei, etc. See Benisti, *Stylistcs...,* Figs. 7, 26, 47, 87, 103, 110, etc.

[15] See Benisti, "Recherches sur le premier art Khmer: I – Les linteaux de Thala Borivat," pp.85-96; Dupont, "Les linteaux Khmers...," pp.30-83:

Briefly, the arguments that support the anteriority of the SPK variant with four arcs are:

• The four arcs on the lintels of the SPK style, through a natural process of reduction, move towards the flattened singular arch of the PK style. The intermediate stages are to be seen on the *toraṇas* from Dambang Dek and Han Chei, for example, where the *toraṇa* arcs are not sharply defined but seem to flow and merge with each other in a wavy fashion.

• By the same reasoning, Dupont states that the Thala Borivat variants also show an intermediate stage in the movement from the SPK style to the PK style. He elaborates this by suggesting that the same reduction towards the single arc PK variant happens at Thala Borivat through the swallowing of the extremities of the arch and half the lateral medallions by the *makaras*. He points to the partially visible rim of the lateral medallions near the jaws of the *makaras* as evidence for this development.

The arguments in favour of the anteriority of the Thala Borivant variant are:
• The Thala Borivat lintels are more "primitive" in appearance; the *makaras* are stocky and bigger, the curves of the garlands underneath the arch delimit areas that are devoid of decoration, a large pendant lotus hangs below the central medallion, and the abacus of the pilaster supporting the lintel is not included in the lintel.

One may add that all these features on the dual-arc variant bring the Thala Borivat *toraṇas* closer to Indian counterparts of the fifth-seventh centuries. By comparison, the SPK variants with four arcs take us a step away from the Indian counterparts.

Also:
• The fact that the wall niches of some SPK sanctuaries are crowned with *toraṇas* of dual arcs clearly indicates that dual-arc forms were well-known during the period when more complex variants with four arcs were employed as *dvāra-toraṇas* at the SPK site (Fig. 5.2).

• The festoons beneath the *toraṇas* with four arcs at SPK (and other sites) are far more advanced than in the Thala Borivat variants. They are intricately carved, a trend that is carried forward in the PK style.

This is often not so in the case of the Thala Borivat variants where the festoons delimit spaces that are empty and devoid of décor.

• Benisti convincingly clarifies that Dupont's assumption that the ends of the arch and the half-medallions are swallowed by the *makaras* in the case of the Thala Borivat variant is incorrect. In support of her argument, she elaborates with the help of other examples from near the Thala Borivat site, such as Prasat Khtop, etc., and shows that the beaded borders near the *makaras'* jaws in the Thala Borivat variants are not related to the lateral medallions of the SPK variants with four-arcs.

• The motif of '*garuḍa-nāgas*' within the central medallion in the Thala Borivat variants is seen in a more developed form at the SPK site (for example, the lintel-fragment from the south group of sanctuaries). The example from Chantabuon (now in the Bangkok Museum) seems to provide an intermediate stage.

• Also, a late sixth-early seventh century stray inscription found at the site of Vat Kantel (in the region of Thala Borivat) which records the foundation of the brother-in-law of Bhāvavarman I supports the anteriority of the Thala Borivat variant.

[16] Benisti, *Stylistcs...,* Fig. 28.

[17] Benisti, "Notes d'Iconographie Khmere, III – Au Sujet D'Un Linteau De Sambor Prei Kuk," pp.71-75.

[18] Whereas Dupont has placed it at the beginning of the SPK style, Dalet and Benisti situate it towards the end of this style, citing stylistic as well as inscriptional reasons. Dupont, "Les linteaux Khmers du VIIe siecle," pp.30-83; Benisti, "Recherches sur le premier art Khmer: VII – Le Probleme De Sambor S.1," pp.25-49.

[19] Those carved on the eastern, northern, and southern door-lintels were found *in situ* by French scholars; the western one was relocated in the Phnom Penh Museum.

[20] The extremely damaged northern lintel of S 1 is also sculpted with a *toraṇa* of four shallow arcs. The southern lintel on this sanctuary has been reported to be fairly similar to the northern one but too damaged for analysis.

[21] Dupont, "Les linteaux Khmers...," pp.30-83.

[22] Also from sites such as Han Chei, Phnom Thom, Dambang Dek, Prasat Preah Theat, Vat Tang Kasang, Tuol Ang Srah Theat, Preah Theat Thom, and Sophas. See Benisti, *Stylistcs...,* Figs. 103-110.

[23] Instances of the mature PK style belong to Vat Eng Khna, Svay Preahm, Prei Kmeng, Vat Khnat, Kuk Roka, Prasat Ko, Robeang Romeah, Ampil Rolum, Vat Baray, Vat Prahar, Udong, and Vat Chum, etc. Benisti, *Stylistcs...,* Figs. 116-125.

[24] Both Dupont and Benisti have studied this transitional phase in some detail. Benisti has successfully traced a continuous, stage-by-stage, advancement of the vegetal PK variant to an evolved KP variant. These successive stages have been identified with the help of *toraṇas* from Robang Romeah, Trapeang Totung Thnay, Svay Preahm, Prasat Ko, Ampil Rolum, Vat Preah Neang, Vat Kakoh, SPK C 1, Prasat Andet, Prasat Sakhla, Vat Prasat, Prasat Khleang, Prasat Phum Prasat, and Kompong Preah. Benisti, "Recherches sur le premier art Khmer: III – Aux Confins Des Styles De Prei Kmeng Et De Kompong Preah," pp.93-111, Figs. 5-26.

[25] Thierry Zephir, though, is of the opinion that the transition between the PK and KP styles should not be considered as gradual. Rather, it is an innovation – one that marks a major departure from earlier norms and sets the trend for all future developments vis-à-vis Cambodian lintels. *See* Zephir, "Khmer Art," in Girard-Geslan *et. al., Art of Southeast Asia,* pp.151-249.

[26] The findings from an excavation in the Maharashtra region, which has revealed *toraṇa* fragments with multiple arcs that stylistically belong to the fifth century time-frame support this surmise. A multi-arc *toraṇa* fragment was brought to the notice of Prof. M.A. Dhaky by Dr. Sripad Keshav Chitale of Kavikulaguru Kālidas Sanskrit University, Ramtek, in May 2005. Several attempts to secure this visual from the source have been unfortunately unsuccessful.

[27] One representation of the *citra-toraṇa* belonging to the latter half of the seventh century, from the Viśvakarmā Cave (no. 10) at Ellora, is significant. Pairs of celestials in attitudes of worship, and moving towards a tree, are shown on the band of the arch. There are no *makaras* at the extremities and the pilasters from which the arch springs bear guardian figures.

[28] Coomaraswamy, *Yaksas: Essays in Water Cosmology,* Schroeder ed., pp.142-154.

[29] *Ibid.,* p.144; Bhartṛhari's *Nītiśataka* (c. fifth century) mentions a connection of *makaras* with pearls and states further that extracting a pearl from the jaws of a *makara* was a proverbial example of courage.

[30] The *garuḍa-nāgas* motif, although seen in Indian art from an early period, gains greater favour in Cambodia and Nepal.

[31] Benisti, *Stylistics of Early Khmer Art,* Vol. 1, p.103.

[32] *Ibid.,* p.104.

[33] *Ibid.,* p.110.

[34] Ellora Cave 15, c. eighth century (Fig. 3.36); Virūpākṣa temple, Pattadakal, 743 CE (Fig. 3.24); and Lakṣmaṇa temple, Khajuraho, 954 CE (Fig. 4.15), to name only three instances.

[35] See endnote 29.

[36] Siribhadra and Moore, *Palaces of the Gods...*, p.85.

[37] Fickle, "Khmer Architecture in Thailand," pp.65-78.

[38] Lunet de Lajonquiere had reported two such pieces from the Chantaboun region near Cambodia's western border. Benisti has published the photograph of one from Vat Thong Thua in the Chantaboun region that is now in the Bangkok Museum. Benisti, *Stylistcs...*, Fig. 295.

[39] Siribhadra and Moore, *Palaces of the Gods...*, p.27.

[40] *Ibid.*, pp.80-83.

[41] *Ibid.*, p.44.

[42] *Ibid. Toraṇa*-lintels have been found, for instance, at Prachinburi, Sathan Phra Narai, and Prasat Pako in Nakhon Ratchasima Province, Pran Ku in Sisaket Province, Prasat Muang Khaek, and Prasat Phnom Wan. Some of them are preserved in the Phimai Museum.

[43] Prasat Damrie Krap in Cambodia, for instance, betrays strong Cham influences.

[44] The capital during the seventh century was at Tra Kieu, near the religious site of Mi Son.

[45] See Benisti, "Representations Khmeres De Visnu Couche," pp.91-117. The Mi Son *toraṇa* comes closest to the one from Tuol Baset (Fig. 3 in Benisti's paper).

[46] For an image of this *toraṇa*-lintel, see Boisselier, *La Statuaire du Champa...*, Fig. 9.

[47] Classification No. 17.8, L: 2.18 m., H: 1.14 m., as given in Guillon, *Cham Art...*, p.72.

[48] *Ibid.* pp.73- 77: Object Classification No. 22.4, Da Nang Museum of Cham Sculpture, Vietnam.

[49] Albert Le Bonheur, "The Art of Champa," in Girard-Geslan *et. al.*, *Art of Southeast Asia,* Figs. 133, 558.

[50] For a visual, *see* J.C. Sharma, *Hindu Temples in Vietnam*, p.43.

[51] *Ibid.* p.122. The Khuong My *kalāns* have been placed by scholars in the period of transition from the Dong Duong to Mi Son A 1 styles.

[52] Guillon, *Cham Art...*, p.48, Fig. 23. Such a motif also acts as the image frame of the famous tenth century Bhagwatī image at Po Nagar of Nha Trang. For a visual, *see* Girard-Geslan *et. al., Art of Southeast Asia,* Fig. 145.

[53] Sharma, *Hindu Temples in Vietnam,* p.128.

[54] For a published image of this *torana*-lintel, see Boisselier, *La Statuaire du Champa,* Figs. 206, 207.

[55] Boisselier, *La Statuaire du Champa...*, Figs. 217-221.

[56] These and probably some architectural drawings and manuals must have provided a base for a similar yet distinctly individualistic architectural style in Java. More recent literature traces the origins of the *Caṇḍī* in Indonesia to the megalithic structures of an earlier period. However, it is the structural and ornamental (visual) correspondences to Indian temples that are addressed here.

[57] For a detailed exposition on the subject of the *kīrttimukha*, see Gangoly, "A Note on the *Kīrttimukha*: Being the Life-history of an Indian Architectural Ornament," pp.11-19 ; Kramrisch, "The Face of Glory: Kirttimukha," in her *The Hindu Temple,* Vol. II, pp.322-331; and Stutterheim, "The Meaning of the *Kāla-makara* Ornament," pp.27-52.

[58] Kramrisch, *The Hindu Temple*, Vol. II, pp.322-331. In the chapter on Rāhucāra in the *Bṛhat Saṁhitā*, Varāhamihira relates the myth of the churning of the ocean for *amṛta,* and of the origin of *kīrttimukha.* Here, *kīrttimukha* is the severed head of Rāhu, son of Siṁhikā the lioness, who having partially partaken of *amṛta,* survived in this beheaded form to bring good fortune. As Rāhu, he is both Tamas – darkness, and Svarabhānu – splendour of radiance; as Kāla, he is time and death.

[59] *Ibid.*

[60] The 17th Chapter of the Kārtikamāsa Mahātmya of the *Skanda-purāṇa (Visṇukhaṇḍa)*, as mentioned in Gangoly, "A Note on the *Kīrttimukha*: Being the Life-history of an Indian Architectural Ornament," p.12. According to the *Skanda-purāṇa*, *kīrttimukha* was born of Lord Śiva, to devour Rāhu, the messenger of Jallandara. When Rāhu pleaded to Śiva, Śiva stopped his fierce creation from devouring Rāhu and instead asked him to satiate his hunger by eating his own nether parts. He was thus left with only his face and earned the name *kīrttimukha*.

[61] Sarnath Museum no. 1788, Chunar sandstone, 130 x 40 cm.

[62] Bernet Kempers, *Ancient Indonesian Art,* p.50.

[63] The works of G. Coedes, A.J. Bernet Kempers, Claire Holt, R. Soekmono, R.C. Majumdar, H. Sarkar,

D.G.E.Hall, J.G. de Casparis, W. F. Stutterheim, Marijke Klokke, and others have enabled a fair assessment of the chronology of Indonesian monuments. For a chronology of Central Javanese rulers, *see* Huntington and Huntington, *Leaves from the Bodhi Tree.,* Appendix III, Chart 6.

[64] For an early assessment of the nature of Indian influence on Indonesian art, see Bosch, "A Hypothesis as to the Origin of Indo-Javanese Art," pp.6-41.

[65] An inscription dated c. 782 CE from Kelurak (Jogjakarta District, Java) refers to the setting up of an image of Mañjuśrī by a royal preceptor from Gauḍa, Kumāraghoṣa. See Majumdar, *Ancient Indian Colonies in the Far East*, Vol. II *(Suvarṇadvīpa)*, Part I, pp.151-152. The Nālandā copperplate inscription dated to year 39 of Devapāla (third quarter of ninth century), records the grant of five villages for the maintenance of a monastery at Nalanda, by the ruler of *Suvarṇadvīpa,* Balaputradeva. See *Epigraphia Indica XVII* (1923-24), pp.310-27. In an analysis of Pāla-Sena sculpture of eastern India, Susan Huntington points to very specific types of contacts between eastern India and regions such as Indonesia, Burma, Tibet, etc. Inscriptional as well as stylistic evidence points to strong contacts shared by Nalanda with Java and Sumatra on the one hand and Bodhgaya and Burma on the other. See Huntington, *The "Pala-Sena" Schools of Sculpture,* p.151.

[66] Tanjore inscription of Rajendra Cōḷa dated in his 19th year (1031 CE) mentions capturing of the *vidyādhara-toraṇa* at the "war-gate" of the extensive city of the enemy, and refers to his conquest of Śrīviṣaya (Śrīvijaya). See App.1, no. 15. Earlier contacts with India are indicated by the inscriptions of King Mūlavarman from East Kālimantan (c. 400 CE) and King Pūrṇavarman from West Java (mid-fifth century). Chinese sources indicate the presence of Buddhist and Hindu pilgrims and missionaries in Indonesia from the early fifth century.

[67] See Girard Geslan *et. al.*, *Art of Southeast Asia*, plate 181, for an illustration.

[68] The pattern carved on the entrance doorframe of Cave 4 at Pitalkhora (c. 100-70 BCE), for example, is very similar to the one seen on this *toraṇa* from Temple no. II at the *Caṇḍī* Gedong Sanga complex. This can also be seen on some of the ornamental arches at the entrances to the cells on the upper level of the Rānī Gumphā, Udaygiri (Khandagiri), Orissa, c. early first century. For visuals, *see* Huntington, *The Art of Ancient India.*, illus. 5.34 & 6.27.

[69] This *toraṇa* is closest to the *nāsī-toraṇas* mentioned in the Dravidian texts and resembles the *gavākṣa* (dormer) motif, although the *toraṇa* is ovoid in shape. The *gavākṣa*, like this *toraṇa* variant, is often depicted with the *kīrttimukha* at the apex and with the *makaras* at the ends.

[70] *Caṇḍī* Kalasan had earlier been dated to c. 778 CE on the basis of an inscription. However, a major part of the monument as it exists today belongs to the mid-ninth century. See Bernet Kempers, *Ancient Indonesian Art*, p.49.

[71] Two exquisite examples of celestial couples in a cloudscape are carved on seventh century ceiling slabs from Aihole, presently displayed in the National Museum, New Delhi.

[72] Bernet Kempers, *Ancient Indonesian Art,* Plates 122-123.

[73] A similar ornament may be seen on a *toraṇa* of the Durga temple, Aihole and on the Kailāsanātha temple, Kanchipuram (Plates 3.19, 3.45).Whereas *toraṇas* with divergent makaras at the ends is the norm in Indonesia, in India, there are fewer examples. In the case of *parikara toraṇas* and those adorning the back-rests of thrones, divergent *makaras* at the extremities, with a *kīrttimukha* at the apex, are prevalent motifs, particularly in eastern Indian sculpture. The outward-facing *makaras* are also encountered on Orissan *toraṇas.*

[74] At Nalanda, Islamic attacks in 1199 resulted in the destruction of libraries that housed illustrated manuscripts. A manuscript of 1015 CE, housed in the Cambridge University Library, shows Prajñāpāramitā seated within a trefoil arch in one instance, and a pentafoil arch in another. In an Aṣṭasahasrikā Prajñāpāramitā palm leaf manuscript (c. 12th century), Buddha is seated in front of a shrine under a *toraṇa* with five semi-circular arcs. The manuscript is now in the Los Angeles County Museum of Art.

[75] A stone piece belonging to the ancient Pyu culture, now in the Hmawza Museum, and datable to the sixth-seventh century, is carved in low relief with a seated image of Buddha flanked by an attendant on each side. The trio is canopied by a faintly visible *parikara-makara-toraṇa* as may be seen on throne-backs in the Indian context. Another stone stele unearthed in Śrīkṣetra in the 1970s, datable to the fifth-sixth century also shows a *parikara-makara-toraṇa* crowning two female figures carrying a throne between them. See Donald M. Stadtner, "The Art of Burma," in Girard-Geslan *et. al., Art of Southeast Asia,* pp.39-91, Figs. 235, 236.

[76] *Ibid.* Fig. 51.

[77] See Gail, *Klöster in Nepal,* Tafel XXII, 1, for a Newari *toraṇa* with *kinnaras* at the ends, at the Buddhist monastery in Patan, Kva Bāhā (Hiraṇyavarṇa-mahāvihāra), c. 1619-1661 CE.

[78] Durgā on the *toraṇa* of the Kumārī temple, Śiva Naṭeśa with *gaṇas* above the door of the Śiva temple in Mangal Bazar in Patan, and Annapūrṇā and

Lokeśvara on the Chusyabahal *toraṇa* may be mentioned as examples.

[79] Gail, *Tempel in Nepal,* Band I, Tafel II, 1-4.

[80] Deo, Shantaram Bhalchandra, *Glimpses of Nepal Woodwork...,* pp.36-37, Plates VII, XXXVI, 1-3, 7-9.

[81] VAM no. IM 142 A and B-1926; 142 A: H: 24 cm, W: 40.7 cm, D: 7.5 cm; 142 B: H: 23.3 cm, W: 38 cm, D: 7.5 cm.

[82] Mevissen, "A Dated Pañcarakṣā *toraṇa...,*" pp.137-149. The temple has another Pañcarakṣā *toraṇa* above the northern false door, which seems to be of a recent date. The eastern and western sides have gilt *toraṇas* that harbour Mañjuśrī in the centre.

[83] *Ibid.*

[84] Coomaraswamy mentions the practice of erecting a gaily ornamented Sanchi type of *toraṇas* at the gateway of a *devale* procession path during *perahera* time, in Sri Lanka. Coomaraswamy, *Mediaeval Sinhalese Art,* p.253.

[85] Ward, "Sinhalese *Makara Toraṇas* in Cleveland," pp.23-27, Figs. 1-2.

[86] *Ibid.* Fig. 3.

[87] Coomaraswamy, *Mediaeval Sinhalese Art,* Plate VIII A.

[88] "*Makara-toraṇa*" at main entrance to *Vihāra* 3 at Dambullā; Wood engraving by Andrew Nicholl in Ceylon by Emerson Tennent (1860), in Bhandaranayake, Mogren, and Epitawatte eds., *The Settlement Archaeology of the Sigiriya-Dambulla Region,* p.50, Fig. 46.

[89] For a detailed anthropological study of the Pattini cult and the rituals involved, see Obeyesekere, *The Cult of Goddess Pattini.* The account of the *toraṇa*-ritual included here is based on his work.

[90] *Ibid.* pp.202-204: Text 13:
"*Sanna* (Exposition):
[The *toraṇa* should be] like the ocean of Brahmā described earlier, 48 leagues [*gavva*, about 3 $^1/_2$ miles] in length, having mounds [?] about half a league in width, having a base about 7 $^1/_2$ leagues high; [the *toraṇa* should be] like the golden jewelled throne of the great Brahmā Sahampati [Mahā Brahmā Sahampati], king of heaven."

[91] *Ibid.* Text 14b.

Overview

Mohinī standing under a *toraṇa*, detail of pillar in the interior of the hall, Belur, Cennakeśava temple, c.1173-1220 CE.

Overview

In India, *toraṇas* are noticed in sacred and secular contexts from about the second century BCE and find mention in several texts and inscriptions of the ancient period. The earliest surviving free-standing examples are seen in association with Buddhist monuments but a cross-section of evidence indicates their contemporaneous presence in other religious and secular settings also. During this period, they are also seen in the relief sculptures from India and regions beyond the present north-western boundaries of India. Even though they did not serve a structural function in a building, *toraṇas* remained popular in ancient and medieval India because of their varied symbolic and aesthetic roles. They were located along the ramparts of a city or a fort, in association with sacred structures, divine images, *maṇḍalas*, thrones, palaces, and residences. At times, they were employed as props for swings, as weighing scales, in association with wells, and also as independent architectural members. They also served as memorials to commemorate a victory, to represent the honour of a city or kingdom, as a ceremonial construct in a ritual, and are known to have been used even in a funerary context. They were made of varied materials such as wood, ivory, flowers, leaves, gems, precious metals, and stone. Available evidence indicates that they shared the rationale of their origins with other ancient and medieval Indian entryways such as the *gopura, pratolī,* and *dvāra*. But fairly early in the ancient period, a differentiation of form and function set apart the *toraṇas* from the other gateways.

Beginning from the fifth century, the increased construction of stone temples and rock-cut caves marked a new phase in the history of Indian architectural expressions. The earlier *toraṇas* gradually made way for newer adaptations in the changed settings. The shared intent and rationale of the *toraṇa* and the *dvāra*, which was merged in the entrance to Nasik *Vihāra* 3, for example, found expression as the *toraṇabandha* on temple door-frames and as the *dvāra-toraṇa* at entrances to caves and temples. The *toraṇas* from the fifth century onwards register several variations in consonance with regional, temporal, religious, and cultural requirements. The general trend is from simpler to complex formulations through repetitions, permutations, combinations, and rhythmic progressions of constituent elements, as well as innovations within the traditional framework, resulting in a range of forms. However, there is not always a strictly linear formalistic progression through time and atavistic tendencies as well as more radical transformations are also in evidence. Representations of deities, minor divinities, the symbolic imagery of hybrid animal forms, jewels (*ratna*), flowers *(puṣpa)*, and leaves *(patra)* are carved on the *toraṇas*. These embellishments relate to the shared symbolism of the monument with which the *toraṇa* is associated and also to the living tradition of tying flowers, leaves, and jewels at the entrances. Narratives of a didactic nature, such as those seen on the Sanchi *toraṇas*, are rarely repeated on those seen in monuments of the succeeding centuries.

Some of the recurring forms were standardized as visual categories that adhered to given principles of composition, and were recorded in the medieval treatises. The textual types were based on form, thematic content, architectural setting, constituent elements and their proportionate arrangement, and other visual criteria. At times the treatises incorporated complex theoretical extrapolations that were not actualized. Often, they recorded general types, which were variously interpreted in practice in response to regional and temporal predilections, the innate creativity of the artist, and other allied factors. A few of the variations mentioned in the early medieval treatises are in evidence on earlier structures, reaffirming the view that practice preceded formal codification. Interestingly, some of the texts also record differentiations in the employment of the various types of *toraṇas*, based on the hierarchical social order of castes.

In the rock-cut caves and structural temples, the *toraṇas* are carved in relief at entrances *(dvāra-toraṇas)*, as image-frames *(parikara-toraṇas)*, or on the entablatures of aisles and vestibules *(antarāla-toraṇas)*. They may be undulating *(āndola)* or of single, twin, or multiple arcs or loops *(illikā)*. They are also located on the outer temple walls *(kuḍya-toraṇas)*, where they crown niches, are placed above latticed windows, or are variously organized on the offsets and intervening recesses. In addition, they also embellish temple interiors and superstructures, assuming complex forms during the later centuries. The constituent elements of *toraṇas* carved in relief are similar to those of the free-standing ones, but the former are executed as miniature versions of the latter. At times, they are placed in front of miniature temple models and frame divinities. Such *toraṇas* are often met in manuscript paintings, sculptures, or are carved in relief on the walls of sacred monuments. Such an arrangement suggests that the deity housed in the sanctum is seen through the *toraṇa* placed at the entrance. A similar message is conveyed by *toraṇas* placed at the sanctum doorways, or those engaged at the entrance to a sacred structure.

Some basic features pertaining to the location, context, typology, and treatment set apart the central and western Indian *toraṇas* from their southern Indian counterparts. The presence of *kuḍya-toraṇas* is comparatively limited in these regions, unlike in southern India. This is due to the differences in the exterior wall definitions of the medieval temples of the two regions. Also, the western and central Indian *toraṇas* are "free-flying," that is, the arch is independent of the matrix of the stone upon which it was carved. This accords an altogether different appearance to the arches in the temple halls and at the entrances, their graceful contours and delicately rendered masses shown to advantage in the elusive play of light and shade. Their southern counterparts are usually carved in relief, but as in the Karnataka temples, one witnesses exquisite formulations rendered in rampant profusion, which enhance the aesthetics of the walls, lintels, door-frames, image-frames, and *nāsīs*. Several subtler and complex processes of form and transformation are observed within this general framework. Although eastern India yields fewer examples, these have a significant bearing on those in the South and Southeast Asian regions.

Free-standing *toraṇas* are noticed more frequently in association with temples, beginning from the 10th century. These are often encountered in western and central India. In southern India, where relatively fewer examples are found, the majority are from Karnataka and Andhra Pradesh. From the 13th century, the *toraṇas* also register their presence in the mosques and mausoleums, while at the same time remaining in evidence in temples, palaces, forts, and other settings. They merge with the newer architectural traditions of Indo-Islamic affiliation and adapt to the requirements of the medieval architectural landscape. For instance, the *illikā-toraṇa* transforms into the engaged cusped arches in the *mihrābs,* screens, and façades of Indo-Islamic and Rajput structures. In western Indian mosques, the *āndola-toraṇas* are made suitable to fit the *mihrāb* pediments. When used as a free-flying arch, as in the Jāmī Masjid in Ahmedabad or at the Rānījī-kī-baorī in Bundi, the *toraṇas* are admirably reinvented as attenuated fragile ornamental arches, devoid of figural embellishment. The diminishing importance of figural embellishment is also noticed on the high medieval temple *toraṇas*.

The many adaptations and visual formulations of the *toraṇa* far outlived its original intent and significance. In some South and Southeast Asian regions, their varied forms gave rise to alternate and parallel expressions. Historical records and living traditions from some of these regions reveal that the term *toraṇa* was also well-known beyond the boundaries of India. Even as far as Japan, the idea and image of the *torii* corresponds with the *toraṇa*.

Appendices

Appendix 1 : Inscriptional Notices
Appendix 2 : Literary Sources
Appendix 3 : References in Treatises
Appendix 4 : Variants in Treatises

Appendix 1
Inscriptional Notices

1.a On a pillar of the eastern *toraṇa* from Bharhut, now in the Indian Museum, Kolkata. The inscription records the name and lineage of the person responsible for the making of the *toraṇa* during the reign of the Śuṅga dynasty:
Inscription no. A 1, 687:
Text: *Suganaṁ raje raño Gāgiputasa Visadevasa*
pauteṇa Gotiputasa Āgarajusa puteṇa
Vāchhiputena Dhanabhūtina kāritaṁ toranāṁ
(toraṇaṁ)
silākaṁmaṁto ca upaṁno.
Tr. During the reign of the Sugas (Śuṅgas), the gateway *(toraṇam)* was caused to be made and the stonework (i.e. carving) presented by Dhanabhūti, the son of a Vāchhī (Vātsī), son of Āgaraju (Aṅgāradyut), the son of a Gotī (Gauptī) and grandson of king Visadeva (Viśvadeva), the son of Gāgī (Gārgī).
Source: *CII* Vol. II, Part 2 *(Bharhut Inscriptions),* ed. Heinrich Lüders, pp. 11-12, Pl. 1.

1.b Fragmentary inscription on the pillar of a gateway:
Inscription no. A 2, 688:
Text: *Sagāna rāja...*
Agaraju...
toraṇaṁ...
Tr. During the reign of the Sugas (Śuṅgas), Agaraju (Aṅgāradyut)... the *toraṇa...*
Source: *CII* Vol. II, Part 2 *(Bharhut Inscriptions),* ed. Heinrich Lüders, p. 14, Pl. XXIII.

1.c Fragmentary inscription on the pillar of a gateway:
Inscription no. A 129, 689;
Text: *hena*
***toraṇaṁ** ca*
kata
The inscription apparently recorded the gift of a *toraṇa* but no connected translation is possible.
Source: *CII* Vol. II, Part 2 *(Bharhut Inscriptions),* ed., Heinrich Lüders, p. 63, Pl. XXVI.

2. On a Jain tablet of homage *(āyāgapaṭṭa)* depicting a *toraṇa* fronting a *stūpa* and punctuating a *vedikā*-railing (Lucknow Museum No. J 255):
Tr. "Adoration to the Arhats; By Sivayaśa, wife of the donor Phaguyaśa ...a tablet of homage was caused to be made for the worship of Arhats." (Donatory inscr.: c. first century).
Source: *EI,* V, II, p. 200.

3. On a door jamb from Mathura. *Toraṇa* in association with a *vedikā*-railing, for a Brahmanical sacred structure, donated by a person for accrual of religious merit to his superior, a person of high-rank:
Tr. By Vasu, a gateway of stone *(lam **toraṇaṁ**...)* and the railing was erected at the great temple of Bhāgvata Vāsudeva. May Bhāgvata Vāsudeva, being pleased, promote (the dominion or the life and strength) of *svāmin mahākṣatrapa Ṣodaśa.*
Source: *EI,* XXIV, pp. 208-209.

4. On a pillar from Mathura, of Jain affiliation. Donated for accrual of religious merit:
Text: _ *mā Ahantānaṁ śramaṇaśrāvikā [ye]*
_ *lahastinīye **toraṇaṁ** prati [ṣṭhāpi]*
saha mātā pitihi saha
saśrū _ *śaśureṇa*
Tr. Adoration to the Arhats! A *toraṇa* has been erected by order of *..lahastinī (Balahastini),* a lay pupil of the ascetics *(śramaṇaśrāvikā)...,* together with her parents, together with her mother-in-law (and) her father-in-law.
Source: G. Bühler, "New Jaina Inscriptions from Mathura," *EI,* I, pp. 371-393, Inscr. 17, p. 390).

5. On a *toraṇa* architrave from Kankali Tila. Donated by a lay person to a Jain temple:
Text: *Samanasa Māharakhitāsa Āntevāsisa*
Vachiputrasa Sāvakāsa Utaradāsakasa
Pāsādotoraṇam (pp. 198-199).
Tr. An ornamental arch for the temple, (the gift) of the lay hearer Utaradāsaka, son of Vacchi and disciple of the ascetic Mahārakhita.
Source: G. Bühler, "Jaina inscriptions from Mathura," *EI,* II, pp. 195-212.

6. On a Buddhist railing-pillar from Mathura. *Toraṇa* punctuating a *vedikā*-railing, donated by a lay-person:
Text: *ka[p]*
bhuti sa...(Vā)ts(ī)-
putrasa...sa
Dhanabhūtisa dāna[ṁ] vedikā
***toraṇāni** ca ratnagṛh[e] sa-*
rvabudhapujāye saha mātāpi-
tihi sahā[ca] catu[hī]pariṣāhī
Tr. The gift of Dhanabhūti, the..., the son of (Vā)ts(ī), ... bhūti... (consisting in) a railing and gateways ***(toraṇāni)*** at the jewel house in honour of all Buddhas, together with his parents and together with the four assemblies.
Source: *CII,* Vol. II, Part 2 (Bharhut Inscriptions), ed., Heinrich Lüders, pp. 12-14.

7. On a rail bar *(sūci)* from Mathura, now in a private collection in America. Donated for a Buddhist establishment. Suggests the presence of stairways leading up to a *stūpa* enclosed by a *vedikā* and *toraṇas*:
Text: *..**toraṇāni** sopānāni ca ratana-g(ṛ)he sahā mātā-pitihi sahā catu(nā) pariṣāhi sarva-budha-pūjāye ācariyānaṁ mahāsa(ṁ)ghiyana(m) parigrahe*
Tr. gateways and stairways with jewels in the jewel house (were donated) for the worship of all Buddhas, with mother, father, and the four assemblies, for the acceptance of the Mahāsāṅghika teachers.
Source: Bhattacharya, Gouriswar, "Two Donations in favour of the Mahāsāṅghikas of Mathura," pp.421-427.

8. ***Tr.*** Imprecation against him who takes away or causes to be taken away an arch ***(toraṇa)*** or rail *(vedikā)* from this [Kakana]va, or causes it to be transferred to another temple of the teacher *(ācāriyakula)*.
Source: *Appendix to Epigraphia Indica and Record of the Archaeological Survey of India,* Vol. X, ed. Heinrich Lüders, p. 41, no. 340.

9. At Halebidu, above the southern doorway of the Hoysaḷeśvara temple. Cites the name and acquired titles of the artist who carved the *makara-toraṇa* and also of a master artist for whom he worked in the reign of the Hoysala king Narasiṁhadeva:
Text: *Svasti śrīmatu-pratāpa-Hoysaḷa-Nārasiṁha-Dēvana rūvāri Kēdārōjaṅge mala-vara-gaṇḍa biruda-rūvāri-giri-vajra-daṇḍa rūvāri-Kāḷidāsi geyda*
makara-toraṇa/
maṅgalaṁ śrī/
Tr. For pratāpa-Hoysaḷa-Nārasiṁha-Dēva's sculptor, Kēdārōja, the sculptor Kāḷidāsi, champion over the proud, a thunderbolt to the rock *(vajra-giri)* titled sculptors, made the *makara-toraṇa* (or carved the head-piece for the lintel).
Source: *EC,* V, Part I, Supplement, Belur Taluq, no. 239, pp. 592 and 275*;* (Date about 1140 CE).

10. At Halebidu, on a stone-slab of the Doḍḍa-Basavaṇṇa temple, belonging to the Hoysaḷeśvara temple. Cites the name of the artist who carved the door-frame (including the *toraṇa* on the door-lintel?) on the eastern side of the Hoysaḷeśvara temple:
Text: *mūdaṇa-bāgilavāḍava Dēmōja gēda//*
Tr. Dēmōja made the frame of the eastern door.
Source: *EC,* V, Part I, Belur Taluq, no. 241, p. 592 and Vol. V, Part I, Supplement, Belur Taluq, no. 241, p. 275; (Date about 1140 CE?).

11. At the ruined Harṣanātha temple at Harshagiri. The inscription records the erection of a temple complex of Śiva (here, Harṣa) on the hill Harsha by the Śaiva ascetic Allaṭa, and its completion by Allaṭa's disciple Bhāvadyota. It describes the temple's *toraṇa* in two separate verses, mentioning the bull (Nandī) and many gods that were sculpted on it. The name of the chief architect who authored the temple and the *toraṇa* is also mentioned:

11a. v. 12, p. 121:
Text: *Meroh śriṅgopamānaṁ*
*sughaṭitavṛṣasat**toraṇa**dvāraramyaṁ/*
Nānāsaṁbhogayuktaṁ jayati bhagavato
*Harṣadevasya//*12
Tr. p. 126: (Glorious is the mansion of holy Harṣadeva...)
Surpassing in height the peak of Meru, it is beautified by a well-made *toraṇa* at which a bull is skilfully carved, and is endowed with manifold objects of enjoyment.

11b. vv.43-44, pp.123-124:
Text: *Vīrabha[dra]sutaḥ khyātaḥ sūtradhāritra Caṇḍaśiva*
Viśvakarmeva sarvagñyo vāstuvidyā[ṁ]
[ye]na nirmitamidaṁ manoharaṁ śankarasya bhavanaṁ samaṇḍapaṁ
*[sa]rva-deva-maya-cāru-**toraṇaṁ** svarga-khaṇḍaṁ iva vedhasā svayam/*
Tr. p. 128: The architect in this (work) was Caṇḍaśiva, the famed son of Vīrabhadra, omniscient like Viśvakarman in the art of building houses... He built this delightful house of Śaṁkara, with its chapels (and) the beautiful *toraṇa* that harbours all the gods, like a portion of heaven made by the creator himself.
v. 47, p. 124, tr. p. 129:
The temple was completed on the 13th day of the bright half of Āṣāḍha of the year VS 1013 (956 CE).
Source: F. Keilhorn, "Harsha Stone Inscription of Cāhamāna Vigraharāja, VS 1030," *EI,* II, pp. 116-130.

12. From Kumbhariya, an inscription of 1125 CE from the Mahāvīra temple, originally from the main sanctuary of the Pārśvanātha temple, recording the dedication of a *toraṇa* for Pārśvanātha by a *śrāvaka*:
Text: *Samvat 1181 Kārtik Sudi 15 Su(Śu)kradine Śrīpārasva(rśva)nāthadevasya Sāmbā Ṣeḍhā Srā(Śrā)vakena **Toraṇam** Kārāpitaṁ//*
Source: Dhaky and Moorti, *The Temples in Kumbhāriyā,* p. 111, Inscr. no. 19.

13. From Kumbhariya, the dedication of a *toraṇa* for accrual of religious merit to the donor's mother, dated 1231 CE:
Text: *Samvat 1287 Varṣe Māgha sudi 10 Budhe Śrīnābhinandanadevasya Mātālakṣmīśreyorthaṁ Sre. Sajjanena* ***Toraṇam*** *Kāritaṁ//*
Source: Dhaky and Moorti, *The Temples in Kumbhāriyā,* p. 118, Inscr. no. 76.

14. On the pillar of a *toraṇa* originally erected in front of the Mahāvīra temple at Osian, which records the date (978 CE or 1018 CE?) of its establishment. Note the prefix *'Śrī'* before *'toraṇam'*:
Text: *Saṁ 1035 Āṣāḍha sudi 10 Ādityavāre Svātinakṣatre* ***Śrī toraṇaṁ*** *pratiṣṭhāpitamiti/*
Source: Handa, *Osian: History, Archaeology...* pp. 46-47.
D.R. Bhandarkar had earlier read it as:
Saṁ 1075 Āṣāḍha sudi 10 Ādityavāre Svātinakṣatre..., and mentioned that the inscription recorded the names of two individuals credited with the construction of the *toraṇa.* Their names were not legible.
Source: *ASIAR* 1908-09, p. 108.

15. Rajendra Coḷa's inscription of 1034 CE refers to his conquest of the kingdom of Kidara, and the amassing of booty including the ***Vicchādira (Vidyādhara/ Vicitra?) toraṇa*** at the war gate of the enemy's extensive city. Capturing the enemy's *toraṇa* and carrying it away as war booty signified the appropriation of the kingdom and honour of the enemy.
Tr. (Who), (Rajendra Coḷa) - having despatched many ships in the midst of the rolling sea and having caught Saṁgrāma Vijayottuṅga-varman, the king of Kaḍāram, along with (his) vehicles, *(viz.)* rutting elephants, (which were as impetuous as) the sea in fighting, - (took) the large heap of treasures, which (that king) had rightfully accumulated; the (arch called) *vidyādhara-toraṇa* at the "war-gate" of the extensive city of the enemy; the "jewel gate," adorned with great splendour; the gate of large jewels;" Vijayam, of great fame...
Source: *South Indian Inscriptions,* Vol. II, Part 1, ed. E. Hultzsch, (Tanjore) Inscription No. 20 (Inscription of Rajendra Coḷa 1), pp. 105-109.
For amendments, see *EI,* IX (1907-08), eds. E. Hultzsch and Sten Konow, p. 231:
"In conclusion I would like to add a few words on the later conquests of Rajendra Coḷa I which are registered in the Tanjore inscription No. 20. Mr. Venkayya has shown that my identification of Kaḍāram with a place in the Madura district must be wrong, because the Chola king despatched an expedition to it on ships by sea... Instead of the first, which I had translated by 'Vijayam of great fame,' an inscription at Kaṇḍiyūr near Tanjore reads *niṛai-śrīvishayaimum,* 'the prosperous Śrīvishaya.' This may be the correct reading, for according to the larger Leiden grant (1.80), Śrīvishaya was the name of the country ruled over by the king of Kaṭāha or Kaḍāram."

16. The inscription contains a *praśasti* composed at the consecration of five *liṅgas* in Somanathapattana (Devapattana or Prabhas), the famous Śaiva *tīrtha* in Kathiawar (Veraval) (1287 CE). Suggests a *prākāra-toraṇa* at the enclosure wall of a temple-complex:
Text: *Ātma bāhu yuga sauhṛd-āṁcita-stambha-saurabha-śubhaṁ su-****toraṇam/*** *Dūram-asta-duritastad-uttaradvāra-bhūparisare cakāra yaḥ//* v.46, p. 284
***Tr.*:** The inscription states that Tripurāntaka built five temples, dedicated five statues and erected an auspicious and beautiful *toraṇa* supported by two pillars. The temples were erected to the north of the hall of the temple of Someśvara. The *toraṇa* was erected in the region before the northern gate of the five temples. This suggests that the temples were surrounded by a wall and that the arch adorned the principal entry into the enclosure which had to be made on the north side as the great temple of Someśvara lay to the south and east, and to the west lay the sea. (pp. 271-276)
Source: G. Bühler, "The Cintra Prasasti of the reign of Sarangadeva," *EI,* I, pp. 271-287.

17. On a pillar at Devapattana or Somanathapattana, near Veraval. The inscription eulogises the temple and town of Somanatha, Śrīdhara-the representative of the Vastrākula family in VS 1273 who built several temples at Devapattana, the Śaiva ascetic Vimalaśiva, and the Caulukya kings. The names of the author of the *praśasti* and the architect of the temples are unfortunately lost. The erection of *toraṇas* is mentioned here along with a list of other pious acts that were traditionally believed to accrue religious merit.
Text: *vāpikūpataḍāgakuṭṭimamaṭhaprāsādasatrālayan sauvarṇadhvaja****toraṇā****paṇa-puragrāmaprapāmaṇḍapān/* v.10, p. 440
Tr. The inscription mentions that the king commissioned the sons of a pious astrologer to look after the supervision of his charities and the digging of wells and tanks as well as the erection of houses of

refuge, colleges, temples, and alms-houses, gilt flagstaffs, *toraṇas*, markets, towns, villages, drinking fountains and halls (pp. 438-439).
Source: G. Bühler, "Sridhara's Devapattana Prasasti," (1273 VS/ 1216 CE), *EI,* II, pp. 437-446.

18. At Sundha Hill in the Jodhpur District of Rajasthan. The primary object of this inscription is to glorify the Cāhamāna chief Cacigadeva (VS 1319/ 1262 CE) and also to give a general eulogistic account of the Cāhamānas of Naḍḍula. A golden *toraṇa* is mentioned in a commemorative role – to mark a victory:
Text: *ma-nṛpater=mānahṛt-sainyasiṁdhuḥ/ nirbhidy=ōccaiḥ prava(ba)la-kalitaṁ yas=Turushkaṁ vyadhatta śrīSōmēśāspada mukuṭavat=**tōraṇam kāṁcanasya**//*v.34
Tr. Verse 34 of this inscription states that (Cāhamāna) Kelhaṇa defeated the southern King Bhilima (Devagiri-Yādava Bhillama), and after destroying the Turushka, erected a golden *toraṇa*, like a diadem for the abode of holy Someśa.
Source: F. Keilhorn, "Sundha Hill Inscription of Cacigadeva; [Vikrama] Samvat 1319," *EI,* IX (1907-08), pp. 70-79.

19. Inscription dated 3rd May 1032 on a slab erected to the south-east of the fort of Koppal (of the Aśokan Edict fame), describing a lofty, curved free-standing *makara-toraṇa* carved with geese and in association with a stairway (perhaps on a hill). Note the usage of *yamaka,* the poetic figure of speech:
Text and ***Tr.*** The worshipper of the feet of Parama-śrī-jinadharmma-ratnanidhi Gollacarya' Taḷagarasānta... ***Tōraṇamam*** (the *toraṇa)-karāḷa* (formidable/greatly curved or crooked)-***makarālam*** (*makara*=crocodile; *ālam*=to the extent or (with) extensive crocodile) *kōkamam* (with or including ruddy goose or *jakkavakki*)- *celva vettire* (radiating a beauty)-*sopāna kaḷāpamam* (with an ornate step-way) *Kopaṇa-tīrtha-sthānadoḷ* (in the sacred centre of Kopaṇa) *nāḍe* (greatly/excessively) *bittaradim-māḍisi* (greatly/extensively) *māḍisi* (caused to be made) *kīrtiyam* (glory) *nilisidam* (erected in upright) *śāntam (śānta) diśāntabaram* (filling the direction)
Source: *Kannada University Epigraphical Series-II,* Koppal District (Hampi-Vidyaranya, 1999), Inscr. no. 120)

20. Erection of a Śiva temple on a hill and a *toraṇa* at its enclosure wall *(*textual *prākāra-toraṇa)* by Mādevī of royal blood, as a pious act (1179 CE):
Text: *...arundavāmpurinda śindaiyāl-āgiy-irund-araññ-jeyivaradiyāl penna eṇ..ṇi śuṟṟum puriśaiyun-**tōraṇa**-vāyadaluṅ-gaṟṟaḷiy-aduvuṅ-gavin peṟava-amaittu nandana-vanamuntirumaḍaippaḷḷiyum... Umaiyoḍu Śaṅkaran-ṟannai tāpittanaḷē.*
Tr. (Mādevī, the daughter of a great king... having come to the firm conclusion that wealth, rank and all things of this wide world are fleeting, practised severe austerities, and with a desire to do some act of charity), built a beautiful stone-temple with the *toraṇa* -gate and the surrounding walls. Having provided the temple with a flower-garden, kitchen, pond, suitable environs, musical instruments (two named) and ornaments (some named)... she set up... the god Śankara together with his consort Umai near the hill on which the fragrant Vilva trees grew...
Source: *EC,* X, Inscriptions in the Kolar District (Taluk), ed. B.L. Rice, 1905, inscr. no. 132, text p. 54, *tr.* p. 49.

21. *Makara-toraṇa* constructed in front of a temple:
Tr. In front of the *basadi* of Nokkijabbe, the family goddess of her husband, Vīra-Śantara, she had a ***makara-toraṇa*** made.
Source: *EC,* VII, part 1, Nagar Taluk, no. 47, *tr.* p. 151, para 2 (as mentioned in Acharya, *A Dictionary...,* p. 252).

22. *Makara-toraṇa* and *gopura* constructed as part of a re-built temple (It was widely believed that the restoration or re-building of temples with *toraṇas,* tanks, gardens, etc. led to the accrual of religious merit):
Tr. Pulling down the temple which had fallen to ruin, had it securely re-built with a *gopura,* a ***makara-toraṇa*** for the god Durgīśvara and god Vṛśabha.
Source: *EC,* III, Tirumakuḍlu-Narasīpur Taluk, inscr. no. 103, text p. 170, *tr.* p. 88 (as mentioned in Acharya, *A Dictionary...,* p. 253)

23. At Kuruvangi (Hubli?) on a *vīragal* (hero-stone) to the south of the Malleśvara temple, in the reign of Hoysaḷa Vīra Narasiṁhadeva: Mention of a movable *toraṇa* as an honorific gift given to the wife and children of Bāsi-Seṭṭi to honour his heroic death. Date 1287 CE:
Text: *... bīragaḷu ā Bāsi-Seṭṭiya heṇḍaru makkaḷige ā-mahājanaṅgaḷu mechchi Bāsi-Seṭṭiya makkaḷu makkaḷu dapada-daṇḍige **toraṇa** saluvudu*
Tr. (... when Bāsi-Seṭṭi... fought with the people of Hiriya-Muguḷi and Basavanahaḷḷi, and died like a hero); his *bīragaḷ*; Those Brahmans, pleased with

Bāsi-Seṭṭi, gave to his wife and children a large palanquin and a *toraṇa* to descend to his children's children.
Source: *EC,* Vol. VI, Inscriptions in the Kadur District, Chikmagalur Taluk, ed. B.L. Rice, 1901, Inscr. no. 44, text p. 104, *tr.* p. 39.

24. *Makara-toraṇa* as a movable, honorific insignia:
Tr. We grant you in addition, throne, crown, palanquin, white umbrella, *cāmaras* on both sides, ***makara-toraṇa*** (a kind of arched canopy), fan, daylight torch, yellow and red flags and such insignia, with cymbals...
Source: *EC* VIII, part I, Nagar Taluk, no. 67, *tr.* p. 157, line 14f (as mentioned in Acharya, *A Dictionary...,* p. 252).

25. *Makara-toraṇa* as a movable insignia:
Tr. White *cāmaras*, the crown-banner, ***makara-toraṇa,*** herds of camels.
Source: *EC* IX, Channapatna Taluk, no. 85, tr. p. 150 (as mentioned in Acharya, *A Dictionary...,* p. 252).

26. *Makara-toraṇa* as a movable, honorific insignia:
Tr. The Vīra-bhikshavatī-udāna-svāmī honoured the svāmī of Gāḷipūje throne with the following: a palanquin with silver mountings, a pearl necklace, a golden umbrella, the double-*cāmaras,* a ***makara (toraṇa)*** canopy..., for the feet, a Mukkanna drum, a Basava drum, a Nandī flag, etc.
Source: *EC,* VI, Chikmagalur Taluk, no. 109, text p. 124, line 8f, tr. p. 51, para 2 (as mentioned in Acharya, *A Dictionary...,* p. 254).

27. Text: *kanaka-maṇimaya-**toraṇa** kalpa-vṛkṣa.*
Tujañaru, 1323 CE, E. Java.
Tr. Gold and gem studded *toraṇa*, (as a?) wish-fulfilling tree.
Source: H.I.R. Hinzler, "Terms for building and buildings in Old Javanese in inscriptions," Workshop, Old Javanese, Royal Institute of Linguistics, KITLV, Leiden, 1998 (Unpublished).

28. From the door-lintel of the temple of Avalokiteśvara in Bungamati, dated Nepal Samvat 792/ 1672 CE:
Text: *Svarṇa-dvāraṁ sthāpitaṁ **toraṇena** sārddhe Srimal-Lokanāthasya gehe*
Tr. 'Placed a golden door and *toraṇa* in the temple of glorious Lokanātha.'
Source: Inscriptions from Nepal, no. 21, Inscription of Srinivasa, *Indian Antiquary,* Vol. IX, p.192, note 62.

29. Dated (NS 922/ 1802 CE), dedicatory inscription on a wooden Pañcarakṣā *toraṇa* at the site museum on Svayambhūnāth Hill near Kathmandu:
Text: *(siddhi) o(ṁ) namo ratnatrayāya// śubha// saṁva 922 pauṣa kṛṣṇa... 6 ādityavāra kuhnū... ṅata pithyā tuṁccheyā turādhra bhājuman parivāra samūcayana... śrī 3 hāratī pitina... thva toraṇa dohalapā jūro// śūbha...m bhūyāt*
Tr. [Siddhi] (symbol) O (ṁ), homage to the three jewels! Blessing! On the 6th lunar day of the dark [fortnight of the month of] Pauṣa, Sunday, [in the year] 922 of the [Nepal] era, this tympanum was donated with devotion to the thrice blessed Hāratī by Bhājuman Tulādhar collectively with his family at Pithyā Tuṁche of Ṅata. Let [all] be blessed!
Source: Mevissen, Gerd J.R., "A Dated Pañcarakṣā *toraṇa...,* pp.137-149.

30. Dated (NS 949/ 1828-29 CE), dedicatory inscription on a gilt Pañcarakṣā *toraṇa* above the main entrance on the southern side of the Hāratī Temple at Svayambhūnāth near Kathmandu. It harbours the *rakṣā* goddesses and mentions that the *toraṇa* was donated by Bekhasinh Tulādhar Nyata Tunche, as a replacement of the wooden *toraṇa* with a golden one, at the Hāratī temple. The donor's name as well as his caste and address may indicate that he was a descendant of the Tulādhar merchant Bhājuman of Ṅata Pithyā Tuṁche who donated the wooden *toraṇa* (here, inscr. no. 29).
Source: Mevissen, Gerd J.R., "A Dated Pañcarakṣā *toraṇa...,* pp.137-149.

Appendix 2
Literary sources

1. *Kauṭilīyaṁ Arthaśāstram,* ed. T. Ganapati Sastri Part I, 2: 3 *(Durga Vidhānam)*:

*Dvayoraṭṭālakayormadhye saharmya dvitalāmadhyārdhāyāmāṁ pratolīṁ kārayet/*p.122
*dvi hastaṁ toraṇa śiraḥ/*p.125

2. *The Miliṅdapanho,* ed. V. Treckner

Atthi Yonakānaṁ nānāpuṭabhedanaṁ Sāgalan-nāma nagaram... vividha-vicitra-dalham-aṭṭāla-koṭṭakaṁ varapavara-gopuratoraṇaṁ gambhīraparikhā-paṇḍara-pākāra-parikkhittantepuraṁ... (p.1)

3. *The Jātaka,* ed. V. Fausboll

Samgāmavacara Jātaka (182), Vol. II, p.95:
Samgāmavacaro sūro balava iti vissuto/
Kin nu toraṇaṁ asajja patikkamasi kuñjara/
Ommada khippaṁ palighaṁ esikani ca abbaha/
Toraṇāni pamadditvā khippaṁ pavisa kuñjara/

Vidhurapaṇḍita Jātaka (545), Vol. VI p.276:
Puraṁ uddāpasampannaṁ bahupākārātoraṇaṁ/
*Siṁghāṭakesu bhūmiyo maṇimhi passa nimmitaṁ/*1190
Passa toraṇamaggesu nānādijagaṇā bahū/
*Haṁsa koñcā mayūrā ca cakkavākā ca kukkuhā/*1192

4. *Mṛchchhakaṭika* of Śūdraka, p.156 (canto 4):

gaganatalāvalokankautūhalādūronnamitaśīrsasya dolāyamānavalambitairavanahastabhramayita mallikādāmaguṇālankṛtasya samucchṛta dantidantatoraṇavabhāsitasya... toraṇadharaṇastambhavedikānikṣipta samullasaddharitacūtapallavalalāmaśatika maṅgalakalaśābhirāmobhayapārśvasya...

5. Aśvaghoṣa's *Buddhacarita,* v.52, p.52:

Avalambya gavākṣapārśvamanya śayitā cāpavibhugnagātrayaṣṭiḥ/
Virarāja vilambicāruhara racitā toraṇaśālabhañjikeva//

6. *Rājapraśnīya Sūtram*

p.3, *sūtra* 1:
pāgāra-parikkhittā kavisīsayavaṭṭaraiya-saṇṭhiyavirāyamāṇā aṭṭālaya-cariya-dāra- gopura-toraṇa.

p.6, *sūtra* 2:
candanaghaḍasukaya-toraṇapaḍiduvāradesabhāye

p.26 *sūtra* 26:
Tesi ṇaṁ tisovāṇapaḍiruvagāṇaṁ purao patteyaṁ patteyaṁ toraṇaṁ paṇṇattaṁ, tesi ṇaṁ toraṇāṇāṁ ime eyāruve vaṇṇāvāse paṇṇatte, tanjahā-toraṇā ṇāṇāmaṇimayā ṇāṇāmaṇimaesu...

p.27 *sūtra* 27:
Tesi ṇaṁ toraṇāṇāṁ uppim aṭṭhaṭṭha maṅgalagā paṇṇattā...

p.27 *sūtra* 28:
Tesiṅ ṇaṁ toraṇāṇāṁ uppiṁ bahave kiṇhacāmarajjhayā...

p.27, *sūtra* 29:
Tesiṅ ṇaṁ toraṇaṇaṁ uppiṁ bahave chattātichatte, paḍāgāyipaḍāge, ghanṭājugale, uppalahatthaye, kumuda-ṇaliṇa-subhaga-saugandhiya-pauṇḍarīya-mahāpauṇḍarīya-satapatta-sahassapattahatthaye, savvarayaṇamaye acche jāva paḍirūve viuvvati/

p.32, *sūtra* 45:
Taye ṇaṁ se Ābhiyogiye deve... ettha ṇaṁ mahaṁ picchāgharamaṇḍavam viuvvai, aṇegakhambhasaya-sanniviṭṭhaṁ Abbhuggayasukayavaraveyiyā toraṇavararayiyasālabhanjiyāgaṁ... uvaciyacandaṇakalasaṁ, candaṇaghaḍa-sukayatoraṇapaḍiduvāradesabhāgaṁ...

p.70-71, *sūtra* 132:
Tesi ṇaṁ dārāṇaṁ ubhao pāse solasa solasa toraṇā pannattā, ṇāṇāmaṇimayā ṇāṇāmaṇimayesu khambhesu.

Tesi ṇaṁ toraṇāṇaṁ patteyaṁ purao do do sālabhanjiyāo pannattao...

Tesi ṇaṁ toraṇāṇaṁ purao do do cittā rayaṇakaraḍagā pannattā, se jahaṇāmaye ranno cāuranta-cakkavaṭṭissa citte rayaṇakaraṇḍaye veruliyamaṇiphalihapaḍalapaccoyaḍe sāte pahāte te patese savvato samanta obhā sati ujjoveti tavati pabhāsati, evameva te vi cittā rayaṇakaraṇḍagā sāte pabhāte te payese savvao samantā obhāsanti, ujjoventi, tavanti pabhāsanti.

Tesi ṇaṁ toraṇāṇaṁ purao do do tellasamuggā, pattasamuggā, coyagasamuggā, tagarasamuggā... acchā jāva paḍiruvā.

7. *The Mahābhārata*

Vol.I, Part 2: *The Ādi Parvan*:
Dvāratoraṇaniryūhairyuktamabhracayopamaiḥ/
Prāsādasātasambādhaṁ mahendrapurasannibham//
I. 102. 8, p.463

Prākāraparikhitopeto dvāratoraṇamaṇḍitaḥ/
Vitānena vicitreṇa sarvataḥ samavastṛtaḥ//
I.176.17, p.717

Vol. II, *The Sabhāparvan*, ed. Franklin Edgerton, BORI, Poona 1944;
Yudhiṣṭhira sabhā divyā varuṇasya sitaprabhā
Pramāṇena yathā yāmyā śubhaprākāratoraṇā//
II. 9. 1, p.47

Vol. III, *The Āraṇyakaparvan* (Part 1), ed. Vishnu S. Sukthankar, BORI, Poona 1942:
Purī samantādvihitā sapatākā satoraṇā/
Sacakra sahuḍā caiva sayantra khanakā tathā//
III. 16. 5, p.54

Vol. IV, *The Āraṇyakaparvan* (Part 2), ed. V.S. Sukhtankar, BORI, Poona 1942
Rāvaṇaśca vidhiṁ cakre Laṅkāyāṁ śāstranirmitaṁ/
Prakṛtyaiva durādharṣā dṛḍhaprākāratoraṇā//
III. 268. 2, pp.934 - 935

Vol. VI, *The Udyogaparvan*, ed. Sushil Kumar De, BORI, Poona 1940:
Mānsaśoṇitavarṣaṁ ca vṛṣṭaṁ devena mādhava/
Tathā gandharva nagaraṁ bhānumantamupasthitaṁ/
Saprākāraṁ saparikhaṁ savapraṁ cārutoraṇam//
V. 141. 21, p.507

Tatra sthūṇasya bhavanaṁ sudhāmṛttikalepanaṁ/
Lājollāpika dhūmāḍhyamuñcaprākāratoraṇaṁ//
V. 192. 21, p.641

Vol. X, *The Karṇaparvan*, ed. P.L. Vaidya, BORI, Poona 1954:
Ekaikaṁ yojanaśataṁ vistārāyāmasammitaṁ/
Gṛhāṭṭālakayutaṁ bṛhatprākāratoraṇam//
VIII. 24. 16, p.184

Vol. XIII, *The Śāntiparvan*, ed. S.K. Belvalkar, BORI, Poona 1961:
Yathā Duryodhanagṛhaṁ tathā Duḥśāsanasya ca/
Prāsādamālāsamyuktaṁ hematoraṇabhūṣitam//
XII. 44. 8, p.182

Vol. XVIII, *The Aśvamedhikaparvan*, ed. R.D. Karmarkar, BORI, Poona 1960:
Stambhānkanakacitrānśca toraṇāni bṛhanti ca/
Yajñāya tanadeśeṣu datvā śuddhaṁ ca kāñcanam//
XIV. 86. 14, pp.317 – 318

Dadṛśustoraṇānyatra śātakumbhayāni te/
Śaiyāsanavihārānśca subahūnratnabhūṣitān//
XIV. 87. 3, pp.319 – 320

Vol. XIX, *The Āśramavāsikaparvan*, ed. S.K. Belvalkar, BORI, Poona 1959:
Puraṁ ca te suguptaṁ syāddṛḍhaprākāratoraṇaṁ/
Aṭṭālakasambādhaṁ ṣaṭpathaṁ sarvatodiśam//
XV. 9. 16, p.28.

The Harivaṁśa

Vol. I, *Viṣṇuparva*
Maṇistambhasahasrāṇāmyutairvidhṛtaṁ sitaṁ/
Toraṇairjvalanaprakhyairmaṇividrumarājataiḥ/
Tatra tatra prabhāsadbhiścitrakāñcanavedikaiḥ//
94. 2, p.606.

8. *The Rāmāyaṇa* (*cf.* Cock): as mentioned in P.K. Acharya, *A Dictionary of Hindu Architecture,* p. 250:

II. 91,32: *Harmya prāsāda samyukta toraṇāni/*
I. 5, 10: *Rāma veśma maṇi vidruma toraṇaṁ/*
II. 15,32: *Hema-kakṣya puri ramya vaidurya-maya-toraṇa/*
V. 3, 33: *Nagarīṁ Laṅkāṁ satta-prākāra-toraṇam/*
V.4, 24: *Gṛhaṁ .. mahā-hāṭaka-toraṇam/*
See also IV. 33, 17; V.2, 18, 51; V. 6, 4; V. 18, 8; V. 27, 31; V. 37, 39; V. 41, 21; V. 42, 27; V. 39, 42; V. 44, 6; V. 42, 6; V. 46, 20, 41; V. 47, 7, 38; V. 53, 39; V. 55, 32, VI. 25, 24, 30; VI. 26,12; VI. 41,3, 56, VI. 42, 15; VI. 75, 21, VII. 3, 27; VII. 5, 25; VII. 13, 5; VII. 14, 24, 27, 28, 29; VII. 15, 36; VII. 38, 17.

9. *Matsya Purāṇa*
(Chap. 264, v. 15), as given in Acharya, *Dictionary...*, p.250:

Caturbhis toraṇair yukto maṇḍapa(h)syāc caturmukhaḥ// Chap. 264, v. 15, and
Aiṣṭaka dar(a)vās caiva śaila vā syuḥ sa-toraṇā//
Chap. 269, v. 46

10. *Vāyu Purāṇa*
(Part I, Chap. 39, v. 36, 51, 60), as given in Acharya, *Dictionary...*, p.250:

Harmya-prāsāda-kalilaḥ prāmśu-prākāra-toraṇaḥ//
Āsity-amara-pury-ābha mahā-prākara-toraṇaḥ//
Pāṇḍure-cāru-śikhare mahā-prākāra-toraṇe//

11. *Works of Kalidāsa,* Volume II

Meghadūta, Uttaramegha 12, p. 28.
Tatrāgāraṁ Dhanapatigṛhānuttareṇāsmadīyaṁ dūrāllakṣyaṁ surapatidhanuścāruṇā toraṇena/

Kumārasaṁbhava, 7.3, p.100.
Bhāsa jvalatkāñcanatoraṇānāṁ sthānāntaraṁ svarga ivāvabhāse/

Raghuvaṁśa
Śreṇibandhādvitanvadbhirastambhāṁ toraṇasrajāṁ/
Sārasaiḥ kalanirhṛādaiḥ kvacidunnamitānanao//
1.41, p.9

Tāvatprakīrṇābhinavopacāram
indrāyudhadyotitatoraṇāṅkaṁ/
varaḥ sa vadhvā saha rājamārgaṁ prāpa
*dhvajacchāyanivāritoṣṇaṁ//*7. 4, p. 119

Dhanvinao tamṛsimanvagacchatām
pauradṛṣṭikṛtamārgatoraṇao// 11. 5", p. 196.

Appendix 3
References in Treatises

1. *Bṛhat Saṁhitā*
See Bhatt, *Varāhamihira's Bṛhat Saṁhitā* and Saramana, *Varāhamihira Viracita Bṛhat Saṁhitā*, verses XXX.6, XXXVI.2; XLIII.25; XLIV.3,8; XLVI.20,70,74; LIII.25; LX.I; LXXI.13; XCVII.8,11.

2. *Viṣṇudharmottara Purāṇa*
See Shah ed., *Viṣṇudharmottara Purāṇa,* Third Khaṇḍa, Vol. I, pp. 352-53.

3. *Samarāṅgaṇasūtradhāra (Nagarādisaṁjñā,* 18.35-38)
हर्म्यद्वारे गृहद्वारे तथा हर्म्यावलोकने।
प्राकारान्तरपृष्ठे तु या च प्रासादिका भवेत्॥ ३५ ॥
पार्श्वयोरुभयोरेषां फलकद्वयमुच्छ्रितम्।
उपर्युपरि संक्षिप्तमर्धचन्द्रद्वयाकृति॥ ३६ ॥
आनने द्वे यथा चास्मिन् श्लिष्टैरग्र्यैर्महाधरैः।
तयोरुपरि सन्धौ च तारकाकृति मण्डलम्॥ ३७ ॥
harmyadvāre gṛhadvāre tathā harmyāvalokane|
prākārāntarapṛṣthe tu yā ca prāsādikā bhavet||35||
pārśvayor-ubhayor-eṣāṁ phalaka-dvayam-ucchṛtaṁ|
uparyupari saṁkṣiptamardhacandradvayākṛti||36||
ānane dve yathā cāsmin śliṣtair-agryair-mahādharaiḥ|
tayor-upari sandhau ca tārakā-kṛti-maṇḍalam||37||

4. *Samarāṅgaṇasūtradhāra* (68.54)
सुखलीलाशनार्थं तत् सप्रवेशं सनिर्गमम्।
sukhalīlāśanārthaṁ tat sapraveśaṁ sanirgamam||54||

5. *Samarāṅgaṇasūtradhāra* (46.1-5, 9)
पुरातनं नवं वापि कृतं वाथार्धनिर्मितम्।
देवतानां नृपाणां च तोरणं निपतेद् यदि॥ १ ॥
भज्यते दह्यते वाथ नमते सज्जतेऽथवा।
देवविद्युज्जलाद्यैर्वा हन्यते तत् कदाचन॥ २ ॥
तत्र मृत्युभयं विद्याद्दुर्भिक्षं चापि निर्दिशेत्।
तस्मात् प्रशमहेत्वर्थं विधिं कुर्यादिमं बुधः॥ ५ ॥
तोरणं भज्यते चेत् तद्राष्ट्रभङ्गं विनिर्दिशेत्॥ ९ ॥
purātanaṁ navaṁ vāpi kṛtaṁ vāthārdha nirmitam|
devatānāṁ nṛpāṇāṁ ca toraṇaṁ nipated yadi||1||
bhajyate dahyate vātha namate sajjate 'thavā|
devavidyujjalādyairvā hanyate tat kadācana||2||
tatra mṛtyubhayaṁ vidyād durbhikṣaṁ cāpi nirdiśet|
tasmāt praśamahetvarthaṁ vidhiṁ kuryād imaṁ budhaḥ||5||
toraṇaṁ bhajyate cet tadrāṣṭrabhaṅgaṁ vinirdiśet||9||

6. *Īśānaśivagurudevapaddhati* (30.35-41)
कायश्चाप्यनुकायश्च प्रासादाङ्गं द्विधा स्मृतम्॥ ३५ ॥
अधिष्ठानं तथा स्तम्भो भित्तिः कुम्भश्च मण्डिकाः।
पोतिका स्याद् भारतुला जयन्तय इति क्रमात्॥ ३६ ॥
अनुमार्गाश्च कायः स्यादनुकायोऽथ कथ्यते।
उत्तरं वाजनं श्रेणी बलीकं कर्णपत्रिका॥ ३७ ॥
सन्धिद्वारकपाटानि योगः प्रच्छादनानि च।
कुम्भवल्ली तोरणानि मुष्टिबन्धाष्टमङ्गलैः॥ ३८ ॥
मृणालिका दण्डिका च नीप्रहाराश्च नासिकाः।
पट्टिका वलभी बन्धवेदिका जालकानि च॥ ३९ ॥
कर्णकूटास्तथा कूटा नीडकोष्ठादयोऽपि च।
ऊर्ध्वप्रच्छादविन्याससुधालोष्टेष्टकादयः॥ ४० ॥
अनुकायाभिधानानि सामान्यानि भवन्ति हि।
देशोचितानि क्षुद्राल्पविमानानि भवन्ति हि॥ ४१ ॥
kāyascāpyanukāyaśca prāsādāṅgaṁ dvidhā smṛtam||35||
adhiṣṭhānaṁ tathā stambho bhittiḥ kumbhaśca maṇḍikāḥ|
potikā syād bhāratulā jayantaya iti kramāt||36||
anumārgāśca kāyaḥ syād anukāyo 'tha kathyate|
uttaraṁ vājanaṁ śreṇī balīkaṁ karṇapatrikā||37||
sandhidvārakapāṭāni yogaḥ pracchādanāni ca|
kumbhavallī toraṇāni muṣṭibandhāṣṭamaṅgalaiḥ||38||
mṛṇālikā daṇḍikā ca nīprahārāśca nāsikāḥ|
paṭṭikā valabhī bandhavedikā jālakāni ca||39||
karṇakūṭāstathā kūṭā nīḍakoṣṭhādayo 'pi ca|
ūrdhvapracchādavinyāsa sudhāloṣṭeṣṭakādayaḥ||40||
anukāyābhidhānāni sāmānyāni bhavanti hi|
deśocitāni kṣudrālpavimānāni bhavanti hi||41||

7.a *Samarāṅgaṇasūtradhāra* (68.54)
(गन्द्राग्रे सुकाग्रे) च प्रतोल्यग्रे तथैव च।
तोरणं त्रिविधं ज्ञेयं कनीयोमध्यमोत्तमम्॥ ५४ ॥
(gandrāgre sukāgre?) ca pratolyagre tathaiva ca|
toraṇaṁ trividhaṁ jñeyaṁ kanīyomadhyamottamam||54||

7.b *Aparājitapṛcchā* (115.39)
गण्डाग्रे शुण्डिकाग्रे च प्रतोल्यग्रे तथैव च।
तोरणं त्रिविधं ज्ञेयं ज्येष्ठमध्यकनिष्ठकम्॥ ३९ ॥
gaṇḍāgre śuṇḍikāgre ca pratolyagre tathaiva ca|
toraṇaṁ trividhaṁ jñeyaṁ jyeṣṭhamadhyakaniṣṭhakam||39||

8. *Aparājitapṛchhā* (81.24)
अन्येषां स्वल्पराज्यानां ये स्मृताश्चान्यसंज्ञकाः।
तेषां च तोरणं दद्यात् सिंहद्वारविवर्जितम्॥ २४ ॥
anyeṣāṁ svalpa-rājyānāṁ ye smṛtāścānya-saṁjñakāḥ|
teṣāṁ ca toraṇaṁ dadyāt siṁha-dvāra-vivarjitam||24||

9. *Aparājitapṛchhā* (115.41-42)
ब्रह्मस्थानादिगर्भे च स्तम्भगर्भे च तोरणम्॥ ४१ ॥
स्तम्भगर्भे भित्तिगर्भे तन्मध्ये च विचक्षणः।
brahmasthānādigarbhe ca stambhagarbhe ca toraṇam||41||
stambhagarbhe bhittigarbhe tanmadhye ca vicakṣaṇaḥ|

10. *Kāśyapaśilpa* (14.25, 30)
कुड्यतोरणमाख्यातं द्वारतोरणमुच्यते॥ २५ ॥
लोहैर्दारुशिलान्तर्वा कर्तव्यं द्वारतोरणम्।
द्वारतोरणमेवं हि स्तम्भतोरणमुच्यते॥ ३०॥
kuḍyatoraṇamākhyātaṁ dvāratoraṇamucyate||25||
lohairdāruśilāntarvā kartavyaṁ dvāratoraṇam|
dvāratoraṇamevaṁ hi stambhatoraṇamucyate||30||

11. *Kāśyapaśilpa (Nāsikālakṣaṇam)* (22.12)
चित्रचित्राख्यमकरैस्तोरणाख्यमथापि वा।
तोरणाभ्यन्तरे लक्ष्मीः साभिषेकाम्बुनासिका॥ १२॥

citracitrākhyamakaraistoraṇākhyamathāpi vā|
toraṇābhyantare lakṣmīḥ sābhiṣekāmbunāsikā||12||

12. *Mānasāra* (XLVI.1-2)
देवानां भूपतीनां च भूषणार्थे(गृहादीनां) च तोरणम्।
आसनोपरि विन्यस्य(सेत) सर्वेषामपि तोरणम्।
विस्तारे मध्यसूत्रस्य चापरे तोरणा[नि] न्यसेत्॥ २॥
devānāṁ bhūpatīnāṁ ca bhūṣaṇārthe
(? gṛhādīnāṁ) ca toraṇam|
āsanopari vinyāsya (seta) sarveṣāmapi toraṇaṁ|
vistāre madhyasūtrasya cāpare toraṇā (ni) nyaset||2||

13. *Aparājitapṛchhā* (194.1-3)
तोरणाः पञ्चधा वत्स... ।
उत्तुङ्गं मालाधरं च विचित्रं चित्ररूपकम्।
मकरध्वजस्तथा प्रोक्तस्तोरणः पञ्चमस्तथा।
toraṇāḥ pañcadhā vatsa...|
uttuṅgaṁ mālādharaṁ ca vicitraṁ citrarūpakam|
makaradhvajastathā proktastoraṇaḥ pañcamastathā|

14. *Aparājitapṛchhā* (194.4-9)
पीठं प्रासादपीठस्य किञ्चिन्न्यूनं तु कारयेत्।
पट्टं पट्टानुसारेण पट्टं दद्यात्तु तोरणे॥ ४॥
पादोन द्व्यंशकं पीठं भागेनैकेन कुम्भिका।
तदूर्ध्वे तु विधातव्यः स्तम्भः पञ्चांशकोदयः॥ ५॥
भागार्धे भरणं चैव शिरः पादोनभागिकम्।
पादोनद्व्यंशा गडवी शिरोच्छालस्तु पूर्ववत्॥ ६॥
एकभागं तथा पट्टं तदूर्ध्वे खूं(कू)ट छाद्यकम्।
तिलकं स्तम्भगर्भे स्यान् मकरो दिक्षु चोन्नतः (चतुर्दिक्षु समुन्नतम्) ॥७॥
तिस्रस्तिस्रस्तथा कार्या इल्लिका वलणैर्युताः।
सदाशिवं मध्यदेशे ब्रह्मविष्णु याम्योत्तरे॥ ८॥
तदूर्ध्वे क्षणोद्भवा! (क्षोभणा) कार्या इल्लिकाना मलङ्कृतिः।
उत्तुंगं नाम विख्यातं तोरणं प्रथमं विदुः॥ ९॥ इत्युत्तुङ्गः॥
pīṭhaṁ prāsādapīṭhasya kiñcinnyūnaṁ tu kārayet|
paṭṭaṁ paṭṭānusāreṇa paṭṭaṁ dadyātu toraṇe||4||
pādona dvayaṁśakaṁ pīṭhaṁ bhāgenaikena kuṁbhikā|
tadūrdhve tu vidhātavyaḥ stambhaḥ
pañcāṁśakodayaḥ||5||
bhāgārdhe bharaṇaṁ caiva śiraḥ pādonabhāgikam|
pādona dvayaṁśā gaḍavī śirocchālastu pūrvavat||6||
ekabhāgaṁ tathā paṭṭaṁ tadūrdhve
khūṁ(kū)ṭacchādyakam|
tilakaṁ stambhagarbhe syān makaro dikṣu connataḥ
(caturdikṣu samunnatam)||7||
tiśrastiśrastathā kāryā illikāvalaṇairyutāḥ|
sadāśivaṁ madhyadeśe brahma viṣṇu yāmyottare||8||
tadūrdhve kṣaṇodbhavā! (kṣobhaṇā)
kāryā illikānāmalaṁkṛtiḥ|
uttuṅgaṁ nāma vikhyātaṁ toraṇaṁ
prathamaṁ viduḥ||9|| ityuttuṅgaḥ||

15. *Aparājitapṛchhā* (194.10)
तद्रूपाकारादग्रे तु युग्माकारै र्द्वितीयकः।
मालाधरस्तदा नाम तोरणश्च द्वितीयकः॥ १०॥ इति मालाधरः॥
tadrūpākārādagre tu yugmākārair dvitīyakaḥ|
mālādharastadā nāma toraṇaśca dvitīyakaḥ||10||
iti mālādharaḥ||

16. *Aparājitapṛchhā* (194.11)
तस्योपरि पदानि(च) चतुष्काकार संस्थितम्।
पूर्वापरयाम्योत्तरे इल्लिकाश्च चतुर्दिशम्॥ ११॥ इति विचित्रम्॥
tasyopari padāni (ca) catuṣkākāra saṁsthitam|
pūrvāparayāmyottare illikāśca caturdiśam||11||
iti vicitram||

17. *Aparājitapṛchhā* (194.12-13)
स्तम्भोभयपक्षौ तु मत्तावरणवेष्टितौ।
चित्ररूपं तदा नाम कर्तव्यं तोरणं शुभम्॥ १२॥ इति चित्ररूपकम्॥
षड्भिः स्तम्भैस्तु रूपाढ्यै र्मत्तावरणवेष्टितैः।
मकरध्वजनामा तु तोरणस्त्रिपुरान्तके॥ १३॥ इति मकरध्वजः॥
इति पञ्चतोरणाः॥
stambhobhayapakṣau tu mattāvaraṇaveṣṭitau||
citrarūpaṁ tadā nāma kartavyaṁ toraṇaṁ śubham||
iti citrarūpakam||12||
ṣadbhiḥ stambhaistu rūpāḍhyair mattāvaraṇaveṣṭitaiḥ|
makaradhvajanāmā tu toraṇastripurāntake||13||
iti makaradhvajaḥ|| iti pañcatoraṇāḥ||

18. Unpublished Omnibus Manuscript
स्तम्भांतरेषु च कृता नवचन्द्रभागा
ऊर्ध्वे शिवांश उदितो निर्गमांश कोणात्।
स्थाप्यम् तथांतरविभाग ललामशोभा
रूपांवितामरगणांविततोरणेषु॥ (वसन्ततिलका)
आंदोलम् विधि तोरणेस्य उदितम् स्तम्भांतरेन्दुस्त्रिभिः
भक्ते षोडशचैव लुम्बिपरतो यवतपट्टपेटकम्
तन्मध्ये तिलकम् प्रवेशम् उदयोवेदांशरगै संस्थिताः
तस्मान्निर्गममुच्छ्रयेषु निर्गमम् स्थाप्यम् तथैवः क्रमात्॥
(शार्दूलविक्रीडित)
ऊर्ध्वं (यन्कत) शोभितं सप्तसंख्यया आंदोलोस्तिः रागसंख्ये ललामः
(...) वंस्वम् मूर्ध्यत्तिर्यगाधौ त्रिभागाः देवागारे कार्य+मग्ने विचित्रं
वृत्ताव्या अष्टगुणितोकै भारिताप्तश्च सुपैः तदग्रासांकैर्गुणितोष्टभाजितै
(लघ्र) वृत्तम्॥
stambhāntareṣu ca kṛtā navacandrabhāgā
ūrdhve śivāṁśa udito nirgamāṅśa koṇāt|
sthāpyam tathāntaravibhāga lalāmaśobhā
rūpānvitāmaragaṇānvitatoraṇeṣu|| (Vasantatilakā)
āndolam vidhi toraṇesya uditam
stambhāntarendustribhiḥ
bhakte ṣodaśacaiva lumbiparato yavatapaṭṭapeṭakam|
tanmadhye tilakam praveśam
udayovedāṅśaragaisaṁsthitāḥ
tasmānnirgamamucchrayeṣu nirgamam sthāpyam
tathaivaḥ kramāt|| (Śārdūlavikrīḍita)
ūrdhvaṁ (yaṅkata?) śobhitaṁ saptasaṁkhyayā
āndolostiḥ rāgasaṁkhye lalāmaḥ
(...) vaṁsvam mūrdhyattiryagādhau tribhāgāḥ
devāgāre kārya+magne vicitraṁ
vṛttāvyā aṣṭaguṇitokai bhāritāptaśca supaiḥ
tadagrāsāṅkairguṇitoṣṭabhājitai (laghra) vṛttam||

19. *Rūpamaṇḍana* (*Ṣaṣṭodhyāyaḥ*, 36-39)
दैर्घ्ये तु प्रतिमातुल्य तयोरूर्ध्वे तु तोरणम्॥
वहिका बाह्यपक्षे तु गोसिंघैः अलङ्कृता।
कर्तव्या द्वारशाखा तु तत्तन्मूर्तिसम्युता॥
तोरणं पञ्चधा प्रोक्तं रथिकायां च देवता।
ललितं चेति(ल्लि)काकारं त्रिरथं वलितोदरं
श्रीपुञ्जं पञ्चरथिकम् सप्तवानन्दवर्धनम्।
जिन गौरी गणेशश्च स्वे स्वे स्थाने सुखावहा॥
dairghye tu pratimātulya tayorūrdhve tu toraṇam||
vahikā bāhyapakṣe tu gosiṅghaialaṅkṛtā|
kartavyā dvāraśākhā tu tattanmūrtisamyutā||
toraṇaṁ pañcadhā proktaṁ rathikāyāṁ ca devatā|

lalitaṁ ceti(lli)kākāraṁ trirathaṁ valitodaraṁ|
śrīpuñjaṁ pañcarathikam saptavānandavardhanam|
jina gaurī gaṇeśaśca sve sve sthāne sukhāvahā||

20. *Mānasāra* (XLIV.15-18)
देवानां भूपतीनां च स्थानकस्यासनस्य च ॥ १५ ॥
वृत्तं वाथ त्रियुग्मं वा चार्धचन्द्राकृतिस्त(त)था ।
जना(त्रिधा) चाप(पा)कृतिर्वा(वा)पि यथेष्टाकारं तोरणम् ॥१६ ॥
मध्यात्तु भ्रामयेच्छिल्पी वृत्ताकारं च तोरणम् ।
तदर्धे नासिकादौ तद् भ्रामयेदर्धचन्द्रकम् ॥१७ ॥
तदर्धेन द्विपार्श्वे तु भ्रामयेद्धनुराकृतिम् ।
त्रिभुजं तत्समं नीत्वा तोरणं युक्तितो न्यसेत् ॥ १८ ॥
devānāṁ bhūpatīnāṁ ca sthānakasyāsanasya ca||15||
vṛttaṁ vātha triyugmaṁ vā cārdhacandrākṛtis(ta)thā|
janā (tridhā) cāpa(pā)kṛtirvā(vā)pi yatheṣṭākāraṁ toraṇam||16||
madhyāttu bhrāmayecchilpī vṛttākāraṁ ca toraṇam|
tadardhe nāsikādau tad bhrāmayedardhacandrakam||17||
tadardhena dvipārśve tu bhrāmayeddhanurākṛtim|
tribhujaṁ tatsamaṁ nītvā toraṇaṁ yuktito nyaset||18||

21. *Samarāṅgaṇasūtradhāra* (18.38-39)
तत् तोरणमिति प्रोक्तं यञ्च तेन परिष्कृतम् ।
सुवर्णतोरणं च स्यान्मणितोरणमेव च ॥ ३८ ॥
पुष्पतोरणमप्येतत् क्रियते पुष्पकादिभिः ।
tat toraṇamiti proktaṁ yañca tena pariṣkṛtam|
suvarṇa toraṇaṁ ca syān maṇi toraṇameva ca||38||
puṣpa toraṇamapyetat kriyate puṣpakādibhiḥ|

22. *Mayamatam (Toraṇādividhānam)* (21.68-80)
तोरणं त्रिविधं पत्रतोरणं मकरान्वितम् ।
चित्रतोरणमित्येषां मण्डनं त्वधुनोच्यते ॥ ६८ ॥
बालचन्द्रनिभं पत्रैश्चित्रितं पत्रतोरणम् ।
द्वयोर्मकरयोर्वक्त्रस्थित मध्यमपूरितम् ॥ ६९ ॥
नानाविधलतायुक्तमेतन्मकरतोरणम् ।
तदेव पार्श्वयोर्मध्यं पूरिमध्यं द्वयोस्ततः ॥ ७० ॥
नक्रतुण्डं प्रगृह्यैव द्वयोरास्यविनिर्गतैः ।
विद्याधरैश्च भूतैश्च सिंहैर्व्यालैश्च हंसकैः ॥ ७१ ॥
बालैः स्रग्दामकैरन्यैर्मणिबन्धैर्विचित्रितम् ।
चित्रतोरणमेतत् स्याद् देवानां भूभुजां वरम् ॥ ७२ ॥
गुहासु प्रतिमास्तासु पार्श्वपादयुतानि च ।
तोरणान्युत्तराधस्तात् प्रयोज्यानि विचक्षणैः ॥ ७३ ॥
स्तम्भोच्चे पञ्चषट्सप्तद्वयंशोच्चं तोरणाग्रकम् ।
शेषं पादोदयं पादं चतुरश्राष्टवृत्तयुक् ॥ ७४ ॥
कुम्भमण्ड्यादिसंयुक्तं पोतिकारहितं तु वा ।
उत्तरं वाजनं साब्जक्षेपणं क्षुद्रवाजनम् ॥ ७५ ॥
पोतिकोपरि वा कुर्याद् वीरकाण्डस्य चोपरि ।
उत्सन्ध्यन्तानताग्रं तु कुर्यान्मकरविष्टरम् ॥ ७६ ॥
तुङ्गार्धं त्रिचतुष्पञ्चदण्डतोरणविस्तृतम् ।
द्वारतुल्योन्नतं व्यासान्तरं स्तम्भद्वयोरपि ॥ ७७ ॥
उत्तरोत्तर युक्ताष्टमङ्गलोर्ध्वस्थनक्रवत् ।
फलकं पञ्चवक्त्रं तु तदूर्ध्वे शूलसंयुतम् ॥ ७८ ॥
छत्रकेतुपताकाश्रीभेरी कुम्भं च दीपिका ।
नन्द्यावर्तेन चाष्टौ हि सर्वेषामष्टमङ्गलम् ॥ ७९ ॥
एवं प्रोक्तं चतुर्भेदं देवादीनां तु तोरणम् ।
पद्मासनोर्ध्वे कुम्भस्य तिर्यक् चारुलताकृतिः ॥ ८० ॥
toraṇaṁ trividhaṁ patratoraṇaṁ makarānvitam|
citratoraṇam ityeṣāṁ maṇḍanaṁ tvadhunocyate||68||
bālacandranibhaṁ patraiścitritaṁ patratoraṇam|
dvayormakarayorvaktrasthita madhyamapūritaṁ||69||
nānāvidhalatāyuktametanmakaratoraṇam|
tadeva pārśvayormadhyaṁ pūrimadhyaṁ dvayostataḥ||70||
nakratuṇḍaṁ pragṛhyaiva dvayorāsyavinirgataiḥ|
vidyādharaiśca bhūtaiśca siṁhairvyālaiśca haṁsakaiḥ||71||
bālaiḥ sragdāmakairanyairmaṇibandhairvicitritam|
citratoraṇaṁ etad syād devānāṁ bhūbhujāṁ varam||72||
guhāsu pratimāstāsu pārśvapadayutāni ca|
toraṇānyuttarādhastāt prayojyāni vicakṣaṇaiḥ||73||
stambhoñce pañcaṣaṭsaptadvayaṁśoccaṁ toraṇāgrakam|
śeṣaṁ pādodayaṁ pādaṁ caturaśrāṣṭavṛttayuk||74||
kumbhamaṇḍyādisaṁyuktaṁ potikārahitaṁ tu vā|
uttaraṁ vājanaṁ sābjakṣepaṇaṁ kṣudravājanam||75||
potikopari vā kuryād vīrakāṇḍasya copari|
utsandhyāntānatāgraṁ tu kuryānmakaraviṣṭaram||76||
tuṅgārdhaṁ tricatuṣpañcadaṇḍatoraṇavistṛtam|
dvāratulyonnataṁ vyāsāntaraṁ stambhadvayorapi||77||
uttarottara yuktāṣṭamaṅgalordhvasthanakravat|
phalakaṁ pañcavaktraṁ tu tadūrdhve śūlasaṁyutam||78||
chatraketupatākāśrīrbherī kumbhaṁ ca dīpikā|
nandyāvartena cāṣṭau hi sarveṣāmaṣṭamaṅgalam||79||
evaṁ proktaṁ caturbhedaṁ devādīnāṁ tu toraṇam|
padmāsanordhve kumbhasya tiryak cārulatākṛtiḥ||80||

23. *Kāśyapaśilpam (Toraṇalakṣaṇam)* (12.6-11, 13, 25, 30-34)
पत्राख्यं तोरणमेकं द्वितीयं (म)करतोरणम् ।
तृतीयं चित्रसंज्ञं तु त्रिविधा तोरणाकृतिः ॥ ६ ॥
अर्धचन्द्रमिवाऽऽकारं पत्रराजिविराजितम् ।
पत्रतोरणमाख्यातं ततो मकरमुच्यते ॥ ७ ॥
पञ्चवक्रसमायुक्तं पार्श्वयोर्मकरास्यकम् ।
मध्ये पूरीमसंयुक्तं नानाफललतान्वितम् ॥ ८ ॥
नानालंकारसंयुक्तं वृत्तं मकरतोरणम् ।
तदेव पार्श्वयोर्मध्ये पुरीमस्य द्वयोरपि ॥ ९ ॥
नक्रतुण्डं प्रकर्तव्यं भूतविद्याधरास्तथा ।
सिंहव्यालकहंसाद्यैर्बलाग्रन्मुक्तमादकैः ॥ १० ॥
अन्यैश्च विविधैश्छत्रै रत्नसंघैश्च भूषयेत् ।
चित्रतोरणमेवं स्यात्प्रोच्यते तोरणत्रयम् ॥ ११ ॥
बोधिकारहितं यत्तत् स्तम्भं तु गलता स्मृता ।
स्तम्भतोरणवन्मूर्ध्नि कर्तव्यं तोरणद्वयम् ॥ १३ ॥
कुड्यतोरणमाख्यातं द्वारतोरणमुच्यते ॥ २५ ॥
लोहैर्दारुशिलान्तर्वा कर्तव्यं द्वारतोरणम् ।
द्वारतोरणमेवं हि स्तम्भतोरणमुच्यते ॥ ३० ॥
पादोच्चं तु त्रिधा भज्य द्विभागं चरणोदयम् ।
पादं सर्वाङ्गसंयुक्तं पोतिकारहितं कुरु ॥ ३१ ॥
उत्तरं वाजनाब्जं च क्षेपणं निम्नवाजनम् ।
तदूर्ध्वे च(झ)षकर्णं तु नानापत्रैर्विचित्रितम् ॥ ३२ ॥
तोरणं मकरात्यं (रव्यं)तु मृणाल्याद्वि(ऽन्वि)तकंधरम् ।
सर्वालंकारसंयुक्तमेतत्स्यात्स्तम्भतोरणम् ॥ ३३ ॥

पादान्तरे हारायां वा कर्णप्रासादमध्यमे ।
शालामध्यान्तराले वा कर्तव्यं सर्वधामसु ॥ ३४ ॥

patrākhyaṁ toraṇamekaṁ dvitīyaṁ (ma)karatoraṇam|
tṛtīyaṁ citrasaṁjñaṁ tu trividhā toraṇākṛtiḥ||6||
ardhacandramivā 'kāraṁ patrarājivirājitam|
patratoraṇamākhyātaṁ tato makaramucyate||7||
pañcavaktrasamāyuktaṁ pārśvayormakarāsyakam|
madhye pūrimasaṁyuktaṁ nānāphalalatānvitam||8||
nānālaṁkārasaṁyuktaṁ vṛttaṁ makaratoraṇam|
tadeva pārśvayormadhye purīmasya dvayorapi||9||
nakratuṇḍaṁ prakartavyaṁ bhūtavidyādharastathā|
siṁhavyālakahaṁsādyairbalāgran muktamādakaiḥ||10||
anyaiśca vividhaiścchatrai ratnasaṁghaiśca bhūṣayet|
citratoraṇamevaṁ syārprocyate toraṇatrayam||11||
bodhikārahitaṁ yattat stambhaṁ tu galatā smṛtā|
stambhatoraṇāvanmūrdhni kartavyaṁ toraṇadvayam||13||
kuḍyatoraṇamākhyātaṁ dvāratoraṇamucyate||25||
lohairdāruśilāntarvā kartavyaṁ dvāratoraṇam|
dvāratoraṇamevaṁ hi stambhatoraṇamucyate||30||
pādoccaṁ tu tridhā bhajya dvibhāgaṁ caraṇodayam|
pādaṁ sarvāṅgasaṁyuktaṁ potikārahitaṁ kuru||31||
uttaraṁ vājanābjaṁ ca kṣepaṇaṁ nimnavājanam|
tadūrdhve ca(jha)ṣakarṇaṁ tu nānāpatrairvicitritam||32||
toraṇaṁ makarātyaṁ(khyaṁ)tu mṛṇālyādvi('nvi)takaṅdharam|
sarvālaṁkārasaṁyuktametatsyāt stambhatoraṇam||33||
pādāntare hārāyāṁ vā karṇaprāsādamadhyame|
śālāmadhyāntarāle vā kartavyaṁ sarvadhāmasu||34||

24. *Kāmikāgama* (55.61-66, 79, 87-88)

तोरणं त्रिविधं प्रोक्तं तोरणं मकरान्वितम् ।
चित्रतोरणमित्येषां मण्डनं त्वधुनोच्यते ॥ ६१ ॥
बालचन्द्रनिभं भद्रैः चित्रितं पत्रतोरणम् ।
तयोर्मकरयोर्वृत्तं सत्तमध्यमपूरितम् ॥ ६२ ॥
नानाविधलतायुक्तं एतन्मकरतोरणम् ।
तदेव पार्श्वयोर्मध्यं पूरिमस्य द्वयोरपि ॥ ६३ ॥
नक्रतुण्डप्रगृह्यैश्च तयोरास्यविनिर्गतैः ।
विद्याधरैश्चभूतैश्च सिंहेभव्यालहंसकैः ॥ ६४ ॥
बालैस्सृन्मन्तामकैरन्यैर्मणिबन्धैर्विचित्रितम् ।
चित्रतोरणमेतत्स्यात् देवानां भूभृतां वरम् ॥ ६५ ॥
गृहासु प्रतिमाद्यासु पादास्सर्वाङ्गशोभितः ॥ ६६ ॥
एवं तोरणमाख्यातं पर्वित्ति(भित्ति)मध्ये विशेषतः ।
गळे वा द्वारदेशे वा द्वारतोरणमिष्यते ॥ ७९ ॥
देवद्विजनरेन्द्राणां तोरणं मकराख्यकम् ।
तोरणं चित्रसंज्ञन्तु वैश्यानां प्रविधीयते ॥ ८७ ॥
पद्माख्यतोरणं शूद्रैः सर्वं सर्वत्र वा मतम् ॥ ८८ ॥

toraṇaṁ trividhaṁ proktaṁ toraṇaṁ makarānvitam|
citratoraṇamityeṣām maṇḍanaṁ tvadhunocyate||61||
bālacandranibhaṁ bhadraiḥ citritaṁ patratoraṇam|
tayormakarayorvṛttaṁ sattamadhyamapūritam||62||
nānāvidhalatāyuktaṁ etanmakaratoraṇam|
tadeva pārśvayormadhyaṁ pūrimasya dvayorapi||63||
nakratuṇḍapragṛhyaiśca tayorāsyavinirgataiḥ|
vidyādharaiśca bhūtaiśca siṁhebhavyālahaṁsakaiḥ||64||
bālaissṛnmantāmakairanyair maṇibandhairvicitritam|
citratoraṇametatsyāt devānāṁ bhūbhṛtāṁ varam||65||
gṛhāsu pratimādyāsu pādassarvāṅgaśobhitaḥ||66||
evaṁ toraṇamākhyātaṁ parvitti(bhitti)madhya viśeṣataḥ|
gaḷe vā dvāradeśe vā dvāratoraṇamiṣyate||79||
devadvijanarendrāṇāṁ toraṇaṁ makarākhyakam|
toraṇaṁ citrasaṁjñyantu vaiśyānāṁ pravidhīyate||87||
padmākhyaṁ toraṇaṁ śūdraiḥ sarvaṁ sarvatra vā matam||88||

25. *Īśānaśivagurudevapaddhati (Toraṇādilakṣaṇam)* (32.1-10)

तोरणं त्रिविधं ज्ञेयं मकरं चित्रपत्रके ।
देवद्विजनृपाणां तु शस्तं मकरतोरणम् ॥ १ ॥
विशां तु चित्रसंज्ञं स्याच्छूद्राणां पत्रतोरणम् ।
पार्श्वयोः पृष्ठतश्चापि प्रकुर्यात् कुड्यतोरणम् ॥ २ ॥
प्रतेरुत्तरसीमान्तं तोरणोदय ईरितः ।
तदर्धेनास्य विस्तारस्तद्व्यासेऽथ शरांशके ॥ ३ ॥
त्रिभिर्मकरयुग्मं स्यादंशाभ्यां पादयोः स्थितिः ।
यथा शोभान्तरं तत्र गुहावेशो भवेदपि ॥ ४ ॥
अर्धेन्दुसदृशैः पत्रैश्चित्रितं पत्रतोरणम् ।
नक्रयोर्वदनासक्तमध्यपूरिममण्डितम् ॥ ५ ॥
चित्रतोरणमुद्दिष्टं मध्यपूरिमपार्श्वयोः ।
विगृह्य मकरस्योत्थरत्नमालाधिरोपितैः ॥ ६ ॥
भूतविद्याधरव्यालसिंहैश्चारूढबालकैः ।
विलम्बितं तूभयतो भवेन्मकरतोरणम् ॥ ७ ॥
गुहासु तोरणानां तु यथार्हं प्रतिमास्तथा ।
न्यस्येन्नारीनरादींश्च यथाशोभं विचित्रितम् ॥ ८ ॥
हारासु वलभीमध्ये प्रमाणभवनेऽपि वा ।
कुड्येषु तोरणानि स्युस्तत्कुड्यं पञ्चधा स्मृतम् ॥ ९ ॥
शिलामयं चैष्टकं च जालकमयमित्यपि ।
फलकमयमप्यंत्यं मृण्मयं चापरम् क्रमात् ॥ १० ॥

toraṇaṁ trividhaṁ jñeyaṁ makaraṁ citrapatrake|
devadvijanṛpāṇāṁ tu śastaṁ makaratoraṇam||1||
viśāṁ tu citrasaṁjñaṁ syācchūdrāṇāṁ patratoraṇam|
pārśvayoḥ pṛṣṭhataścāpi prakuryāt kuḍyatoraṇam||2||
prateruttarasīmāntaṁ toraṇodaya īritaḥ|
tadardhenāsya vistārastadvyāse 'tha śarāṁśake||3||
tribhirmakarayugmaṁ syādaṁśābhyāṁ pādayoḥ sthitiḥ|
yathā śobhāntaraṁ tatra guhāveśo bhavedapi||4||
ardhendusadṛśaiḥ patraiścitritaṁ patratoraṇam|
nakrayorvadanāsaktamadhyapūrimamaṇḍitam||5||
citratoraṇamuddiṣṭam madhyapūrimapārśvayoḥ|
vigṛhya makarasyottharatnamālādhiropitaiḥ||6||
bhūtavidyādharavyālasiṁhaiśvārūḍhabālakaiḥ|
vilambitaṁ tūbhayato bhavenmakaratoraṇam||7||
guhāsu toraṇānāṁ tu yathārhaṁ pratimāstathā|
nyasyennārīnarādiṁśca yathāśobhaṁ vicitritam||8||
hārāsu valabhīmadhye pramāṇabhavane 'pi vā|
kuḍyeṣu toraṇāni syustatkuḍyaṁ pañcadhā smṛtam||9||
śilāmayaṁ caiṣṭakaṁ ca jālakamayamityapi|
phalakamayamapyaṁtyaṁ mṛnmayaṁ cāparam kramāt||10||

26. *Mānasāra* (XLVI.19-32)

पत्रं पुष्पं च रत्नं च चित्रतोरणमेव च ।
एवं चतुर्विधं प्रोक्तं देवानां च त्रिमौलिनाम् ॥ १९ ॥

अन्येषां भूपतीनां च पुष्पं रत्नं च तोरणम्।
पत्रवल्यादि(भिः) संभूष्य पत्रतोरणमीरितम्॥ २०॥
नानापुष्पैरलङ्कृत्य पुष्पतोरणमेव च।
सर्वरत्नैरलङ्कृत्य कर्तव्यं रत्नतोरणम्॥ २१॥
नानालङ्कारसंयुक्तं यक्षविद्याधरादिभिः।
तच्चित्रतोरणं प्रोक्तं पूर्वोक्तानां तु संमतम्॥ २२॥
सर्वेषां तोरणमध्ये चोर्ध्वे तुम्बु(म्ब)रुनारदम्।
तत्प्रदेशे द्विपार्श्वे तु मकरादिविभूषितम्॥ २३॥
तोरणस्याग्रमूले तु गृहा(ग्राह)पत्रैश्च भूषितम्।
तोरणाद्यं तु पत्रादिभूतवल्यासनान्वितम्॥ २४॥
पादानां च द्विपार्श्वे तु व्याल(लं)तोरणधारिणम्।
पत्रतोरणमित्युक्तं शेषं युक्त्या प्रयोजयेत्॥ २५॥
तदेव रत्नपुष्पैश्च नानालङ्कारसंयुतम्।
यक्षविद्याधराद्यैश्च युक्तं स्याच्चित्रतोरणम्॥ २६॥
ग्राहकिम्ब(न्न)रीसंयुक्तं चित्रपद्मादिभिर्विना।
सर्वाङ्गं पुष्पसंयुक्तं सर्वालङ्कारसंयुतम्॥ २७॥
पुष्पतोरणमित्युक्तं मकरन्दैश्च पुष्पकम्।
सर्वाङ्गं नवरत्नैश्च ग्राहकिन्नरभूषितम्॥ २८॥
ग्राहपुच्छादिसर्वेषां सर्वरत्नेन बन्धयेत्।
रत्नतारागणैर्युक्तं कुक्षि रा(चा)वृतलम्बितम्॥ २९॥
तोरणस्योपरि देशे तु भुजङ्गपादद्वयोरपि।
ग्राहान्तं सर्वरत्नैश्च पूरितं श्रेणिसंयुतम्॥ ३०॥
रत्नतोरणमित्युक्तं सर्वालङ्कारसंयुतम्।
(तोरणस्य) कृतं मध्ये कमलां(लं) कुर्यात् (तु) वारणम्॥ ३१॥
तन्मध्ये कल्पयेल्लक्ष्मीं नानालङ्कारभूषित(ता)म्॥ ३२॥

patraṁ puṣpaṁ ca ratnaṁ ca citratoraṇameva ca|
evaṁ caturvidhaṁ proktaṁ devānāṁ ca trimaulinām||19||
anyeṣāṁ bhūpatināṁ ca puṣpaṁ ratnaṁ ca toraṇam|
patravalyādi(bhiḥ) saṁbhūṣya patratoraṇamīritam||20||
nānāpuṣpairalaṁkṛtya puṣpatoraṇameva ca|
sarvaratnairalaṁkṛtya kartavyaṁ ratnatoraṇam||21||
nānālaṁkāra saṁyuktaṁ yakṣavidyādharādibhiḥ|
taccitratoraṇaṁ proktaṁ pūrvoktānāṁ tu saṁmatam||22||
sarveṣāṁ toraṇamadhye cordhve tumbu(mba)runāradam|
tatpradeśe dvipārśve tu makarādi vibhūṣitam||23||
toraṇasyāgramūle tu gṛhā(grāha)patraiśca bhūṣitam|
toraṇādyaṁ tu patrādibhūtavalyāsanānvitam||24||
pādānāṁ ca dvipārśve tu vyāla(laṁ)toraṇadhāriṇam|
patratoraṇamityuktaṁ śeṣaṁ yuktyā prayojayet||25||
tadeva ratnapuṣpaiśca nānālaṁkāra saṁyutam|
yakṣavidyādharādyaiśca yuktaṁ syāccitratoraṇam||26||
grāhakimba(nna)rīsaṁyuktaṁ citrapadmādibhirvinā|
sarvāṅgaṁ puṣpasaṁyuktaṁ sarvālaṁkāra saṁyutam||27||
puṣpatoraṇamityuktaṁ makarandaiśca puṣpakam|
sarvāṅgaṁ navaratnaiśca grāhakinnarabhūṣitam||28||
grāhapucchādisarveṣāṁ sarvaratnena bandhayet|
ratnatārāgaṇairyuktaṁ kukṣī rā(cā)vṛtalambitam||29||
toraṇasyopari deśe tu bhujaṅgapādadvayorapi|
grāhāntaṁ sarvaratnaiśca pūritaṁ śreṇisaṁyutam||30||
ratnatoraṇamityuktaṁ sarvālaṁkārasaṁyutam|
[toraṇasya] kṛtaṁ madhye kamalāṁ(laṁ) kuryāt [tu] vāraṇam||31||
tanmadhye kalpayellakṣmīṁ nānālaṁkārabhūṣita(tā)m||32||

27. *Samarāṅgaṇasūtradhāra* (57.23, 98-99)
इति(ल्लि)कातोरणयुक्तं चतुर्दिक्षु मनोरमम्।
पुरतो मण्डपं कुर्यात् सर्वलक्षणसंयुतम्॥ २३॥
(मेर्वादिविंशिका] श्रीधरः)
कुर्याद् भागं सविस्तारं तोरणं चतुरुन्नतम्।
वरालमकरैर्युक्तं स्तम्भेषु स्यात् तथेल्लिकाः॥ ९८॥
(मेर्वादिविंशिका] हंसध्वजप्रासाद)
समैर्भागैश्च पत्रैश्च विकटैः पद्मपत्रकैः॥
हस्तितुण्डैर्वरालैश्च शालभञ्जीभिरण्डकैः।
(इ)मल्लिकातोरणैश्चैव भूषणीया चतुष्किका॥
द्वारे कार्यौ प्रतीहारौ भय(इ)ल्लिकातोरणास्तथा॥ ९९॥
itikā(lli)kātoraṇayuktaṁ caturdikṣu manoramam|
purato maṇḍapaṁ kuryāt sarvalakṣaṇasaṁyutam||23||
(Mervādiviṁśikā, Śrīdharaḥ)
kuryād bhāgaṁ savistāraṁ toraṇaṁ caturunnatam|
varālamakarairyuktaṁ stambheṣu syāt tathellikāḥ||98|| (Mervādiviṁśikā, Haṁsadhvajaprāsāda)
samairbhāgaiśca patraiśca vikaṭaiḥ padmapatrakaiḥ||
hastituṇḍairvarālaiśca śālabhañjībhiraṇḍakaiḥ|
(i)mallikātoraṇaiścaiva bhūṣaṇīyā catuṣkikā||
dvāre kāryau pratīhārau bhaya(i)llikātoraṇāstathā||99||

28. *Jina Saṁhitā* (33.191-196)
लक्षणं तोरणादिनामुक्तानामधुनोच्यते।
तोरणं त्रिविधं पत्रतोरणादिविकल्पनः॥
अर्धेन्दुसदृशाकारं नानापत्रैर्विचित्रितम्।
पत्रतोरणमेतत्स्यात् शूद्रगेहे तदेवसत्॥
द्वयोर्मकरवक्त्रासक्त मध्य सपूरिमम्।
नानाविध लतोपेतं यत्तन्मकरतोरणम्॥
तदेन पार्श्वयोर्मध्ये पूरिमस्य द्वयोरिति।
द्वयोर्मकरयोरस्य ...
विद्याधरैस्तथा सिंहै हंसे व्यालकुञ्जरैः।
मालाभिर्मणिबन्धैश्च चित्रितं चित्रतोरणम्॥
देवालये तथा राजगृहेऽपीदं वरं भवेम्।
अधस्तादुत्तरस्यात् गुहास्वेतत्तु तोरणम्॥
lakṣaṇam toraṇādināmuktānāmadhunocyate|
toraṇaṁ trividhaṁ patratoraṇādivikalpanaḥ||
ardhendusadṛśākāraṁ nānāpatrairvicitritam|
patratoraṇametatsyāt śūdragehe tadevasat||
dvayormakaravaktrāsakta madhya sapūrimam|
nānāvidha latopetaṁ yattanmakaratoraṇam||
tadena pārśvayormadhye pūrimasya dvayoriti|
dvayormakarayorasya...
vidyādharaistathā siṁhai haṁse vyālakuñjaraiḥ|
mālābhirmaṇibandhaiśca citritaṁ citratoraṇam||
devālaye tathā rājagṛhe ’pīdam varaṁ bhavem|
adhastāduttarasyāt guhāsvetattu toraṇam||

Appendix 4
Variants in Treatises

TABLE 1

Variants based on sculptural embellishment of *toraṇas*

S.No.	*Maya-mata*	*Prayoga-mañjarī*	*Sama-rāṅgaṇa Sūtra-dhāra*	*Kaṭaka-bhūṣaṇa*	*Īśānaśivaguru devapaddhati*	*Aparājita-pṛcchā*	*Kāmik-āgama*	*Kāśyapa-śilpa*	*Suprabhed-āgama*	*Jina-saṁhitā*	*Mānasāra*
1.	*Patra*	*Patra*	–	–	*Patra*	*Patra-mālā*	*Patra*	*Patra*	*Patra*	*Bhadra*	*Patra*
2.	*Makara*	*Makara*	–	*Makara*	*Makara*	–	*Makara*	*(Ma)kara*	*Makara*	*Makara*	–
3.	*Citra*	*Citra*	–	–	*Citra*	–	*Citra*	*Citra*	*Citra*	*Citra*	*Citra*
4.	–	–	*Maṇi*	–	–	–	–	–	–	–	*Ratna*
5.	–	–	*Puṣpa*	–	–	–	–	–	–	–	*Puṣpa*
6.	–	–	*Suvarṇa*	–	–	–	–	–	–	–	–

TABLE 2

Variants based on *Toraṇa* Forms and Shapes

S.No.	*Mayamata*	*Samarāṅgaṇa sūtradhāra*	*Īśānaśivaguru devapaddhati*	*Aparājita pṛcchā*	*Kāmik-āgama*	*Kāśyapa-śilpa*	*Jinasaṁhitā*	*Mānasāra*	*Rūpamaṇḍana*
1.	*Vṛttākāra*	–	–	–	–	–	–	*Vṛttākāra*	–
2	*Bālacandra nibham*	*Ardhacandra dvayākṛti*	*Ardhendu*	–	*Bālacandra nibham*	*Ardha candrākāra*	*Ardhendu*	*Ardha candrākāra*	–
3	–	–	–	–	–	–	–	*Cāpākāra Dhanurākṛti*	–
4	–	–	–	*Uttuṅga*	–	–	–	–	–
5	–	–	–	*Mālādhara*	–	–	–	–	–
6	–	–	–	*Vicitra*	–	–	–	–	–
7	–	–	–	*Citrarūpaka*	–	–	–	–	–
8	–	–	–	*Makaradhvaja*	–	–	–	–	–
9	–	–	–	–	–	–	–	–	*Lalitam*
10	–	–	–	–	–	–	–	–	*Illikākāram*
11	–	–	–	–	–	–	–	–	*Śrīpuñjam*
12	–	–	–	–	–	–	–	–	*Valitodaram*
13	–	–	–	*Illikāvalaṇa Illikākāra*	–	–	–	–	*Nandavardhana*
14.	–	–	–	–	–	–	–	*Triyugmam tribhujam*	–

Glossary

adhiṣṭhāna-toraṇa : non-textual, actual *toraṇa* type located at the base mouldings of temples
aiṣṭaka : brick
amaragaṇa : gods
antarāla : vestibule
antarāla-illikā-toraṇa : composite *toraṇa* type made of loops and placed in the vestibule
antarāla-patra-toraṇa : composite *toraṇa* type made of leaves and placed in the vestibule
antarāla-toraṇa : *toraṇa* at the vestibule entrance
antarapaṭṭa : a recessed band between different temple mouldings
añjali hasta : hands folded in adoration
ardhacandrākāra : half-moon shape
ardhacandrākṛti : textual and actual type of half-moon shaped *toraṇa*
ardhapadma : half-lotus motif
ardhaparyaṅkāsana : a seated posture employed in the iconography of divinity or royalty
ardharatna : half-diamond motif
aṣṭadikpālas : eight directional divinities
aṣṭamaṅgalas : eight auspicious symbols
aṭṭālaka : defence tower at the gatehouse
āmalaka : ribbed member usually found on the northern Indian temple spire
āndola-toraṇa : textual and actual type of sinusoidal or wave-like *toraṇa*
āsthāna maṇḍapa : pilgrim's hall
āyāgapaṭṭa : tablet of homage
āyudhapuruṣas : personified attributes (of a deity)

bālacandra : *(toraṇa)* in the shape of a half- or crescent-moon
bahirdvāram outer entrance
banaspati (*vanaspati*) : lord of the woods
bhadras : central offsets
bharaṇa : fluted portion of a pillar
bhāraputrakas : load-bearing figures
bhūta : elemental
brahmakānta : pillar type with square cross-section

caitya-gavākṣa : dormer motif often found on *caitya* façades
caitya : excavated hall or shrine for worship, usually Buddhist
cakra : disc or wheel
cakravartin : sovereign king
candraśālikā : miniature dormer
caṇḍī : Indonesian monument
cāmara : whisk
cāmara-dhvajas : fly whisks
cāpākāra parikara-toraṇa : composite textual and actual type of bow-shaped *toraṇa* used as image-frame
cāpākāra-toraṇa : textual and actual type of bow-shaped *toraṇa*
chatra : parasol
chatrī : parasol or structure with a parasol-like roof
chepu : Newarī *kīrttimukha*
citrakhaṇḍa : pillar with variegated cylindrical and cubical sections
citra-ratna-toraṇa : composite textual and actual type of *toraṇa* with figures and jewels
citrarūpaka-toraṇa : A textual type of free-standing *toraṇa* mentioned in the *Appr.*

dalān-toraṇa : Newarī *toraṇa* placed between pillars
dantidanta-toraṇa : ivory *toraṇa* mentioned in the *Mṛcchakaṭika*
daṇḍacchādya : eave
darpaṇa : mirror
daru : wood
devakulikā : subsidiary shrine
dhanurākṛti (toraṇa) : textual and actual type of bow-shaped *(toraṇa)*
dharmacakra : wheel of law (Buddhist)
dikpāla : directional divinity
dvāra : door
dvāra-aṭṭālaka : gate tower
dvāra-illikā-toraṇa : composite *toraṇa* type made of loops and placed at the entrance
dvāra-toraṇa : textual and actual type of *toraṇa* placed at entrances
dvitala parivārālayas : double-storied shrines of family or adjunct deities
dyo-toraṇa : Newarī *toraṇa* placed above the doors
ḍolā yātrā : ritualistic procession of deities on swings

ekādaśa-candrabhāgā : eleven crescent-shaped arcs

gagāraka : *fleur-de-lis* motif
gagārapaṭṭī : *fleurs-de-lis* or inverted scout-badge sequence
gaja- or *hasti-toraṇa* : non-textual, actual type of *toraṇa* with elephants carved at the ends
gajakrānta-siṁha : 'lion on elephant' motif
gajapīṭha : elephant band carved at the socle of a monument
gajasiṁha : hybrid lion with elephant head
gajavyālas : hybrid elephant and leonine creature
gammaḍuva : a sacred village ritual
gandharvas : celestial musicians
gaṇas : goblin-dwarfs
garuḍa-toraṇa : non-textual, actual type of *toraṇa*

with the *garuḍa*-bird at the ends or apex
gavākṣa : dormer
gavākṣa-toraṇa : actual type of *toraṇa* shaped as a dormer
gāḍha : central circular cavity within dormer motifs or arches
ghaṇṭa : bell
ghaṭa : vase
ghaṭapallava : 'vase and foliage' motif
gopura : temple gateway or city gateway
gopura-toraṇa : textual and actual type of *toraṇa* as part of gateway
grāsa : gorgon
grāsakiṅkiṇikā : gorgon and bell motif
grāsamukha : gorgon face
grāsapaṭṭikā : gorgon band
grāsa-toraṇa : non-textual, actual type of *toraṇa* with a prominent gorgon face at the apex
gūdhamaṇḍapa : closed hall

haṁsa : goose or gander
haṁsamālā : a band or sequence of geese
haṁsa-toraṇa : non-textual actual type of *toraṇa* with geese at the ends
hastiśālā : elephant hall
hāṭaka-toraṇa : textual and actual type of golden *toraṇa* mentioned in the *Mahābhārata*
hema-toraṇa : textual and actual type of golden *toraṇa*
hiṇḍola : swing
hiṇḍola-toraṇa : non-textual, actual type of *toraṇa* used as a frame or peg to suspend a ceremonial or common swing
hitimanga : Newarī *makara*
hīraka : roll (bracket of a pillar)

ihamṛga : an imaginary animal
illikākāram : shaped as a curvilinear segment of an arc or loop
illikā-toraṇa : textual and actual type of *toraṇa* comprised of successive loops (lit. emulating the gait of a caterpillar)
illikāvalaṇa : undulating pediment

jāḍyakumbha : inverted cyma recta
jagati : elevated platform upon which a temple stands
jaṭā : matted locks
jālavātāyana : latticed window
jhal-toraṇa : Newarī *toraṇa* placed above windows
jhaṣa : big fish or crocodile

kakṣāsana : seat-back member on the walls of a temple's open hall
kalān : sacred monument in Southeast Asia
kalaśa : vase or vase-shaped moulding
kalikā : bud motif
kalpavallī : vine creeper
kapilī : connecting wall
kapota : eave cornice
kapotālī : eave moulding
kapotapālikā : eave-cornice moulding
karimakara : hybrid dolphin-elephant creature
karṇa : corner offset
karṇadardarikā : serrated or saw-tooth course
karṇaka : arris
karṇikā : knife-edged arris
kāla-makara-toraṇa : (Indonesian) *toraṇa* with prominent *kālamukha* and *makaras*
kālamukha : gorgon face
khura-kumbha : base mouldings
kibihi : Sinhalese *kīrttimukha*
kinnara : half human-half bird creature
kinnara-toraṇa : non-textual, actual type of *toraṇa* with *kinnaras* at the ends
kīrti-toraṇa : non-textual free-standing *toraṇa* type erected for signifying honour
kīrttimukha : gorgon face
kuḍya-illikā-toraṇas : composite textual and actual type made of loops and placed on walls
kuḍya-muktā-toraṇa : composite textual and actual type with pearl strands placed on walls
kuḍya-stambhas : wall-pilasters
kuḍya-toraṇa : textual and actual type of wall *toraṇa*
kumāra : young man or atlantid figure
kumārikā : maiden
kumbhī : high basal moulding with curved shoulder
kumbha : base moulding
kumbhaka : pillar base
kuṇḍa : tank
kūṭa : miniature shrine
kūṭacchādya : eave or awning of miniature shrine or niche
kūṭastambhas : pilasters topped by miniature shrine models

lalāṭa-bimba : image on central part of a temple's door-lintel
lalitam(toraṇa) : *toraṇa* type mentioned in the *Rūpamaṇḍana*
laśuna : curved shoulder element of a pillar
lumbī : pendant motif

madala : S-shaped segment of a *toraṇa*
mahā-abhiniṣkramaṇa : the great departure of Siddhartha
mahāparinirvāṇa : the great emancipation or salvation of the Buddha
makaradhvaja-toraṇa : textual type of free-standing *toraṇa*
makara : hybrid crocodile-dolphin creature
makara-toraṇa : textual and actual type of *toraṇa* with *makaras* at the extremities
maṇḍala : sacred or charged field
maṇḍapa : hall
maṇḍapikā : hall
maṇi toraṇa : textual and actual type of bejewelled *toraṇa*
maṇibandha : a sequence or string of jewels
maśūraka : cushion moulding
mayūra-toraṇa : non-textual, actual type with peacocks at the extremities
mālādhara-toraṇa : textual and actual type of free-standing *toraṇa* mentioned in the *Appr.*
mālāvidyādhara : garland bearing celestial
meghamaṇḍapa : storied hall
mihrāb : prayer-niche in Islamic monuments
miśraka : (pillar) composite pillar
mithunas : loving male-female couples
mīna-yugala : a pair of fish – auspicious symbol
mukhacatuṣkī : front porch resting on four pillars
mukhamaṇḍapa : front porch
mukhapaṭṭī : frontal ornamental band
muktāgrāsa : gorgon emitting pearl strands
muktā-toraṇa : non-textual, actual type made of pearl strings or strands
mukula : bud-like knob

Nandī-*maṇḍapa* : pavilion for Nandī
nandīpada : auspicious symbol
nandavardhana (toraṇa) : *toraṇa* type mentioned in the *Rūpamaṇḍana*
narapīṭha : sequence or band of human figures at the socle level of a temple
naucaukī : Jain temple vestibule with nine bays
nava-candrabhāgā : nine crescent-shaped arcs
nāga : serpent
nāgapāśa : entwined serpents motif
nāsī : dormer motif often found at gable-ends
nāsī-toraṇa : textual and actual type of *toraṇa* carved at the dormer on temple superstructures
nidhi : treasure
nirvyūha : horizontal salient of a *pratolī-toraṇa*

padmāsana : cross-legged yogic posture
padmapīṭha : lotus-socle
pañcāyatana : temple-complex of five temples
pañcarakṣā toraṇa : *toraṇa* harbouring five *rakṣā* goddesses
parṇapaṭṭī : bands of foliage
parikara-citra-toraṇa : composite textual and actual type with varied figures and which frames images
parikara-ratna-toraṇas : composite textual and actual type with jewels and which frames images
parikara-toraṇa : textual and actual type of *toraṇa* which frames images
patra : leaf or leafy motif
paṭṭaśālā : cloister of a Jain temple
pāgāra : (Pālī) enclosure wall
pāli-maṇḍi : dish-shaped echinus
pedyā : lower portion of doorjambs
phaṁsa-kūṭa : tiered pyramidal aedicule
phaṁsanā : tiered pyramidal roofed shrine
potikā : bracket
prabhā : aureole
prabhā-maṇḍala : aureole
prabhāvalī : aureole
pradeśa : region or territory
pramatha : goblin
pratibhadra : intermediate projection adjacent to the central wall offset
pratiratha : intermediate wall offset
pratolī : gateway
pratolī-toraṇas : arched portals or brackets as part of a gateway
prākāra-toraṇa : *toraṇa* punctuating the city enclosure walls
prekṣāgṛha : auditorium
puṣpa-ratna-toraṇa : composite textual and actual type with floral and jewel motifs
puṣpa : flower
puṣpa-toraṇa : textual and actual type of *toraṇa* made up of flowers or floral motifs
puradvāram : city gate
puṣpapaṭṭī : floral band
pūrṇakalaśa : vase of plenty
pūrṇakumbha : vase of plenty

raṅgamaṇḍapa : open-hall of temple
rathikā : framed niche harbouring divinities
rathyā : main street
ratna : jewel
ratnakaraṇḍaka : bejewelled crown
ratna-makara-toraṇa : composite textual and actual type made of jewels with *makaras* at the ends
ratnapaṭṭī : band or sequence of diamonds

ratna-toraṇa : textual and actual type of bejewelled *toraṇa*
rāmba-toraṇa : *toraṇa* made of plantain trunks
rūpaśākhā : doorjamb with figural sculpture
ṛṣi sage or ascetic

salilāntara : recess between wall projections
sapta-candrabhāgā : seven crescent-shaped arcs
sarvatobhadra : structure with entrances on all four sides
siṁhāsana : lion throne
siṁha : lion
siṁha-toraṇa : non-textual, actual type with lions at the ends
stambha-śākhā : pilaster door-jamb
stambha-toraṇa : pillared *toraṇa* or *toraṇa* carved on a pillar
stambhī : pillarette
stūpī : vase-finial
stūpa : sacred monument, often Buddhist, housing relics
surasundarī : celestial maiden
suvarṇa-toraṇa : *toraṇa* made of gold or golden *toraṇa*
sūtradhārā : (lit. cord -bearer) chief architect
swastika : auspicious symbol
śaila : stone
śakti : female power
śaṅkha : conch
śālabhañjikā : dryad, *śāla* (tree) plucker
śikhara : temple tower, spire (North India)
śrāvaka : Jain lay-adherent
śrīkāra : a variety of pillar with circular (lathe-turned?) sections
śrīpuñjam : *toraṇa* type mentioned in the *Rūpamaṇḍana*
śūrasenaka : trifoliate dormer patterns

taraṅga-śīrṣa : roll-bracket
tilaka : miniature niche-shrine
toraṇa : arched portal or festoon
toraṇabandha : post-lintel and eave-cornice type of *toraṇa* as part of a doorframe
toraṇamālā : *toraṇa* garland
toraṇasphaṭika : *toraṇa* made of crystals or creepers
toraṇa-śālabhañjikā : bracket-dryad seen in association with a *toraṇa*
torii : Japanese entryway with vertical posts and horizontal beam(s)
trika : columnar vestibule with three bays
triratna : the three jewels (of Buddhism)
triyugmam : of three or six sections
tulābhāra-toraṇa : non-textual, actual type of *toraṇa* employed as a weighing scale
turaṅga : horse

udadhikumāras : minor water divinities
udgama : pediment
uttaraṅga : upper portion of the doorframe
uttuṅga-toraṇa : textual and actual type of free-standing *toraṇa*
ūrdhvacippikā : upturned cyma with lotus leaves

valitodaram(toraṇa) : *toraṇa* type mentioned in the *Rūpamaṇḍana*
vandanamālā : festoon or garland
vandanamālikā : festoon or garland
varāha : boar
vasantapaṭṭī : floral scroll
vāhana : vehicle
vedikā : railing
vetāla : ghoul
viśikhā : main street
vicitra-toraṇa : textual type mentioned in the *Appr.* (rare in practice)
vidyādhara : angelic semi-divinity
vidyādhara-toraṇa : *toraṇa* with celestials at the ends (mentioned in an inscription)
vihāra : cave structure used by monks for meditation and rest
vimāna : (usually) southern Indian main-temple
vīthikā : veranda
vṛkṣa : tree
vṛṣabha : bull
vṛttam : circle
vṛttākāra : circular
vṛttākāra citra-toraṇa : composite textual and actual type of (semi) circular *toraṇa* with variegated figural and non-figural carvings
vyāla : leonine creature

yajñopavīta : sacred thread
yakṣī : female nature spirit
yakṣa : male nature spirit

Abbreviations and Conventions

AIIS: American Institute of Indian Studies, Gurgaon
App.: Appendix
Appr.: *Aparājitapṛcchā*
ARADH: Annual Report of the Archaeological Department of Hyderabad
ASI: Archaeological Survey of India
ASIAR: Archaeological Survey of India, Annual Report
ASWI: Archaeological Survey of Western India
BM: British Museum, London
BORI: Bhandarkar Oriental Research Institute, Pune
CII: Corpus Inscriptionum Indicarum
EC: Epigraphia Carnatica
EI: Epigraphia Indica
EITA: Encyclopaedia of Indian Temple Architecture
Inscr.: Inscription
IsIAO: Istituto Italiano per l'Africa e l'Oriente, Rome
ISP: *Īśānaśivagurudevapaddhati*
JISOA: Journal of the Indian Society of Oriental Art
JS: *Jinasaṁhitā*
KA: *Kāmikāgama*
KS: *Kāśyapaśilpa*
MG: Musée national des arts Asiatiques (Guimet), Paris
MM: *Mayamata*
MS: *Mānasāra*
NM: National Museum, New Delhi
NMI: National Museum Institute, New Delhi
OIOC: Oriental and India Office Collections, British Library, London
DR: *Devatāmūrtiprakaraṇam* and *Rūpamaṇḍanam*
SS: *Samarāṅgaṇasūtradhāra*
VAM: Victoria and Albert Museum, London

Diacritical marks have not been used for names of places. Names of texts, monuments, technical terms, and words in languages other than English, however, appear with diacritical marks.

Unless otherwise specified, dates refer to the Common Era.

A few examples from Nepal and Sri Lanka are included in the final chapter even though the title of the book does not convey the same.

Image Credits

Figures

© **American Institute of Indian Studies, Gurgaon (AIIS)**: 1.2, 1.4, 1.7-1.11, 1.19-1.22, 1.28, 1.29, 3.1-3.16, 3.18-3.20, 3.24-3.26, 3.32-3.42, 3.44, 3.48-3.54, 3.56-3.76, 3.79-3.90 (also p. 37), 3.92, 3.99, 3.102-3.103, 3.105-3.118, 3.120-3.123, 3.125-3.135, 4.1, 4.3-4.10, 4.12, 4.14, 4.18, 4.20-22a, 4.25 (also pp. ii-iii), 4.26-4.28, 4.34 (also p. 111), 4.36-4.40, 4.53, 4.56-4.60, 4.64-4.66, 4.71, 4.72, 4.77-4.81, 4.83-4.92, 4.95-4.98, 4.100-4.102, 4.104-4.107, 4.109-4.125, 4.128-4.131, 5.27-29, 5.32-5.38, 5.40, 5.41, 5.43, 5.44, 5.48, 5.50-5.53, 5.58, and 5.59.

© **Chedha Tingsanchali:** back cover image, 1.12, 1.15, 1.27, 3.17, 3.21-3.23, 3.30, 3.31, 3.45-3.47, 3.77, 3.91, 3.93-3.98, 3.100 (also p. v), 3.101, 4.35, 4.47, 4.68-4.70, 4.99, 4.126, 4.127, 5.1, 5.2, 5.4, 5.5-5.7, 5.9, 5.12, 5.13, 5.15, 5.17-5.20, 5.22, 5.24-5.26, 5.30, 5.31, 5.39, 5.42, 5.45-5.47 (also pp. xii, xvi), 5.49, and pp. 213, 273.

© **Parul Pandya Dhar and Sanjay Dhar:** front cover image, 1.1, 1.5, 1.6, 4.11, 4.13, 4.15-4.17, 4.19, 4.23, 4.24, 4.29, 4.30, 4.34a, 4.41, 4.43-4.45, 4.48-4.52, 4.67, 4.76, 4.82, 4.93, 4.94, 4.108 (also p. xviii), 5.55, and 5.56.

© **Musée national des arts Asiatiques (Guimet), Paris (MG):** 1.13 (also p. 7), 1.14, 5.3, 5.8, 5.10, 5.11, 5.14, 5.21, and 5.23.
© **V and A Images, Victoria and Albert Museum, London (VAM):** 4.32, 4.33 (also pp. vi-vii), 4.133 (also p. viii), and 5.54 (also p. 277).
© **Archaeological Survey of India (ASI):** 3.27-3.29, 3.43, and 3.119.

© **National Museum, New Delhi (NM):** 1.18, 3.78, 3.104, and 4.132.

© **British Museum, London (BM):** 1.23, 1.24, and 1.26.

© **Istituto Italiano per l'Africa e l'Oriente, Rome (IsIAO):** 1.16 and 1.17.

© **Indian Museum, Kolkata:** 1.3, 4.46, and 4.135.

© **M.A. Dhaky:** 4.55, 4.61-4.63, 4.73, and 4.74.

© **Gerd Mevissen:** 4.134, 4.136, and 5.57.

© **Joachim Bautze:** 4.75 and 4.103.

© **A.K. Sharma:** 4.2.

© **A.K. Singh:** 4.31.

© **Government Museum, Chennai:** 1.25.

© **ACP, Alkazi Foundation, New Delhi:** 3.124.

© **Institut Français de Pondichèry:** 3.55.

Drawings

© OIOC, British Library, London: D.2

After Fergusson and Burgess (1880: Pl. XX): D.1

After Bhandarkar (1920: 137-140): D.3

After Burgess and Cousens (1903: Pl. XLIV, 2): D.5

Adapted from a photograph by M.A. Dhaky: D.12

Prepared by Suman Lata: D.4, D.13-D.27, D.29-D.51, D.54 (also p. 27), D.55

Prepared by N. Ravi and S. Pandian: D.6-D.11, D.52, D.53, D.56

Courtesy Rodolfo Lujan Lunsford: D.28

After (Bhandaranayake *et.al.* eds. 1990: Fig. 46): D.57

Bibliography

Primary Sources

Śāstras, Āgamas, Saṁhitās, Purāṇas, Sūtras, and other texts

Aparājitapṛcchā of Bhuvanadeva, ed. P.A. Mankad, Gaekwad Oriental Series (G.O.S.), No. CXV, Oriental Institute, Baroda, 1950.

Architecture of Mānasāra, Vol.4, tr. from original Sanskrit by P.K. Acharya, Oxford University Press, London, 1934.

Aśvaghoṣa's Buddhacarita or Acts of the Buddha, ed. E.H. Johnston, Motilal Banarasidass, New Enlarged Edition, Delhi, 2004 (reprint).

Mānasāra on Architecture and Sculpture, Sanskrit Text with Critical Notes, Vol. 3, ed. P. K. Acharya, Oxford University Press, London, 1934.

Devatāmūrtiprakaraṇam and Rūpamaṇḍanam (Manuals of Indian Iconography and Iconometry), ed. Upendra Mohan Sankhyatirtha, Calcutta Sanskrit Series No. XII, Metropolitan Printing and Publishing House Ltd., Calcutta, 1936.

Dīpārṇava, ed. P.O. Sompura, Palitana, 1960.

Īśānaśivagurudevapaddhati of Īśānaśivagurudeva, Vols. I-IV, ed. T. Ganapati Sastri, Bharatiya Vidya Prakashan, Delhi – Varanasi, 1988.

Jinasaṁhitā, Transcript, 32-37 Pariccheda 291 of 1883-84 in Government Mss. Library at BORI, Poona (transcript: A.I.I.S. Library, Gurgaon).

Jīvājīvābhigama Sūtra [Part I] (Original Text, Hindi Version, Introduction and Appendices, etc.), ed. Shri Rajendra Muni, Jinägama Granthamālā Publication No. 30, Shri Agam Prakashan Samiti, Rajasthan, VS 2046/ June 1989.

Kāmikāgama, (copied by) Visvanatha S. Sarma, (transcribed in 1966-67 from a manuscript preserved in the Government Oriental Manuscripts Library, Madras R. No. 12966 (transcript: A.I.I.S. Library, Gurgaon).

Kāśyapaśilpam, ed. Vinayaka Ganesha Kṛṣṇarāya Apte, Anandāśrama Sanskrit Granthāvalī No. 95, 1926.

Kaṭakabhūṣaṇam, Transcribed in 1966-67 from a manuscript preserved in the Government Oriental Manuscripts Library, Madras, under R. No. 3846; (transcript: A.I.I.S. Library, Gurgaon).

The Arthaśāstra of Kauṭilya, Vol. I, ed. T. Ganapati Sastri, Bharatiya Vidya Prakashan, Delhi-Varanasi, 1984

Kṣīrārṇava, ed. P.O. Sompura, Palitana, 1960.

Mayamatam, Treatise of Housing, Architecture and Iconography, Vols. I & II, ed. Bruno Dagens, (Original Sanskrit text edited and translated), IGNCA, New Delhi and Motilal Banarasidass, Delhi, 1994.

Mṛchchhakaṭika of Śūdraka, (ed. and tr.) M.R. Kale, Motilal Banarasidass, Delhi, 1994.

Prāsādamañjarī by Sūtradhāra Nāthjī, ed. P.O. Sompura, Palitana, 1965.

Prayogamañjarī, transcribed in 1966-67 from a manuscript preserved in the Government Oriental Manuscripts Library, Madras, under R. No. 3029; (transcript: AIIS Library, Gurgaon).

Rājapraśnīya Sūtram, ed. Yuvāchārya Śri Mishrimalji Maharaj 'Madhukar', Jināgama Granthamālā Publication No. 15, Sri Agam Prakashan Samiti, Rajasthan, VS 2039/ 1982 CE.

Samarāṅgaṇasūtradhāra of Bhojadeva of Dhāra, ed. T. Ganapati Sastri, G.O.S. No. XXV, 2nd revised edition, Baroda, 1966.

Samarāṅgaṇasūtradhāra, Bhavananiveśa-Prathama Bhāga, text and translation, D.N. Shukla, Delhi, 1965.

Śilpa Smṛti Vāstuvidyāyām, Pūrvārdha and *Uttarārdha,* ed. N.C. Sompura, Palitana, 1979.

The Harivaṁśa (Being the Khilā or the supplement to the Mahābhārata), Vol. I (Critical Text) ed. P.L. Vaidya, Bhandarkar Oriental Research Institute (BORI), Poona, 1969.

The Jātaka or Stories of the Buddha's former births, Vol. II, ed. E.B. Cowell, at the University Press, Cambridge, 1895.

The Jātaka Together with its Commentary (being tales of the anterior births of Gotama Buddha), Vols. II & VI, ed. V. Fausboll, , Kegan Paul Trench Trubner & Co. Ltd., London, 1896.

The Mahābhārata, eds. Vishnu S. Sukthankar and S.K. Belvalkar *et. al.*, BORI, Volumes I-XIX, Poona, 1933-1961.

The Miliṅdapanho (Being the dialogues between King Miliṅda and the Buddhist sage Nāgasena), The Pali Text edited by V. Treckner, The Royal Asiatic Society, London, 1928.

The Questions of Milinda, translated from Pali by Rhys Davids, T.W., Sacred Books of the East Volume XXXV, edited F. Max Mueller, Motilal Banarasidass, Delhi, 1965 (reprint).

Varāhamihira Viracita Bṛhatsaṁhitā, ed. Pandit Shri Achyutananda Jha Saramana, Vidyabhavan Sanskrit Granthamala 41, Chowkhamba Vidyabhavan, Varanasi, 1959.

Varāhamihira's Bṛhat Saṁhitā, Parts I & II, ed. M. Ramakrishna Bhat, Motilal Banarasidass, Delhi-Varanasi-Patna, 1981, 1982.

Viṣṇudharmottara Purāṇa, Third Khaṇḍa, Vols. I & II, ed. Priyabala Shah, G.O.S. no. 137, Oriental Institute, Baroda, 1958, 1961.

Works of Kalidāsa, Vol. II, ed. C. R. Devadhar, Motilal Banarasidass, Delhi, 1993 (reprint)

Lexicons

Abhidhānacintāmaṇiḥ (of Shri Hemacandracarya), ed. Pt. Haragovinda Sastri, Vidyabhawan Sanskrit Granthamala 109, Chowkhambha Vidyabhavan, Varanasi, 1964.

Amarakośa [I], with the unpublished South Indian commentaries, *Amarapadavivṛti* of Liṅgayasūrin and the *Amarapadapārijāta* of Mallinātha, ed. A.A. Ramanathan, The Adyar Library and Research Centre, Madras, 1971.

Halāyudhakośaḥ (Abhidhānaratnamālā), ed. Jayashanker Joshi, Hindi Samiti Granthamala-150, Hindi Samiti, Lucknow, 1967 (second edition).

Halāyudha's Abhidhānaratnamālā, A Sanskrit Vocabulary, ed. Th. Aufrecht, Indian India, Delhi, 1975 (first Indian reprint).

Nāmaliṅgānuśāsana or Amarakośa of Amarasimha, ed. Pt. Haragovinda Sastri, The Kashi Sanskrit Series 198, The Chowkhambha Sanskrit Series Office, Varanasi, 1970.

Vaijayantīkośaḥ of Sri Yadavaprakāśācārya, ed. Pandit Haragovind Sastri, The Jaikrishnadas-Krishnadas Prachyavidya Granthamala 2, Varanasi, 1971.

Dictionaries and Encyclopaedia

A Sanskrit-English Dictionary, Monier, Monier-Williams, Motilal Banarasidass Publishers Pvt. Limited, Delhi, 1990 (reprint) (First Published by Oxford University Press 1899).

A Dictionary of Hindu Architecture, P.K. Acharya, London, 1927.

Encyclopaedia of Indian Temple Architecture (EITA), Vol. I, Pt. 1 (Text and Plates), South India: Lower Drāviḍadeśa, 200 BC- AD 1324, ed. Michael W. Meister, AIIS and University of Pennsylvania Press, New Delhi and Philadelphia, 1983.

Encyclopaedia of Indian Temple Architecture (EITA), Vol. I, Pt. 2 (Text and Plates), South India: Upper Drāviḍadeśa, Early Phase AD 550-1074, eds. Michael W. Meister and M.A. Dhaky, AIIS and University of Pennsylvania Press, New Delhi and Philadelphia, 1986.

Encyclopaedia of Indian Temple Architecture (EITA), Vol. II, Pt. 1 (Text and Plates), North Indian Style, c. 250 BC-AD 1100, eds. Michael W. Meister, M.A. Dhaky, and Krishna Deva, AIIS and Oxford University Press, New Delhi and Princeton, 1988.

Encyclopaedia of Indian Temple Architecture (EITA), Vol. II, Pt. 2 (Text and Plates), North Indian Style: Period of Early Maturity, c. AD 700-900, eds. Michael W. Meister and M.A. Dhaky, AIIS and OUP, New Delhi and Princeton, 1991.

Encyclopaedia of Indian Temple Architecture (EITA), Vol. I, Pt. 3 (Text and Plates), South India: Upper Drāviḍadeśa, Later Phase, A.D. 973-1326, ed. M.A. Dhaky, AIIS and IGNCA, New Delhi, 1996.

Encyclopaedia of Indian Temple Architecture (EITA), Vol. II, Pt. 3 (Text and Plates), North Indian Style: Beginnings of Medieval Idiom, c. A.D. 900-1000, Dhaky, M.A., ed., AIIS and IGNCA, New Delhi, 1998.

Encyclopaedia of Indian Temple Architecture (EITA), Vol. I, Pt. 4-A (Text and Plates), South India: Drāviḍadeśa, Later Phase A.D. 1289-1798, ed. George Michell, AIIS, New Delhi, 2001.

Others

Annual Bibliography of Indian Archaeology, Vols. XV (for 1940-47), Vol. XVI (for 1948-53), Vol. XVII (for 1954-57), Vol. XXI (for 1964-66), Kern Institute, E.J. Brill, Leyden.

WD 1061, *Antiquities at Amaravati 1816 – 1817,* Drawings W. Cat. ccxxiii 9, India Antiqua Illustrata or An Essay to Illustrate The Ancient History, Inscriptions and Religion of India by Drawings of remarkable Sculptures, Inscriptions, Buildings, Coins and other existing remains of Antiquity. 82 (+ 4) Drawings, in the Prints and Drawings section, Oriental and India Office Collections (OIOC), British Library, London.

Secondary Sources

Agrawala, V.S., *Mathura Museum Catalogue: Architectural Pieces in the Mathura Museum,* Prithvi Prakashan, Varanasi, 1963.

Annual Reports of the Archaeological Department of H.H. the Nizam's Dominions (ARADH) 1925-26 & 1934-35.

Appendix to Epigraphia Indica and Record of the Archaeological Survey of India, Vol. X, ed. Heinrich Lüders, Calcutta, 1912.

Archaeological Survey of India, Annual Reports (ASIAR), 1908-09 and 1909-10.

Asher, Frederick M., *The Art of Eastern India, AD 300-800,* Oxford University Press, Delhi, 1980.

Bandyopadhyay, Sudipa, *Architectural Motifs in Early Mediaeval Art of Eastern India (Pala-Sena Period),* Indological Rare Book Sellers, R.N. Bhattacharya, Kolkata, 2002.

Benisti, Mireille,
-"Representations Khmeres De Visnu Couche," *Arts Asiatiques,* Tome XI, Fascicule 1, Paris, 1964, pp.91-117.

-"Notes d'Iconographie Khmere, III – Au Sujet D' Un Linteau De Sambor Prei Kuk," *Bulletin De L' Ecole Francaise D' Extreme-Orient,* Tome LVIII Fasc. 1, Paris 1966, pp. 71-75.

-"Recherches sur le premier art Khmer. I – Les linteaux de Thala Borivat," *Arts Asiatiques,* XVIII, 1968, pp. 85-96.

-*Rapports Entre Le Premier Art Khmer et L'Art Indien,* Publications De L' Ecole Francaise D'Extreme-Orient, Tomes I & II, Paris, 1970.

-"Recherches sur le premier art Khmer: III – Aux Confins Des Styles De Prei Kmeng et De Kompong Preah," *Arts Asiatiques,* XXIII, Paris 1971, pp. 93-111, Figs. 5-26.

-"Recherches sur le premier art Khmer: VII – Le Probleme De Sambor S1," *Arts Asiatiques,* XVIII, Paris 1977, pp. 25-49.

-*Stylistics of Early Khmer Art,* Volumes I & II, Indira Gandhi National Centre for the Arts and Aryan Books International, New Delhi 2003.

Bernet Kempers, A.J., *Ancient Indonesian Art,* Harvard University Press, Cambridge, Massachusettes, 1959.

Bhandaranayake, Senake, Mats Mogren, and Seneviratne Epitawatte, eds. *The Settlement Archaeology of the Sigiriya-Dambulla Region* Post Graduate Institute of Archaeology, University of Kelaniya, 1990.

Bhandarakar, D.R.
-*Progress Report of the Archaeological Survey of India, Western Circle,* for the months July 1905 to March 1906, inclusive, Bombay, 1906.

-"Two Sculptures at Mandor," *ASIAR 1905-06,* Superintendent Government Printing, Calcutta, 1909, pp. 135-140.

-"The Archaeological Remains and Excavations at Nagari," *Memoirs of the Archaeological Survey of India,* IV, Calcutta, 1920, pp. 137-140.

Bhattacharya, Gouriswar, "Two Donations in favour of the Mahāsāṅghikas of Mathura," in Arundhati Banerji ed. *Hari Smriti: Studies on Art, Archaeology and Indology,* Vol. I, Kaveri Books, New Delhi, 2006, pp. 421-427.

Boisselier, Jean, *La Statuaire du Champa, recherché sur les cultes et l'iconographie, BEFEO,* Paris, 1963.

Bosch, F.D.K., "A Hypothesis as to the Origin of Indo-Javanese Art," *Rupam,* 17, ed. Ordhendra C. Gangoly, Calcutta, 1924, pp. 6-41.

Brolin, Brent C., *Architectural Ornament: Banishment & Return,* W.W. Norton and Company, New York & London, 2000 (First published in 1985 as *Flight of Fancy: The Banishment and Return of Ornament*).

Brown, Percy, *Indian Architecture (Islamic Period),* D.B. Taraporevala Sons and Co. Private Limited, Bombay (3rd edition) (First edition, 1942).

Burgess, J.,
-*The Buddhist Stupas of Amaravati and Jaggayyapeta in the Krishna District, Madras Presidency surveyed in 1882,* with translations of the Asokan inscriptions at Jaugada and Dhauli by Georg Bühler,(Archaeological Survey of Southern India), Indological Book House, Varanasi, 1970 (Reprint).

-*The Temples of Satruñjaya Pālitānā in Kathiawar,* Jain Bhavan, Calcutta, 1977 (Revised edition).

Burgess, James and Henry Cousens, *The Architectural Antiquities of Northern Gujarat, more esp. Baroda State,* Archaeological Survey of Western India (ASWI), Vol. IX, London, 1903.

Chandra, Pramod, *Stone Sculpture in the Allahabad Museum,* American Institute of Indian Studies, New Delhi, 1970.

Chandra, Pramod, ed., *Studies in Indian Temple Architecture,* American Institute of Indian Studies, New Delhi, 1975.

Chihara, Diagoro, *Hindu-Buddhist Architecture in South East Asia (Studies in Asian Art & Archaeology),* tr. Rolf W. Giebel, E.J. Brill, Leiden-New York-Köln, 1996.

Codrington, K. de B.,
-*Ancient India: from the earliest times to the Guptas with notes on the architecture and sculpture of the medieval period,* Ernest Benn Limited, London, 1926.

-*An Introduction to the Study of Medieval Indian Sculpture,* Edward Goldston, London, 1929.

Coomaraswamy, A.K.,
-*Symbolism of Indian Architecture,* Historical Research Documentation Programme, Jaipur, 1983.

-"The Makara," *Yakṣas: Essays in the Water Cosmology,* ed. Paul Schroeder, IGNCA and OUP, Delhi *et. al.*, 1993, pp. 142-154.

-*Mediaeval Sinhalese Art,* Munshiram Manoharlal Publishers Pvt. Limited, New Delhi, 2003 (reprinted from the second edition, 1956).

Corpus Inscriptionum Indicarum Vol. II, Part 2 (Bharhut Inscriptions), ed. Heinrich Lüders, revised by E. Waldschmidt and M. A. Mehendale, Government Epigraphist for India, Ootacamund, 1963.

Cousens, Henry,
-*Bijapur and its Architectural Remains (with an historical outline of the Adil Shahi Dynasty),* Archaeological Survey of India, Volume XXXVII, Imperial Series, Bombay, 1916.

-*The Architectural Antiquities of Western India,* The India Society, London, 1926.

-*The Calukyan Architecture of the Kanarese Districts,* Archaeological Survey of India, New Imperial Series 42, Calcutta, 1926.

-*Bijapur: The Old Capital of the Adil Shah Kings; a guide to its ruins with historical outline,* Scottish Mission Industries, Poona, 1923.

Cunningham, Alexander,
-*The Stūpa of Bharhut,* Munshiram Manoharlal Publishers. Pvt. Ltd., New Delhi, 1998 (reprint of 1879).

-*Mahābodhi, or the Great Buddhist Temple under the Bodhi Tree at Buddha-Gaya,* London, 1892.

- *Archaeological Survey of India Report,* X, Indological Book House, Varanasi, 1969 (Reprint).

Czuma, Stanislaw J., *Kuṣāṇa Sculpture: Images from Early India,* The Cleveland Museum of Art, Cleveland, 1985.

Dalet, R., "Notes sur les styles de Sambor Prei Kuk, de Prei Kmeng, de Kompong Preah et du Kulen," *Bulletin de la Societe des Etudes Indichinoises,* 1944, 2e trimestre.

Dehejia, Vidya, ed., *Unseen Presence: The Buddha and Sanchi,* Marg Publications, Mumbai, 1996.

Deo, Shantaram Bhalchandra, *Glimpses of Nepal Woodwork, The Journal of the Indian Society of Oriental Art (JISOA), New Series,* Volume III, ed. Umakant P. Shah, Calcutta, 1968-69.

Deshpande, M.N., "The Rock-Cut Caves of Pitalkhora in the Deccan," *Ancient India no. 15*, 1959, pp. 66-93.

Desai, Vishakha N. and Darielle Mason eds., *Gods, Guardians and Lovers: Temple Sculpture from North India, AD 700-1200,* The Asia Society Galleries New York in association with Mapin Publishing Pvt. Ltd., Ahmedabad, 1993.

Dhaky, M.A.,
-"The Influence of *Samarāṅgaṇasūtradhāra* on *Aparājitapṛcchā*," *Journal of the Oriental Institute (JOI),* Vol. X, No. 3, ed. B.J. Sandesara, Baroda, March 1961, pp. 226-234.

-"The Chronology of the Solaṅkī Temples of Gujarat," *Journal of the Madhya Pradesh Itihasa Parisad (JMPIP),* No. 3, ed. Krishna Deva, Bhopal 1961, pp. 1-83, Plates I-XVI.

-"The Date of the Dancing Hall of the Sun Temple, Moḍherā," *Journal of the Asiatic Society of Bombay (New Series),* Dr. Bhāu Dājī Special Volume (Volume 38), ed. P.V. Kane, 1963, pp. 211-222, Figs. 1-10.

-"Kirāḍu and the Maru-Gurjara Style of Temple Architecture," *Bulletin of the American Academy of Benaras (AAB),* Volume 1, 1967, pp. 35-45, Figs. 59-75.

-"Some Early Jaina Temples in Western India," *Sri Mahavira Jaina Vidyalaya Golden Jubilee Volume* (English section), Bombay, 1968, pp. 290-347, Figs. 1-24.

-"Genesis and Development of the Maru-Gurjara Temple Architecture," *Studies in Indian Temple Architecture,* ed. Pramod Chandra, American Institute of Indian Studies, New Delhi, 1975, pp. 114-165.

-"The Western Indian Jaina Temple," *Aspects of Jaina Art and Architecture*, eds. U.P. Shah and M.A. Dhaky, Ahmedabad, 1975, pp. 319-384, Plates 1-25.

-*The Indian Temple Traceries,* American Institute of Indian Studies and D.K. Printworld (P) Limited, New Delhi, 2005.

Dhaky, M.A. and U.S. Moorti, *The Temples in Kumbhāriyā,* American Institute of Indian Studies, New Delhi, and Lalbhai Dalpatbhai Institute of Indology, Ahmedabad, 2001.

Dhāṅkī, Madhusudana (Dhaky, M.A.) and P. Sompura, *Bhāratīya Durga Vidhāna,* Bombay, 1971.

Dhāṅkī, Madhusudana (Dhaky, M.A.) (Gujarātī),
-"Gujarāt nī Toraṇa Samṛddhi," *Kumāra,* No. 400, August 1965, pp. 298-308.

-*Tīrthādhirāja Śrī Śatruñjaya, Ṭunk Paricaya*, Śeṭh Ānandajī Kalyāṇajī, Amdāvād, 1995.

-*Kalādhām Delvāḍa,* (Gujarati), Śeṭh Ānandajī Kalyāṇajī, Amdāvād, 1997.

-*Ārasī Tīrtha Ārāsaṇa (Kumbhāriyājī),* Śeṭh Ānandajī Kalyāṇajī, Amdāvād, 1997.

-*Jagavikhyāta Jaisalmer Tīrtha,* Śeṭh Ānandajī Kalyāṇajī, Amdāvād, 1997.

-*Māhātīrtha Ujjayantagiri (Girnār Tīrtha)*, Śeṭh Ānandajī Kalyāṇajī, Amdāvād, 1997.

-*Varkāṇā Tīrtha,* Śeṭh Ānandajī Kalyāṇajī, Amdāvād, 1997.

-*Tribhuvana Tilaka Śrī Rāṇakpur Tīrtha,* Śeṭh Ānandajī Kalyāṇajī, Amdāvād, 1997.

Dhar, Parul Pandya,
-"Morphology of Transformation: *Toraṇa* in Cambodian Architecture (c. 5th-9th century AD)," *Indo-Koko-Kenkyu – Indian Archaeological Studies*, No. 26: 2004-2005 (A bilingual journal in Japanese and English), eds. M.A. Konishi and H. Shudai, Indian Archaeological Society, Tokyo, 2005, pp. 33-50.

-"Text, Context and Architectural Practice: with reference to entryways in ancient & medieval India," *Vanamālā: A.J. Gail Festschrift,* eds. Gerd J.R. Mevissen and Klaus Bruhn, Weidler Buchverlag, Germany, 2007, pp. 59-66.

-"*Kāla-makara-toraṇas*: Javanese Expressions of a Shared Motif," *Sacred Landscapes in Asia: Shared Traditions, Multiple Histories*, ed. Himanshu Prabha Ray, Manohar, New Delhi, 2007, pp. 257-281.

-"Some Early *toraṇa* Representations from the Maharashtra Caves," *Pragñyādhara: Essays on Asian Art History, Epigraphy and Culture in honour of Gouriswar Bhattacharya,* eds. Gerd J.R. Mevissen & Arundhati Banerji, Kaveri Books, New Delhi, 2009, pp. 169-176 and Plates 17.1-17.13.

Donaldson, Thomas E., *Hindu Temple Art of Orissa,* Vols. I-III, (Studies in South Asian Culture Vol. XII, ed. Janice Stargardt), E.J. Brill, Leiden, 1985-86-87.
Dubey, Lal Mani, *Aparājitapṛcchā- A Critical Study,* Allahabad, 1987.

Dubreuil, G. Jouveau, *Pallava Antiquities,* I and II, London, 1916 (reprint 1994: New Delhi and Madras, Asian Educational Services, Eng. tr. by V.S. Swaminadha Dikshitar).

Dupont, Pierre, "Les linteaux Khmers du VIIe siecle," *Artibus Asiae,* XV, 1/2, 1952, pp. 30-83.

Epigraphia Carnatica, Vol. V, Part I, Inscriptions in the Hassan District, ed. B. Lewis Rice, Mysore Archaeological Series, 1902.

Epigraphia Carnatica, Vol. VI, Inscriptions in the Kadur District, Chikmagalur Taluk, ed. B. Lewis Rice, Mysore Archaeological Series, 1901.

Epigraphia Carnatica, Vol. X, Inscriptions in the Kolar District (Taluk), ed. B. Lewis Rice, Mysore Archaeological Series, 1905.

Epigraphia Indica Vol. I, ed. Jas Burgess, The Superintendent of Government Printing, Calcutta, 1892.

Epigraphia Indica Vol. II, ed. Jas Burgess (1894), Motilal Banarasidass, Delhi *et. al.,* 1970 (reprint).

Epigraphia Indica, Vol. V, Part II, ed. E. Hultzsch, Superintendent of Government Printing, Calcutta, 1898-99.

Epigraphia Indica Vol. IX (1907-08) eds. E. Hultzsch and Sten Konow, Archaeological Survey of India, New Delhi, 1981.

Epigraphia Indica, Vol. X (1909-1910), Archaeological Survey of India, New Delhi, 1984.

Epigraphia Indica, Vol. XVII (1923-24), pp. 310-27: Sastri, Hiranand, "The Nalanda Copper Plate of Devapaladeva."

Epigraphia Indica, Vol. XXIV, Archaeological Survey of India, New Delhi, 1984.

Facenna, D. *Sculptures from the Sacred Area of Butkara I (Swat, W. Pakistan),* Part 2, Istituto Poligrafico dello Stato, Rome, 1962.

Fergusson, James and James Burgess, The *Cave Temples of India,* Allen, Trübner & Griggs, London, 1880.

Fickle, Dorothy, "Khmer Architecture in Thailand," *Art from Thailand,* ed. Robert Brown, Marg Publications, Mumbai, 1999, pp. 65-78.

Foekema, Gerard,
-*Calukya Architecture: Medieval temples of Northern Karnataka built during the rule of the Calukyas of Kalyana and thereafter, A.D. 1000-1300,* 3 Volumes, Munshiram Manoharlal, New Delhi, 2003.

-*Architecture Decorated with Architecture: Later medieval temples of Karnataka, 1000-1300 A.D.,* Munshiram Manoharlal, New Delhi, 2003.

Forbes, A.K., *Ras Mala, Hindu Annals of Western India with particular reference to Gujarat,* New Delhi, 1973 (reprint).

Gail, Adalbert J.,
-*Tempel in Nepal* (Band I), Akademische Druck, Graz, 1984.

- *Klöster in Nepal,* Graz, 1991.

Gangoly, O.C., "A Note on Kīrttimukha: Being the Life-History of an Indian Architectural Ornament," *Rupam* No. 1 ed. Ordhendra C. Gangoly, Delhi 1920, pp. 11-19.

Ghurye, G.S., *Rajput Architecture,* Popular Prakashan, Bombay, 1968.

Girard-Geslan, Maud, *et. al., Art of Southeast Asia,* (Tr. from the French by J.A. Underwood), Harry N. Abrams, Inc., Publishers, New York, 1997.

Guillon, Emmanuel, *Cham Art, Treasures from the Da Nang Museum, Vietnam,* Thames and Hudson, London, 2001.

Hagmüller, Gotz, *Patan Museum: The Transformation of a Royal Palace in Nepal,* Serindia Publications in association with Patan Museum, London, 2003.

Hall, D.G.E., *A History of Southeast Asia,* 4th edition, Macmillan, London, 1987

Handa, Devendra, *Osian: History, Archaeology, Art and Architecture,* Sundeep Prakashan, Delhi, 1984.
Hardy, Adam, *Indian Temple Architecture: Form and Transformation, The Karṇāṭa-Drāviḍa Tradition, 7th to 13th Centuries,* IGNCA and Abhinav Publications, New Delhi, 1995.

Hinzler, H.I.R., "Inscriptions: Terms for buildings and temples," Workshop, Old Javanese, Royal Institute of Linguistics, KITLV, Leiden, 1998 (Unpublished).

Holt, Claire, *Art in Indonesia: Continuities and Change,* Cornell University Press, Ithaca, New York, 1967.

Huntington, Susan,
-*The Art of Ancient India: Buddhist, Hindu, Jain,* Weatherhill, New York and Tokyo, 1999 (third reprint).

-*The "Pala-Sena" Schools of Sculpture,* E.J. Brill, Leiden, 1984.

Huntington Susan L. and John C. Huntington, *Leaves from the Bodhi Tree: The Art of Pala India (8th-12th centuries) and Its International Legacy,* The Dayton Art Institute in association with The University of Washington Press, Seattle and London, 1990.

Indian Antiquary, Vol. IX, ed. Jas. Burgess, 1880.

Indian Antiquary, Vol. XIV, eds. J.F. Fleet and R.C. Temple, 1885.

Jarrige, Jean-Francois and Pierre Cambon, *Afghanistan - les trésors retrouvés. Collections du musée national de Kaboul,* Musée national des Arts asiatiques - Guimet, 6 décembre 2006 - 30 avril 2007, Editions de la Réunion des musées nationaux, Paris, 2006.
Kannada University Epigraphical Series-II, Koppal District, Hampi-Vidyaranya, 1999.

Knox, Robert, *Amaravati: Buddhist Sculpture from the Great Stupa,* British Museum Press, London, 1992.
Kramrisch, Stella, *The Hindu Temple,* Vols. I and II, Motilal Banarsidass, Delhi-Varanasi- Patna, 1976 (reprint of 1946 edition).

Lajonquiere, Lunet de, *Inventaire descriptif des monuments du Cambodge,* 3 tomes et 1 cartable, Paris, 1902, 1907, and 1912.

Lipsey, Roger, *Coomaraswamy: Selected Papers, Traditional Art and Symbolism,* Princeton University Press, Princeton, 1977.

Lobo, Wibke, *The Sun Temple at Modhera - A Monograph on Architecture and Iconography,* Verlag C.H. Beck, München, 1982.

Losty, Jeremiah P., "An Early Indian Manuscript of the Karaṇḍavyūhasūtra," *Studies in Art and Archaeology: Nalinīkānta Śatavārṣikī, Dr. N.K. Bhattasali Centenary Volume (1888 – 1988),* eds. Debala Mitra and Gouriswar Bhattacharya, Delhi, 1989, pp. 1-21, Figs. 1-77.

Majumdar, R.C.,
-*Ancient Indian Colonies in the Far East,* Vol. II *(Suvarṇadvīpa),* Part I, The Punjab Sanskrit Book Depot, Lahore, 1937.

-*Influence of Indian Culture in Southeast Asia,* Gujarat Vidya Sabha, Ahmedabad, 1969.

Majumdar, R.C., ed.,
-*The Struggle for Empire (The History and Culture of the Indian People,* Vol. V), Bharatiya Vidya Bhavan, Bombay, 1979 (3rd edition).

-*The Age of Imperial Kanauj, (The History and Culture of the Indian People,* Vol. IV*),* Bharatiya Vidya Bhavan, Bombay, 1984 (3rd edition).

-*The Delhi Sultanate, (The History and Culture of the Indian People,* Vol. VI*),* Bharatiya Vidya Bhavan, Bombay, 1960.

Marchel, Henri, "Le Décor et la Sculpture Khmers," *Etudes d'art et d'ethnologie Asiatiques,* III, Vanoest Editions d'art et d' historiere, 1951.

Marshall, John,
-*A Guide to Taxila,* 4th edition, at the University Press, Cambridge, 1960.

-*Taxila* (3 Vols.), Vol. I: *Structural Remains*; Vol. II: *Minor Antiquities*; Vol. III: *Plates*, at the University Press, Cambridge, 1951.

Marshall, J.H. and Dayaram Sahni, "Excavations at Mandor," *ASIAR 1909-1910,* ed. J.Ph. Vogel, pp. 93-96.

Meister, Michael W., ed.,
-*Ananda Coomaraswamy: Essays in Early Indian Architecture,* IGNCA, Delhi-Bombay- Calcutta-Madras, 1992.

-*Ananda K. Coomaraswamy: Essays in Architectural Theory,* Indira Gandhi National Centre for the Arts (IGNCA), New Delhi, 1995.

Mevissen, Gerd J.R., "A Dated Pañcarakṣā *toraṇa* from the Hāratī Temple at Svayambhūnāth, Nepal, and Related Matters," in *Vanamālā: A.J. Gail Festschrift,* eds. Gerd J.R. Mevissen & Klaus Bruhn, Weidler Buchverlag, Germany, 2007, pp. 137-149.

Michell, George, ed. *Vijayanagara: Splendour in Ruins,* Mapin Publishing and the Alkazi Collection of Photography, Ahmedabad, 2008.

Mohapatra, R.P., *Udaygiri and Khandagiri Caves,* D.K. Publications, Delhi, 1981.

Mukherjee, B.N., *East Indian Art Styles: A study in parallel trends,* K.P. Bagchi & Company, Calcutta, 1980.

Nanavati, J. M. and M. A. Dhaky, *The Ceilings in the Temples of Gujarat, Bulletin of the Baroda Museum and Picture Gallery,* Vols. XVI- XVII, ed. B.L. Mankad, Baroda, 1963.

Panigrahi, K.C., *Archaeological Remains at Bhubaneswar,* Orient Longmans, Bombay, 1961.

Parmentier, H., *L'art Khmer Primitif,* 2 tomes, Paris, 1927.

Pramar, V.S., *A Social History of Indian Architecture,* Oxford University Press, New Delhi, 2005.

Prasad, B. Rajendra, *Art of South India: Andhra Pradesh,* Art of South India Series, Vol. II, Sundeep Prakashan, Delhi, 1980.

Paranavitana, S., *The Art and Architecture of Ceylon: Polonnaruva Period,* Arts Council of Ceylon, 1954.

Rao, Manjushree, Sushmita Pande, and Bhaskar Nath Misra, *India's Cultural Relations with South-East Asia,* Sharada Publishing House, Delhi, 1996.

Rea, Alexander, *Pallava Architecture*, Archaeological Survey of India, New Imperial Series, Vol. XXXIV, Indological Book House, Delhi-Varanasi, 1970.

Remusat, G. de Coral,
-"De l'origine commune des linteaux de l'Inde Pallava et des linteaux Khmers preangkoriens," *Revue des Arts Asiatiques,* VIII (Numéro IV), 1934, pp. 242-250.

- *L'art Khmer, les grand etapes de son evolution,* 1940.

Rosenfield, John M., *The Dynastic Arts of the Kushans,* University of California Press, Berkeley and Los Angeles, 1967.

Rowland, Benjamin, Jr., *Ancient Art from Afghanistan: Treasures from the Kabul Museum,* The Asia Society Inc., Harry N. Abrams, New York, 1966.

Sankalia, H.D., *The Archaeology of Gujarat (including Kathiawar),* Natwarlal and Co., Bombay, 1941.

Sarkar, H., *Corpus of Inscriptions of Java,* Vols. I and II, K.L. Mukhopadhyaya, Calcutta, 1972.

Sastri, K.A. Nilakanta, *The Coḷas*, University of Madras, Madras, 1955 (second edition).

Settar, S.,
-*The Hoysaḷa Temples*, Vols. I and II, Karnataka University (Dharwar) and Kala Yatra Publications, Bangalore, 1992.

-*Hoysaḷa Sculptures in the National Museum,* Copenhagen, National Museum Ethnographical Series, Vol. XV, Copenhagen, 1975.

-*Śravaṇa Belgoḷa: An Illustrated Study,* Rūvāri, Dharwad, 1981.

Schwindler, Gary J., "A Sculpture of *Ardhanārī* from Srinivasanallur," *Oriental Art*, n.s. 26, no. 3, Autumn 1980.

Shah, U.P., "Some Medieval Sculptures from Gujarat and Rajasthan," *Western Indian Art, (JISOA Special Number)*, eds., Shah, U.P. and K.K. Ganguli, Calcutta, 1965-66, Pl. XXXI, Fig. 4.

Sharma, J.C., *Hindu Temples in Vietnam,* Sankalpa Publications, 1997.

Sharma, R.C., *Art and Museum: Perspectives in Indian Art and Archaeology, No. 1,* D.K. Printworld (P) Limited, New Delhi, 1994.

Sharma, R.C., *Buddhist Art: Mathura School,* New Age International, New Delhi, 1995.

Singh, Amar, "On *Toraṇa* Architecture," *Prāgdhara: Journal of the U.P. State Archaeology Department,* No. 10, ed. Rakesh Tiwari, Lucknow, 2000, (pp. currently unavailable).

Smith, V.A., *The Jain Stupa and other Antiquities of Mathura,* Government Press, Allahabad, 1901.

Siribhadra, Smithie and Elizabeth Moore, *Palaces of the Gods, Khmer Art and Architecture in Thailand,* Thames and Hudson, London, 1997.

Sompura, K.F., *The Structural Temples of Gujarat (up to 1600 AD),* Gujarat University, Ahmedabad, 1968.

Sompura, Prabhashankar Ogadabhai, *Album of Indian Architectural Designs (Vāstu Kalānidhi),* The Late Shri Balwantrai Prabhashankar Sompura, Ahmedabad, 1977.

Soundararajan, K.V., *Cave Temples of the Deccan,* A.S.I., New Delhi, 1981.

South Indian Inscriptions, Vol. II, Part 1, No. 20, ed. E. Hultzsch, Navrang Publications, New Delhi, 1983 (reprint of ASI, 1892).

Spink, Walter,
-"On the Development of Buddhist Art in India," *The Art Bulletin* 40, no. 2, 1958, pp. 95-104.

-"Ajanta to Ellora," *Marg,* 20, no. 2, Bombay 1967.

-Ajanta: History and Development, Volume I (The End of the Golden Age), Brill, Leiden and Boston, 2005.

- Ajanta: History and Development, Volume V (Cave by Cave), Brill, Leiden and Boston, 2007.

Spooner, D.B. "The Bodh-Gaya Plaque," *Journal of the Bihar and Orissa Research Society,* no. 1, 1915, pp.1-4.

Srinivasan, K.R., *Cave- Temples of the Pallavas,* Architectural Survey of Temples, No. 1, Archaeological Survey of India, New Delhi, 1964.

Srivastava, Gyanendra Nath, "*Toraṇa* in Art and Architecture of Orissa," *Kṛṣṇa Pratibhā: Studies in Indology, Prof. Krishna Chandra Panigrahi Commemoration Volume,* Vol. I, eds. H.C. Das, S. Tripathy, and B.K. Rath, Sundeep Prakashan, Delhi, 1994, pp. 83-88.

Stern, Philippe, "Evolution du linteau Khmer," *Revue des Arts Asiatiques,* VIII, Numéro IV, 1934, pp. 251-256, Figs. 1-20.

Stevenson, Rev. J., "Historical Names and Facts Contained in the Kānherī (Kenery) Inscriptions; with Translations Appended," *Journal of the Bombay Branch of the Royal Asiatic Society*, No. 5, Bombay 1857, pp. 1-34.

Stutterheim, "The Meaning of the *Kāla-makara* Ornament," *Indian Art and Letters, N.S.* Vol. III, No. 1, The India Society, London 1929, pp. 27-52.

Tarr, Gary, "Chronology and Development of the Chalukya Cave Temples," *Ars Orientalis,* 8 (1970), pp. 155-184.

Tillotson, G.H.R., *The Rajput Palaces, The Development of an Architectural Style, 1450-1750,* Oxford University Press, Delhi 1987.

Tissot, Francine, *Catalogue of the National Museum of Afghanistan,* 1935-1981, UNESCO, Paris 2006

Tod, James, *Annals and Antiquities of Rajasthan (of the Central and Western Rajput states of India),* New Impression, Two Volumes, unabridged, 1960 (Reprint), First Published 1829.

Tranet, Michel, *Sambaour-Prei-Kuk, Monuments d'Isanavarman I (615-628),* Vols. I and II, Toyota Foundation, 1996-1997.

Tripathi, L.K., *The Temples of Bārolī,* Amitabha Prakashan, Varanasi, 1975.

Vatsyayan, Kapila, *The Square and the Circle of the Indian Arts*, Roli Books International, New Delhi, 1983.

Vatsyayan, Kapila, ed., *Concepts of Space: Ancient and Modern,* IGNCA and Abhinav Publications, New Delhi, 1991.

Venkataranga Raju, K., "Cola Temples in Pudukoṭṭai," *Journal of the Indian Society of Oriental Art (JISOA),* V (1937), pp. 78-90.

Vogel, J. Ph.,
-Archaeological Museum at Mathura, Indological Book House, Delhi, 1971.

-Catalogue of the Archaeological Museum at Mathura, Allahabad, 1910.

Wagoner, Phillip B. and Rice, John Henry, "From Delhi to Deccan: Newly Discovered Tugluq Monuments at Warangal-Sultanpur and the Beginnings of Indo-Islamic Architecture in Southern India," *Artibus Asiae,* Vol. LXI, No. 1, Zurich, 2001, pp. 77-116.

Ward, William E., "Sinhalese *Makara Toraṇas* in Cleveland," *The Ceylon Historical Journal,* Vol. II, 1952, eds. Sumana Saparamadu, Swets & Zeitlinger N.V., Amsterdam, 1965, pp. 23-27.

Williams, J.G., *The Art of Gupta India: Empire and Province,* Heritage Publishers, Delhi, 1988.

Index